The New World of Economics
of
Economics

5th Edition

The New World of Economics

5th Edition

Richard B. McKenzie
University of California, Irvine

Gordon Tullock
University of Arizona

McGraw-Hill, Inc.
College Custom Series

New York St Louis San Francisco Auckland Bogotá
Caracas Lisbon London Madrid Mexico Milan Montreal
New Delhi Paris San Juan Singapore Sydney Tokyo Toronto

The New World of Economics

1 2 3 4 5 6 7 8 9 0 DOC DOC 9 0 9 8 7 6 5 4

ISBN 07-045667-4

Editor: Julie Kehrwald

Cover Designer: Mark Anderson

Printer/Binder: R. R. Donnelley & Sons Company

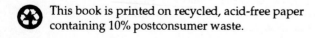 This book is printed on recycled, acid-free paper containing 10% postconsumer waste.

For

William and Barbara Albers

Preface

Economics traditionally has been defined by both its methods and its subject matter. That is to say, there are economic methods—models and statistical tests—based on a set of assumptions about the way people interact. The world of "business" has been studied extensively by economists.

As may be obvious from the table of contents, we believe that the economic methods that have been used successfully to study business issues can also be applied to many other areas of human behavior. These new applications make the study of economics more exciting, more interesting, and more relevant.

When *The New World of Economics* was first published in 1974, it was controversial because many economists were not then comfortable extending the application of economic methods to, for example, politics, sex, crime, and learning. We are pleased to say that *The New World of Economics* has helped to change a lot of professional minds. It was the first introductory economics text to discuss (among a host of other subjects) public choice economics, the economics of marriage and family, and law and economics. Noble prizes have since been given for economists' work in those areas. Indeed, the book is being reissued because many professors of economics want to show their students the "new worlds" of economic inquiry that have emerged practically within the last generation of economists and how the principles they discuss in class are applicable to the everyday experiences of their students and to a variety of issues studied in other courses.

Most introductory economics texts are, literally, encyclopedias of just about everything known in the subject. We believe that the first and most important principle in economics should be economy in the principles that are taught and studied. Accordingly, students will be relieved to know that we introduce a relatively small number of principles, but we make those few principles work, applying them broadly, to just about every nook and cranny of human behavior. We strive to keep the analysis simple in order to make the learning process productive.

The *New World of Economics* is developed on the premise that economics is, at its disciplinary core, *a way of thinking*. We believe that students will *want* to read this book, and by the end of the book, they will be thinking much like economists. We have been told numerous times that the book simply *works*.

We are, of course, indebted to our many colleagues around the country who have contributed directly or indirectly to the development of chapters in this volume. We are also immensely indebted to our students; they have taught us much that is reflected in our work. Nothing helps improve a book like this one more than classroom use, and this book has been used in most of the country's colleges and universities and in many foreign universities. We have been given much advice. We encourage all users—professors and students alike—to let us know how future editions of *The New World of Economics* can be further improved and remain worthy of its title. Get on the electronic highway and let us hear from you. Our electronic addresses are below. We return messages for one simple reason: Doing so makes good economic sense.

Richard B. McKenzie

Fax: (714) 725-2604
Internet: RBMCKENZ@UCI.EDU

Gordon Tullock

Fax: (602) 621-8450
Internet: GTULLOCK@BPA.ARIZONA.EDU

Contents

PART ONE

An Introduction to the New World of Economics

The economists' stock-in-trade—their tools—lies in their ability and proclivity to think about all questions in terms of alternatives. The truth judgment of the moralist, which says that something is either wholly right or wholly wrong, is foreign to them. The win-lose, yes-no discussion of politics is not within purview. They do not recognize the either-or, the all-or-nothing, situation as their own. Theirs is not the world of the mutually exclusives. Instead, it is the world of adjustment, of coordinated conflict, of mutual gains.

James Buchanan*

*James M. Buchanan, "Economics and Its Scientific Neighbors," in *The Structure of Economic Science: Essays on Methodology*, ed. Sherman Roy Krupp (Englewood Cliffs, N.J.: Prentice-Hall, 1966), p. 168.

CHAPTER 1
Economic Thinking

Economics is a constantly changing discipline. This can be said about most disciplines, but it is particularly applicable to economics. At one time students could think of economics as being neatly contained within the sphere of commercial life, and most courses and books on the subject have traditionally revolved around such topics as money, taxes and tariffs, stocks and bonds, and the operation of the market as it pertains to the production and sale of automobiles and toothpaste.

Over the past two decades, however, economists have greatly expanded their field of concern, and, as a result, the boundaries of economics as a discipline are rapidly expanding outward, encroaching on areas of inquiry that have historically been the exclusive domain of other social sciences. The change in direction and scope of the discipline has been so dramatic that the economists who have been involved in bringing about the change are no longer inclined to debate the issue of what is or is not economic in nature. They merely ask What can economics contribute to our understanding of this or that problem?

This book reflects that expanded vision. Accordingly, we will introduce you to topics and points of discussion you may never have imagined would be included in an economics book. We will talk about family life, child rearing, dying, sex, crime, politics, and many other topics.[1] We do this not because such topics add a certain flair to the book, but rather because we believe that these are extraordinarily important areas of inquiry and that economic analysis can add much to our understanding of them. In addition, we are convinced that you will learn a good deal about economics through their consideration.

In dealing with such topics, we cannot avoid coming to grips with human behavior and making it the focus of our concern. The simple reason is that crimes cannot be committed, children cannot be reared, sex cannot be had, and governments cannot operate without people's "behaving" in one respect or another. We argue that before we can ever hope to understand

---

[1]Actually, Adam Smith was concerned with several of these problem areas in *The Wealth of Nations*, published in 1776. He would not be surprised that economists are now giving such topics more attention.

social phenomena, we must understand why people behave the way they do. To do this, we must have some perception, or model, of how behavior is motivated and organized from which the revealed actions of people can be interpreted. Economists have such a model, which has been developed and refined since the days of Adam Smith, and it is because we employ this model in our discussion, that we consider this to be a book on economics. All we intend to do here is to extend the application of this model into unconventional areas.

This is not to say, however, that economics can give a complete understanding of these problem areas. Other social scientists have long considered many of the topics included in this book, and their contributions to our understanding of human behavior cannot be overlooked. By viewing these topics strictly through the thinking process of economists, we must be ever mindful that what we are dealing with is one particular point of view, which can be complemented by many of the findings in other disciplines.

You may at times have reservations about accepting what we have to say, but this is not necessarily unwelcome to us. We could easily write a book with which the reader would readily agree; however, we imagine that such a book might deal only with trivial issues and very well be a monumental bore. We take the view that at any given time, there are many important issues that are to some degree unsettled; we believe that learning requires not only that an individual know the settled issues but also that he be able to explore those issues over which there may be some disagreement.

You do not need to have a large reservoir of economic knowledge to understand what we have to say. We will provide you with the necessary principles on which later discussion will be founded. Furthermore, we do not intend to waste your time with a lot of esoteric theory that will never be used. We understand that you want to make as efficient use of your time as possible, and we intend to cooperate with you. Remember, this is a book on economics!

The principles that we do develop and the points that we make will at times be very subtle and a little tricky to handle—we cannot escape this. You may be pleasantly surprised, however, at how few the principles are and at how useful they will be in thinking about topics that are and are not included in this book. First we need to lay the foundation—to explain how economists look at their subject and at human behavior.

THE MEANING OF ECONOMICS

For nearly 200 years, economists have periodically struggled with the problem of defining economics, and it is still a live issue. At times the subject has been defined as "what economists do," as that part of human experience that involves money, or as a study of how men attempt to maximize their material well-being. Different people perceive a discipline in different ways; therefore no one can ever claim to offer readers *the* definition of the subject.

All we can hope to accomplish is to lay out our own perception of the subject and in that way suggest how we will proceed.

The approach taken in this book is to define economics as a mental skill that incorporates a special view of human behavior characteristic of economists.[2] It is, in short, a thought process, or the manner in which economists approach problems, rather than an easily distinguishable group of problems that sets an economist apart from others. Sociologists and political scientists have dealt with many of the problems considered in this book, but the reader may notice that our approach to these problems is substantially different from theirs. This mental skill or approach has several distinctive characteristics that can be discussed separately as follows.

THINKING IN TERMS OF ABSTRACTIONS

First and foremost, economists are prone to think, as are all other scientists, in terms of abstractions, not in the sense that the notions are vague or nebulous, but rather in the sense that their first impulses are to reduce reality to the relationships that are important and that bring the inquiry down to manageable proportions. The ideal approach to the study of human and social phenomena would be to treat the world as we confront it. However, the world is terribly complex. At any point in time it encompasses literally billions of bits of information and tens of thousands (if not millions) of relationships. On the other hand, the human mind has a limited capacity to handle such data; it can consider only so much at any one time. It is, therefore, literally impossible for a person to think about the world in its totality and deduce anything meaningful. As a consequence, scientists must restrict the information they do consider. They must abstract in the sense that they pull out from the total mass of information a limited number of relationships that they think are important and that they can handle.

This means that the analysis that then follows will lack a certain degree of realism. It must be that way because the analysis is based on abstractions that represent only a small portion of what we might call the real world. The expectation is, however, that such an approach will increase our understanding of the real world and will increase our ability to predict events in it.

In thinking about the social world around them, economists heed the principle concisely laid out by economist Kenneth Boulding: "It is a very

---

[2]In fact, it is the thought process or the mental skill developed below that defines an economist. Indeed, in the context of the discussion that follows, there are no doubt many people who call themselves economists but who do not meet the description offered here, and there are many persons in other disciplines who can, according to our definition, accurately be classified as economists. However, given the differences in policy conclusions of economists and noneconomists, it is apparent that not everyone possesses the mental skills developed in this book. By the same token, economists are well advised to develop some of the skills possessed by other social scientists.

fundamental principle indeed that knowledge is always gained by the orderly loss of information; that is, by condensing and abstracting and indexing the great buzzing confusion of information that comes from the world around us into a form which we can appreciate and comprehend."[3]

Take a moment and think about this. If you have difficulty understanding the world we live in, we suggest that your problem is likely to be that you are attempting to consider too much information, not too little.

Since the theory or model that is handled is by its very nature "unreal," the test of its acceptability is not dependent solely on the degree of its realism but also on the extent to which the model is able to accomplish its purpose— that is, to explain events in the real world and to make correct predictions.

At times, the reader is likely to think to himself that our analysis is, in one respect or another, unreal or that the model we employ does not represent the "fullness of the human experience." To such a comment we agree, but we must follow with the question, Are our conclusions not borne out in the real world? Are our predictions not more accurate than can be obtained by other means?

There is a story of an economics professor who was lecturing on a very esoteric topic before his graduate class. In the middle of the lecture, he was interrupted by a student who said, "Sir, I hate to break in, but in the real world . . . " The professor snapped back, "Mr. Waldorf, you must remember that the real world is a special case, and, therefore, we need not consider it!" Before one gets the impression that we may be taking the same view as that professor, let us emphasize that everything we say, although it may be discussed in terms of models, is directed at our understanding of the real world, and we believe that economics has a very efficient way of doing that

THINKING ABOUT VALUES

The approach of the economist tends to be (but is not always) amoral. Economics is not so much concerned with what should be or how individuals should behave, as it is with understanding why people behave the way they do. Accordingly, our analysis is devoid of our own personal values—as much as possible. We treat each topic as something that is to be analyzed and understood, and to do that, we must avoid the temptation to judge a given form of behavior as contemptuous, immoral, good, or bad. Therefore, in the context of our analysis, the services of a prostitute are treated the same as the services of a butcher; they are neither good nor bad—they exist and are subject to analysis. Criminal activity is considered in a manner similar to that of legitimate enterprise, and religion is treated as *a good* (in the sense of anything that yields satisfaction to the user) that is sought after and procured.

---

[3]Kenneth E. Boulding, *Economics as a Science* (New York: McGraw-Hill, 1970), p. 2.

Our reason for taking this tack is that in this book, we are not interested in telling people how they should behave or what is good or evil; we are interested in gaining understanding of the behavior of others, given *their* values. Further, we are interested in evaluating the effects of institutional settings on human behavior and in suggesting how institutions may be rearranged to accomplish whatever objective is desired. Note that our intention is to suggest changes in institutions and not in behavior.

Like everyone else, we have our own value systems, and we could easily make recommendations regarding how people's behavior should be changed to accomplish what we, as humanists, think is right. We also recognize that you have your own values, and we in no way wish to suggest that you dispense with them. You may violently disagree with prostitution or with political corruption—we do not quarrel with this. All we ask is that you allow us the opportunity to address the question of why such phenomena occur. In the process, you may find a solution to the problem that is more consistent with your values than the solution you may now perceive.

Further, economic analysis may suggest that some value can be achieved, but that the cost would be so much as to make it undesirable. In the early part of this century, many well-intentioned Americans objected to the consumption of alcoholic beverages. They succeeded in getting the Constitution amended to prohibit the sale of alcohol.

By the 1930s most of them had given up because they discovered how difficult it was to enforce the law. If backers of prohibition had consulted economists, we are sure they would have been told that the law would be very difficult and expensive to enforce. With this advice they might have decided not to undertake the program of moral elevation. The same considerations (involving the costs of enforcement) should, perhaps, be taken into account now in evaluating the efficacy of contemporary laws against hard drugs or pornography.

THINKING ABOUT PEOPLE

The focal point of the study of economics is the individual person. It is the individual who possesses values, makes choices, and if given the freedom, takes actions. All group decisions and actions are thought of in terms of the collective decisions and actions of individuals. Social goals are considered only to the extent that they reflect the collective values or choices of individuals.

All too often we hear such expressions as "society disapproves of this or that," "Congress is considering legislation," or "government has made a decision to enforce a given policy." If the expressions are meant to suggest that individuals are involved, we have no qualms; if, on the other hand, the expressions are intended to suggest that these bodies have a behavior of their own that is independent of the behavior of individuals, we must take issue.

We ask how can a group act? What is group behavior if it is not the behavior of individuals? How can a society, as an independent organism, have a value? Where must the values come from?

Do not misinterpret us; we are interested in understanding group behavior. However, we argue that to do this, we must first understand the behavior of the individuals that make up the group. We take it as a given that only individuals can act.

THINKING ABOUT RATIONALITY

Economists begin their analysis of human behavior with the assertion that *human beings act* and do so with a purpose. That purpose, in general terms, is to improve their lot—to change the situation from something less desired to something better, as economist Ludwig von Mises put it:

> Acting man is eager to substitute a more satisfactory state of affairs for a less satisfactory. His mind imagines conditions which suit him better, and his actions aim at bringing about this desired state. The incentive that impels a man to act is always some uneasiness. A man perfectly content with the state of affairs would have no incentive to change things. He would have neither wishes nor desires; he would be perfectly happy. He would not act; he would simply live free from care.[4]

This is the ultimate foundation of economics as a discipline. Such a position has several implications. First, in economics people are assumed to be rational in the sense that they are able to determine within limits what they want and will strive to fulfill as many of their wants as possible. People are, in other words, able to offset environmental, social, and biological forces that would otherwise determine what they do. To what extent they are able to accomplish this depends on the resources at their command and the intensity of desire to overcome forces that are obstructing the achievement of their goals.

Although taken for granted by many, these points need to be made because not all social scientists agree with this perspective. Many will argue, at least for purposes of their theories, that a factor such as the immediate environment *determines*—not influences—human behavior. The economist, on the other hand, looks at such factors as the immediate environment as constraints within which the individual's preferences can operate.

The economist's assumption of rational behavior sometimes annoys people from other branches of the social studies who apparently feel that people act irrationally (or nonrationally) much of the time. The actual difference here, however, may be largely a matter of definition. In assuming that people behave rationally, the economist does not mean that human beings are nec-

---

[4]Ludwig von Mises, *Human Action: A Treatise on Economics* (New Haven, Conn.: Yale University Press, 1949), p.13.

essarily cold, calculating machines, who always pursue selfish interest with perfect precision. Indeed the economics of information, which deals with the question of how much information people should gain before they make a decision, is one of the rapidly developing fields of economics. Thus, the prospect that people make mistakes because they're not properly informed is now very much alive in economic theory.

Furthermore, the religious hermit who lives in semistarvation to achieve oneness with God could be quite rational. The kamikaze pilot who crashes his plane into a carrier could be no less rational. They both may be using their resources in the best way they know how to fulfill their goals.

Thus the statement that people behave rationally is not a terribly strong statement about how people behave. It merely means that people attempt to achieve their goals and that they devote at least some thought, some of the time, to how to do it. It turns out that this assumption, modest though it is, permits a great deal of careful analysis.

Further, it also turns out that people are not the only living beings that behave rationally, at least some of the time. As discussed in a later chapter, experimental animals behave rationally. They may be dumb but they are not irrational! On the basis of this view, that man behaves rationally in this very limited sense, economists have been able to construct a very elaborate detailed theory. Of course, the fact that it is elaborate and that its basic assumptions seem sensible does not prove that it is true. In order to tell whether any given theory is true, we must contrast it with reality, either through statistical manipulation or through experiments.

Economists from Adam Smith on always looked to the real world to test their theories. Since about 1950, with the development of modern computers, this study has become predominantly a matter of careful statistical analysis. Very recently laboratory experiments have begun to be performed. All of these studies seem to indicate that the basic theory, founded on assumptions of rationality, is correct much of the time.

Rational behavior implies that the individual will always choose more of what he or she wants rather than less. It also means that he or she will choose less of what he or she does not want than more. For example, if the individual desires beer and pretzels and is presented with two bundles of these goods, both with the same amount of pretzels and one with more beer, the rational individual (that is, college student!) will take the bundle with the greater number of beers. If he or she does not like beer, then that is another matter. In a similar vein, if one bundle contains a greater variety of goods or goods with a higher quality than the other bundle, the individual will choose that bundle with the greater variety or higher quality. For all intents and purposes, goods of differing quality can be treated as distinctly different goods.

If there is some uncertainty surrounding the available bundles, the individual will choose that bundle for which the expected value is greatest. People do make mistakes mainly because they have incomplete information, but this does not negate the assumption of rational behavior. We only assume that the individual's motivation is to do that which he or she expects will improve his or her station in life, not that he or she always accomplishes this. There are such things as losers.

Economists are often criticized for assuming that man is wholly materialistic—that man wants material things. The criticism is unjustified. All we have assumed from the start of this section is that an individual has desires. These desires may be embodied in material things, such as cocktails and clothes. However, we also fully recognize that human beings want things that are aesthetic, intellectual, and spiritual in nature. Some people do want to read Shakespeare and Keats and to contemplate the idea of beauty. Others want to attend church and worship as they choose. Even a few may want to read this book! We have no quarrel with this (particularly with those who are interested in this book). We accept these as values with which we must deal in our analysis. They are part of the data we handle. We emphasize, however, that what we have to say regarding material things is also largely applicable to those values that are not material. We may talk in terms of goods, but what we mean are those things people value.

THINKING ABOUT COST

Another implication of our basic position is that as far as the individual is concerned, Nirvana will never be reached. The individual will never obtain a perfect world and, as a result, must accept second best, which is to maximize utility through behavior. This suggests that the individual will undertake to do that for which there is some expected net gain. He or she will in this sense pursue his or her own self-interest. This does not mean that the individual will necessarily lack concern for fellow human beings. One of the things that he or she may want is to give to others. Such behavior can yield as much pleasure as anything else, and if so, it will be done.

Why do people give gifts, say, at Christmas time? There are many motives that can be separated out; however, we suggest that the overriding reason is that the person involved gets some pleasure (gain), in one form or another, from doing it. Even the Bible admonishes that "it is better to give than to receive," indicating that there are gains to be had for acts of charity. Can you think of anything done by you or anyone else that the actor did not expect would make him or her happier? (Remember, you have no doubt made a mistake and lost, but this is not involved in the question.)

Certainly there have been instances in which direct self-satisfaction was not the basis for your action. However, we wish only to make the point that much, but certainly not all, human action is founded on the desire of people to gain from what they do. To the extent that they behave the way we assume they do, then our predictions about their behavior should be accurate.

If we are seeking to maximize our utility, then it follows that we must make choices between relevant alternatives. It also follows that in the act of choosing to do one thing, we must forgo doing or having something else. There is no escaping this. Although often measured in terms of dollars, the cost of doing or having something is the value of one's best alternative forgone when a choice is made.

Therefore, for every act there is a cost, and it is this cost that will determine whether (or how much) something will be done. Cost is the constraint on action. In other words, is there anything such as a free lunch? Free TV? Free love or sex? How can these things be had if choices are involved? No money may have changed hands, but again, cost is not money. Money (or more properly, dollars) is just one means of measuring cost. To have such things, we have to give up something in the way of time, psychic benefits, or resources that may be used for other purposes.

In an attempt to explain social phenomena we will, throughout this book, address the question of the costs and benefits of any given form of behavior. In understanding behavior, cost is a very powerful explanatory factor, as we will see. Consider the following problems:

1. Why do the poor tend to ride buses and the rich tend to fly?

It may be that there are differences in the educational and experience levels of the two groups that result in different behavior patterns. It may also be that the rich, being rich, can afford such extravagances as airplane tickets. All these factors may explain part of the behavior; but we wish to stress that it may be cheaper for the poor to take a bus than to fly and cheaper for the rich to fly than to take the bus. Both rich and poor pay the same price for equal tickets; consequently, the difference in cost must lie partly in the difference in the value of the time of the rich and the poor.

If by rich person we mean someone whose wage rate is very high, it follows that the rich person's time is much more valuable (in terms of wages forgone) than the poor person's time. Since it generally takes longer to take a bus than to fly, the cost of taking the bus, which includes the value of one's time, can be greater to the rich than the cost of flying. The poor person's time may be worth very little in terms of what he could have earned. Therefore, the total cost of a bus ride can be quite inexpensive. As a case in point, consider Johnny Carson, who makes well over $1 million per year, and a poor man who is unemployed. Determine the total cost for each to take the bus and to take the plane from Washington to Chicago. You may think that Johnny Carson has a lot of free time for sunbathing on the beach. Actually, Johnny Carson could be making money instead of playing on the beach. He is spending very large amounts, in terms of income forgone, for his pleasure on the beach. It is understandable why a wealthy man might choose to do this, but it is hard to say why a wealthy man would choose to spend his valuable time by riding a bus.

2. Why do the British use linen table napkins more often than Americans do?

In part, the answer may be that the differences in culture have had an effect on the willingness of people to use one form of napkin or another. However, one should also realize that the British have to import virtually all of their paper or pulpwood and that paper is relatively expensive there. Paper napkins are much less costly in the United States. Furthermore, linen napkins require washing and ironing, and since wages are generally higher in the United States, the cost of using linen napkins is much greater to Americans than to people of Britain. Again the difference in costs provides a partial explanation.

3. Why do some people resist cheating on their examinations?

It may be that they fear being caught and suspended from school, which means they attribute a cost to cheating. Barring this, they may have a moral code that opposes cheating, at least in this form. If they cheat, they would have to bear the psychic cost of going against what they consider right. This does not mean that all those with a moral code or conscience will not cheat to some degree. (Why?)

4. Why do some men forgo asking women out on dates?

They may be shy (or gay), or they may feel that the cost of the date in terms of the money and time expenditure is too great. They may also be reluctant to ask women out because in doing so they have to incur the risk cost of being turned down.

5. Why are people as courteous as they are on the highways?

They may have a streak of kindness in their hearts, but they may also be fully aware of the very high cost they can incur if their rudeness ends in an accident.

When trying to sum up the economist's view of human behavior, we are reminded of a little ditty for which, unfortunately, we do not have the source:

> Oh, little girl with your nose pressed up against
>   the windowpane of life,
> There is no jelly doughnut.

At least, there is no jelly doughnut without a cost, which is why economists often say, "There is no such thing as a free lunch."

THINKING ABOUT THE MARGIN OF COST

In determining how many units of a given good we will consume, we must focus on the additional cost of each additional unit. Another name for this cost concept is *marginal cost*. In other words, before we can proceed to the consumption of the next unit, we must, at each step along the way, ask how much that additional unit costs.

If we are allowed time to make choices, there is substantial reason to believe that, as a general rule, the marginal cost of successive units we provide for ourselves or others will rise. At any point where a choice must be made, we are likely to have a whole array of opportunities we can choose to forgo to do this one thing. These opportunities are likely to vary in their value to us. In making the choice to consume the first unit of a good, which opportunity will we give up? We will forgo that opportunity we value least, and we will forgo that opportunity if the value of the unit produced is greater than the value of the opportunity forgone.

Since cost (or as in this case, marginal cost) is the value of that opportunity given up, this means that the cost of the first unit is as low as possible. If we then wish to produce or consume a second unit, we will have to give up that opportunity that is second to the bottom in value. This means that the marginal cost of the second is greater than the first. Given this choice behavior, we should expect the marginal cost of successive units to rise progressively. Therefore, if we were to describe the relationship between the unit of the good provided and the marginal cost, we would expect to have a curve that is upward sloping to the right as in Figure 1–1. In this graph, marginal cost is on the vertical axis, and the quantity of the good is on the horizontal axis. We economists refer to such a curve as the *supply curve*. Because of this

FIGURE 1–1

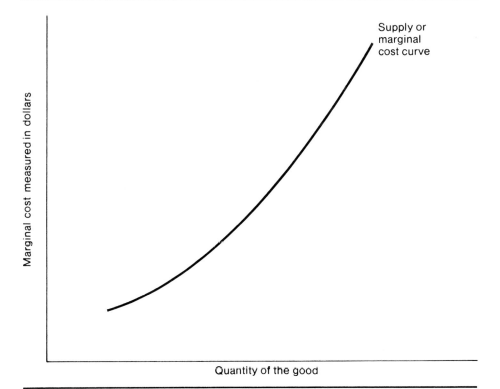

FIGURE 1–2

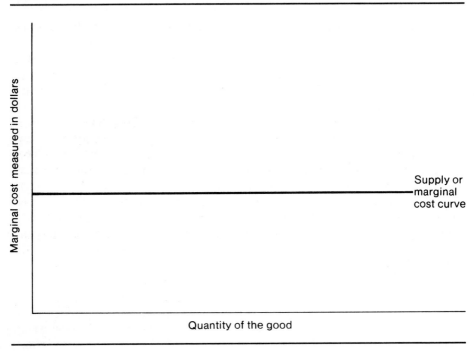

relationship, we can argue that the higher the benefits (or price) received per unit, the more units of the good that we can justify providing.

There are cases in which the marginal cost of providing additional units is constant. More units of the good can be provided by forgoing alternatives that are equal in value. (Can you think of such cases?) In this event the supply curve will be horizontal. See Figure 1–2.

There is no reason to believe that the supply curve will remain stationary over time and under all conditions. Basically, the curve is set where it is because of a given cost structure of providing the good. It follows that anything that changes this cost structure will cause the curve to shift in one direction or the other. If the cost (which means the value of alternatives) of providing the good rises, then the curve will shift upward and to the left. If the cost goes down, the curve will move downward and to the right.[5] (Can you think of changes that would change the cost structure?)

---

[5]For a more detailed discussion on the concept of supply, see any standard textbook on principles of economics. For example, see David Kamerschen, Richard B. McKenzie, Clark Nardinelli, *Economics* (Boston: Houghton Mifflin, 1989), chap. 3.

THINKING ABOUT DEMAND

The assumption that the rational individual maximizes his utility implies that he or she will fully allocate income among those things wanted. When we say income, we mean full income, which includes not only what a person can earn on a conventional job and that can be measured in terms of dollars, but also what a person can earn by doing things for himself or herself outside of work, such as cooking meals.

How can a person not fully allocate his income? Even when a person saves, he is allocating his income and generally doing it for a purpose. That purpose may be to acquire a certain degree of security for himself or his family or to buy something he wants in the future. We might rightfully argue that by saving the person is buying something.

The assumption also implies that the individual will continue to consume a given good until the marginal cost (MC) of the last unit obtained is equal to the last unit's marginal utility (MU). (As in the concept of marginal cost, *marginal utility*, or *benefit*, is the additional utility on each additional unit of the good.) That is to say, the individual would consume until $MU = MC$. If this were not the case and the marginal cost of the next unit of the good were less than the marginal utility of it (or $MC < MU$), the individual could increase his or her level of satisfaction by consuming additional units. He or she could get more additional satisfaction from the additional unit or units than would be forgone by not consuming something else.

Note that the marginal cost is the value of that which is forgone. If the marginal cost exceeds the marginal utility, the individual can increase his satisfaction by consuming at least one unit less. (Can you explain why?)

This so-called equimarginal rule ($MC = MU$) is readily applicable to production and consumption decisions involving, say, carrots or candy, but we suggest that it has a much broader application than may be first realized. If you are a student, what rule do you follow in determining how much you study for a given course? We expect that you will follow the $MC = MU$ rule developed above. You will continue to study until the marginal cost of an additional minute spent studying is equal to the marginal utility gained from studying that unit of time. If the marginal utility of an additional minute is greater than the marginal cost, is not this another way of saying that you would gain more by studying this particular course than doing whatever else you could do with the time? Would you, therefore, not study the additional minute?

Mini skirts are in. But how mini is mini? In determining the length of her skirt, what rules does a woman follow? Again we argue that she will shorten the skirt until the marginal utility of taking it up one additional inch is equal to the additional cost. (What are the costs and benefits of shortening the skirt?) For different people in the same situation and for the same people in different situations, the costs and benefits of a skirt's length are different. Therefore, we would anticipate a variety of skirt lengths.

Consider a person—yourself, if you like—who is preparing to eat dinner. What rule do you use in determining how many beans you will dish onto this plate? By now, you should have it; you will add beans to your plate until the marginal cost of the additional bean is equal to the marginal utility.

No individual is really able to act in as precise a manner as the above discussion may imply. Each person may not have the capacity to do so and the benefits to be gained from such precision may not be worthwhile. (Explain.) Actually, we are interested only in making the point that the rational individual will approximate this kind of behavior.

When considering more than one good, say, two goods such as beer and pretzels, the utility-maximizing condition of $MC = MU$ translates into the following condition:

$$MU_b/P_b = MU_p/P_p$$

where

MU_b = marginal utility of beer
MU_p = marginal utility of pretzels
P_b = price of beer
P_p = price of pretzels

If this is not the case and MU_b/P_b is greater than MU_p/P_p, then we can show that the person will not be maximizing his or her utility. No one really knows what a *util* of satisfaction is, but for purposes of illustration, let us assume that utils exist and that the additional satisfaction acquired from the last unit of beer (MU_b) is 30 utils, the additional satisfaction of the last unit of pretzels (MU_p) consumed is 10 utils, and that the price of beer and pretzels is $1 each. It follows that

$$MU_b/P_b > MU_p/P_p \text{ or } 30 \text{ utils/\$1} > 10 \text{ utils/\$1}$$

The individual can change his consumption behavior, consume one less unit of pretzels, and use the $1 to consume one additional unit of beer. He would give up 10 utils of satisfaction in the consumption of pretzels, but he would gain 30 utils of satisfaction in beer. He would be better off, and he would continue to reorganize his purchases until the equality set forth above is met. (You may find this a little tricky. Do not hesitate about rereading what you have just finished. It is imperative that you understand what has been said above before going ahead to the next point.)

Now, let us suppose that the individual has fully maximized his satisfaction and that $MU_b/P_b = MU_p/P_p$. Further, suppose that MU of beer and of pretzels is 20 utils and that the price of beer falls to, say, $0.50 and the price of pretzels remains at $1. This means that ($MU_b/P_b > MU_p/P_p$) or (20 utils/$0.50 > 20 utils/$1) and that the individual can get two units of beer (40 utils) for the price of one unit of pretzels; he can gain utility by switching to more beer. Notice what we have said: if the price of beer goes down, the rational individual will buy more beer. This all falls out of our general assumption that the individual is simply out to maximize his utility.

This inverse relationship between price and quantity is extremely important in economic theory and in the analysis of this book—so important that economists refer to it as the *law of demand*. It is important because it adds an element of prediction to economic analysis. We can say with a great deal of confidence that if the price of a good or service falls, *ceteris paribus* (or Latin for everything else held constant), people will buy more of it. It is, perhaps, the strongest predictive statement a social scientist can make with regard to human behavior.[6]

The law of demand can be graphically depicted by a downward sloping curve as in Figure 1–3. As the price for the good falls from P_2 to P_1, the quantity purchased rises from Q_1 to Q_2.

Courses in economics generally deal with the law of demand in the context of conventional goods and services such as peanut butter, detergent, and meals at a restaurant. Although we agree with such application, we wish to stress that the law has a much broader application. In fact, we go so far as to assert that the law of demand applies to a wide range of things that people value and the procurement of which is revealed in human behavior. Consequently, we argue that the law of demand can be applicable to such "goods" as sex, honesty, dates, highway speeding, babies, and life itself! We predict that if the price of any one of these things goes up, the quantity demanded will diminish and vice versa.

We will spend much of our time in this book discussing how the law of demand applies to areas such as these. For purposes of illustration at this point, let us consider the demand for going to church. Many people do place a value on going to church, and as strange as it may seem, there is a price to church attendance. The church may not have a box office outside its doors selling tickets, but people have to pay the price of their time, and they do understand that they are expected to contribute something to the operations of the church. (How many well-established people in the community would feel comfortable taking their families to church week after week without contributing anything to the church?) Through stewardship, sermons, and visitations the church does apply pressure, as mild as it might be, to get people to contribute. To that extent they extract a price.

Suppose that the minister and the board of elders decide to raise significantly their demands on the congregation. What do you think will happen to the church's membership, holding all other things constant? The membership may be on the rise for a number of reasons. What we maintain is that because

---

[6]The relationship called *demand* is held with such complete confidence that one prominent economist has reportedly argued that if an empirical study ever reveals that people buy more when the price is increased, there must be something wrong with the empirical investigation. Other economists like ourselves, taking a more moderate view, may recognize possible exceptions to the rule but argue that they are extremely few.

FIGURE 1–3

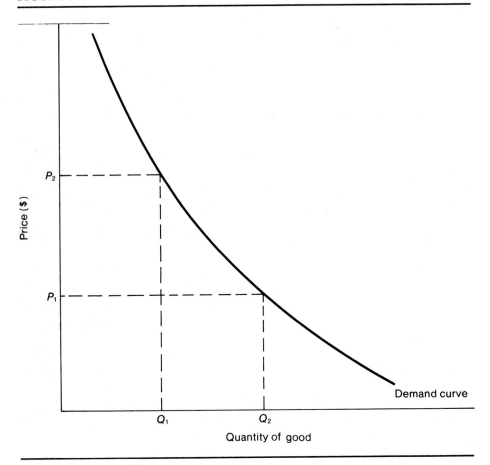

of the greater price, the membership will rise by less than otherwise. In that sense, the "price" increase reduces the membership. This does not necessarily mean that people would be less religious; it may only mean that some will react to the price change and make use of other ways of expressing and reinforcing their beliefs.

Suppose we return to the days when men were expected to be the ones who asked women out on dates. (In recent years, as many of the readers of this book can attest, this social institution has broken down to a significant degree.) Given all the attributes of a given group of women, men placed, as they do now, some value on having dates with them. In other words, they had a demand for dates. (In the event that you are concerned with the approach we are taking, we could easily reverse the example and talk about women's demand for dates. We only intend to use this situation as an example. We do not wish to judge it as being good or bad.)

Clearly, the utility-maximizing men will date women, if they can get the dates, until the marginal utility of the last date during some specified period of time is equal to the marginal cost of the date. There is an implicit price to most dates. For the man, if men are expected to bear the expense, it is equal to the money spent on transportation, entertainment, and refreshment, plus the value of his time. (There is also a price to the woman, even when women do not pay. The question is, what does the price include?)

Suppose that during this epoch when men were expected to pay for dates, a group of women collude; they get together and decide that the humdrum dates of yesterday are no longer up to their standards. They decide to collectively require the men to spend more on them. They in effect agree to raise the price of dates. If such a collusive arrangement were to stick, what do you think would have happened to the number of invitations issued to this group of women? No doubt it would fall. It may fall because the men would then have an incentive to substitute other women for the women that were taking part in the cartel. Additionally, the increase in price of dates can induce several men to consume other goods such as watching Saturday night television or having a cold beer at a local tavern.

As the number of calls for dates begins to fall off, there would very likely be women who would begin to chisel on the collusive agreement by effectively lowering their demands (price). Thus, the agreement would tend to break down. Competition, as we will see on a number of occasions, will play a role in determining exactly what demands are made in areas of social interaction.

Many people value speeding in their cars. If caught speeding they may pay a fine of, say, $50. If they expect to be caught one out of every 100 times that they speed, the price they pay per incident of time speeding averages out to $.50. Given this price, they will find a certain quantity of speeding desirable.

Suppose, now, that the fine is raised to $10,000 per speeding conviction. The average price paid per speeding incident would then rise to $100. Do you think that the people would speed less as the concept of demand predicts? Suppose that the probability of being caught is increased. This can be accomplished by putting more patrolmen on the roads. What would be the effect?

THINKING ABOUT MARKETS

One of the more interesting questions asked by economists is, how much will a person, or a whole lot of people, consume, of a given good? We have stated in so many words our answer for the individual: An individual will continue to consume a good until the marginal cost and marginal benefit of the last unit equal one another.

That rule of behavior can be depicted graphically with the aid of the supply and demand curves we have just developed. Since both curves are price-quantity relationships, we can draw both the demand (or marginal benefit) curve and the supply (or marginal cost) curve on the same graph (see Figure 1–4). In taking this step we have constructed an abstract model of human behavior, but such an abstract model can be quite revealing and useful in many contexts. We will repeatedly demonstrate this throughout the book.

For now, we need only point out that the maximizing individual will choose to produce and consume Q_1 units of this particular good. It does not matter what the good is or where the curves are positioned; the individual will choose that consumption level at the intersection of the two curves. It is at this point that marginal cost is equal to marginal benefit.

If the individual chooses to restrict consumption to Q_2, note that the marginal benefit, which is indicated by the demand curve and represented by MB_1, is greater than the marginal cost, which is indicated by the supply curve and is MC_1. This is true of every unit between Q_2 and Q_1. Therefore,

FIGURE 1–4

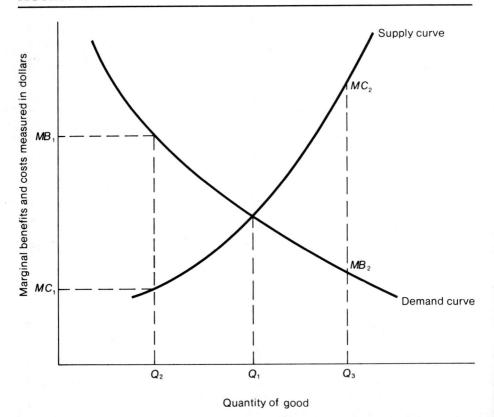

the maximizing individual can raise his or her utility by consuming them. Beyond Q_1, the reverse is true; the marginal cost is greater than the marginal benefit. For example, for the unit consumed at Q_3, the marginal cost is MC_2 while the marginal benefit is less, MB_2.

Implicitly, we have assumed the maximizing person is trading with himself—giving up units of one thing for more units of another. Quite often, however, people find that it is less costly to trade with someone else than to produce the good themselves. To understand a social setting in which there are many producers and consumers trading for a particular good, we need to construct a model involving a market supply curve and market demand curve. We can derive a market supply curve by adding together what all producers are willing to offer on the market at each possible price. If each individual producer is willing to offer a larger quantity at higher prices, the market supply curve, like the individuals' supply curves, will be upward sloping.[7] To obtain the market demand curve, we can add the amounts demanded by all the consumers at each and every price. Since the individuals' demand curves are downward sloping, the same will be true of the market demand curve. The market supply and demand curves are depicted in Figure 1–5. The quantities involved in this graph are much greater than in Figure 1–4.

In a highly competitive market situation—one in which many consumers have many sources for obtaining a given good—we will still expect the market to offer that quantity of the good (Q_1) that is at the intersection of the market supply and market demand curves. The simple reason is that if the price is P_1 and if only Q_2 units (which is fewer than Q_1) are provided on the market, there will be many more units demanded (Q_3) than will be available (Q_2). Also note that there are consumers who are willing to offer the producers a price that exceeds the P_1 of producing the additional units. These consumers, who are represented by positions on the demand curve up and to the left of Q_3 on the demand curve, can be expected to bid the price up, just to obtain the quantity they want.

As a result of the competitive bidding process, the suppliers can be induced to expand their production from Q_2 to Q_1. Beyond Q_1, the marginal cost of providing an additional unit is greater than what any consumer is willing to pay for it. If one producer refuses to expand production, the consumers can, since we are talking about a competitive market, turn to other producers who may be in the market or may be enticed into it by the higher price.

In a monopoly market, one in which there is only one producer of the good, the consumers do not have the option of turning to another producer

---

[7]Strictly speaking, the market supply curve is not equal to the horizontal summation of the individuals' supply curves. Nothing is lost for our purposes, however, by leaving this refinement for more advanced treatments of the theory of supply.

FIGURE 1–5

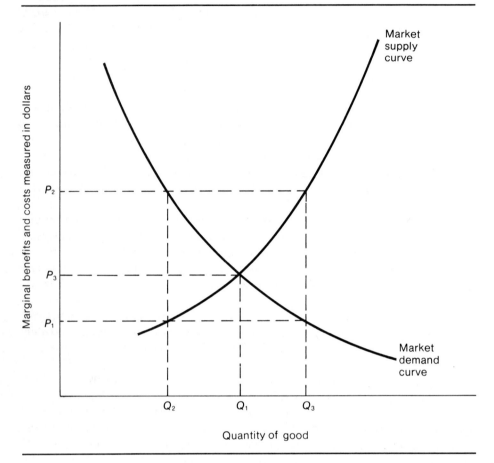

(i.e., competitor). To that extent, the monopolist has control over the market: the monopolist can restrict the number of units provided and thereby demand a higher price from the consumer. By restricting output, the monopolist can reduce the total cost of production and can receive greater revenues. (Can you explain why?)

Similarly, the number of units produced and consumed will adjust toward Q_1 if the suppliers initially try to sell more than Q_1 at price P_2. Suppose they try to offer Q_3 in Figure 1–5. The only way they can justify doing that is to charge a price higher than what consumers are willing to pay. Note that at Q_3 the marginal cost of the last unit is greater than the price the consumers are willing to pay for it. There will, as a result, be more units offered (Q_3) than will be purchased by consumers (Q_2) at the price (P_2) required for suppliers to cover their marginal cost.

Hence, the suppliers will be in a dilemma. They can either cut back on production and lower the price to the point that consumers will buy what is produced, or they can continue to produce more than can be sold at the price necessary to cover the cost of production. The suppliers can also produce the good and sell it at a price less than the cost incurred. Which option do you think the rational producers will choose? They will cut production back to Q_1, of course, and lower the price to P_3 in order to sell that quantity.

To the extent that the competitive market produces where marginal cost equals marginal benefit, which is the optimizing condition of individuals as explained above, economists say that it is "efficient." This means that producers sell all of those units of a good that are worth more to consumers than to producers. It also means that all trades are mutually beneficial to consumers and that producers have been exhausted, which is to say that no one can gain by further trades (beyond Q_1).

Now that we have outlined the basic framework of the economist's model, we can use it to consider changes in market conditions (meaning environmental, social, or whatever). We consider such changes in the discussion of most topics in this book. You name it—sex, family, organ transplants, school, politics, lying—and we will probably discuss it, either with supply and demand curves drawn out or with the curves in the back of our minds as points of analytical reference. We hope that through repeated reconsideration of market topics you will learn a great deal not only about the topics themselves but also about the intricacies of the laws of supply and demand.

THE LIMITS OF ECONOMIC THINKING

Although we consider many diverse dimensions of human experience in this book, we do not suggest that economic analysis can be used to explain all human behavior. The interaction of individuals in a social state, with each reacting to actions of the others, is indeed very complex. Some would say that it is so complex that precious little or nothing can be gained by the scientific study of it. We, of course, dispute such a claim. On the other hand, we must approach the complex task that we have before us with full recognition of our limited ability to understand social behavior, and we should be careful that we do not exaggerate the importance of the insights we gain from our study.

Scientific insights about people's behavior achieve a degree of prominence not so much because they rank high on some absolute scale of useful knowledge as because they say a little something we may not otherwise have known. In short, these insights should always be kept in perspective; they are not, for the most part, monumental and unchanging truths but tentative statements of the way we perceive the world at this time. And they should be coveted as small nuggets because of their relative durability in the give-and-take of scientific debate.

You now know that economic analysis is founded on an assumption that people know what they want or, what amounts to the same thing, that they have values. People make choices consistent with the values they hold, and we can talk about the logic people follow in maximizing the attainment of what they want—as we have done.

An obvious limit to economic analysis is implied in what we have just said, because much human experience is founded less on the attainment of what we want than on trying to figure out just what we want in the first place. The late University of Chicago economist Frank Knight made the point with more flair several decades ago:

> Since economics deals with human beings, the problem of its scientific treatment involves fundamental problems of the relations between man and his world. From a rational or scientific point of view, all practically real problems are problems in economics. The problem of life is to utilize resources "economically," to make them go as far as possible in the production of desired results. The general theory of economics is therefore simply the rationale of life—insofar as it has any rationale! The first question in regard to scientific economics is this question of how far life is rational, how far its problems reduce to the form of using given means to achieve given ends. Now this, we shall contend, is not very far; the scientific view of life is a limited and partial view; life is at bottom an exploration in the field of values, an attempt to discover values, rather than on the basis of knowledge of them to produce and enjoy them to the greatest possible extent. We strive to "know ourselves,"" to find out our real wants, more than to get what we want. This fact sets a first and most sweeping limitation to the conception of economics as a science.[8]

Economics, unfortunately, has very little to say about what people value or why they value what they do. Values are the type of basic data that must be given or assumed as a part of the analysis. Once the values or goods are defined, then the individual can be assumed to maximize the attainment of those goods.

However, note that this approach leaves little room for the individual, in the course of the maximizing process, to redefine what he wants; it leaves little room for spontaneous actions that spring from raw emotions. We do not mean to suggest that economic analysis is useless, only that, as might be reasonably expected, it has its limitations. It can explain only a part of human experience, whether that experience involves crime, politics, sex, the family, education, or any other subject broached in this book. We must look to the other social sciences, philosophy, and the humanities for help in our quest

---

[8]Frank H. Knight, "The Limitations of Scientific Method in Economics, " in *The Ethics of Competition and Other Essays* (New York: Harper & Row, 1935), p. 105.

for understanding human behavior. And even with this help, we will probably always conclude that there is much about human behavior that is incomprehensible.[9]

CONCLUDING COMMENTS

How a person views the world and interprets the information he receives from it depends on the preconceived model he or she has of it. The preceding has been an outline of how economists perceive the real world. For sure, this has been an incomplete description of the economists' way of thinking; there are many more refinements that can be made.[10]

Because of this model—because of the concepts of supply and demand—the economists' first inclination is not to think in terms of absolutes, of whether something will be done or left undone, or whether or not a goal will be sought.[11] Most things have a price at which they may be obtained, and adjustments in behavior are made according to the price (benefit) that is charged (received).

By concentrating on the general goal of utility maximization (and when talking about the firm, profit maximization) rather than on specific objectives, economists are continuously seeking out new and nonobvious alternatives and thinking in terms of the substitutability, on the margin, of specific means of reaching the general goal. Years of life are therefore viewed as a possible substitute for cigarette smoking; low-quality medical service in large quantities is one alternative to high-quality service in more limited quantities; ice cream is a possible substitute for good dental care.

Because economists view the individual as fundamentally seeking ways of gaining, whenever a person proposes a solution for any problem, economists instinctively ask, are there private interests involved? Economists are trained to separate private interests from the fabric of proposals offered as solutions for social concerns, and they are trained to pull out value judgments from arguments that are put forth as matters of logic. The economists' proclivity to think in this way sets them and their discipline apart from others. We hope that after you have read much of this book, you will reread this chapter and understand better both the benefits and limitations of economic thinking.

---

[9]For more on the limits of economic analysis, see Richard B. McKenzie, *The Limits of Economic Science* (Boston: Kluwer-Nijhoff Publishing, 1983).

[10]Because of space restrictions a book of this nature forces upon the authors, we have attempted to extend and refine the model until we thought the marginal benefits of an additional point was equal to the marginal cost of making the point.

[11]See the quote by James Buchanan at the beginning of Part 1.

QUESTIONS TO PONDER

1. What role does utility maximization play in economic theory? Why does the economist not assume that the individual strives for something less than maximum utility?

2. What is the decision rule an individual will follow in determining the distance he will drive behind another car? What will be the effect of a reduction in the speed limit on the distance between cars? Explain.

3. If in the so-called *economy-size* box of detergent, a consumer can actually get more detergent per penny, why do people buy smaller boxes? What are the costs and benefits of various box sizes?

4. The authors could provide the readers with a more complicated and sophisticated economic theory than the one they have developed to this point. What are the costs and benefits of doing so? Why do they not do it? How complicated should a theory be?

5. "If a theory can explain everything, then it can predict nothing." Do you agree? Explain.

CHAPTER 2

Anything Worth Doing Is Not Necessarily Worth Doing Well

In the previous chapter, we stressed the role cost plays in guiding human behavior. In this chapter, we offer specific examples of the influence of cost. We seek to show you how economic analysis can help us develop surprising conclusions about the way people behave.

ANYTHING WORTH DOING

From early childhood, most of us have been taught that anything worth doing is worth doing well. If we were asked today if we still agree with the statement, many of us would say that we do.[1] It is only natural for a person to prefer a job that has been done well to one that has been done not so well. Indeed, such a preference for quality is fully consistent with the basic assumption in economics that more is preferred to less. It is also easy to see why a person may not like to redo something that he or she has already done, particularly if the combined time involved is greater than the time that would have been required to do it right in the first place.

Obviously, people do not behave the way they profess they should. There is probably not a minister around who has not written what he considered at the time to be a poor sermon, and one of the authors recently built a bookcase that was more or less thrown together. Wives and husbands have cooked dinners they knew in their hearts were seriously deficient in one respect or another. Students regularly choose to work for a grade of C (or a grade point average far less than 4.0) instead of going all out for an A. This is true even though the A is the preferred grade. How many, do you suppose, of the students who are reading this have written a paper that by their own standards fell far short of a well-done paper? In fact, can you say at this point that you have read the last few pages well?

---

[1]James M. Buchanan has suggested that an economist can be distinguished from a noneconomist by his reaction to the statement. "Economics and Its Scientific Neighbors," in *The Structure of Economic Science: Essays on Methodology,* ed. Sherman Roy Krupp (Englewood Cliffs, N.J.: Prentice-Hall, 1966) p. 168.

Admittedly, people do some things well, but the point we wish to emphasize is that they frequently do things less than well, not because they do not want to do better, but because of the additional (or marginal) cost involved in improving the quality of whatever they are doing. Given the student's ability—which, as a matter of fact, is limited at any time—writing a good A paper generally requires more effort and time than writing a C paper. If the student spends additional time on the paper, he or she has less time for doing other things—less time to study the subject matter in other courses—which may mean doing less well in another course or even failing it. He or she cannot use the added time for physical exercise, cannot spend the time in bed, or out on dates. To reiterate, there is usually an additional cost that must be borne for a higher quality paper, and it is because of this cost that the student may rationally choose to turn in a paper that may just get by. (Even so, the student may still hope for an A. Can you explain why?)

If the cost is not greater for higher quality work, then one must wonder why the job would be done poorly. The student would be able to have a higher quality paper without giving up anything. The problem of the poorly done work may be one of perception; that is, the student may perceive the additional cost to be greater than what it actually is (in which case he or she should respond appropriately if provided with accurate information). Or the student may inaccurately assess the benefits of a better performance.

Quite often one person will admonish another to do a good job. For example, professors may be distressed at the quality of the papers they receive and may honestly feel that if their students are going to write a paper they should write a good one. The professors may be even more upset if they find out that their students spent the last few days doing very little or just having a good time.

The values the professors and the students place on different activities obviously differ. Professors may view the paper as being of greater value than do the students; they may view the other activities as being of less value. Consequently, they believe it is in the students' best interest to do better papers. However, since students view the value of the other activities as being higher, they in effect, view the cost of doing the better paper as being higher. Of course, it is clearly rational for professors to want the students to turn in better papers, but if they had to bear the costs, they might change their minds.

The same line of argument can be used to explain why the preacher's sermon is of low quality even though he or she may have the ability to do better. By writing a better sermon, the minister may have to bear the cost of not seeing the parishioners at the hospital or of giving up something else that is considered valuable. To cook a better meal, the homemaker may have to forgo writing letters, discussions with neighbors, or hauling Little Leaguers to practice.

What should be the quality level toward which a person should strive? The utility-maximizing individual should raise the quality of whatever he or she does until the marginal benefit received from an additional unit of quality

FIGURE 2–1

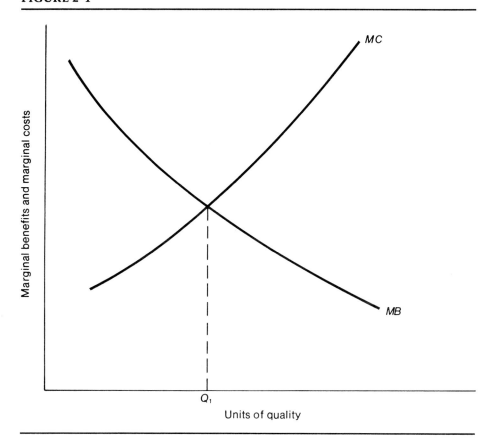

Units of quality

is equal to its marginal cost. Suppose that the marginal benefits (marginal utility) for units of quality diminishes as the total quality of the work goes up. Assume also that the marginal cost of additional units increases as the quality level is raised. The diminishing marginal utility assumption is represented by the downward curve (which is equivalent to the demand curve) MB in Figure 2–1. The upward sloping curve MC represents the increasing marginal cost. Notice that we have labeled the horizontal axis as units of quality. (The actual good or service involved can be anything.)

The utility-maximizing quality level is Q_1. Before Q_1, the marginal utility of an additional unit of quality is greater than the marginal (or additional) cost.[2] By expanding the quality toward Q_1, person can arise utility. If the

_____

[2]Marginal cost can be viewed as the utility forgone in some alternative activity. Therefore when $MU > MC$, by consuming more quality, the individual can acquire more utility than he gives up in some other activity.

person extends the quality level beyond Q_1, notice that the marginal cost of doing so will be greater than the marginal utility. The result is that the person's total utility level will be less than it would be at Q_1. An outside observer (such as a teacher) may feel that the quality of the work done by the student at Q_1 may be quite low—and it may even be low by the standards of the student—but this does not make his behavior any less rational. In other words, anything worth doing is not necessarily worth doing well!

WHY THE YOUNG GO TO COLLEGE

College classes are predominantly made up of young adults between the ages of 18 and 22 years. A small percentage are in their middle or late 20s, but people who are over 50 constitute an extremely small minority. Why do the young go to college whereas older adults, as a general rule, do not? The list of answers conventionally cited may include (1) the young, having recently graduated from high school, are more accustomed to the routine and peculiar demands of the educational process; (2) the young do not have the family responsibilities that the older people have; (3) the young, as a rule, realize the value of education more than do their elders; and (4) the young are more intellectually alive than their parents.

All of these factors can have an influence in determining the composition of college classes, although our experience suggests the last two reasons are invalid.[3] Although rarely cited, the difference in cost to the two groups may be equally important in explaining the composition of college classes.

The cost of a college education is more than the direct monetary expenditures made by the student at the start of each year or academic session. The total cost is the sum of all that the student must forgo. In addition to university charges, this total may include the loss of income one may experience while in the classroom and studying, the transportation expense associated with going to and from the campus, the additional postal and telephone expenditures one must make to stay in contact with friends and family, the cost of books and materials, and the cost of fitting in culturally with the college community.

Although there may be several differences, the essential difference to the young and old is the opportunity cost of their time. This, of course, will mean that the total costs will differ. Suppose, for example, that total university charges are $5,000 per year (approximately the average for all public univer-

---

[3]Two to three decades ago psychology professors often taught that people's mental capability peaked in the mid-twenties; that is to say, people's IQs rose until about 25 years of age and then declined. However, it appears that psychologists based their conclusion on a cross-sectional study of all age groups, and it happened that people in the study group who were in their mid-twenties were the most intelligent. Later studies of the same people as they age indicate that people's IQs continue to rise until at least the 60s or even 70s at which point they tend to level off.

TABLE 2–1   Cost of Four Years of College at Present-Day Prices

	Young Adult	Middle-Aged Adult
University charges	$20,000	$ 20,000
Opportunity cost	40,000	120,000
Other costs	8,000	8,000
Total costs	$68,000	$148,000

sities in the country in 1987) and that all costs other than opportunity cost of time are $2,000 per year. (We realize that the older people may be inclined to spend less on such things as college decals.) A younger person just out of high school can, over the course of the following four years, probably earn, at the best job he can get, about $40,000 for an average of $10,000 per year.

On the other hand, the man who is 45 years old can conceivably earn about three times as much, $120,000, or even more. This means that the total cost to the young adult is about $68,000 for four years of college education; the cost to the older person is approximately $148,000 (see Table 2–1).

Even if we assume that the two groups have the same values and are equal in every respect with regard to college education, we would expect a larger quantity of education to be demanded by the young than by the old. For example—and only as an example—assume that the demand for college by the young is exactly equal to the demand by the old, as depicted in Figure 2–2, A and B. Since the price of a college education to the older person (P_b) is

FIGURE 2–2

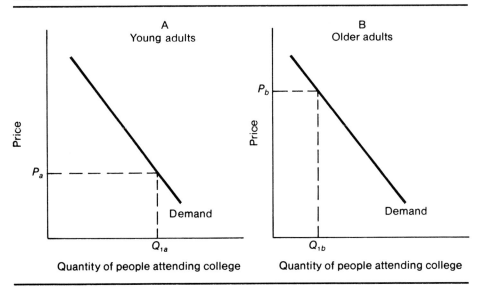

A
Young adults

B
Older adults

Quantity of people attending college   Quantity of people attending college

far greater than the price paid by the young (P_a), we would expect that the quantity of education demanded by the young would be greater. In the example of Figure 2–2, the quantity of education demanded by the young would be Q_{1a}, which is greater than the quantity demanded by the old, Q_{1b}.

In addition, the young have a much longer period of time to reap the benefits of a college education. The 45-year-old man or woman has only 20 to 30 years left in his or her working life, whereas the 22-year-old college graduate has 43 to 53 years left until retirement. Therefore, the investment expenditure by the young is likely to be much more profitable. Finally, we should note that the total cost to the young can be much less than we calculated, since their parents may foot the university bills. This is less likely to be so for much older persons.

WHY STUDENTS WALK ON THE GRASS

Walking on the grass may not appear to have anything to do with economics or to be sufficiently important to warrant discussion. We suggest, on the contrary, that the decision to walk on the grass, for example on the campus mall, is an aspect of human behavior and, therefore, of economics. A study of the decision to walk on the grass can be revealing about the causes of pollution and human action in general.

Why do students walk on the grass? More to the point, why do people who may dislike seeing paths form on campus or courthouse lawns walk in places where paths exist or are likely to exist? To answer these questions, one must begin by recognizing that there are benefits to walking on the grass. It can be a shortcut across campus and can save time; the walk may also be personally gratifying, particularly in the spring and without shoes.

The individual who strongly favors campus beautification must, in making the decision to walk on the grass, weigh these expected benefits against the expected cost. Before stepping onto the grass, the student must quickly reflect on the benefits and then calculate the costs involved. She may calculate that if she walks on the grass she will be responsible for killing several blades of grass but that it is very unlikely that anyone would be able to notice even if she regularly walked in the same places. Even if the student dislikes paths on lawns, she may reasonably expect the cost of the walk to approximate zero since each individual walk does not materially affect the environment under normal circumstances. Consequently, the calculated benefits exceed the cost, so she walks and does it rationally![4]

The problem is that everyone independently making similar calculations may do the same thing she did. The result is that a path forms, an eyesore is

---

[4]Before readers become unduly disturbed by this statement, they should check the economic meaning of rational action in Chapter 1.

created. This does not mean that it is rational for any one individual not to walk even after the path has formed: Since the student cannot control the walking of everyone else, the results of one's individual walks cannot be detected by anyone hence, the rational choice to take the benefits of cutting across the lawn. If the path is there, one can reason that if one does not walk, no one will be able to tell that one did not—that is, the nature of the path will not be affected. So one walks, and everyone else walks, and the path remains and continues to deepen and possibly spread. This in miniature illustrates the evolution of a form of pollution.

Following this line of argument, one can deduce that if a private cost is incurred by the individual, then the logical thing to do may be to take the sidewalk or another route. If the lawn or path is prone to become a quagmire when it rains, then private costs are imposed for walking. The student who walks on the grass will have to clean her shoes, and since time is involved in doing that, there is a cost. The cost for some may still not be as great as the benefits, but, significantly, when such conditions exist, there is less walking on the lawns than on sunny days.

The connection between walking on the lawns and pollution of other forms should be clear. A person or firm may litter because of calculating that there are certain benefits to getting rid of a piece of paper. One may reason that a piece of paper by itself will not significantly affect the environment or materially affect anyone's sensibilities, and will therefore discard the paper. The problem, again, is that if everyone follows suit, an environmental problem will develop. If the individual can control the behavior of all others, she may not pollute herself, but given her inability to control others, polluting may be rational. Also, cleaning up can be irrational; one may reason he cannot do enough to affect the general environment, particularly since others will be littering as he cleans up. (See footnote 4.) (In fact, his attempts to clean up can reduce the cost of polluting to everyone else—the environment is less affected—and therefore, one might anticipate, without an intervening change in people's values, more littering by some.) As a result he does not receive the full benefits of his actions and to that degree is less likely to clean up.

The analysis can be extended to conversations at a crowded cocktail party. If the reader has ever been at such a gathering, he or she probably remembers that often the sound level starts off low and then increases, even though the number of people in the room has not changed. The reason for the crescendo in conversation volume is that at the start people may be able to understand one another at a low volume, but, as everyone else begins to talk, the general volume begins to rise; this means that the volume that any one individual must use to be understood by the next person must be increased. Because she and everyone else increase their volume, talking louder can be rational. The result may be (as it has been time and time again) that all persons in the room end up virtually shouting at one another. If each were to lower his or her own individual volume, then all could have a more pleasant conversation. But the question is whether it is rational for any one individual to lower their volume. The answer is no; they could not be heard, because they cannot control the volume of the others in the room. In addition, they may not significantly affect the general volume level. Therefore, no one changes the volume.[5]

These problem areas point to the usefulness of some form of collective action, the purpose of which may be to impose private costs on the actions of individuals so that they may be expected to act in the general interest shared by all (which can also be in their own interest). In the case of walking on the grass, the government (university) can plant hedges or thorny bushes along the edge of the sidewalks. If students want to walk on the grass, they will have to incur the cost of jumping the bushes or of damage to stockings or pants. In the case of industrial pollution, taxes or fines for polluting can be imposed. Since people's demands for these activities slope downward, the quantity demanded will be reached.

THE ECONOMIC CALCULUS OF PANICS

To panic in a burning theater, falling stadium, or sinking ship often appears to be a dumb—irrational—thing to do. If all people in the theater or stadium or on the ship remained orderly, far fewer lives would be lost. Instead, often in such situations, people panic and dash for the exits or the lifeboats, sometimes in a wild frenzy. Unable to get through the exits or on the lifeboats at more or less the same time, panicky people stack up at the doors or turn over or overload the lifeboats. Needless deaths occur. Unfortunately, in many fires more people die from not being able to get out than from the fire itself.

Certainly, panics are frequently thought to be totally outside economic analysis. After all, it is commonly believed that people could be caught up in panics only if they lose their "cool," or worse, their brains—meaning their ability to calculate the consequences of what they are doing. Indeed, panics are explained as the spontaneous, unthinking behavior of people responding to survival instincts, which may be true in some situations. To us, however, many panics (but certainly not all) panics can be understood in terms of the economic calculus of costs and benefits. Panicky behavior can be quite rational.

---

[5]One qualification: as the volume goes up, several may decide to leave the room, keeping the volume from going as high as it otherwise would. Additionally, the higher general volume can make the party more tiring and can cause it to end more quickly for some. The host could conceivably get up and ask that everyone quiet down; the immediate effect can be a sharp reduction in volume. This is, however, likely to be a short interlude before the sound increases again.

Admittedly, if everyone remained calm and collected in the presence of a crowded and burning theater, then all *may* be able to exit without harm. People could walk single file out the limited number of exits. However, each person in the theater has little or no control over the entire group. Each has to reflect on what he or she should do, given what others are expected to do when no one can control the entire group. Each person can reason that he or she has a very good chance of getting out of the theater alive if everyone else acts orderly and walks out calmly. But each can also reason that he or she has an even better chance of survival by running for the exit, regardless of whether the other do or do not run.

The person in the middle of a theater looking up at the burning roof may rightfully reason that he or she has the poorest chance of getting out alive and therefore has the most to gain from "panicking." However, those closest to the exits are not without cause for panicking. They too can improve their chances of survival if they run; they get out more quickly. In addition, they can quickly conclude that others far removed from the exit have rational reasons to run for the exit and can run over the people closest to the exits. Indeed, many people in the theater can be expected to contemplate a pileup at the doors, which is all the more reason to panic: they must attempt to get out before the doors are clogged with trampled dead bodies.

If there were some personal cost to running for the exit, then all within the theater would be less likely to run. The cost itself would reduce their interest in running directly (downward sloping demand curves still exist in burning theaters). Furthermore, each person can reason that others will be less inclined to run, which reduces the incentive of everyone to run. The threat of a pileup at the doors is reduced. This line of reasoning explains why panics are reduced when someone—the police, the manager of the theater, or the captain of the ship—takes charge when panics are real possibilities. The person taking charge effectively says that he or she will exact a significant toll on the people who get out of hand. The captain of a sinking ship may go so far as to say that he will blow the brains out of anyone who tries to improve his position in the cue for the boats. In effect, the captain says I will make running for the lifeboat a bad deal: "If you try to improve your chance of survival by panicking, I will worsen it with the gun in my hand!"

Unfortunately, many panics occur because no one is in a position to take charge. For example, no one has a gun to threaten everyone. In addition, many may refuse to take charge because taking charge can be an irrational thing to do. If a person stops to try to convince the crowd that they should walk orderly to the exits, then he or she can be the one with the worst chance of survival. Besides, each can reason that no one (or an insufficient number) will listen, making the calls for order worthless. The moral of the analysis: if you intend to control in a potential panic, you had better have a very big stick—but a gun might be better!

Is there any way of telling whether the economic explanation does explain the type of behavior observed in panics? Or should we deduce that panics reflect a breakdown of the economic calculus we call rationality? Evidence is difficult to come by, simply because it is hard for researchers to intrude on panics to gather data. There is tentative evidence, based on an experiment run in the early 1950s that, although it does not conclusively settle matters, it does cast a great deal of light on it. A professor of sociology tied a knot on one end of each of a large number of pieces of string. He placed these knots, one by one, in a bottle in such a way that the end of each string stuck out. The neck of the bottle was such that it was easy to pull the strings out, including the knot, if only one or two were passing through the neck at a time. However, the knots were sufficiently large that if all of the strings were pulled at more or less the same time, the knots would clog the neck of the bottle.

The professor then gave the free ends of the strings to his students and told them he was running an experiment and that all of the students who pulled their strings completely out of the bottle (that is, pulled the knot out) within 30 seconds would receive a nickel. Clearly, there was no cause for panic here—the students were not in any way in danger; but on the other hand, the economic arguments developed above with regard to panics would apply. Those who did not pull on the strings and let other people pull theirs out first had less chance of getting a nickel. On the other hand, if everyone pulled on the strings, none of them would get their strings out, and no one would get paid.

As we suppose the reader has already guessed, all of the students pulled on their strings immediately.[6] In effect, the neck of the bottle resembled the door of a burning theater when panic had set in.

THE SOCIAL DILEMMA: CONSERVING ENERGY

In the 1970s, most people were concerned about the developing shortage of energy. Many attempted to conserve by turning down their thermostats a few degrees and perhaps driving a little more slowly. The effects of such voluntary actions were, however, not sufficient to eliminate the shortage. Drastic government action in the form of rules on speed limits, thermostats, and fuel consumption in automobiles was necessary to partially remedy the situation.

Why did people who were concerned about the energy crisis leave their lights burning and continue to zip along the highways at high speeds? Was it solely because people did not care (as many did not)? Why were price increases on energy necessary to get people to cut back on their energy use at home and in the automobile?

---

[6]The authors have repeated the experiment with the students in their classes with essentially the same result.

Imagine, for the moment, John sitting in an overstuffed chair watching television. He knows that a light has been left on in an adjoining room, but he does not get up and turn it off. Leaving the light on for an additional half hour until he happens to walk by the room will increase his electric bill, but we must also recognize that getting up requires effort and diminishes the entertainment value of the television program. In other terms, turning the light off is costly. Moreover, given relatively low rates on the use of electric power, John may calculate that the cost of turning the light off is greater than the increase in the electric bill.

If John is concerned about the total community consumption of fuel through the generation of electric power, he may still reasonably assume that his decision to leave the light on, or even leave every light in his house on, will not appreciably affect the total amount of fuel consumed by the power company. During the winter of 1977 and 1978, natural gas supplies were in critically short supply. Many workers were being laid off because of the gas shortage. All during this period, the gas streetlights in a townhouse development in Blacksburg, Virginia, (as well as elsewhere in the country) were left on day and night! The townhouse residents met to consider turning them off; they decided to leave them on, however, because an "insignificant" quantity of gas was being used.

The problem, as in previous examples, is that many people, viewing the situation only in individual terms, may decide to leave their electric and gas lights on, in which case, significantly more fuel will be consumed by the generating facilities. The reader should understand that we do not necessarily condone this behavior; we are merely attempting to explore the logic of what can be considered a deplorable circumstance.[7]

If you question the legitimacy of this explanation, suppose then that John knew that leaving lights on for the duration of the program would cost him $50. Would you expect him to get up and turn it off? Suppose the price of natural gas had been three or four times higher, what would the townhouse residents have decided to do?

When the shortage of gasoline began emerging in the spring and summer of 1973, Exxon and other petroleum companies advertised a saving in gas consumption if a driver were to drive at 50 miles per hour instead of 70. The Exxon commercial demonstrated that a car going 70 miles per hour would use a 20-gallon tank in 253 miles; if the car went 50, the 253 miles could be covered with four gallons of gas to spare. Should Exxon or anyone else have expected the ad to make a significant dent in total gasoline consumption? Not really, because it would take the driver approximately one and a half hours longer to travel the 253 miles at 50 than it would at 70. The value of the gasoline saving

---

[7]We recognize that there are times when a person will get up and turn the light off; our purpose here, however, is to explain why at times he may not.

(at the time) was $.60 per gallon, approximately $2.40. This means that the driver would have had to value his time at $1.60 per hour (or far less than the minimum wage at the time) to justify (on purely economic grounds) slowing down. If he had had the public interest at heart, he might have slowed down, but he would have done so without materially affecting the long-run fuel problem of the United States. Also it is very difficult for anyone to slow down in the public interest while others, including public officials, are cruising along at higher speeds.

If the price of gasoline were to rise to $2.00 per gallon, several effects can be predicted. First, and as a generality, a greater private cost will be incurred for energy consumption. Second, the savings from going 50 miles per hour (instead of 70) would be $8.00 (four gallons times $2.00). This means that anyone who would then value his time at less than $5.32 per hour would find going slower economical; economists would expect more to do so. (Why?)

Third, economists would also expect that, since the demand curve for travel is downward sloping, people will drive fewer miles, buy smaller cars, use more car pools, and make greater use of mass transportation. All this would be expected to further reduce the amount of energy consumed. (And consumers responded to the gas price increase in the 1970s in all of these ways.)

Fourth, since people would also be expected to go slower and the highway fatality rate declines with lower speed, there should be fewer deaths on the highways. The dollar value of damage per wreck would also be expected to fall, causing a reduction in insurance rates. Not having made a detailed study of the possible effects, we cannot say how great the effects would be expected to be in the aggregate, but we would predict (as we did predict in the first edition of this book, published in 1975) with confidence the favorable direction of the effects and that the "shortage" would be eliminated with some increase in price. (Why?) By 1980, the price of a gallon of gasoline rose in some areas to $1.50 and above, and all the above consequences had been observed.

No one likes to see prices of things increase. The problem is that when the quantity demanded exceeds the quantity supplied, how is the shortage to be eliminated? How is the available quantity of gasoline, natural gas, and fuel oil going to be distributed among the potential buyers? The pricing system has drawbacks. The real income of many people is going to be reduced: many people will be unable to buy as much. The question is not, however, whether the pricing system is perfect for allocating supplies but rather how its advantages and disadvantages stack up against alternative systems.

The pricing system may not be fair, but is a formal gas coupon rationing system (which was frequently proposed during the energy crises of the 1970s) fairer by your own definition? The question that then emerges is How do we distribute the coupons? Do we distribute the coupons according to the number of cars that a person has? If we do, wealthy people (who tend to have more cars) will be getting disproportionate shares of the gasoline. Do we give the people who live 2 miles from work less than the people who live 20 miles away? Do we give the family with six children and one car less gasoline than the person with two children and two cars? Do sales representatives get more gasoline than college students who commute to and from school? Can we really say that being able to go to work for a middle-aged worker is more important, in some sense, than an afternoon ride for an elderly couple who may have no other principal form of entertainment?

These questions have no easy answers, but if the pricing system is not employed, these questions and many, many others like them must be addressed. If we do adopt a nonmarket rationing system, then it follows that the price of the good will be kept lower than otherwise but that there will still be people who are willing to violate the rules and sell the gas on the black market at a higher price. Control of black markets is likely to be necessary.

If an economist ever suggests that the price should be raised to reduce the quantity demanded, he or she will normally be confronted by the argument that the rich will be able to continue to buy all the gas that they need, but the poor will not, and the poor need the gasoline to go to work. We are inclined to believe that both rich and poor will cut back on their gasoline consumption. In addition, it is not at all certain that the poor will, under a coupon system, end up with the gasoline. If the price of gasoline goes to $2.00 per gallon and the poor are unwilling to buy at that price, will they not be willing to sell their coupons at that price? If they do, they will have more money, but they will not have the gasoline which, as suggested, they need.[8]

RECKLESS DRIVING: AIR BAGS AND DAGGERS

There are many drivers on streets and highways who are, for all practical purposes, numskulls. They do not know how to drive, are drunk when they do, or generally do not think about what they are doing behind the wheel. Others take out all of their pent-up aggressions when driving their cars.

We can attribute a large percentage of the deaths that occur each year from automobile accidents to that type of driver. There are, on the other hand, many conscientious people who are careful and continually think about the consequences of their driving behavior. They are the ones who purposefully stay on their side of the road, observe speed limits, do not tailgate, or in general, do not do things that may be deemed reckless because they calculate the costs of having an accident to themselves and the other

---

[8]If the government is interested in setting up a coupon system to minimize people's disutility under a bad situation, then they should permit people to sell their coupons. By the fact that people freely choose to buy or sell coupons, we must conclude that they are better off by doing so. Otherwise, we must wonder why they make the trade. If coupons are sold, it means that the price of gasoline will, in effect, rise.

people in the car. They are careful because the costs of being less careful are greater than the benefits that can be achieved.

Actually, the cost of driving recklessly is not necessarily equal to the cost incurred from any given accident but, rather, is equal to the cost of the accident discounted by the probability of having the accident. Granted, the probability of having an accident under such conditions is very close to one; however, under other conditions (for example, driving 85 miles an hour on a freeway), the probability of having an accident can be far removed from unity. The calculated costs of reckless driving is correspondingly lower. The reader should think in terms of the probability of having an accident as well as the cost of the accident if it occurs. When discussing reckless driving, too often people tend to think only in terms of the cost of the accident *if it occurs;* consequently, they tend to overestimate the cost and fail to understand why so many people drive recklessly.

Those people who weigh the costs and benefits of driving recklessly should respond in a predictable way to changes in the expected costs and benefits. If the benefits of going faster, making U-turns in the middle of the street, and driving on the wrong side of the road were to increase, then obviously driving of this nature from drivers as a group would increase. For example, if a child were to have a serious head injury requiring immediate medical attention, would you not expect the parents to break speed limits, ignore stop signs, and generally take more chances attempting to get the child to the emergency room than they otherwise would? This is a clear example of an increase in benefits from reckless driving; we suggest that similar responses will occur even if the change in the benefits were less dramatic. Take, for example, a person who may be late for an important meeting. How would she behave, relatively speaking, behind the wheel? At least, would you not expect drivers as a group to respond in the way an economist would predict?

In a similar manner, we would expect people to respond to changes in the expected costs of reckless driving. There should be less reckless driving when the expected cost of driving so goes up and more when the cost goes down. If these statements are reasonable, the reader should agree that one reason for the large volume of accidents on highways is that the expected cost to the drivers is relatively low.[9] This is simply another application of the law of demand.

Admittedly, not everyone will respond to changes in cost—for example, those who do not think about what they are doing, and those who do not

---

[9]We recognize that although in an absolute sense the cost of an accident may be quite high, the cost that the driver will operate on is the cost of the accident discounted by the probability of having the accident. Besides, we are merely suggesting in different words that if the costs were even higher, the quantity of reckless driving would be lower.

consider the cost as a factor—but so long as there are people who do consider cost as a factor, the downward sloping demand curve should hold. The number of people who think or act randomly will determine the position of the demand curve and not the slope.

To illustrate this basic point, would the reader not agree that students have more collisions in the hallways of their classroom buildings than they do on the streets when they are in their cars? It appears clear to us that, although students are involved in large numbers of automobile accidents, the number of hallway accidents is far greater. One explanation for the difference in the accident rate is possibly that bumping in the halls does not cost the persons bumping very much, whereas automobile collisions can be considerably more costly. If the student knew that if he bumped into someone in the hall, he would be fined $50, would you expect the same amount of bumping or less? Would your answer not apply to people's behavior in traffic?

Finally, there is an ironic implication of our argument for automobile safety policy. In 1987, the then secretary of transportation, Elizabeth Dole, came out in favor of the mandatory installation of air bags in cars. The secretary's concern was that people were losing their lives because of their failure to buckle up. But the secretary should have considered the predicted economic consequences of the recommended policy.

Safety devices such as seat belts, padded dashes, and air bags reduce considerably the probability of death and the severity of injury in the event of an accident. By making such equipment mandatory, the government is in effect reducing the expected total cost of an accident to those in the car, thereby reducing the cost of reckless driving.

Therefore, required seat belts and other similar internal safety devices should, contrary to the good intentions of those who supported the legislation, increase the amount of reckless driving. The effect may not be very great (just how great it is will depend on the elasticity of demand), *but it should still be positive.* This means that there will be a tendency for people who have such devices to inflict a greater cost on the drivers around them. This was not, undoubtedly, what the secretary had in mind when the air bag policy was recommended.

We have suggested that mandatory seat belts and air bags will reduce the private cost incurred from reckless driving and increase the *social cost*— that is, the cost of one's own reckless driving borne by others. If the government is interested in reducing the social cost from automobile travel, then it might consider (the costs and benefits of) developing requirements for proper headlights and brakes and annual safety inspections. Ironically, the private cost to the driver of having an accident can be increased by making the inside of the car less safe. As an extreme example of the point being tendered, suppose the government were to require that a dagger be mounted on the steering column pointed at the driver's chest. Would the driver not be inclined to drive more safely? We are not proposing that such devices actually be required. We are merely attempting to make the more general point concerning how people may respond as a result of automobiles being made more or less safe inside.

CONCLUDING COMMENTS

Our central point in this chapter has been relatively simple: People respond to cost in a predictable way, which is represented by the demand curve. The concept of demand is so ingrained in economists that they call it a *law*—the law of demand. This does not mean to suggest that the law of demand holds in all situations, but economists hold to the concept so firmly that their first reaction is to assume it applies.

A subsidiary point of the chapter is that the actions of individuals are often inconsequential. Consequentially, *pollution* (undesirable collective behavior) of many forms may emerge without some form of control. Most students assume that unwanted behavior must be controlled directly by government rules. A major point of this chapter is that the pricing system is an important alternative control mechanism in many situations. It might not work in panics, but it can work very well in the use of, for example, energy.

QUESTIONS TO PONDER

1. Is life priceless? What evidence can you offer to support your contention?

2. In the fall and winter of 1973, gasoline production was falling behind consumption partially because of the Arab embargo of oil shipments to the United States. State governments were beginning to order cutbacks in speed limits for cars to 55 miles per hour. CBS News reported (November 28, 1973) that the cutback in speed could result in approximately 14,000 fewer deaths on the highways. Given this benefit, why would the states not reduce the speed limits under more normal circumstances?

3. In most democratic organizations, such as student governments and faculty senates, motions will pass and candidates will be elected if they secure a simple majority of all votes. Provide an economic explanation as to why such organizations would generally be opposed to the adoption of a rule that required unanimous consent.

4. Explain why there is congestion on many highways. Explain why water shortages often emerge during long dry summers.

5. In the mid-1980s, delays in the takeoffs and landings of airplanes at major airports around the country began to escalate. As an economist, what would you expect to be the cause? Why would an appeal to airlines to reschedule their flights not be expected to solve the delay problem?

6. Give an economic explanation for unruly (and criminal) behavior of people during riots.

CHAPTER 3

Hierarchy of Needs and Demand: A Digression into Psychology

A. H. Maslow, a psychologist, argued that basic human needs can be specified with reasonable clarity and can be ranked according to their importance in providing motivation and influencing behavior.[1] Embedded in Maslow's hierarchy of needs is a theory of human behavior that is to some degree foreign to the economist's way of thinking. In this chapter, Maslow's system will be outlined so that we may be able to use it for comparative purposes.

Our discussion of Maslow's "hierarchy of needs" is, admittedly, a digression of sorts, but we think it is an important one because we have a suspicion that Maslow's system (at least in terms of its basic structure) is not terribly dissimilar to the views of many laymen in economics. In addition, Maslow's hierarchy (or some similar structure of needs) underlines the research in several other disciplines, including business courses.

MASLOW'S HIERARCHY

Maslow's need hierarchy is pictured in Figure 3–1. The importance of the needs, in terms of how powerful or demanding they are in affecting human behavior, ascends as one moves downward through the pyramid; that is, the most fundamental or prepotent needs, which are physiological in nature, are on the bottom. This category of needs includes on one level all attempts of the body to maintain certain chemical balances (such as water, oxygen, and hydrogen ion levels) within the body. On a higher level, the physiological needs include the individual's desires for food, sex, sleep, sensory pleasures, and sheer activity (meaning the need to be busy).

The need for safety, which is next in prepotence, may include the desires of the individual for security, order, protection, and family stability. The next category, belongingness and love needs, may include, among other things,

---

[1]A. H. Maslow, *Motivation and Personality* (New York: Harper and Row, 1954). See primarily chap. 5.

FIGURE 3–1

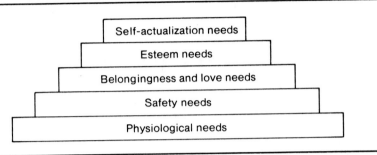

the desire for companionship, acceptance, and affection. Maslow lists under the heading of esteem needs the individual's desire for achievement, adequacy, reputation, dominance, recognition, attention, appreciation, and importance. He argues that the need for self-actualization "refers to man's desire for self-fulfillment, namely, to the tendency that might be phrased as the desire to become more and more what one is, to become everything that one is capable of becoming."[2]

Maslow stresses that such an individual may indicate she (or he) is striving after one need when in fact she is pursuing something else. For example, the individual may say that she is hungry because by doing so and going out to dinner, she can acquire companionship, affection, and attention. This may be the case because the individual may find it useful to deceive another person or because she does not consciously know what her true motivation is. In addition, Maslow argues that certain preconditions, such as the freedom to express oneself, are necessary before basic needs can be satisfied. Consequently, individuals can be motivated to establish the necessary preconditions; they may not appear to be attempting to satisfy basic needs.

Maslow does not hold rigidly to the ordering of needs as indicated in Figure 3–1. He specifies this particular ranking because it appears to him to be descriptive of the people with whom he has associated and because it appears to be a reasonably good generality concerning human motivation. Because of cultural or environmental factors or because, for example, love has been denied in the past, some people may place more emphasis on esteem needs than on the need for love. He also suggests that "There are other apparently innately creative people in whom the drive to creativeness seems to be more important than any other counter-determinant. Their creativeness might appear not as self-actualization released by basic satisfaction, but in spite of the lack of basic satisfaction."[3]

---

[2]Ibid., pp. 90-92.
[3]Ibid., pp. 98.

Although he qualifies his argument, the core proposition in Maslow's theory of human behavior is the argument that a person will first satisfy her most basic needs (physiological needs) before she attempts to satisfy needs of higher order. He writes:

> If all the needs are unsatisfied, the organism is then dominated by the physiological needs, all other needs may become simply nonexistent or be pushed into the background. It is then fair to characterize the whole organism by saying simply it is hungry, for consciousness is almost completely preempted by hunger. All capacities are put into the service of hunger-satisfaction, and the organization of these capacities is almost entirely determined by the one purpose of satisfying hunger. . . . Capacities that are not useful for this purpose lie dormant, or are pushed into the background.[4]

If the most basic needs are satisfied, "At once other (and higher) needs emerge and these, rather than physiological hungers, dominate the organism. And when these in turn are satisfied, again new (and still higher) needs emerge, and so on."[5] One gets the impression from reading Maslow that the individual will not attempt to satisfy her second most prepotent needs until the most prepotent needs are almost fully satisfied; she will not move to the third tier in the hierarchy until the needs at the second tier are "fairly well gratified."[6] Apparently, the individual will not attempt to effect any self-actualization until she has moved through all former tiers. If any tier in the hierarchy is skipped entirely, it is because of insurmountable environmental or physiological barriers.[7]

ECONOMICS AND THE HIERARCHY

Maslow's approach to human motivation and behavior resembles the approach of economists in several respects. First, they are similar because the essence of both theories is an assumption that the individual is able to rank all of his wants (or needs) according to their importance to him. In the Maslow system, anything that is not directly a basic need is ranked according to how close it is to a basic need. Other needs beyond the five categories mentioned, such as the need to know or understand and the need for aesthetic

---

[4]Ibid., p. 92

[5]Ibid., p. 92.

[6]"If both the physiological and safety needs are fairly well gratified, there will emerge the love and affection and belongingness needs." Ibid., p. 89. Maslow never explains what will keep the individual from fully satisfying any given need level before moving on to a higher tier.

[7]Admittedly, this is an interpretation of Maslow and may be an unfair statement of what his true position is, however, he does tend to write in black and white terms—either the barriers are there or they are not.

quality, can be handled by adding additional tiers.[8] As pointed out in Chapter 1, the economist simply starts with an assumption that the individual knows what she wants and is able to rank all possible goods and services that are able to satisfy her wants.

The two systems are dissimilar, however, when it comes to specifying of the ranking. Maslow is willing to argue that in general the basic needs and their ranking can also be identified; that is, he can say what the individual's needs are and is willing to venture a statement about their relative importance. On the other hand, an economist would generally take the position that the relative importance of the needs varies so much from person to person that a hierarchy of needs, although insightful for some limited purposes, does not move us very far in our understanding of human behavior.

The economist may specify whether a good or service may add to or subtract from the individual's utility and will argue that more of something that gives positive utility is preferred to less; but he would be unwilling to try to say exactly where the good (or need) may lie on some relative scale. We must presume that the specificity Maslow seeks is to him a useful, if not necessary, basis for predicting human behavior. Economists believe that they can say a great deal about human behavior without actually specifying the relative importance of the things people want. We certainly admit that the economist's inability to specify the relative importance of needs is a limitation to economic theory. (Given some of the areas into which economists are now delving, more and more economists are beginning to wish that they could somehow specify the ordering of people's preferences.)

The two systems are similar to the extent that they view the individual as consuming those things that give the greater satisfaction. Even in the Maslow system, which lacks a direct statement to the effect, there is the implicit assumption that the individual is a utility maximizer. Maslow also assumes diminishing marginal utility as more of the need is consumed; if this is not the case, it is difficult to understand how the individual can become fully or almost fully satisfied at any need level.

The systems are different because of their views of the constraints that operate on the ability of the individual to maximize his utility. The constraints in the Maslow hierarchy include environmental and cultural factors and the individual's character, or his beliefs about what is right and wrong. There is no mention of the individual's productive ability or income (unless these are implied in the environmental or cultural constraints) or of the costs of the means by which his basic needs can be fulfilled. These considerations are basic constraints in the economist's view of human behavior.

---

[8]Maslow, in his 1954 book, is less certain about the relative positions of the need to know and the need for aesthetic quality because of the limited research that had been done on the subject at the time he wrote the book.

By not considering cost, Maslow appears to assume either that there is no cost to need gratification or that (in spite of an implicit assumption concerning diminishing marginal utility) the demand curve for any need is vertical (or perfectly inelastic). This means that the quantity of the need fulfilled is unaffected by the cost. An implied assumption of the vertical demand curve is that the basic needs are independent of one another. They are not substitutes; for example, a unit of an esteem need fulfilled does not appear in the Maslow system to be able to take the place of even a small fraction of a unit of physiological need.

Maslow recognizes that most people have only partially fulfilled their needs at each level. He writes:

> So far, our theoretical discussions may have given the impression that these five sets of needs are somehow in such terms as the following: if one need is satisfied, then another emerges. This statement might give the false impression that a need must be satisfied 100 percent before the next need emerges. In actual fact, most members of our society who are normal are partially satisfied in all their basic needs and partially unsatisfied in all their basic needs at the same time. A more realistic description of the hierarchy would be in terms of decreasing percentages of satisfaction as we go up the hierarchy of prepotency. For instance . . . it is as if the average citizen is satisfied 85 percent in his physiological needs, 70 percent in his safety needs, 50 percent in his love needs, 40 percent in his self-esteem needs, and 10 percent in his self-actualization needs.[9]

Maslow does not, however, explain why this will be the case, nor does he provide an explanation for why a person will not fully satisfy the higher needs before he moves to the next tier.

THE RELEVANCE OF DEMAND

The economist might concede for purposes of argument, as we do, that the demand for a physiological need is greater (and more inelastic) than the demand for a safety need, which in turn is greater than the demand for a love need. However, it does not follow that, as Maslow suggests, the love need will be less fulfilled in percentage terms than the safety or physiological needs. To what extent the different needs are gratified depends on the cost or price of each unit of the means for satisfying a need and the elasticity of demand of each need. To illustrate, consider Figure 3–2. The demand for a means of gratifying a physiological need is depicted as being greater (meaning it is further out to the right) than the other demands. (For the sake of simplicity we consider only three needs.) We assume that any given need is

---

[9]Maslow, *Motivation and Personality*, pp. 100–101.

FIGURE 3–2

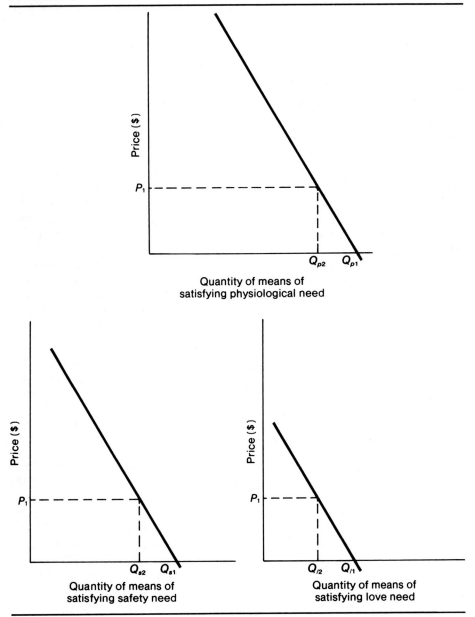

Quantity of means of
satisfying physiological need

Quantity of means of
satisfying safety need

Quantity of means of
satisfying love need

fully satisfied if the quantity of the need purchased is equal to the quantity at the point where the respective demand curves intersect the horizontal axis.[10]

If, as in this example, the cost of satisfying each need is the same, P_1, the individual will consume Q_{p1} of the means of satisfying his physiological need. As far as units are concerned, this is greater than the quantity of units consumed for satisfying the other needs; however, the percentage of the need gratified does not have to be greater. If demand for the physiological need were sufficiently inelastic, the percentage of the need gratified could be greater.

It is doubtful, however, that the costs of satisfying the different needs are the same. The availability of the resources needed for satisfying the different needs can easily be different; consequently, the costs of need gratification can be different. If the cost of fulfilling the physiological need were substantially greater, even though the demand for the need were greater, the percentage of the physiological need fulfilled could be less than the percentage of the other needs fulfilled.

In Figure 3–3, the prices (or cost per unit) of the means by which a physiological need can be satisfied (P_p) are greater than the prices of the means for satisfying the other needs. The price of satisfying the safety need (P_s) is assumed to be greater than the price of satisfying the love need (P_1). The result in this case is what we suggested it could be; the individual will fulfill a lower percentage of his physiological need than she will fulfill of her other needs. In fact the order of need fulfillment is reversed from the order suggested by Maslow: the individual fulfills a higher percentage of her love need than of the other needs.

CONCLUDING COMMENTS

Maslow apparently has observed that people fulfill a higher percentage of their physiological needs than of other needs. Our line of argument suggests that this may have been the case because the price of physiological need fulfillment is lower than the prices of fulfilling the other needs.[11] The important point we wish to make is that a change in the price (or cost) structure can bring about a change in the extent of need gratification at each level. In such an event, our (and psychologists') definition of what may be considered normal as far as need gratification is concerned should be reconsidered.

---

[10]At the quantity, the marginal utility is zero, implying that the person's utility level from the consumption of that need is at its maximum.

[11]It may also be that the demand for physiological satisfaction is more inelastic than the other demands. This could be considered normal as far as need gratification is concerned.

FIGURE 3–3

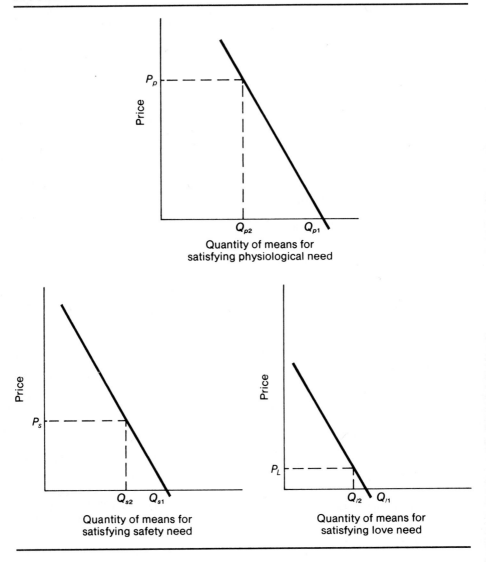

People's behavior need not have changed in any fundamental sense; they may merely be responding to different prices, while their basic preferences and attitudes remain the same.

QUESTIONS TO PONDER

1. Do people you observe fully satisfy their physiological needs before they attempt to satisfy other needs? Can you offer any evidence?

2. Attempt to make rough estimates of the cost of obtaining an additional unit of some physiological need and some self-actualization need. (What is the relationship between their cost?) What difficulties do you encounter in making those estimates?

3. In the chapter, we assumed for simplicity that the demands for three methods of satisfying needs were the same. Is this a reasonable assumption? Why or why not?

4. Are people willing to make trade-offs in satisfying their needs? If they are, does this mean that the Maslow or the economic approach to consumer behavior is the more descriptive of people's behavior?

CHAPTER 4
Rationality in Experimental Economics

In Chapter 1, we outlined the economic approach to human behavior. One of the foundations of this approach is the assumption that human beings are rational. As we pointed out in that chapter, the standard of rationality is not a very high one; nevertheless economists do believe in the essential intelligence of human beings in the very limited sense that their demand curves slope downward and that they will select the preferred choice over the less preferred.

Among scholarly critics of economics, this rationality assumption is perhaps the most frequently criticized aspect of economics. Economists have answered this criticism in a number of ways, first by pointing out that the requirement of rationality in economics is actually a very low requirement. Second, Gary Becker has argued that the demand and supply relationship can be generated by random behavior; hence people do not have to be rational to fulfill the basic postulates of economics.[1] This argument by Becker was criticized in part by Israel Kirzner, but the basic point is generally accepted.[2] It is not true that all of the participants in a market process have to be rational.

In this chapter, we turn to the experimental evidence of the rationality assumption. We begin with discussion of the experimental economics in which special experiments are set up for normal human beings. The outcome of these experiments is consistent with the rationality hypothesis. Indeed, Vernon Smith, one of the pioneers in the area, regards these experiments as the first real proof of both rationality and what we normally refer to as consumption theory. It should be said, however, that these experiments were originally designed for other purposes and their proof of rationality is a

---

[1]Gary S. Becker, "Irrational Behavior and Economic Theory," *Journal of Political Economy* 70 (February 1962), pp. 1–13.

[2]Israel M. Kirzner, "Rational Action and Economic Theory," *Journal of Political Economy* 70 (August 1962), pp. 380–85. See also, Gary S. Becker, "A Reply to Kirzner," *Journal of Political Economy* 71 (February 1963), pp. 82–83.

secondary consequence. Nevertheless, they do support the presumption that at least a great many people behave rationally.

After we have discussed these examples of experimental economics, we turn to another set of experiments that deal with rationality in quite a different way. This set demonstrates that rationality in the sense that it is used in economics characterizes not only human beings but human beings who are formally judged insane (and therefore are hospitalized), as well as birds, rats, and a group of microscopic animals called rotifers. We do not know if these animals are rational, but they certainly behave as if they are. In other words, their demand curves slope downward. They try to buy in the cheapest market, adjust consumption in terms of prices, and so on.

EXPERIMENTAL ECONOMICS

Let us then turn to some very simple experiments that support the idea that markets tend to equilibrium and that this equilibrium is an efficient one. These experiments were originally carried out by University of Arizona economist Vernon Smith, and they can be duplicated in any class with no great difficulty.[3] They are less enlightening than some of the later experiments to be discussed for a number of reasons, the most important of which is that the students were simply asked to play the game of buying and selling without having any real money riding on their action. Later experiments, many of them also devised by Smith, have provided the students with cash they can earn by efficient performance in this experimental market.

In the original experiment, students are divided into sellers and buyers. Then they are given a card that tells them their minimum sale price if they are the sellers or their maximum purchase price if they are the buyers. One student, for example, might receive a sale card with $2.50 as the lowest price at which he or she can sell, and another might receive a purchase card with $3.50 as the highest purchase price at which he or she can buy. They are also told how many units they can buy or sell. For simplicity, this is usually one unit.

The students are then instructed to buy and sell to each other in a simulated market. Each one is to attempt to maximize his or her profit. The profit is defined as the amount by which the price the seller receives exceeds his or her minimum price. The converse rule applies to the buyer.

The technique is very informal. The students simply announce an offer to buy or sell whenever they feel like it, and some other student may then accept the offer, or perhaps no student will accept it. In professional markets—for example, the grain exchange—that operate on roughly these rules, the procedure appears to be very disorderly, with a great deal of shouting

---

[3]See Vernon Smith, "An Experimental Study of Competitive Market Behavior," *Journal of Political Economy* 70 (April 1962), pp. 111–37.

and a set of hand signals. But for classroom purposes, it is sensible to provide some rule that guarantees that everyone understands what everyone else is saying. For example, the students could hold up their hands if they want to make or accept an offer, and the professor may indicate which one of the several raised hands will be recognized. This is some departure from the real world, but it is a little easier to follow.

The cards that have been distributed to the students are normally arranged in these experiments so that there is an equilibrium price. For example, see Figure 4–1.[4] Each of the dashes on the line marked *DD* represents a student holding a demand card for the price shown. Similarly, each dash on the line *SS* represents a student holding a seller's card for the price shown. The equilibrium price is a trifle less than $3.50, and the number of units that will be sold is 15. A few students will be left with transactions left uncompleted, but this is true of the market also.

The game is played until there are no longer any acceptable offers. Normally the price and quantity at which this occurs can be predicted quite accurately by anyone who knows the shape of the demand and supply curves represented by the cards distributed to the students. The student experimental subjects do not know this; hence, their information is incomplete. Under the circumstances, it takes a little while to establish equilibrium. On the right half of Figure 4–1, we show the process through time of the price of transactions. You will note that the prices start at the left with considerable variance, but toward the right end of the chart (after some experience has been accumulated), they are quite stable.

The method in which these time charts are produced is fairly simple. The individuals play the game until there are no more offers that are acceptable. This is called a period, and, for example, the first such play is shown as period 1.

Once there are no more acceptable offers forthcoming, the beginning round of the game is declared finished, and each student is then told the game will start again. He will still use in the second round of the game the same prices and designation of seller and buyer that he used in the first round. In the second round of the game, however, each of the students has more information about the structure of the market than in the first round, and therefore, we would expect that the variance of prices would be lower in period 2 than in period 1. Examination of Figure 4–1 indicates that this is what happens. In this particular experiment, only three rounds of the game were played, and the reason is obvious from observation of the transaction chart in period 3. By period 3 with this rather simple structure, almost everyone was well enough informed so that the price was extremely stable. Smith

---

[4]This is a mildly revised version of Smith's fig. 2, ibid., p. 118.

FIGURE 4–1

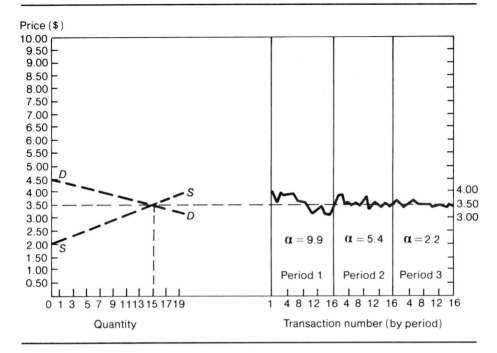

Price ($)

felt that little was to be gained from further repetitions at this point, and he stopped the game.

All that we have learned so far from these experiments is that the price does indeed approach the equilibrium but that it does not do so instantaneously, because people do not have adequate information. This will surprise very few students of economics, but some noneconomists have expressed doubt on this point.

However, there is a little more information to be obtained from our very simple experiment. We could make measures of the speed with which equilibrium is approached, and this is a topic upon which formal economics has very little to contribute. Economists have normally said that equilibrium would be achieved but not very fast.

As a matter of fact, in the article from which this experiment was drawn, Smith proceeded to test a number of hypotheses having to do with the stability of the market price and the speed at which equilibrium was approached, depending on such matters as the steepness of the demand and supply curves, whether they have roughly the same slope or one is fairly flat and the other is steep, and so forth. Not surprisingly, in general, the flatter the demand and supply curves, the faster equilibrium was approached. Although there had been speculation on this matter beforehand, the information obtained was the first real evidence.[5]

Of course, a game in which nothing really rides on success in trading is really not very close to the real world. In fact, it is surprising how good the results are. After Smith had done the initial work, he was able to interest the National Science Foundation in funding more elaborate experiments in which the participants actually had something to gain from efficient behavior. Students really made a cash profit.

Cards were distributed in much the same way as in the earlier experiment. However, the individuals received a money payment equal to the difference between their minimum sale price or maximum purchase price and the actual transaction price (if they were sellers), or below their maximum purchase price and the actual transaction price, assuming that the price was above their minimum sale price (if they were sellers), or below their maximum purchase price (if they were buyers).

Smith mainly used these funds for more complicated experiments than the one described above. But Cal Tech economist Charles Plott, building on Smith's work, duplicated the above experiment using cash payments in this manner. The principal difference between Plott's experiments and Smith's is, we suppose, readily predictable. When there was something actually riding on the results, the people engaged in the game were more careful and paid closer attention, with the result that they approached equilibrium more rapidly.

Notre Dame economist Barry Keating, as a by-product of teaching managerial economics, produced some further experimental data along these same lines. In his class, the students are divided into 15 "companies," each with a small board of directors (three to five students). These companies routinely make decisions on various management policy matters including price and production schedules. The experiment is intended to be realistic in the sense that market conditions change, so that the students can never be perfectly informed about the demand situation, just as real-world companies are never perfectly informed. The students are rewarded in grades if their company is "profitable."

Keating's result would surprise no economist. The companies responded to changes in the basic underlying market conditions by experimental activity

---

[5]Some of this work had been foreshadowed in S. Siegel and L. Fouraker, *Bargaining and Group Decision Making* (New York: McGraw-Hill, 1960). One nice feature of this set of experiments, however, is that they do not require any complicated setup or sizable resources; hence, any economics class that wishes can duplicate them and indeed develop more complicated hypotheses to be tested by the same method. A word of caution, however, is necessary. From personal observation of Vernon Smith, the students playing these games tend to become bored. This is not surprising, since the games are not designed for entertainment: but a rapid boredom rate means that it is undesirable to do very much of this experimentation, even though one or two rounds of the game would probably be a good way to break up the classroom routine.

with new prices and production schedules. Since different companies tried different prices and production rates, this would lead to an increase in the spread of their policies. Rather quickly, however, the spread between different companies' prices and policies narrows. Note that it never actually gets down to zero, since some of the companies are always searching to determine whether market conditions have changed. These findings, of course, are very consistent with experience in real markets.

Plott continued his experiments into more difficult areas. One of these areas, voting procedures, was the subject of a set of experiments that rather neatly confirmed the basic proposition to be developed in Chapter 17. In that chapter, we argue that in a two-party system, even with more than one issue, the two parties tend to be very close together and at approximately the middle of the distribution.

Plott also dealt with the problem of regulating pollution. By an ingenious technique, he generated a pollutant in his experiment; that is, each individual completing a transaction imposed a cost on all other individuals, but the cost was, for him or her, lower than his or her gain. As any economist would predict, the equilibrium reached by the experiment was socially inferior, although it was privately optimal. The individuals, like real-world polluters, maximized their own profit and ignored the injury they inflicted on others, with the result that all of them were worse off than they would have been had they each taken the well-being of others into account.

In such a situation, economists usually argue that a properly calculated tax is the optimal policy, but in the real world, governments very commonly rely on regulations, a pollution standard, for example. Plott tried both of these techniques and found, as no economist would be surprised to hear, that the tax achieved the socially optimal number of sales in an efficient manner, and the pollution standard achieved the same number but with a good deal of waste.

Another interesting and rather counter intuitive result developed by Plott emerged from a study of the market for advice. We are continuously in the situation where we must depend on advice from a doctor, garage mechanic, and so on, in areas which vitally concern us but where our own information is poor. Most economists, certainly the authors of this book, had always assumed that this gave the people with this special information an advantage and the capacity to cheat on occasion.

Plott constructed an experiment in which some people were in essence customers who did not understand their car, and other people were garage mechanics who knew what was wrong. It was discovered that in his reasonably competitive market the traditional economic rule of one price was supplemented by a rule of one advice. In other words, the "mechanics" gave the best advice to their customers, apparently with the theory that the customer would just go somewhere else if they received poor advice. The result is surprising and obviously requires other testing and further experiments.

CRAZY BUT NOT IRRATIONAL

The experiments discussed above were intended to demonstrate various economic propositions and test rationality as a sort of by-product. Further, normal, presumably sane human beings (students) were used. Let us now turn to the evidence that indicates that abnormal, officially insane, human beings and at least some animals are also rational.

Let us begin with the insane. Most patients in mental hospitals do not require any kind of physical restraint, although their behavior may be peculiar at times. Further, most are in reasonable physical health. As a consequence, the management of most mental hospitals usually tries to get a certain amount of maintenance work from their patients. For example, the patients may be asked to make up their beds, keep the area around their beds (or their room, if they have one) clean and orderly, perhaps assist in other tasks, such as mopping the hall floor. Since most of the patients are free to associate with each other, a certain amount of disciplinary control is also desirable. In particular, patients are restricted from doing things likely to irritate the other patients in their wards.

Traditionally, hospitals have found it difficult to get the patients to cooperate. Lately, however, the introduction of "token economies" has led to significant improvements in patient behavior, with very little effort on the part of the hospital management.

The system is fairly simple. A special money (token) is issued by the hospital management. Since theft is frequently a major problem, the tokens are usually similar to traveler's checks in the sense that each token is issued to one particular patient and only that patient can use it.[6] Thus, if one of the patients steals the tokens of another, it does him no good.

These tokens may be used to purchase small comforts within the hospital community. For example, there may be a ward shop selling candy, cigarettes, and so forth. Further, it may be possible for the token holders to "buy" better-than-standard meals, the use of recreational facilities, visits to town, and so forth.

It should be said that this new technique was not originally introduced to make the life of hospital managers easier. It began as a rather controversial method of treating patients. Although there is still some controversy about the procedure, it does seem in many cases to cure (or at least suppress the symptoms of) some mental diseases. Unfortunately, although it works in many cases, it does not work in all.

The individuals under treatment would be paid in tokens for an activity the doctors thought would benefit them. For example, a patient suffering from agoraphobia (fear of open spaces) might be given a token for walking 10 yards out into an open field and then back. After several days in which

---

[6]Raymond C. Battalio, "A Test of Consumer Demand Theory Using Observation of Individual Consumer Purchases," *Western Economic Journal* 11 (December 1973), pp. 411–28.

tokens were earned this way, the distance the patient had to go would be increased. This rather simple technique, believe it or not, does cure a fair number (unfortunately not all) of the cases of agoraphobia.

But our purpose here is not to discuss the use of token economies as a technique for curing mental illnesses but as a way of obtaining economically rational behavior from the patients in mental hospitals. After using tokens as a curative measure for a time, the caretakers of mental hospitals soon realized that the token economy could also be used for improving inmate behavior in other ways. The patient might be given a token, for example, for bedmaking, be paid in tokens for mopping the floor or assisting in other routine tasks. Indeed, in some cases the patients can actually be "employed" in simple, factory-like assembly jobs. It should be said that in general these jobs were assigned not because the institution wanted to make money but because it was thought desirable both to keep the patients busy and to give them continuing work experience, in order that they can support themselves when and if they are released. Nevertheless, in a number of cases, institutions have in fact made modest profits on the operation, although in most cases there are losses if the curative aspects of the project are disregarded.

Disciplinary problems became relatively unimportant with the token economies. Further, when difficulties did arise, in general they could be dealt with very simply and easily by changing the price. For example, in one hospital, the patients objected to mopping the floor. The caretakers simply raised the wage for floor mopping and found themselves deluged with volunteers.

Psychologists tend to be interested in improving their art; hence they perform experiments. Changing the price of goods in the patients' shop turns out to lead to exactly the kind of behavior that economists would anticipate. For example, in one rather elaborate experiment, prices of various commodities were changed at unannounced intervals.[7] The patients in general adjusted just the way that economic theory would predict for rational beings; that is, they increased their purchases of things whose prices had gone down and reduced their purchases of those that had gone up. In some cases, the change was slow rather than immediate (which would indicate that a learning process was involved), and in some cases, errors in observation threw a good deal of sand into the procedure. Still, in general these people who had been certified as insane behaved quite rationally.

In another case, the management of an institution had the patients employed in various activities for which they were paid. As an experiment, the management gave the patients a "paid vacation." The patients were given opportunities and encouragement to continue their work during their vacation, but they would be given no additional payments. Needless to say, this

[7] T. Allyon and N. H. Azrin, "The Measurement and Reinforcement of Behavior of Psychotics," *Journal of Experimental Analysis of Behavior* 8 (November 1965).

was an experiment, and the results are not surprising. The patients all chose not to work, thus indicating that their previous work had been a rational effort to obtain the tokens and not the result of conditioning or some other irrational characteristic. The same management also arranged a set of experiments in which individuals were first trained for a number of different jobs and then given the choice of the jobs with token payment. After they had become accustomed to the job, they were then suddenly informed that the payment would be discontinued for their preferred job but that they could earn the same wage in a less-preferred job. As would be expected, all but one of the patients instantly changed to the less-preferred job, and the one exception changed after a day or so of experience of getting by without a "wage."[8]

R. C. Winkler, working with chronically psychotic female patients, tested more complex behavior patterns.[9] He distinguished luxury items from necessities and measured the responsiveness of the patients to price changes of several items, reaching the standard conclusion that the demand for necessities was "price inelastic," meaning that the patients were relatively unresponsive to price changes and that the patients had greater total expenditures when the price of the necessities went up. They also found that the demand for luxuries was "price elastic." This means that the patients made lower total expenditures on the luxuries when their prices were raised.

In the above experiments, nothing in the way of age, IQ, educational level, type of mental disorder, or length of time in institutions seemed to affect the results. In other words, even seriously disturbed or very stupid people with no education who had been institutionalized for long periods of time behaved as if they were rational. It is only those people who were so seriously disturbed or so mentally impaired that they had only a few available behavior patterns—and were therefore not capable of earning and spending tokens—who did not respond, in a rational way to the types of experiments described above.

In general, what these experiments indicate is that standards of rationality required for economic behavior are so low that certified patients in mental hospitals—sometimes, certified basket cases—meet them. The argument that economics assumes rationality and that people are not rational is not, strictly speaking, refuted by these observations; but they certainly cast doubt on it.[10]

---

[8]*Ibid.*

[9]R. C. Winkler, "An Experimental Analysis of Economic Balance: Savings and Wages in a Token Economy," *Behavior Therapy* 4 (January 1973), pp. 22–40.

[10]For a general survey of token economies, see David G. Tarr, "Experiments in Token Economies: A Review of the Evidence Relating to Assumptions and Implications of Economic Theory," *Southern Economic Journal* 43 (October 1976), pp. 1136–43.

THE RATIONALITY OF ANIMALS

Let us proceed to consider some other entities normally thought to be even less rational—specifically, laboratory rats. Recently, a few economists, particularly John H. Kagel and Raymond C. Battalio of Texas A & M University, have been borrowing experimental techniques from the psychologists and using them to test whether behavior of nonhuman species is similar in restricted ways to that of human beings.[11] Since the research has only been under way for less than two decades, they have so far tested only some of the simplest propositions of economics. It should be said at the start, however, that in these special, simple areas, rats seem to behave rationally.

Let us consider briefly the existing experimental technique in which the rats are confined individually in separate cages. We will in fact talk about only one rat, although Kagel and Battalio have, of course, tested their hypothesis on more than one. The box used to test the rats in these experiments is a bit of standard psychological apparatus. It consists of a box that has an internal environment wholesome enough so that the rats can be kept there indefinitely provided that food and water are supplied and the box is regularly cleaned. Attached to the box is a small computer that can be used to meter the behavior of the experimental animal and to carry out whatever provision of food or other stimuli to the animal the experimenter has planned; that is, the computer keeps track of all things going in and can be instructed to deliver various items under various conditions.

Since the rat would have great difficulty in handling token currency, the experiments charge the rat prices not by giving it a small collection of tokens and having it insert them in a slot but by having the rat push a bar at the back of the cage. The pushes on the bar are the payments made by the rat, and this leads the computer to meter out to it, let us say, a small quantity of root beer, cherry cola, or whatever else the experimenters choose. They change the price of the various commodities by changing the amount delivered each time the bar is pushed. Thus, the price of 0.1 cc of cherry cola might be one bar-push, or two, or four.

Suppose, then, we consider one of their experiments in which a rat is given an adequate supply of food and water automatically by the machine and, in addition, is confronted with two bars: pushing one provides root beer and pushing the other provides cherry cola.

The computer can now be instructed to change the price of root beer and cherry cola by changing the amount received each time the bar is pressed. In one experiment, for example, the amount of root beer delivered per bar-push was held constant, but the amount of cherry cola per bar-push was changed.

---

[11]John H. Kagel et al., "Demand Curves for Animal Consumers." (Paper presented at Southern Economic Association meeting, Atlanta, Georgia, November 1976.)

FIGURE 4–2

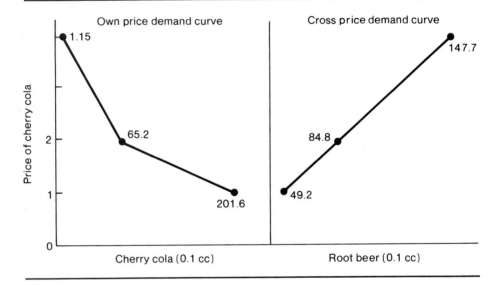

It was found that when the payoff to a bar-push was 0.025 cc of cherry cola, the rat consumed only a little over 0.1 cc per day. When the price was lowered so that the rat could get 0.5 cc per push, it consumed 65, and at one bar-push per 0.1 cc, it consumed 200. Of course, the rat changed its consumption of root beer at the same time; that is, since the price of root beer was being held constant in real terms, the exchange ratio between the root beer and cherry cola was improving. Hence, the rat reduced its consumption of root beer and increased its consumption of cherry cola.

The rat's consumption of both cherry cola and root beer at varying prices of the cherry cola can be seen in Figure 4–2.[12] It can be seen that for the rat, root beer and cherry cola were substitute goods; that is, the more it consumed of one, the less it consumed of the other. There was, however, an element of complementarity (that is, the two goods are not perfect substitutes) in that the rat did not reduce its consumption of root beer at exactly the same rate as it increased its consumption of cherry cola.

Apparently the rat was behaving rationally. Its consumption of a given product increased as the price went down, and it lowered its consumption of a competing product at the same time, just as we assume rational human consumers do. The rat was equally rational in dealing with necessities. At one point, instead of being given as much water as it wished to drink and

---

[12]Kagel et al., "Demand Curves for Animal Consumers," fig. 5.

then the choice of two luxury drinks, the rat was required to push the bar to get water. It turned out that it drank almost as much water per day at a low price as at a high price. Water was clearly a necessity, not something it drank for pleasure. Hence, it pushed the bar enough to get its daily demand for water and no more. We can say that the rat had an elastic demand for cherry cola and root beer but an extremely (almost perfectly) inelastic demand for water.

Thus, it seems that the minimum rationality assumption normally used by economists is met by quite simple animals. Those who say that human beings are not able to behave in an economically rational manner may be saying we are as dumb as rats or dumber! Note, however, that we are discussing behavior and not the actual preferences of the rat. But we do, for subjective reasons, believe that a downward sloping demand curve reflects a desire to obtain some goal, and action is taken to that end.

The other view is possible. The prominent behavior psychologist, B. F. Skinner, said:

> A rat could be said to know when to press a lever to get food, but it does not press because it knows that food will be delivered. A taxi driver could be said to know a city well, but he does not get around because he possesses a cognitive map.[13]

Skinner, of course, believes that rats and human beings are very similar in that neither one engages in what we might call rational thought and both respond to conditioning. The authors of this book believe that both behave rationally in attempting to achieve goals they value. From the standpoint of economics, however, the issue is not an important one, and either point of view can perhaps be held.

Let us go a little further. One of the authors (Tullock) investigated theoretically the behavior of an English bird called a coal tit. He explained the bird's behavior on the theory that the bird is rationally allocating its time between two different kinds of searches for food in order to get the most food with the least effort.[14] Kagel and Battalio repeated on pigeons the experiments similar to those performed on rats. The results were similar also. Even such simple animals as snails seem to have at least some ability to make rational choices.[15]

David Rapport has investigated a microscopic animal *Stentor coeruleus*, and he finds that the behavior of the stentors he studied is simple-minded

---

[13]B. F. Skinner, *About Behaviorism* (New York: Alfred A. Knopf, 1974), p. 139.

[14]Gordon Tullock, "The Coal Tit as a Careful Shopper," *The American Naturalist* 105 (January/ February 1971), pp. 77–80.

[15]Gordon Tullock, "Switching in General Predators: Comment," *Bulletin of the Ecological Society of America* 51 (September 1970), pp. 21–24.

but still rational.[16] Since this very small animal has practically nothing that we would recognize as a brain or even a nervous system, it obviously has only very limited abilities to make rational choices. Nevertheless, when it was confronted with different types of food under circumstances in which the effort it had to undertake to consume each varied, it responded as would human beings or rats. When its preferred food was hard to get, the stentor made do with second-rate food. However, when the cost of the "better" food was lowered, the stentor would spit out the less-preferred food and concentrate on the more preferred.

Although the experiments summarized above raise the question of rationality, it seems to be a rather general feeling among biologists that all animals behave this way. It should be said, however, that biologists normally do not use the same language as do economists. Rapport, who performed the experiment on stentor mentioned above, wrote two articles in which he attempts to introduce his fellow biologists to the vocabulary and methods of economics.[17] In these articles, he presents standard economic models, with appropriate introduction for the biologist. Toward the end of one of these articles, he says:

> The use of optimization principles has been implicit in much of theoretical biology. As Rosen points out, "that idea that nature pursues economy in all her workings is one of the oldest principles of theoretical science" (Rosen, 1967). The assumption of optimizing food selection behavior appears valid provided natural selection is efficient in "weeding out" species or individuals which failed to make optimum food choices.[18]

Rapport goes on to discuss the deductions that can be drawn from this rational model for biology and methods of testing them. He then performed some of the tests in the articles listed above and confirmed the theory.

SOCIOBIOLOGY

That some animals have fairly complex social orders has been known for a very long time. The ant was held up as an example in the Old Testament, and beekeeping seems to be an immensely ancient human profession. The study of animal societies has, of course, always been part of biology. In recent years, however, a new subdiscipline within biology, called *sociobiology*, has

---

[16]D. J. Rapport and J. E. Turner, "Determination of Predator Food Preferences," *Journal of Theoretical Biology* 26 (1970), pp. 365–72; and David J. Rapport, Jacques Berger, and D. B. W. Reid, "Determination of Food Preference of *Stentor Coeruleus*," *Biological Bulletin* 142 (February 1972), pp. 10–39.

[17]David J. Rapport, "An Optimization Model of Food Selection," *The American Naturalist* 105 (November/December 1971), pp. 757–87.

[18]Rapport, "Optimization Model of Food Selection," pp. 583–84; inner quote by Rosen refers to R. R. Rosen, *Optimality Principles in Biology* (London: Butterworths, 1967).

been developed. It studies the social interactions of nonhuman species, not so much from the experimental method as from simple observation of what the species do.[19]

The popular press has given sociobiology a good deal of attention, with prominent sociobiologists such as E. O. Wilson and Robert L. Trivers appearing on the cover of *Time* or being interviewed on talk shows. It is of great interest to economists, and indeed, economists have made contributions to the sociobiological literature. The types of things learned by sociobiologists can be illustrated by the research on insects, mainly ants and termites. However, as you will see, the study of insects raises as many questions as it provides answers.

Although we are apt to feel somewhat more at home in dealing with the societies of other warm-blooded animals, particularly the primates, and also to feel at least some fellow feeling for other vertebrates, the most interesting social organizations are probably those found among the insects. There are wasps, bees, and ants, which are all related to each other; the social spiders (a little-known group); and the termites. Of these, the oldest and in some ways best developed are the termites. Termites are a rather primitive family of insects related to the cockroach. Although they are something of a nuisance in the United States, their highest development can be found in the tropics. Indeed, the traveler in some parts of Africa can actually take his direction from the tall, blade-like termite nests, which are always rigidly oriented north and south.

Such a nest may have up to 2 million termites in it. The nest itself is, of course, only the center from which a large number of tunnels go off in all directions to permit the termites to find and consume dead wood. The nest and the tunnels are full of busy worker termites who are engaged in collecting wood, in some cases bringing water into the nest (although that is not always necessary), and maintaining the nest itself. They will be guarded by a special caste of soldier termites who are equipped with quite a wide variety of different kinds of defensive armament. Perhaps the most interesting ones are those provided with a sort of nozzle on the top of their heads from which they can spray a sticky substance. Others have large jaws, and in some cases, the head of the soldier is specially designed for blocking the entrance into the tunnels of the nest. The workers have much to do in addition to bringing in wood. The nest itself requires maintenance and repair, and the ventilation of the nest is important.

---

[19]For example, see Gordon Tullock, "Biological Externalities," *Journal of Theoretical Biology* 33 (December 1971), pp. 565–76; "Altruism, Malice, and Public Goods," *Journal of Social and Biological Structures* 1 (January 1978), pp. 3–9. See also Paul A. Samuelson, "Complete Genetic Models for Altruism, Kin Selection, and Like-Gene Selection," *Journal of Social and Biological Structures* 6, no. 1 (January 1983), pp. 3–16, and Jack Hirschleifer, "Natural Economy versus Political Economy," *Journal of Social and Biological Structures* 1, no. 4 (October 1978), pp. 319–37.

The termite inside the nest of one of the large African colonies lives in an environment that is remarkably stable. First, the atmosphere in the nest is a great deal more moist than the outside air and contains much more carbon dioxide. It is also quite stable in temperature. The nest is built in such a way that there is a regular circulation of air through it driven by the heat generated in the nest, and there are arrangements so that the speed of circulation can be changed by termite workers so that the amount of heat radiated through the upper portion of the blade-like structure can be adjusted; hence, the temperature of the nest is kept quite stable. The inside of a termite nest is not quite as stable in temperature as the interior of a heat-regulating mammal such as the human being, but it is a good deal more stable than the interior of a lizard or a fish. Last, but by no means least, the termite reproductives are, of course, the heart of the nest. Normally, there is a king or queen, but in some cases, a number of pairs of so-called secondary reproductives may be found.

The termites have another peculiarity, which is that most of them, indeed all except the highest termites, don't actually digest the wood themselves. They have in their intestine colonies of small single-celled animals that do the actual digestion. Thus in a way, there is a colony inside the colony. Further, some of the termites engage in gardening. They build fairly large caverns in their nest in which they raise a special type of fungus.

It can be seen that the termite nest is a complex social organization with a great deal of division of labor. Further, except for the reproductives and the specialized soldier classes, the division of labor among the termites does not depend on their physical constitution. Most of the termite workers are capable of carrying on any of the tasks in the nest. How then are the termites allocated to their jobs?

Theoretically, it could be, of course, that they simply come out of the egg with instruction for some to repair walls, others to attend to the royal pair, and so forth. We know that this is not true, however, because the number of termites engaged in any activity changes depending on the needs of the nest. If you damage the nest, for example, the number of termites engaged in repair and reconstruction immediately rises sharply. In times of drought, more termites are involved in obtaining water.

Again, it might, of course, be that the termites are simply randomly distributed among their various activities, but if this were so, the termite nest would be highly inefficient. We do not have any positive proof that termites, ants, and so forth are highly efficient, but there is fairly good evidence that they are from the role they play in the world. Next to man, the social insects are probably the most successful single group of species on the planet. Further, the fact that both the ants and the termites, two totally unrelated species using different food sources, have found much the same social organization is some, albeit rudimentary, evidence of their efficiency.

One form of evidence of the efficiency of ant colonies can be established by watching them gather food. An ant alone in the wood may appear to be engaged in a random walk—and indeed, that may often be so, for the ant may not always know at the start of its search where the food is. Nonetheless, it knows how to return to the mound by the scents it leaves in its trail. Upon finding food, it returns to the nest by backtracking. Once it communicates the location of the food to other ants, all of the ants will follow the scented trail. However, they will not continue to follow the trail as it was originally developed. They will gradually cut off the corners and eventually straighten (to the extent possible) the trail to the food, presumably in an effort to minimize the cost of collecting the food. Again, they may not be thinking like economists when they straighten their food trails, but they surely act like it!

There is further evidence of the efficiency of these social insects, in this case taken from the ants. E. O. Wilson examined the division of ants among the various castes, specifically workers and soldiers, in his test. To understand this test the reader should know that workers and soldiers are produced by the nest through different feeding and care of otherwise identical larvae. Thus, the ratio between them is something determined by the nest just as the ratio between those ants engaging in repairing the walls of the nest and those seeking food are determined by the nest.

Wilson, using complicated statistical (linear programming) techniques, investigated the efficient proportion of worker and soldier ants in a number of species. In all cases, he found the actual allocation was close to the allocation that his calculation showed to be efficient. It was not perfect, but this is as likely to be because his calculations did not perfectly fit the real world as it was because the ants were themselves inefficient.

Similar tests have not been carried on with respect to most other aspects of the efficiency of ant and termite nests; nevertheless, we think that they are indeed efficient and that the allocation of labor within the nest between the various tasks is tolerably well carried out.

How is this allocation controlled? It certainly is not controlled by a central planning board, nor is there a system of formal orders transmitted from some center of the nest that says in essence: "the temperature in the nest has risen by one half a degree, open ventilation channels 13a, 26b, and 45c." Before answering this question we should keep in mind that a somewhat similar puzzle exists inside the human body. Within us are white corpuscles that are amoeba-like entities in our bloodstream. These cells attack and ingest foreign matter in the bloodstream, particularly bacteria. If a human being suffers an injury, let us say, a cut to a finger, the white blood corpuscles will immediately congregate at that spot where they provide what amounts to guard force against infection. How are they guided to the right locations?

It is certainly not true that they are ordered to the right location by the brain, because the white corpuscles have no connection with the nervous system. They will go to areas the injury has affected even if, due to the injury itself, the nerves have been severed in that area. The simple explanation seems to be that these corpuscles are self-motivated in the sense that they "decide" where they will go and are provided with some kind of drive or motivation to ingest things in the blood that should not be there. We can regard this as a "taste." Further, they are motivated to seek out places where such things are particularly common. Probably the clues they follow are chemical. It seems likely that a cut releases into the bloodstream various bits of cell debris and chemicals from the cells which are normally not found there, and it is these chemicals and bits of debris that attract the white corpuscles. It is easier to assume that the white corpuscles are programmed to respond to these stimuli and do so than to assume that they receive special orders.

Probably the same is true with the termites. In part, they are no doubt responding to chemicals, particularly chemicals exuded by the queen, which get transmitted around the nest from termite to termite whenever they are in close contact. But this message system can hardly control the temperature of the nest.

If, on the other hand, we assume that termites respond to temperature, then temperature changes could affect their behavior. Assume that a termite in the upper part of the nest feels that it is too hot. There is immediately available an opportunity to lower the temperature both for itself and for the nest by opening a few more ventilation channels. Similarly, if the termite feels too cold, the reverse behavior is called for. The same termite if deep down in the nest, even if he was too warm, would not be stimulated to do anything about the temperature because there would be no ventilation channels in the immediate vicinity to deal with. By complicating this set of drives and assuming that each termite has quite a number of them, we can produce something that is roughly analogous to a human-utility function for each termite. The termite (again using the human analogy) attempts to maximize this utility function, with the particular action it undertakes being determined by the immediate environment. This pattern of behavior could be elaborated into a complete structure for controlling any of the social insects' behavior.

Although this explains why the individual termite behaves in a manner that is efficient from the standpoint of the nest, it does not explain why evolution has given the termites this set of drives. After all, many social insects (termite soldiers, for example) will sacrifice themselves for the good of the nest without, as far as one can see, the slightest hesitation or doubt. This would superficially appear to be a counterevolutionary pattern of behavior.

Once again, if we consider the human body, the explanation is fairly simple. The human body has a very small set of cells that are involved in reproducing other human beings, but the bulk of the body cells exist simply to keep the body as a whole alive. Your skin cells sacrifice themselves by the millions every day for your well-being. Evolution has selected the human being as a complicated mechanism in which most of the cells have the duty of protecting those few cells that can reproduce. The nonreproducing cells have no effect at all on evolution in the future, because they simply won't be around.

The same is true with the termite. Only the reproductives are involved in transmitting the genes to future generations. Therefore, there is no reason why the genes should be programmed so that there is any self-protection drive for the workers or the soldiers, and as far as we can see, they are not so programmed.

The analogy between the termite's nest and the human body is strong enough so that a great many biologists tend to think that in the case of the termite the actual nest should be regarded as the individual rather than the termite itself. They refer to a *superorganism.* Certainly, the termite nest with its controlled internal environment does have a great deal of resemblance to the warm-blooded animal, but there seems no point here in quarreling about words. We can easily tell a termite from a termite nest and we can talk about them separately. But there are many gaps to fill in our knowledge of termites and, indeed, of all other social animals. In many of them, the gaps are much more prominent than the few places where we have knowledge. The social spiders would be a good example. A general science of society can be developed, with human society and the various animal societies being merely specific instances of the theory. We cannot say for certain that this is untrue, but what we can say is that if we are going to have such a general theory, we have to know a great deal more about nonhuman societies than we do now.

CONCLUDING COMMENTS

Thus, human beings in experimental situations, microscopic animals, birds, rats, and inhabitants of mental hospitals choose to buy in the cheapest market. Obviously, it does not follow directly from all of this that everyone is rational in his or her daily life. What we have attempted to demonstrate in this chapter is not that human beings are necessarily rational (although we do believe that they are quite rational) but that the requirement of rationality used in economics is a very modest one. We are not saying anything very complimentary about human beings when we say that they are economically rational. On the other hand, people who say that human beings are not rational are saying something extremely insulting. They are saying that microscopic animals are more capable than is the average human being.

QUESTIONS TO PONDER

1. Design a simple experiment to test some additional economic propositions.
2. In what sense is the concept of rationality different from the concept of intelligence?
3. Can you think of any reasons why the evolutionary process would tend to develop animal behavior patterns that demonstrate what we call rationality?
4. How would you account for the fact that many critics of economics attack the rationality assumptions?

PART TWO

The New World of Households

CHAPTER 5

The New "Home Economics"

The family is generally considered to be the basic building block on which social order is founded. However, even with all the attention that social scientists and others have given it, the family remains perhaps one of the least understood institutions.

The purpose of this chapter is to develop insights into the marriage and family processes. Our approach is somewhat unusual. Certainly we recognize the importance of love in marriage and the family. However, we also recognize that in considering the establishment of a family, individuals are driven by a variety of motives. Some of these are not fundamentally different from those that lead people to buy a car or new clothes.

In addition, we will treat the family in its function as a producing unit. It is a "firm" that takes resources, including labor from within the family and the goods that are purchased, and produces things desired by family members. We want to look inside the family unit and analyze its behavior in terms of the behavior of its members. In the process, we are able to make observations regarding the importance of the marriage contract, the difficulty of divorce, the economic implications of love, and organizational principles underlying the family structure.

THE MARRIAGE CONTRACT

Marriage can be defined in many different ways,[1] but for our purposes, we view it as a legally enforceable contract between a man and woman (or between two parties of the same sex if homosexual marriages are ever legalized). Each party explicitly or implicitly makes certain commitments as to his or her responsibilities within the family. He and she agree to recognize certain rights and privileges of the other, and both agree, again explicitly or

---

[1]*Webster's* defines marriage as "the institution whereby men and women are joined in a special kind of social and legal dependence for the purpose of founding and maintaining a family." *Webster's Ninth New Collegiate Dictionary*, 1986, s.v. "marriage" (Springfield, Mass.: G. & C. Merriam Company, 1981).

implicitly, to a set of rules by which household decisions and changes in the contract are to be made. This last provision is necessary because not all issues concerning the relationship are ever likely to be settled before the vows are said and because conditions do change.

Such provisions of the contract may be only vaguely understood and recognized as such, but they are nevertheless generally present in one fashion or another. The couple may simply have an understanding that they will work things out together, tacitly realizing from their knowledge of the other's behavior what this means.

The process of marriage may be compared with the development of a constitution and bylaws for any firm or organization. As in the case of any one organization, the rules of the game can be as restrictive or as flexible as the people involved desire. In fact, the central purpose of dating and engagement may be to give the couple a chance to work out such provisions and to develop the contract by which both agree to live. (Not all couples, however, avail themselves of this chance to the same degree.)

The contract, for example, may incorporate a provision on whether children will be included (or how many), who will do the housework and mow the lawn, and which decisions will be democratically determined by the whole family and which decisions will be administratively determined. Although we might like to think that everything regarding the marriage should hinge on love, the division of the responsibilities and rewards may be greatly influenced by the relative bargaining power of the two involved.

Without the opportunity to develop such provisions, or if the couple leaves them undetermined, considerable disagreement can arise in their future and result in divorce. Because people have different views on what a marriage should be, the marriage may never take place and very often does not. This is true because the couple involved cannot agree on what the contract should be. In this sense, the dating process screens out some of those marriages that would otherwise fold. Resources are used in dating, but at the same time, the process saves resources from being tied up (albeit temporarily) in an unsatisfying marriage.

Divorce can often be the result of insufficient resources (time, energy, and emotional hassle) being invested by the couple in developing the marriage contract. This may be because the two misjudge how many resources are required. It may also be that either or both of the parties calculate that the expected gain from spending more time and energy on the contract will not be worth the cost

Except in the case of divorce, most provisions of the marriage contract generally do not have the force of law. Occasionally there are cases in which a wife or husband takes her or his spouse to court (for example, for lack of support), but these are indeed relatively rare events. One reason is that the mutually agreed-upon contract is vague and rarely written down. Another is that the cost of one spouse's taking the other to court can be considerable in terms of time and lawyer's fees and can be easily greater than any benefits that may be achieved.

So many of the violations of the contract are of a trivial nature, such as one party's refusal to take out the garbage, to spend time with the children, or to refrain from flirting with other men or women. The potential benefits are just not that great, even if the court will consider the case. In addition, the court fight itself, which may generate a great deal of antagonism, can represent considerable cost.

If provisions have any meaning, it is mainly because of the moral obligation such agreement engenders, the pressures that can be brought to bear on the parties involved by either party or by friends and others, and the threat of one party retaliating by shirking his/her responsibilities. The main role of the court has generally been one of refereeing the division of the family assets (children included) between the husband and wife at the time of divorce. On occasion, the court does attempt to bring about reconciliation.

This role of the court in the divorce process is one that is not unimportant and not without economic implications. The reason is that the court's intrusion ensures that the husband and wife each has some property rights in the family assets, both tangible and intangible. To this extent, the husband and wife have a greater incentive to invest their time and other resources in the development of family assets and the building of a strong marital relationship. The family is an investment project in the sense that returns can be received over the span of years.

An analogy of an investment in business is useful here. Suppose an entrepreneur is considering an investment in an office building. Will he (or she) be willing to make the investment if he knows that after doing so he has no property rights in the building—that is, someone else can take it over without any objections from the court? Although he may be willing to make some investment in the enterprise and to protect it, he will probably be more willing to do so and invest a larger amount if he has some rights that are protected by the state.

The same line of reasoning can be applied to the willingness of the partners in a marriage to invest in the union. To the extent that the stability and durability of the marriage is favorably affected by such investments, the legal status of the marriage yields benefits to all parties in the family.

There is one problem here. By giving each partner property rights over the family assets and, to some extent, over the other partner, and by making the dissolution of the marriage costly, the husband or wife can, if he or she desires, abuse the other. Since there is a cost involved in divorce, one may allow himself or herself to be exploited because he or she may be better off that way than by incurring the cost. If the abuse is greater than the cost of going through with divorce, it goes without saying that the marriage will be dissolved. If the parties are single and living together, either party can walk away without legal constraints. This capacity to walk away without court objections may force the other party to be more considerate.

THE COSTS AND BENEFITS OF MARRIAGE

We have assumed that people's behavior with regard to marriage is to a degree rational. (Can you think of any reason we should assume differently?) This, of course, means that in choosing a spouse, both sexes are out to maximize their utility. It also means that in the process of becoming married, each individual must address two very fundamental questions: (1) what are the costs and benefits in general of being married as opposed to remaining single, and (2) given these benefits and costs, how long and hard should he or she search for an appropriate mate?

The Costs of Marriage

In assessing the pros and cons of marriage, the individual must reckon with several major cost considerations. One of the most important for some (but by no means all) persons is the loss (cost) of independence. Individuals are never completely free to do exactly what they please; they must consider the effects their actions have on others. However, in the close proximity of the family, the possible effects any one person's action can have on another in the family are more numerous and direct than effects on others that a person who lives alone will have. The result can be that everyone may willingly agree to restrict their own behavior to a much greater extent than would be necessary if they all lived alone.

They may, and very likely will, also agree to make many decisions by democratic or collective action. In taking this step, the members of the household essentially agree to incur future costs, which include the time and trouble of reaching a decision. This is because it is generally more costly to make decisions with a larger number of people involved. For example, it is more costly for McKenzie, who is married, to purchase a new car than for Tullock, who is single. All Tullock has to do in buying a new car is consider his own preferences. McKenzie, on the other hand, must consider not only his own preferences, but also those of his wife. The result can be, and almost always is, that buying a car is a long process for the McKenzies.

Note that if McKenzie and his wife had identical preferences, which, to be sure, is never the case in marriages, their decision cost would be the same as Tullock's. In such event, McKenzie would not have to bring his wife in on the decision to buy the car or anything else, and she would not care that he did not. Because of identical preferences, they both could be assured that whatever he bought each would like as well as the other. We have used just one example of the numerous times in which decision costs are incurred in a family. (Any reader who thinks that such costs are unimportant should try marriage for a convincing empirical study!)

It is because of such decision costs that husbands and wives often agree to have many decisions made administratively by one party or the other. Except under unusual circumstances, one party can be allowed, without consulting the other, to make decisions with respect to, say, the family meals. The other party can determine what clothes will be purchased for the children and what types of flowers to plant in the yard. Each party may make decisions not agreeable with the other; however, the savings in decision costs can yield benefits that more than offset the effects of wrong decisions.

Often wives have the responsibility of making decisions with respect to meals and the interior of the house in general and husbands, of making decisions with respect to the yard and the exterior of the house. This division has been attributed to inculturated values—that is, spouses are merely role playing. Although there may be some truth in the statements, we suggest that such argument does not explain why the responsibilities for decisions are divided in the exact way they tend to be in the first place.

Our analysis indicates that the division of decision-making power within the home can add efficiency to the operation of the household and that if roles are not assumed to begin with, they would tend to evolve. The division of powers may not end up in the same way that we now observe them, but given what they are, there may then be the criticism that inculturated roles are being assumed.

As suggested above, the family is involved to a considerable extent in the production of goods and services shared by all members of the family. These are basically of one type and available in one quantity and quality. Such a good—take for example the car considered above—may not be perfectly suitable for any one individual's tastes, but it is the good everyone agrees to buy. In this instance, and there are many of them, the individual must bear the cost of not getting the good in the amount and quality that is most suitable to her preferences.

This type of cost is not only incurred because of the goods consumed, purchased, or produced by the family—such as cars, television programs, recreation, and family life (which tends to defy definition)—but is also applicable to relationships with other people. Both spouses may agree to associate with certain people, not because either finds the people to be best suited to what they find desirable in friends, but because the selected friends represent compromises for both. This is not to say that each will not have several friends of his or her own, but only that they are likely to agree on mutual friends. To the extent that they associate with mutual friends, there is less time for them to be with their individual friends. We submit that this can be a legitimate cost calculation in marriage.

To the extent that household decisions are democratically determined, members of the household have to have a say on how the burden of the production of the household goods is to be distributed. In this way they can determine who pays, in terms of contributing either money income or time and effort. The family can effectively "tax" family members in a way that is similar to any other collective, governmental unity. Any family member can, like any citizen, be forced to pay for collective goods and projects with which they may not be in perfect agreement. This can be considered a potential cost to a family member. This is evident from the complaints that one may hear in a home when the decision is made to go on a picnic and the burden of preparation is distributed or when one is asked to take out the garbage or mow the lawn.

Other costs associated with marriage and the family in general include the risk cost of developing strong emotional ties with one specific group of individuals and forgoing the opportunity to date and in other ways associate with other people. These factors may be of no consequence to some, and may in fact be an advantage to others. Further, the cost of marrying one particular person can be the loss of the opportunity to have married someone else who is not known at the time of marriage but who, if he or she were sought out, would be a more desirable spouse. The list of costs provided can, of course, be extended.

The Benefits of Marriage

The benefits of marriage and the family are derived mainly from the ability of the family to produce goods and services wanted. First, the spouses have the opportunity to produce things not readily duplicated in nonmarriage situations. Such a list may include children (at least ones that cannot legitimately be called bastards), prestige and status that can affect employment and the realm of friends, companionship that is solid and always there, a family-styled sex life that may be more desirable than sexual associations of which the individual may disapprove, and family life in general, which we indicated above defies definition. Granted, many of these goods can be had in certain quantities and qualities outside of the family; we are only suggesting that they take on special characteristics within the family and for that reason are valuable to people. (We recognize that to some these are costs.)

Second, the family operating as a single household—that is, more than one individual—can produce many goods and services more efficiently than can several single-person households. This is because there are economies of scale in household production.

Take, for example, the problem of cleaning the rug. Although there may be some selection in size and power of vacuum cleaners, generally speaking, the machines available are capable of handling the dirt of several people. However, one cleaner must be purchased. If more people are added to the house, the household need not increase the number, size, or power of the vacuum cleaner proportionally. The same can be said of many of the resources that go into the production of a garden, meals, and other household goods such as washing machines, rakes, mixers, brooms, electric tooth-brushes, and so forth.

Indeed, many of the goods and services provided by individuals in the home are public goods: they benefit everyone involved and do not diminish in quantity or quality if additional people are added to the household. For example, many things done to beautify the house are this kind of good. If a picture that all like is hung on the wall, one person's enjoyment of it does not detract in any significant way from the enjoyment by others. Because they all live under the same roof, they do not each have to produce such goods for themselves individually, meaning that they can raise the quality of the goods that are had or they can divert resources to other purposes.

Such goods may not be enjoyed or appreciated by a very large group of people, and because of the decision costs involved, as explained, there is some point at which the collective group would be too large. Therefore, we would expect some unit in society to develop that would be small enough that people of similar tastes can be together to satisfy their mutual interests and large enough that they can be provided efficiently—yet again, small enough that the decision costs incurred are minimized. By having provision for numerous such family units, individuals are given considerable choice over the type, amount, and quality of these goods.

The efficiency of household production can also be greater because of the opportunities for the parties to specialize and effectively trade with one another. In this way the parties can take advantage of their comparative efficiency in production.

Suppose that, for simplicity's sake only, there are only two things for the household to do—clean a given size house and mow its lawn, which is of a given size. Suppose also that we are given the following information about the abilities of a husband and wife in doing these two things:

	Cleaning the House	Mowing the Lawn
Wife	60 minutes	100 minutes
Husband	100 minutes	300 minutes

What this table shows is that the wife can clean the house in 60 minutes and can mow the lawn in 100 minutes. It takes the husband 100 minutes for the house and 300 minutes for the lawn. If they both live separately and have lawns to mow and houses to clean, it would take them a total of 560 minutes. If they lived together and each cleaned half of the house and mowed half of the lawn, it would take them a total of 280 minutes (80 minutes for the house cleaning and 200 minutes for the lawn).

However, there is a possibility here for the two to specialize, one clean-ing the house and one mowing the lawn. Since each will be doing something for the other, we can, in a sense, say they are trading.

To see this prospect, recognize that every time the wife cleans the house she gives up three fifths of the lawn being mowed: If she spends 60 minutes on the house, those are minutes she cannot be mowing the lawn. Since it takes her 100 minutes to mow the lawn, we can assume that she could have mowed three fifths of the lawn. On the other hand, each time the husband cleans the house, he gives up one third of the lawn being mowed. (Why?) We can thereby argue that it is more costly in terms of the portion of the lawn not mowed for the wife to clean the house.

If we want the cost of production to be minimized, we would then argue that the wife should mow the lawn, the husband clean the house. If they divide the tasks this way, the total time spent by both of them would be 200 minutes. If the wife cleans the house and the husband mows, the total time would be 360 minutes.

Notice what we have demonstrated here: by being under one common roof, the cost of the goods demanded by the members can be minimized by the husband and wife specializing and effectively trading. Notice also that we have made this demonstration even though one spouse, the wife, is actually more efficient in the production of both the mowed lawn and the cleaned house. By specializing, the wife and husband can also avoid many of the costs associated with developing the same skills. Each can concentrate attention on a more limited number of household tasks, improving the efficiency with which the tasks can be done.

This demonstration is important because it indicates that if the husband and wife are interested in maximizing household production or minimizing the cost of household production, which amounts to the same thing, then they will specialize to some degree in the functions of the household. They will have what many derogatorily call roles.

However, these assigned roles need not be the traditional roles for spouses. Further, it indicates that certain roles may be assumed by, say, the wife not because she is necessarily less efficient than the husband in the production of those things the husband does, but rather because her comparatively greater efficiency (called comparative advantage) lies in what she does.[2] The same is true for the husband. (Of course, to acquire the efficiency benefits described here, the husband and wife need to have the appropriate preferences for the assigned tasks.)

Furthermore, if the decision facing the family is the allocation of members' time between work internal to the home and work external to the home and if the family is interested in minimizing the cost of goods produced in the home, then it should use that labor with the lowest value outside of the home. The cost of cleaning the house is equal to the cost of the materials and supplies and the value of the individual's time outside the home who does the cleaning.

---

[2]If the wife takes as much as 180 minutes to mow the lawn and everything else about the example above is the same, it would still be more efficient for the wife to mow the lawn and the husband to clean the house.

Assume that it takes two hours to clean the house, that the wage the wife can earn outside the home is $6 per hour, and that the wage of the husband is $10 per hour. (Here we are only attempting to use a realistic example; it is a fact, which is the subject of considerable complaint by women, that husbands do tend to earn more than their wives.) It follows that it would be cheaper for the wife to do the cleaning. If the man did the cleaning, it would cost an additional $8 since his wage is $4 per hour higher.[3]

Many sociologists and psychologists contend that roles, such as child care, are assumed within the house because of socially determined values. We are unwilling to argue that such forces have no effect on the organization of many households. All we wish to add is that much of what we observe in household relationships may often be the result of a conscious, rational choice on the part of the couples.

Clearly, women do tend to earn less than men in the market, a point made above, either because they are the victims of discrimination or because they are less productive. Given this, which is not something individual households can do much about, it is reasonable to expect households to delegate many responsibilities, such as child care, to wives. In this way, the cost of the child care is minimized, and the output of the family is maximized. If the household production is greater by the wife's staying at home, then one can suggest that the output of the wife is actually greater than what is indicated by her work in the home; she should get some credit for the greater output of the household.

If the discrimination women face outside of the home is reduced and/or they are able to raise their productivity relative to men, we should expect their wages to rise relative to their husbands'. We should then expect to see more and more wives working outside the home and relatively more time being spent by husbands in housework. It is clear that the labor force participation rate of women has been on the rise over the decades; it is equally clear that the labor force participation rate of men has been on the decline. There are many reasons for this, including changes in attitudes of men and women toward women working in jobs. Our point is elementary: The greater wages of women can be another explanatory factor.

There are other possible benefits to marriage and the family, such as the benefit of making communication less expensive. Communication is an

---

[3]The same allocation of wife- and husband-time would result if the wife is substantially more efficient in the production of household goods. Consider the case of the wife being able to earn $10 per hour and the husband earning $6 per hour. Suppose that it takes the wife an hour to do some household task and it takes the husband two hours. If the husband stayed at home to do it, it would cost the family $12 (two hours at $6 per hour). However, it would only cost them $10 (one hour at $10 per hour) for the wife to do it. In such case, the family would choose to have the wife stay home if it were interested in minimizing production costs. Inculturated values would perhaps come into play as an explanatory factor if the couple did not obey these rules for time allocation.

important aspect of any production process. (Can you name other benefits?) The point is that home economics has much to do with how households are organized.

SPOUSE SELECTION

The rational individual in search of a spouse will attempt to maximize utility as in all other endeavors. He (by which we mean he or she) will not pretend to seek the "perfect mate" but only that one individual among those whom he knows and who are willing to marry him that best (not perfectly) suits his preferences. (Who do you know that has married the *perfect person*?)

This means that he will seek to minimize the cost incurred through marriage and the family.[4] If he marries someone who agrees with him, the cost associated with arriving at the marriage contract is less than otherwise. There is not as great a need for (implicit) bargaining. If he marries someone who agrees with him as to what the family should do, what kinds of recreation they should have, and the number and way in which children should be reared, then the cost of having to give up friends and goods that suit his preferences better will be minimized. In other words, we would expect rational individuals to tend to marry persons who have similar values and preferences and are in other ways like themselves. Interestingly enough, this is generally what researchers have found.[5]

Rational behavior has other implications with regard to search for a mate. It implies that the greater the benefits from marriage, the greater the costs a person will be willing to incur in searching for the spouse. This means that the greater the efficiency benefits that are to be achieved in family production or the greater the esteem people give those who marry, the more costs, in terms of time and effort, that a person will apply in looking.

Greater costs may take the form of later marriages and a smaller fraction of the population married. Also, the longer the individual expects the marriage to last and the more stable it is expected to be, the more careful will be the search. This does not mean that mistakes will not be made; it only means that greater costs will be incurred in trying to avoid mistakes.

It also follows that the difficulty (cost) of divorce should affect the extent to which people search for a spouse. It may affect the extent to which people marry, the extent of more informal arrangements, and the availability and economic well-being of prostitution as an institution. If a divorce is made impossible, a man (or woman) knows that if he (or she) chooses the right person, then there are more benefits to be had than if divorce were easier to

---

[4]In searching for a mate, he will extend his search until the marginal cost of extending the search is equal to the marginal benefits.

[5]See, for example, R. F. Winch, *Mate Selection* (New York: Harper & Row, 1958). This conclusion, of course, does not apply to the situation in which one party prefers a mate who will dominate him or her.

come by. The impossibility of divorce will assure him that his spouse cannot freely marry someone else whom she may later prefer. If, on the other hand, he chooses the wrong person, the impossibility of divorce will mean that the decision would carry with it greater cost than if the marriage could be easily dissolved by divorce.

Therefore, as Gary Becker has argued, we would expect the resources applied to search for a mate to be directly correlated with the difficulty of obtaining a divorce, and he writes that "Search may take the form of trial living together, consensual unions, or simply prolonged dating. Consequently, when divorce becomes easier, the fractions of the persons legally married may actually increase because of the effect on the age at marriage."[6] Alan Freiden has in part corroborated Becker's hypothesis in a study of the effects of different state divorce laws. He found that the more costly the divorce process, the smaller was the fraction of women married.[7]

If divorce is made easier, this line of analysis indicates that people will tend to incur fewer search costs, perhaps reflected in a younger age at which people marry. One might reasonably assume that the durability of marriages in general is positively related to the extent to which people search the marriage market before they choose the one. If this can be accepted (and it might be a poor assumption), then making divorce easier can result in more divorces because they are less costly and also because people are expending fewer resources in search of a spouse and, therefore, making more wrong choices.

THE RELEVANCE OF LOVE

For our purposes (in developing an economic analysis of people's behavior), we say that a person loves another if his or her level of satisfaction is in part dependent on the satisfaction level of the other person. In this sense, one person genuinely cares for the other person and cares what happens to her (or him). This is because she (or he) will have greater utility if it is known that the other person is in some sense better off. She will, therefore, be motivated to help improve the situation of the person who is loved. The more intense the love, the stronger is this motivation.

As we have explained, responsibilities are typically delegated to family members, and each member is dependent on the others' fulfilling their end of the bargain. In this way, the welfare of the family members will diminish if any one member shirks responsibilities.[8] Because shirking hurts others, the

---

[6]Gary S. Becker, "A Theory of Marriage: Part II," *Journal of Political Economy* 82, supplement (March/April 1974), p. s22.

[7]Alan Freiden, "The United States Marriage Market," *Journal of Political Economy* 82, supplement (March/April 1974), pp. s34–s54.

[8]A person can shirk by failing to carry out any part of the contract or by making it more difficult (costly) for the other person to see that the contract is obeyed.

person who loves the other will be less inclined to shirk than the person who does not. It is for this reason that a person, if given the choice, would naturally want to marry someone who loves her (or him) and would also naturally want to marry someone whom she loves because what she does for the family will also give her satisfaction to the extent that it makes everyone better off.

Put somewhat differently, the presence of love reduces the costs each spouse must incur in monitoring the marriage contract Almost all contracts require some monitoring. The marriage contract is no exception, especially since it is necessarily involved in legal and emotional terms.

Where love does not exist, we will be more likely to find individuals shirking family responsibilities. This in turn means that family resources will have to be diverted into the "policing" of family members. In this way love has an economic dimension. This does not mean that people will not marry someone they do not love or who does not love them. Because of the benefits of being in a family situation, people may prefer that to the single life. Many people do marry for money as well as other benefits.

All of this adds up to one interesting conclusion, and that is that the efficient marriage is one in which the two are in love and are alike in terms of values and preferences. Oddly enough, this is what most people would readily argue. The interesting thing about this conclusion is that it is derived from the perspective of economics and the family as a producing unit. The greater the love and the closer the preferences of the couple, the closer will the marriage approximate what may be considered the ideal.

However, in the realistic world in which we live, it is clear that the maximizing individual does not always have the opportunity to choose a spouse who loves her (or him) and has similar preferences (at least to any great degree). She (or he) must often choose between a person who may love her very little but who may be in many ways like herself, and the person who loves her but who is very different. All the individual can do is maximize over the range of opportunities.

The discussion suggests that love adds to the efficiency of the household; we also argued earlier that differences in preferences can detract from the efficiency with which the household is operated. If this is the case and the individual is seeking to maximize the output from being in a family, then we must conclude that love is not all that is necessary for a successful family and marriage.

Marriages in which the parties professed to love each other dearly have been known to break up. The problem was that they violently disagreed over what the marriage should be and do and the roles that each was to play. The gulf in preferences could have been so wide that the love, as intense as it was, could not bridge it. In the same way, we might expect that many marriages are held together with little love; the partners' preferences are so much alike, they still find their relationship very beneficial, at least given their next-best opportunities.

CONCLUDING COMMENTS

Marriage and the family are terribly complex subjects to discuss, and you probably detect there is a lot that has been left unsaid. We definitely agree. We believe that the field is wide open for future research. This has been only a sample of what economists are beginning to say about such basic social institutions, and we think that the economic approach shows great promise in contributing to our understanding of the subject.

QUESTIONS TO PONDER

1. Given the analysis in this chapter, would you expect married couples to "invest" more or less in their marriages (in the way of building up a permanent relationship) than people who are simply living together? Explain.

2. Consider the following true-life case: A movie star had been living with a woman for several years. He decided to break the relationship, but when he did, the woman sued him for the division of their common property and for a monetary settlement. The woman won her case. What effect will such a ruling have on the willingness of people to "live together"? On the willingness of people to marry? What effect will such a ruling have on the durability of the relationships that exist between people who are living together? *increased cost*

3. Given the following information, who will mow the lawn and who will clean the house:

	Cleaning the House	*Mowing the Lawn*
Wife	75 minutes	150 minutes
Husband	200 minutes	200 minutes

   (See the example in this chapter involving the division of household chores.)

4. Many states and the federal government are interested of increasing the penalties for failure of the noncustodial parent to make the court-approved child-support payments. What will such changes in the law do to the marriage rate, the birth rate, and the divorce rate? *decrease - increase*

5. What is the likely effect of an increase in the ease of divorce on the birth rate? Explain your answer in economic terms.

6. If because of the way they were reared wives were more productive than husbands in cooking meals, does it follow that women will always cook the meals in an efficient household? Prove your answer with a numerical examples involving the productivity of wives and husbands.

CHAPTER 6

Child Production

Children may be little darlings in their parents' eyes, but they are also economic goods. They can provide considerable benefits to their parents and relatives, and they are the result of a continuously evolving production process. This process involves resource expenditures like everything else that is produced in the home. From an economic perspective, they are a source of consumption and an object of investment.

CHILDREN AS ECONOMIC GOODS

Parents obtain from children a good deal of companionship, resulting in benefits not unlike those received from other goods, such as a new car or a good martini. Children can be someone to talk to or go on a walk with, and they can be ready-made partners for a game of Ping-Pong or checkers (if one can bear the hassle of getting them to do it). Their existence gives parents some hope that they will not be left alone later in life. Children also provide parents with the pleasure that comes from being respected and needed and, at least at some stages of a child's development, adored by someone else. There are very few parents who are not touched when their small children run to them when they return from work or a trip.

Rightly or wrongly, children are used to fulfill parents' goals and to extend themselves beyond their own physical limitations. By having children, parents are able to negate the unspoken criticism of relatives and friends that they are incapable of having or, in some way, loving them. The motivation for having children may include a means of fulfilling a sincerely felt need to make a contribution to society, to explore the unknown, or to test the hypothesis that they can do a better job in rearing children than others. In all these regards, children are consumer goods.

Children, at one time in our history (and this is still true in many undeveloped areas of the world), were a means by which parents could develop their own old-age pension plan. As the children grew up, parents paid into the plan by feeding and clothing their children; in later years, the children took care of the parents when they were unable to provide for themselves.

This, incidentally, was at a time when security markets and insurance companies were not very well developed, particularly in newly opened territories.

This kind of household self-insurance arrangement has not completely dissipated. However, for the most part, today people in the industrialized countries rely much more heavily on the impersonal, financially based retirement plans for old-age income. The reason may be in part that the market has provided alternative retirement schemes that are cheaper than those incorporated in children. As we will see, children can be extremely expensive. Further, the benefits in the financially based plans are contractual and to that degree are more certain or less risky. Another reason may be that the government has forced people to become a part of the social security system, which may have contributed to reduced reliance on children for retirement maintenance.

Last but not least, children can be an important source of labor, particularly for families living on farms and places where child labor is less expensive than mechanization. The parents, in the beginning stages of the children's lives, invest resources in their growth and development in order that they can become workers. When the child is old enough to work, the parents reap the returns from their investment.

Granted, parents in general may not have children for the sole purpose of seeing them become good and loyal workers or for the purpose of gaining a sense of immortality. All of the benefits that can be listed are fused in the typical decision to have a child. But this is true in the decision to buy a new car or house; there are a multiplicity of reasons for buying or producing almost anything.

All of the benefits of having children that can be enumerated add up to one total level of parental satisfaction and, to that degree, to the parents' demand for children. This demand for children—or, perhaps more properly, "child services"—can be reflected in the total number of children or in the quality of the children born and reared. The one thing that can be said at this point is that the greater the benefits reaped from children, the greater the number and quality of children that will be had.

Such a statement assumes, of course, that the cost of the children is held constant and that parents, or at least some of them, look upon the decision to have children in the same rational way as they do everything else. Because some readers will doubt the reasonableness of this latter assumption, we will return to it later.

The cost of rearing a child includes the family expenditures on giving birth, food, clothing, shelter, education, entertainment, medical expenses, insurance, transportation, and so on. Other major cost items, which are often overlooked, are the emotional drain and the value of the parents' time spent on rearing the child. Estimating the cost of children is a difficult problem at best. The actual cost of a child will depend on exactly how much the parents want to spend, and all costs will vary with the economic status and location

TABLE 6–1   The Suggested Cost of a Child

Birth	$ 3,000
Rearing	65,000
College education	24,000
Parents' time (opportunity cost)	374,400
Total cost	$466,400

of the parents. Given these problems, however, any estimate for the late 1980s would include the cost of birth (hospital and doctors' fees, about $3,000), cost of rearing the child through age 18 [$65,000 ($300 per month)], cost of education in a public college or university [$24,000 ($6,000 per year)], and the opportunity of parents' time devoted to child rearing [$374,400 ($20 an hour for 20 hours a week for 18 years)]. These costs are summarized in Table 6–1.

The total cost of $466,400 is probably far greater than might have been expected, primarily because of the inclusion of the opportunity cost of parents' time, which many readers may not have considered.[1] The total cost of a child will vary markedly with the opportunity wage of the parents. The cost of a child to a low-income person can be substantially less than that indicated above. For example, assuming all costs other than the wage rate remain the same as above, the cost of a child to a "poor" person who earns $5 an hour drops to $185,600.

The costs given above are the result of the simple summation of the expenditures made and the earnings forgone during the rearing phase of the child's life. However, the total cost may be lower than that which is indicated. This is because many of the costs will be spread out over a number of years. And $1,000 spent years from now is worth less than $1,000 spent today. The reason is that the $1,000 spent today can earn interest during the course of years if it is deposited in a savings account or invested in interest-bearing securities. Certainly, even after discounting the value of future expenditures, the first child is the biggest single "good" most people are likely to buy during their lives!

The only saving grace in contemplating a family is that many of the costs associated with the first child are fixed, that is, not subject to change with additional children. This only means that the marginal cost of the second child is generally less than the marginal cost of the first.

---

[1]The costs of having children has been much more accurately estimated by Ritchie H. Reed and Susan McIntosh, "Costs of Children," in *Economic Aspects of Population Change: The Commission on Population Growth and the American Future*, ed. Elliot R. Morss and Ritchie H. Reed (Washington, D.C.: U.S. Government Printing Office, 1972), p. 345.

THE DEMAND AND SUPPLY OF CHILDREN

By pointing out the costs and benefits of children, the ᴄ̣
mean to imply that children are just like every other good a family pu̱ᵣ̣
There is substantially more emotion, risk, and uncertainty in having a chı̣ᴌ̣
than in buying a new house or almost anything else. Parents are not able to
see the good (child) before they buy it; in fact, their task is to produce it from
scratch. The child comes with a will of its own from birth. This adds an
element of surprise that is not normally a feature of a new house. In the case
of the house, the buyers can sell if they decide later that it is not what they
want, perhaps recouping their investment and then some. In modern American society, to do the same with a child is frowned upon.

All of this means that the decision to have a child is more difficult than
other decisions a family confronts and that there is more room for error in
child production than in the production of other things. It does not follow
that some parents will not attempt to approach the problem with the same
rational intentions that they approach everything else.

Parents may conceive a child they did not plan to have because the
momentary importance of sex was so great that they forgot to take the necessary precautions. This seems to be very likely if it is recognized that there
are approximately 2.5 billion acts of sexual intercourse between married couples in the United States each year.[2] One could add to that total a substantial
number of acts between those who are unmarried. It is simply a matter
of probability that some goofs will occur—no contraceptive is foolproof. To
the degree that accidents occur, there will be children born and reared who
are not the result of the conscious consideration of the expected costs and
benefits.

However, the important point is that to the extent that there are parents
who consider the costs and benefits in child-bearing decisions, the demand
curve for children will be downward sloping. The cost of a child will influence the fertility level. More children will be had, the lower the cost or price.
Parents will, in addition, rationally balance off the number of children conceived with the quality.

In Figure 6–1 we have illustrated the total market demand for children
(D). In our example Q_1 children will be born and reared because of impulsive
or, in other ways, nonrational behavior on the part of parents. However, how
many children will be had in total will depend also on the supply, which
means cost, of children. If, for simplification, the supply of children is as-

---

[2]Our figure of the number of acts of sexual intercourse is, of course, rough, being based on
the calculations of others for 1965, adjusted for the increase in population through 1986.
Leslie Aldridge Westoff and Charles F. Westoff, *From Now to Zero: Fertility, Contraception, and
Abortion in America* (Boston: Little Brown, 1974), p. 24. This estimate is based on a coital
frequency of 6.7 times a month for all couples.

GURE 6–1

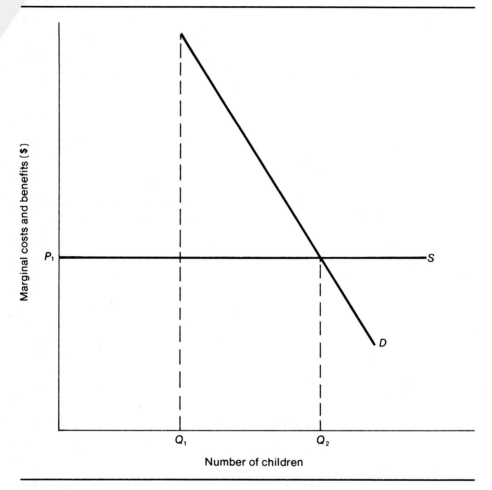

sumed to be horizontal (S)—that is, the marginal cost is constant at P_1—the total number of children had will be Q_2. Of this total, Q_1 will be the result of "accidents" and Q_2–Q_1 will be the result of cost-benefit calculations.[3]

If you are inclined to doubt our assumption that many child-bearing decisions are conscious, rational acts, you should reflect on the number of times you have heard someone or yourself say, "Not me! I can't afford to have another child. There is just not enough time in the day to handle the two that I've got." This is just another way of saying that the cost of the additional

---

[3]It is quite likely that many of the births that are unplanned take the place of births that were planned for a later date. If this is the case, the demand curve will move in to the left. The line of argument, however, remains undisturbed.

child is too great for the expected benefits. We might expect that people who make such statements often go to a great extent to avoid conceiving again.

If the demand for children falls, the economist would predict that the number of children had will fall. This situation is described in Figure 6–2 by a shift in the demand curve from D_1 to D_2. The number of children drops from Q_2 to Q_3. The number of accidentally conceived children remains at Q_1. However, the number of rationally determined children falls, causing the drop in the total.

This change in demand can result from an exogenous drop in people's "taste" for children. It can also result from a decrease in the relative prices of other goods produced and consumed in the home. If the latter happened, rational couples would tend to reallocate their resources toward the cheaper goods and away from children. It may be that one explanation for the declining birthrate has been the growing relative cheapness of goods, such as cars and all forms of entertainment, which may be substitutes for children.

FIGURE 6–2

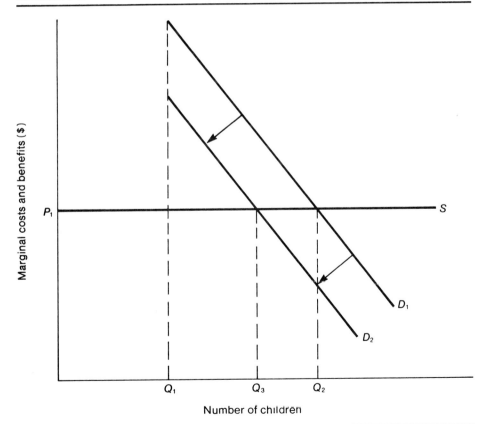

Number of children

In general, the location of the demand curve is dependent on the relative benefits attributable to children and on the family resources. Children who grow up on farms have many more opportunities to contribute to the family's income than children who grow up in an urban setting. One explanation for this is the child labor laws, which do not restrict children from working on farms but do restrict them from working in industry.

For this reason alone, economists would expect the benefits attributable to children and their parents' demand for children to be far greater for farm families than for families living in the cities. In other words, the farm family's demand for children (D_1 in Figure 6–2) will be greater than the demand of urban families (D_2). The result is a tendency for farm families to be larger. If there is a migration of people from the farms to the cities, as there has been over the decades, one would expect birthrates to fall and the population growth rates to taper off somewhat. Interestingly, this is precisely what demographers and economists who have tested these hypotheses have found.[4]

Over time, if there is a reduction in the price of mechanized equipment, *ceteris paribus*, there may be a decrease in the size of farm families if the equipment can take the place of child labor. Cheaper farm equipment would encourage families to buy more equipment and use less labor; that is, have fewer children.

The leftward shift in demand can also be the effect of the availability of cheaper and better contraceptives. Because they are cheaper we may anticipate more extensive use of them and fewer accidental births. The summation of the accidental plus rationally determined births would fall.

Also, people's preferences for children may turn away from numbers to quality, causing the demand curve based on the number of children to shift in. The reader should understand that for parents there is the ever-present decision between using their resources for the purpose of having more children and using them for the purpose of giving the number they have more attention. This can be reflected in what the parents consider a quality improvement.

We have concentrated in this section on a drop in demand for children because that appears to us to be the current trend. The reader may want to extend the discussion by considering possible causes for an increase in demand and the consequences of such developments.

Given our model, anything that reduces the cost of children, *ceteris paribus*, will shift the supply curve downward and increase the number of children had. In the case of Figure 6–3, the supply goes from S_1 to S_2, and the number of children demanded goes from Q_2 to Q_3. The reason for the expan-

---

[4]John D. Kasarda, "Economic Structure and Fertility: A Comparative Analysis," *Demography* 8 (August 1971), pp. 307–17; Stanley Kupinsky, "Non-Familial Activity and Socio-Economic Differentials in Fertility," *Demography* 8 (August 1971), pp. 353–67.

FIGURE 6–3

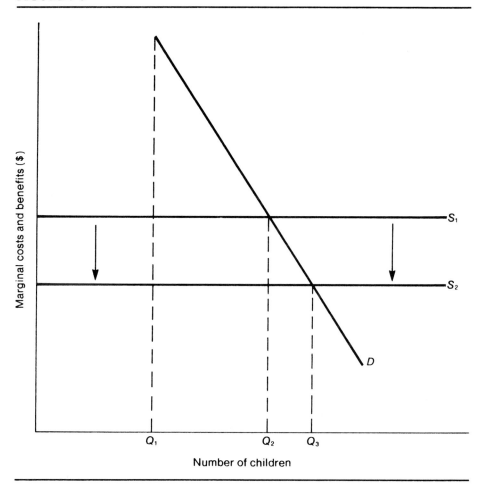

sion is that prior to the cost reduction, the cost of the additional children between Q_2 and Q_3, exceeds the benefits indicated by the demand curve between Q_2 and Q_3. Once the supply curve shifts down, the benefits of the additional children become greater than the cost for those additional children. It is therefore rational for the couple to divert more resources into child production.

Such a change may have been the consequence of an increase in efficiency of rearing children, making the whole process less costly. Also it may have been attributable to a decrease in the prices of those resources purchased from the market that are peculiar to the production of children, or it may be attributable to changes in such exogenous forces as government policy.

As an example of a proposed change in government policy that can affect fertility rates, the personal exemption for income tax is from time to time raised. Clearly, such a policy effectively lowers the cost of having children. If a person were in a tax-rate bracket of 25 percent, a $500 increase in the personal exemption reduces tax liability by $125 ($500 x .25) per year, or by $2,250 (undiscounted) over the first 18 years of the child's life. This may not seem like much of a saving since the undiscounted cost of an additional child can be upwards of $400,000.

Even though such a change in the tax structure is not likely to have an effect on everyone's decision to have a child, it can affect those marginal couples whose estimated costs and benefits of having an additional child are very close or who are more or less indifferent to the idea of having a child but are inclined to hold off. For illustration, suppose that before adjustment in the personal exemption, a couple figured that with the lower exemption per child the undiscounted marginal cost of the additional child was $400,000 and the marginal benefits were $398,000. Since the marginal cost was greater than the marginal benefit, the couple would not have the child.

However, after the exemption was raised, the marginal cost was lowered to $397,500, an amount less than the marginal benefits of $398,500. Such a change in the tax laws will tend to make slightly more difficult the problem of population control. Welfare payments tied to the number of children, including payments for unborn fetuses, and public provision of education and day-care centers can encourage population growth.

In a similar way, high rates of inflation like those experienced in the United States in the 1970s reduce the real value of exemptions, thus increasing the total real costs of having children. With inflation eating away at the value of the tax exemption per child, some parents can be expected to respond by reducing the number of mouths they feed. (Of course, Congress may partially offset the effects of inflation on the birthrate by periodically adjusting the tax exemption for children to the cost of living.)

As seen in Table 6–1, the major cost in the rearing of a child is the opportunity cost of the parents' time. The higher the potential wage of the parents' time outside the home, the higher is this component of the cost. The effect of greater cost can be to reduce the number of children had. This is illustrated in Figure 6–4 by the upward shift in the supply curve and the accompanying reduction in the number of desired children.

On the other hand, the higher wage gives the couple added income to allocate to family purchases, including children. This "income effect" can have a positive influence on the production of children.[5] If this is the case, the net effect of the higher wage depends on the relative strengths of the negative cost effect and the possible positive income effect. The empirical

---

[5]We recognize that children can be "inferior goods," meaning the income effect can be negative.

FIGURE 6–4

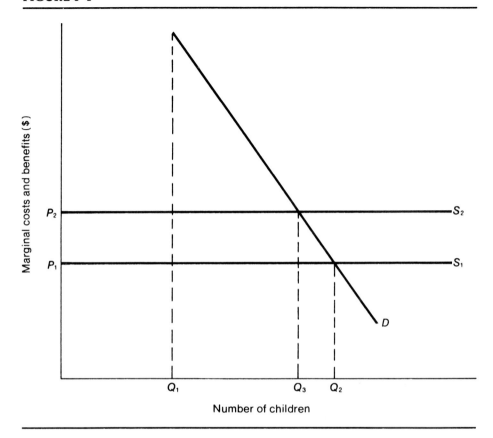

studies that have been done on the subject tend to find a negative correlation between family income and number of children.[6] This suggests, but does not confirm, that the negative cost effect is stronger. As opposed to being reflected in the number of children, of course, the income effect can be realized in the quality of children demanded by people with higher incomes.[7]

---

[6]Bruce Gardner, "Economics of the Size of North Carolina Rural Families," *Journal of Political Economy* 81, supplement (March/April 1973), pp. s99–s122; Dennis N. DeTray, "Child Quality and the Demand for Children," *Journal of Political Economy* 81, supplement (March/April 1973), pp. s70–s95.

[7]Testing the relationship between income and child quality is a difficult task because of the problems associated with defining and obtaining data on quality. Nevertheless, DeTray made an effort by defining child quality as the extent of the child's education. He finds that the education of the mother, which can be mirrored in her opportunity wage, does have an effect on the "efficiency with which child quality is produced." "Child Quality," p. s93.

The discussion of the impact of higher wages on birthrates is interesting and important because it has implications regarding population growth-rate trends in developing countries. If the negative cost effect is stronger than the positive income effect, as empirical studies indicate, and if this relationship holds for underdeveloped countries, then the population explosion that has been the concern of many in recent decades, may fade to some degree if the underdeveloped countries are ever able to develop. The higher opportunity wage, coupled with the greater dependence on industry, could lead to a lower birthrate. All we have argued here, however, is the probable direction of the effect of development on population growth and not how strong the effect is.

EDUCATION AND CHILD PRODUCTION

The education level of parents can influence the child production process in several ways. First, it can change the parents' relative preferences for children by introducing them to things they find more valuable. Second, education can increase the opportunity wage rate of the parents and have the positive income effect and negative cost effect mentioned above.

One of the more firmly established relationships in fertility literature is the negative correlation between the amount of education of the wife and the number of children she has—that is, as the wife's education level rises, the number of children tends to fall.[8] There is some evidence showing that the relationship between the husband's education level and the number of children is positive.[9] One possible explanation for these findings is that, as many studies have found, the wife's time is relatively more important in child production than is the time of the husband, and the cost of her time will accordingly be more influential in child-production decisions. The education of the husband, whose responsibilities have traditionally included earning the money income, has had little cost effect (since the amount of his time involved may not be very great) but has had a positive income effect.

Third, education can increase the efficiency with which the quality of children can be raised. At least one empirical study tends to support this.[10] Even with a higher opportunity wage rate, greater efficiency can make a unit of child quality, however defined by the parent, cheaper to the more educated person.

For example, suppose it takes the parent with an elementary school education two hours to teach his child a certain task that contributes to the child's quality. The parent's market wage rate is $4 per hour. The total cost is $8. On the other hand, if it takes the more educated parent, who earns $20

---

[8]Gardner, "Economics of the Size of North Carolina Families."
[9]Massanori Hashimoto, "Economics of Postwar Fertility in Japan: Differentials and Trends," *Journal of Political Economy* 82, supplement (March/April 1974), pp. s170–s194.
[10]Ibid.

per hour, one quarter hour to accomplish the same thing with his child, the cost is only $5. Everything else being equal, we would expect the more educated person to demand more units of child quality.

Fourth, the effects of education can show up in the parent's knowledge and use of contraceptives and in the number of unwanted children conceived. A number of studies have found a direct relationship between parents' education and their knowledge of and use of contraceptives.[11] More-educated parents tend to use the more effective contraceptive methods and use them to a much greater extent. Robert Michael gives three possible explanations for this:

1. Education makes the technical literature on contraception more easily understood and to that extent lowers contraception costs.

2. Education raises the value of the couple's time and thereby makes more effective methods (which may be more expensive but less time consuming) more economical. (The time expenditure for a couple does vary somewhat from the pill to the use of diaphragms and foam tablets.)

3. Education raises the cost of children by raising the cost of parents' time, and thereby increases the cost of an unwanted child. This makes knowledge and use of contraceptives more valuable.[12]

In the process of developing his argument, Michael makes an interesting point regarding the efficiency of contraceptive devices. He writes, "If a couple used a contraceptive technique that was 'only' 90 percent effective, in a 15-year period their expected fertility outcome would be 2.7 births. . . . Or, if a couple used a contraceptive technique that was 'only' 99 percent effective, the chance of a conception in a five-year interval exceeds 10 percent. 'Good' (but not perfect) contraception does not provide the long-run protection one might think."[13] He also estimated that if a fertile couple does not use any method of contraception for five years, the probability of conception is 100 percent.

CHILD PRODUCTION AND THE "POPULATION BOMB"

Economists are in general agreement that the optimum quantity produced of anything is that quantity at which the marginal cost of the last unit is equal to the marginal benefits of it. This will be the case if all costs and benefits are actually considered by the individual making the decision on the output. And this rule of thumb holds for the production of children.

---

[11]Robert T. Michael, "Education and the Derived Demand for Children," *Journal of Political Economy* 81, supplement (March/April 1973), pp. s123–s164.

[12]Ibid., p. s159.

[13]Ibid., p. s141.

However, if the person making the decision does not consider all costs in the production of children (that is, someone else bears a portion of the cost), the perceived marginal cost will be lower than it really is. Using Figure 6–4, because not all costs are considered by the person making the child production decision, the couple will perceive that the cost of children is represented by supply curve S_1, whereas in fact the true supply curve, considering all costs, is at S_2. Couples will rationally choose to produce Q_2 children. Note that the true marginal cost (P_2), when all costs are included between Q_2 and Q_3, is actually greater than the demand curve. This indicates that the marginal cost of the children is greater than the marginal benefits, and as a result, too many children are produced.

In our present society, there are two basic ways in which couples deciding to bear children can underestimate the cost of their children. They may not consider the added congestion their children can create. This may mean that there are simply more people taking up the same limited area and reducing the freedom all persons have to move about without affecting others, or it may mean that more people are competing for resources other than space and causing another form of congestion. This cost of an additional child is incurred in general by people not involved in the decision to have the child.

The other basic way by which the private decisions of parents can impose costs on others is through governments' budgets. Presently there are many public facilities, such as schools, that are provided with tax money. If the facilities are not free to the user, they are most often subsidized. To this extent, a portion of the total cost of a child is borne by the general taxpayer. The private decision of one couple to have a child can, therefore, increase the tax bill for the rest of the community.

Because these costs may not, and to a substantial degree are not, considered by the child-bearing couple, the costs they consider will be understated, which results in over-production of children. (It is indeed an interesting thought that the tax burden of the general public is partly dependent on the coital frequency of couples!) One way to turn this around is to have the child-bearing couples pay the cost by imposing a tax on them for each birth. To put it mildly, this is not likely to be a popular proposal with those who want children. They no doubt would prefer that the rest of us continue to pay the bill for their fortune or misfortune—as the case may be.

CHILD PRODUCTION AND THE FUTURE

Years ago, Thomas Ireland, in a paper "The Political Economy of Child Production," suggested some interesting prospects (but disturbing to some, we are sure) for the future course of child rearing.[14] If it were not for the

---

[14]Thomas R. Ireland, "The Political Economy of Child Production," paper presented at the annual public choice meeting, University of Maryland (March 1973).

rather dramatic change over the past two decades in the public's acceptance of abortions and surrogate motherhood, we would indeed consider his ideas to be futuristic. But, as it is, Ireland's paper may indicate what is just around the corner.

His paper is based on two main propositions: first, scientists now have the capability to transplant an animal fetus from its mother to a "host mother," with the birth following in due course. There are good reasons for believing that if medical science is not able to do it now, the know-how will be developed in the future to accomplish the same thing in humans. (More will be said on the fetus transplant technology in Chapter 10.)

Second, Ireland recognizes that the problems associated with pregnancies cause some women pain and inconvenience and make many unable to work in the market for several months.

The prospects of fetus transplant provides a potential solution to the dwindling number of adoptable babies and the moral problems surrounding abortions. Because adoptable babies are becoming very expensive, the mother who would like to bear a child but who cannot because of the sterility of the husband, would have some incentive to pay to have an aborted fetus transplanted into herself.[15] This may not sound so crazy if it is remembered that some women (or couples) now pay handsomely for artificial insemination and for the rights to adopt a child. In fact, a public interest group interested in the rights of the fetus's life may be willing to pay another mother to accept the transplant and carry the child to term.

Such a solution may be disgusting to some readers who are concerned about the life of the fetus. Granted, this may be a less-than-ideal solution, but it may be a better solution than one of standing around discussing the question of when life begins while more than a million fetuses a year are being destroyed.

In addition, there are possibilities for payment arrangements whereby the true mother and host mother gain by a fetus transplant. Suppose that there is a mother who earns $60,000 per year, who wants to have a child of her own, but who is not willing to endure the pain and loss of income associated with pregnancy. If there is another woman who earns $12,000 per year and is willing to make a career out of becoming a "surrogate mother," then the true mother can conceive the child and possibly agree through some institution, which is not yet established, to pay a host mother to carry the baby to term, at which time the baby would be transferred back to the original mother.

If the disability associated with the pregnancy is three months, the real mother could be willing to pay (ignoring taxes) as much as or more than $15,000 to the host mother. By making the payment, it will be the host mother

---

[15]Adoptable babies of minority groups are still relatively easy to obtain; but with legalization of abortion, this supply is dwindling.

who will lose time at work, which will cost her $3,000. She can receive from the real mother, say, $6,000 and her income will rise to $15,000.

Furthermore, the total output of the economy can be $12,000 greater than what it would have been if the real mother had lost the time from work. All of this may sound a little coldhearted, but we really do not mean for it to be taken that way. These are, however, solutions that may be more than just attention getters in the relatively near future. We already have cases in which surrogate mothers are artificially impregnated with the sperm of another paying couple and in which eggs fertilized outside the womb are carried to term by surrogate mothers.

CONCLUDING COMMENTS

In recent years, it has been the fad to project the future course of the population trend and accompanying problems. Most of these projections are merely statistical extrapolations of the trends of the recent past. They do not assume that there will be adjustments made in the economy that will alter the course of the trend.

We do not wish to understate the importance of getting the population growth in many countries around the world under control. However, we suspect that the doomsday prophets will be mistaken in their projections because of certain anticipated changes in the child-production process.

First, we expect that as the population grows larger, putting pressure on resources, the cost of producing children will become relatively greater, reflecting back on the private household decisions.

Second, we suspect that as congestion becomes greater, there will be growing pressure on government to change the tax structure and to make abortion and contraceptive devices more readily and inexpensively available to the public.

Third, we expect that with the growing cost of children, there will be a renewed incentive to find new technology for preventing pregnancies. In fact, we view the recent public concern over population growth to be a part of the self-correcting changes we see. Those who are projecting the population are alerting the voting public to the problem and setting the stage for changes in policy.

Regardless, we have tried to demonstrate in this chapter how economics can be used to explain child-bearing decisions. The reader should once again, however, realize that economics cannot yield a complete explanation for these very complex social decisions.

QUESTIONS TO PONDER

1. Suppose that the prices of all goods and services rise faster than the cost of rearing children. What will happen to the population growth rate? Explain. What effect do liberalized attitudes among the young toward hard drugs have on the number of accidental births and planned births?

2. What effect do new technological inventions in child-care services and other goods and services have on the birthrate? *increases*

3. What effect has women's liberation had on the population growth rate? Explain the several ways in which the movement has had an effect.

4. Currently, rights to children borne by surrogate mothers remain an uncertainty. What has this uncertainty done to the birthrate?

CHAPTER 7

Sexual Behavior

If you are at all typical of readers of this book, these are the first words that you have read. We understand why you chose to start at this chapter. However, you must realize that you have skipped over some important introductory material.

In the first six chapters, we have developed several economic concepts that will be used in this chapter, and you may not at times be able to follow the discussion here (unless, of course, you resisted the temptation to read this chapter first). More important, we emphasized in the first chapter that economics cannot explain all dimensions of the human experience. This is a particularly relevant point when we deal with sexual behavior. We demonstrate in this chapter that economic analysis can provide us with several important and interesting insights about people's sexual behavior. However, there is much about people's sexual behavior we simply cannot explain, and several of these areas are, perhaps, the most meaningful. In our dealings with others, we can intuitively grasp the patterns and therefore the sense of other people's behavior. And although we may not be able to explain logically how or why we react, we are indeed able to react—and other people are able to react to our reactions. People's sexual behavior represents very complex patterns of actions and reactions; it involves varying degrees of romance and love, which are patterns of behavior that largely defy explanation.

There is a possible pitfall in trying to explain any pattern of behavior like that of sexual behavior—it is that the writer or reader will assume that those parts of behavior we can explain are more important than those we cannot explain. Unfortunately, this is probably not true with regard to people's sexual behavior. However, we should be able to take the analysis for what it is, nothing more or less. In our view, anyone who thinks that the sexual experience can be fully described and understood with economic analysis is a seriously deprived individual. Having said this, let us proceed.

SEX AND THE ECONOMIST

To those who may be unfamiliar with developments within the field of economics over the past decade, sex—or human sexuality—may appear to be a peculiar topic for discussion among economists and for inclusion in an introductory book on economics. However, for those who view economics as a study of human behavior (as do the authors), concern with sex is not at all peculiar, bizarre, or sensational. Clearly, a major impetus for human action is the sexual drive, and concern with matters relating to sex, in one way or another, occupies a significant portion of most people's time. Indeed, given the dominance of sex in human experience, one must wonder how economists have been able to avoid the topic in their classes and books for so long.

If one thinks about what is normally considered to be within the traditional boundaries of economic science and considers the ramifications of sex as a part of the human experience, the discussion in this chapter and the succeeding one may not appear to be at all out of place. To the layman, economics may be thought of as a discipline that:

1. Is founded on the study of goods and services that yield benefits, or, in the jargon of the profession, utility to the buyers.
2. Concentrates on the give-and-take, exchange, or trading relationships between and among people.
3. Deals with scarce resources and, thereby, with goods and services that involve costs in their production and can command payments from persons who desire them.
4. Is grounded in such concepts as opportunity cost and on such laws as the laws of supply and demand, diminishing marginal utility, and diminishing marginal returns.
5. Is concerned primarily with that domain of human behavior in which the individual is rational—that is, attempts to maximize his or her well-being.

Consequently, economics is normally associated with the development of a theory that is readily applicable to such goods and services as football games, peanut butter, ice cream, brickmaking machines, Rembrandt paintings, and, perhaps on occasion, with prostitution as an institutionalized profession. In the remaining portions of this chapter, an attempt is made to show how the sexual behavior of people other than prostitutes or buyers of the services of prostitutes can be discussed and partially analyzed and understood within the context of economic concepts and theory.

ECONOMIC CHARACTERISTICS OF SEX

As we will see, many of the concepts and reasoning tools employed by economists in their everyday work can be transferred to an analysis of sexual behavior. Certainly, the laws of supply and demand apply. Sex *is* demanded, and sex *is* supplied, often at significant costs.

Sex as a Service

Sex is a classification of a whole range of services one person provides for himself or herself or another that yield utility to the recipients. The list of

services provided under the heading of sex may include such normal heterosexual experiences as holding hands, kissing, petting, and intercourse. A
sexual experience (or service) may also include the stimulation one receives
from watching the girls (or boys) go by, from reading *Playboy*, *Playgirl*, or
National Geographic, and from the tales of those who write to Dear Abby or
Dr. Ruth. For junior high school boys and girls, a gratifying (and permissible)
sexual experience may be nothing more than the frequent and purposeful
bumping and shoving that goes on outside the class. The list of sexual services can be considerably lengthened.

Many people are quick to condemn one sexual practice or another as
inhuman or immoral. Although the authors, and most everyone else, have
their own sexual preferences, they submit that they are just that—their preferences. The issue of what is immoral will not be our concern, mainly because
such a discussion is likely to be worthless to anyone who disagrees with the
writers. Moreover, it would be an unnecessary diversion from the central
purpose of this chapter, which is to explore the question of how people do
behave and not how they should behave.

The utility that one receives from a satisfying sexual experience may in
the psychic realm be similar, but certainly not identical, to the satisfaction a
person receives from eating a good peanut butter sandwich, drinking a choc-
olate milk shake, or watching a performance of Sir Lawrence Olivier in a
Shakespearean play. Indeed, for most people the distinctive, but not the only,
difference between a sexual experience and other more "normal" goods and
services consumed may be in the intensity of the pleasure received. For most
persons, sexual intercourse and all the trappings that go with it probably give
the recipient more satisfaction than a peanut butter sandwich; that is evidenced by the cost a person is willing to incur for sex relative to the cost he
or she is willing to incur for the sandwich. For some people, however, the
sandwich can deliver more utility than intercourse does: not everyone may
consider sex to be within his or her own choice domain just as not everyone
may wish to purchase pickled pig's feet.

Oddly enough, even the person who never engages in sexual activity can
receive considerable utility from sex. He or she may refrain from engaging in
sexual activities because of the extent of the cost. Because of this, it is extremely risky (if not impossible) to make interpersonal utility comparisons
regarding the absolute psychic value of sex just as it is risky to suggest that
the people who attend Shakespearean plays enjoy the plays more than those
who never attend.

Given that sexual experiences can yield utility as other goods do, it
follows that for the fully rational person the quantity of sex demanded is an
inverse function of the price—that is, the demand curve is downward sloping
as in Figure 7–1. If the price goes up, the quantity demanded goes down; if
the price goes down, the quantity goes up. This means, in effect, that given
the price of sex, the consumer will want only so much sex supplied by another and will vary his or her consumption with the price that is charged.
The reason for this relationship is simply that the rational individual will

FIGURE 7-1

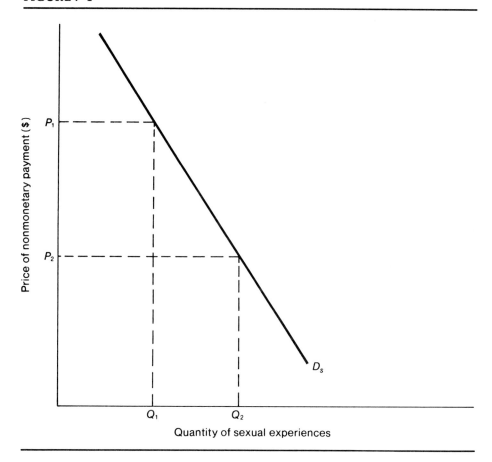

consume sex up to the point where the marginal benefits equal the marginal
n, other goods). If the price of sex rises relative to other goods, the consumer
marginal utility and price, respectively, and where *s* represents sex and *a* and
n, other goods). If the price of sex rises relative to other goods, the consumer
will rationally choose to consume more of other goods and less sex. (Ice
cream, as well as many other goods, can substitute for sex if the relative
prices require it.)

The law of demand, as stated above, is a fundamental principle of business operations that the prostitute cannot ignore. By raising her (or his) price,
the prostitute will not only sell fewer "tricks," but may find that if there are
a number of other readily available competitors, the quantity demanded from
her (or him) can fall to the point that total revenues will fall.[1]

---

[1]The reader should recognize that there are male prostitutes, although they may presently
account for a relatively minor portion of the total membership in the profession.

Revenues can rise if the demand she (or he) faces is inelastic. In other words, the prostitute (he or she) must remember that although the demand for sex in general may be inelastic because of the relative necessity of the services to those who want it, the demand for any particular sex service from any particular person can be highly elastic. (Can you explain why?)

The law of demand is also applicable to the more ordinary sexual relationships. A man may demand very few units of sex from the women he is dating or from his wife, in part because of his sexual preferences. However, closer examination of the individual's circumstances may reveal that the price he would have to pay—although in nonmonetary terms—may be so great that he must rationally choose to be "gentlemanly" and ask for very little. The same may be said for women; in fact, the difference in the quantity of sex demanded by men and women may reflect in part the relative difference in the cost of sex to men and women.

If the price of sex to women were lowered, one might anticipate a relatively larger quantity of sex demanded by them. The problem of men obtaining more sex from women, if viewed this way, becomes one of how to reduce the cost of sex to women (or, in addition, how to increase their preferences for it—that is, increase their demand).

From the perspective of this section, the invention of various forms of contraception (other than "no") and the legalization of abortion have dramatically reduced the price of sex to both men and women. From this perspective, the dispensation of free contraception devices on campus has, no doubt, increased the coital frequency of college students (contrary to what college officials try to tell parents and religious leaders).

The Cost of Sex

Sex is a service that is produced and procured. The sexual experience must be produced by one party for another. Like all other production processes, the production of any sexual experience entails costs. This is the case because not only may some materials, such as contraceptives, be required and a direct expenditure made (as in the case of the prostitute), but also because the participants must generally forgo some opportunity that has value to them. That, by definition, is the cost. The actual experience requires at least a few minutes, and this, of course, implies that one cannot normally do anything else of consequence at the same time. (One can, perhaps, imagine eating an apple or reading a book while producing sex for someone else, but it may be difficult indeed to imagine playing a successful game of pool or efficiently carrying on one's normal business operations.)

The opportunity cost of the time spent in the sexual act in most instances may be a trivial part of the total cost involved in either the production or procurement of sex. The total cost may include such items as the cost of the "wining and dining," which, contrary to the general impression, may often be heavily borne by females. Consider, for example, the number of times the woman may invite her male companion in for coffee and a snack after a date or over to dinner; or consider the possibility that she may be purposefully and skillfully arranging the situation in which the wining and dining may take place. Because the man may pick up the check, he is credited with the wining and dining. However, one must wonder who wined and dined whom. This is not meant to suggest that all such efforts by one party or the other are intended to procure and produce a sexual experience. The motive can simply be to have an enjoyable evening out. We are suggesting, however, that the wining and dining can, for some, be a part of the calculated cost of obtaining or producing a gratifying sexual experience.

The cost may also include the risk cost of pregnancy (which may be disproportionately borne by the female), the expenditure of effort (male orgasm alone requires approximately 200 calories), the psychic cost of violating one's own moral standards, and the damaged reputation cost which may be incurred if one's family or friends find out about the sexual relationship. Lastly, there is the cost incurred in the time spent plotting and maneuvering into a position in which the type of sex desired can be had. Both female and male must assess the "market" to determine which persons and sexual experiences are within their choice domain and must develop a strategy tailored to the selected party or parties. The selected strategy may require a considerable expenditure on clothes, hairdos, makeup, and education. It may also require a time expenditure on being in the right places. The producer may also require the recipient to become involved emotionally as well as physically; coupling marriage with sex is, perhaps, the ultimate form of contracted involvements.

The value of one's time, as approximated by his or her wage rate, will determine the cost of the sexual experience. The higher the opportunity wage, the higher the cost of the experience. Because of the different effects of higher income on sex consumption (and, perhaps, the associated education levels and lifetime experiences) and the different preferences between the high and low income groups, one cannot say theoretically which income groups—high, low, or middle—should be expected to have the higher rate of sexual activity. The economist can say, however, that the difference in cost to the two groups, because sex is labor-intensive, can partly explain the difference in the level of sexual activity that may exist.

Studies have generally revealed that the higher income groups consume as a group more sex than the lower groups. They tend to be more open-minded, are more educated, and have fewer psychological hangups regarding sex.

We can explain these facts by arguing that the demand for sex, because of the nonprice factors, is greater for the higher income groups. This situation is described in Figure 7–2 A and B. The demand in 7–2 A for the higher income groups is greater than the demand in 7–2 B. Given the differences in cost—P_a for the higher income group and P_b for the other group—the difference in revealed sexual activity is $Q_{1a} - Q_{1b}$ where $Q_{1a} > Q_{1b}$. If the

FIGURE 7–2

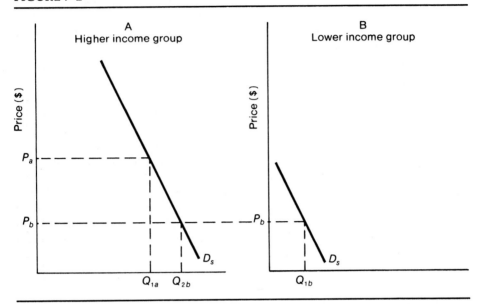

opportunity wage cost had been the same and equal to the wage of the lower income group, the difference would have been greater, $Q_{2a} - Q_{1b}$. The difference in the opportunity wage cost explains $Q_{2a} - Q_{1a}$ of the difference in sexual activity of the two groups.

In summary, a gratifying sexual experience can be quite costly. In economics there is an adage that is probably repeated in almost all principles courses: "There is no such thing as a free lunch." We suggest with equal conviction that there is no such thing as a free love or free sex. Indeed, when looked at realistically, many of us might conclude that sex can be some of the most expensive stuff we purchase, albeit without money.

Sex as a Cooperative Experience

Sexual intercourse is a human experience that must be (for the most part) cooperatively produced and enjoyed. We have, perhaps, written nothing that is more obvious than that. However, stating the obvious can direct our attention to essential points. First, if one party shirks his or her responsibilities in the exercise, then both parties lose in terms of the satisfaction that could have been had. Another way of saying the same thing is that the productivity of one's efforts are integrally related to the efforts of the other person. Understandably, people seeking sexual experiences will try to find other persons who have interests similar to theirs. The search may be costly in terms of time and money expense, but it can be rewarded in terms of finding someone who will energetically apply himself or herself to the sexual experience, thereby increasing the productivity of the efforts of the person doing the searching.

Second, although it may be at times, sex is not always a give-and-take relationship like the relationship that exists between buyer and seller in the market place. In many or most instances, the relationship is fundamentally different from the relationship that exists between traders. Granted, both parties, in the course of the sexual experience, give and take from the other. However, the sexual experience is much more; it is in large measure an exercise in which two (or more) people jointly pursue essentially the same goal. It is probably this dimension of sexual experience that causes people to set it apart from other activities in which they are engaged on a daily basis. In so many activities, people work independently of one another—that is, they work competitively, each trying to undercut, undersell, or outdo the other. There is some competition involved in most any relationship, but because of the nature of the experience, sex is an activity that forces people to work together. This is, no doubt, one of the elements of the experience that causes it to be thought of as more human than other experiences.

Sex as an Exchange Relationship

As much as they may depend on cooperation, sexual experiences can also involve exchanges—one person doing something for someone in return for something else. Generally, when exchanges are involved, the relationship is a barter one—no money is involved. One can provide sex to another in exchange for a similar but different sexual experience. However, the exchange need not always be in kind. One party can provide sex in exchange for security, clothing, candy, kindness, marriage, interesting company, conversation, being a part of a crowd, and entertainment. How many times has one person said or, perhaps, indicated in more subtle terms: (1) "I will give you sex if you will marry me or go out with no one else"; (2) "I will give you sex if you carry out the garbage or vacuum the house for me"; (3) "I will give you sex if you will stay home with me tonight."

In the courting ritual, such implicit dealing is frequently, although not always, present. All such bargains imply nonmonetary payments. Since, as we believe, the supply of sex is upward sloping, the payments should result in a greater quantity of sexual experiences than would occur from strict cooperative efforts. In fact, sex demographers have found that the coital frequency of the American population peaks during the second week in February, suggesting that many (but certainly not all) of the boxes of candy given for Valentine's Day have the desired effect.

Why do exchanges occur in this dimension of interpersonal relationships? The answer must involve the fact that the sexual preferences of the two parties are not identical. Furthermore, the exchanges can increase the utility levels of both parties. Let us explain with references to Figure 7–3.

FIGURE 7–3

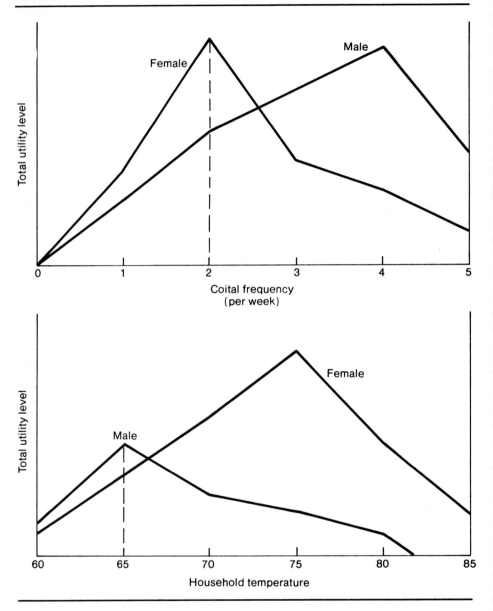

Suppose both parties enjoy sexual intercourse, but they get different levels of satisfaction from different coital frequency rates. As can be seen in the top half of Figure 7–3, the utility level of the female is assumed to rise until her total utility peaks when intercourse is being experienced two times a week. From that point onward, her total utility falls as the coital frequency is raised.

On the other hand, the male's total utility level rises, although less rapidly than the female's, until it peaks at a coital frequency of four times per week. (Remember, the shapes of the two curves in the figure can be anything; by drawing the curves as we have, we mean only to illustrate the fact that sexual partners can differ over coital frequency.)

Given this information, how many times per week will the couple experience intercourse? That is not an easy question to answer precisely. We can say, however, that they will have intercourse at least two times a week. This is simply because between zero and two times per week, both of their utility levels rise, generated directly by the pleasure they receive from the sexual act and indirectly from seeing the other enjoy the experience. Beyond a coital frequency of two, the male's utility level continues to rise, but the female's falls. The female may engage in intercourse more frequently out of a sense of duty or sheer love; however, she may be induced to go even further by exchanges that may be made. Since both of their utility levels are falling beyond a coital frequency of four, we expect the couple to have intercourse between two and four times per week.

In the bottom half of the graph, we have illustrated another dimension of marital life—the temperature setting in the home. (This dimension can really be anything, like the frequency of cleaning the house, or cooking meals, or staying home at night.) In the lower graph, we have illustrated a situation in which the most preferred temperature setting for the female is much higher than the male's. The male would prefer a temperature of 65 degrees, whereas the female would prefer a temperature of 75 degrees. We know that they will cooperatively move to a setting of at least 65 degrees, because both are better off at that level than at any lower level. Again, the temperature may be raised even further for noneconomic reasons.

However, the potential for exchange is indicated in the two halves of the graph. The female may agree to have intercourse more than two times a week if the male will agree to set the thermostat above 65 degrees. So long as the increase in the female's utility from setting the thermostat higher is greater than the loss in utility associated with a higher coital frequency, then she gains by the trade. The same holds for the male but, or course, in the opposite direction. The point of the discussion is that trade can increase the coital frequency over and above what it would otherwise have been, and, in the process, both parties can be better off. The actual trades, however, may not be viewed as such; the two sides of the deal(s) may be discussed in terms of compromises.

Because money is not normally a permissible part of the deal, people who desire heterosexual or homosexual experiences must have double coincidences of wants. One party must be able to provide what the other party wants and must want what the other party has to offer. This implies that the search cost of both parties can be considerable and can result in less sex being exchanged than otherwise. It is because of such search costs alone that people may be willing to make monetary payments to prostitutes.

Sex as a Marketed Product

Sex can be molded, packaged, advertised, and promoted like most other product groups. In the case of *Playboy* and *Penthouse*, the marketing process is direct and open; people know clearly what is being sold. In other instances, such as Dr. Ruth's column, the intentions, which may include the simulation of a sexual experience, are not so obvious. Most watchers of television realize that sex is the medium through which other products are sold. The testimonial of Joe Namath, former all-pro quarterback, in the Brut cologne commercial aired several years ago, which ends with the statement: "If you aren't going to go all the way, man, why go at all?" is a less-than-subtle form of selling Brut by selling sex.

On a personal level, people use many of the same marketing techniques as do major manufacturers—they do package and advertise their sexual products. Short skirts, padded bras, no bras, tank tops, tight slacks, deodorants, and body shirts are all forms of presenting one's sexual services in the best possible light and methods of attracting the attention of possible "buyers." By using such devices and techniques, the individuals involved may be as guilty of fraudulent packaging and advertising as are producers of cosmetics, soaps, and toys. If one views much of the advertising of such products as wasteful, then it would be consistent to view much expenditure on makeup and clothing in the same light.

Why do people incur the costs associated with personal beautification? We must, at the start, admit that there is the prevalent "honorable" reason that people just want to look nice and/or feel good. Be that as it may, we wish to suggest that there are other reasons (which are no less honorable except in an individualistic sense). An individual may want to increase the number of buyers for what he or she has to offer in order to have a larger quantity of sex and a larger group from which to select the services that he or she desires. With an increased choice range, the individual, in all probability, can select a higher quality service, as he or she assesses quality.

By looking attractive, a person can also possibly increase the nonmoney payment received for the sex services that he or she produces or can possibly lower the nonmoney payment that he or she will have to make for the sex services of others. All of these possible benefits can make expenditures on personal beautification rational.

In other words, people may attempt to look more attractive for the same reason that the professional prostitute does, although not necessarily in the same ways; how much expenditures are made depends on the costs, the benefits, and market conditions. The man or woman with no competitors may be expected to expend, *ceteris paribus*, less on improving the quality of his or her sexual services.

There is one other economic explanation for looking attractive. The human mind has a limited capacity to absorb facts and information, such as who may be in our presence and their characteristics. On the other hand, an individual is bombarded by tens of thousands of bits of information. Because the mind is incapable of absorbing, analyzing, and registering all of the information, the individual must, by absolute necessity, make decision rules regarding the facts and information that will be permitted to register in the brain. A result of deciding to ignore some information as a general rule may be that he or she does not notice all the people nearby.

Before a person can have a meaningful relationship in any dimension with someone else, the fact that he or she exists as a distinct entity must register in the mind of someone else. Because of the construction of decision rules regarding which bits of information will actually be allowed to register, the person desiring the relationship must not only be present but also be able to somehow break through the decision rule that presents a barrier. This may mean that his or her actions have to be dramatic or flashy; a simple statement that "I'm present" can be ineffective. The extra nice clothes, the tight skirts, the bulging muscles, the makeup, and the exceptionally nice manners may be means of breaking through the barrier of decision rules.[2] Once this has been accomplished—that is, his or her presence has registered—and the relationship has been established, the individual can drop back into his or her own manner of dressing and behavior.

A MODEL OF SEXUAL BEHAVIOR

The amount of sex that is produced and consumed is not in our view determined by the gods (at least not entirely). Granted, men and women have biological drives, and there are bodily constraints on sexual behavior. Man and woman, however, have some control over these drives (as a general rule) and do not engage in sex to the extent of their biological capabilities. The amount of sex produced and consumed is the result of the interaction of individuals within what we might call social space (or the market). For an explanation of how the amount of sex actually consumed and produced is determined, we must look to some of the forces these individuals bring to bear on this interaction process.

A restatement of principles that have been intrinsic in much of the discussion that has gone before would be helpful. These principles are the laws of demand and supply. We stress, however, that these principles cannot explain all sexual behavior—only a small portion of it. We assume that the demand curve for sex by either males or females is downward sloping and that, as a reasonable generality, the market supply curve of sex is upward

---

[2]Personal beautification, once produced, becomes a public good because persons other than the one who is more beautiful receive benefits from the sense that their surroundings are more pleasant. This may mean that since people may consider only the private benefits from the personal beautification and not the total social benefits, there may be an underinvestment in such beautification.

FIGURE 7–4

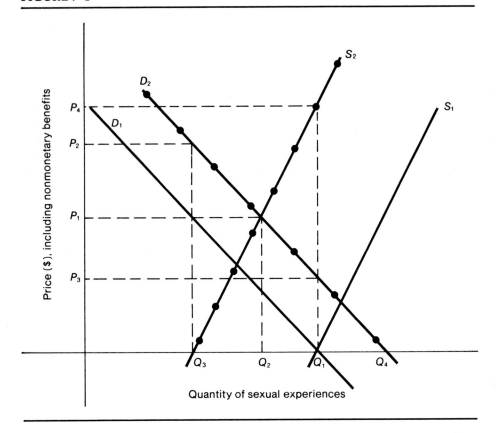

sloping. Therefore, the quantity of sex supplied will increase with the price paid for it. As in Figure 7–4, which depicts the demand for sex by men and the supply of sex by women, the relative positions of these curves depend on such factors as the relative preferences of the sexes and the relative costs of the sexual experience(s) borne by them.[3]

If the supply and demand for sex were determined solely by biological drives and if these drives were equal for men and woman (which may or may not be the case), the supply and demand curves could be so positioned on the graph that their interaction is on the horizontal axis; the price, or non-

---

[3]In the event that you think our talking about the male's demand for sex and the female's supply of sex is "sexist," everything said with reference to Figure 7–4 could be restated (if space permitted) with the labels on the supply and demand curves reversed. Indeed, the model can be reversed by holding Figure 7–4 up to a mirror. Then, the male's demand curve becomes the supply curve, and the female's supply curve becomes the demand curve. Try it.

money payment, paid for the sex would be zero, as is the case with S_1 and D_1 in Figure 7–4. This does not mean that no costs are involved to the parties; there are, as discussed above. It only means that there will be no need for extra nonmoney payments or direct money payments made by one party to the other. The gratification one receives from the experience will compensate him (her) for the cost incurred in providing the sex.

Such a circumstance does not, however, realistically reflect the general state of the world. Women and men are often restricted from fully revealing their biological drives. Women bear a substantial portion of the risk cost associated with pregnancy (men, it must not be forgotten, bear a part of the cost). Although general standards have changed drastically over the past three or four decades, many women and men still view sex as an activity in which they are not supposed to engage except under the umbrella of marriage.

Many women, because of their training from childhood, look upon sex as something dirty and not to be enjoyed. Virginity, in and of itself, can have positive value so that giving it up is an added cost of sex. Men, on the other hand, generally look upon sex as a service that is to be pursued for purposes other than the pleasure received directly from the experience. In tribal Africa, men may achieve status within the tribe from killing a lion barehanded. In more modern and less barbaric places, men can achieve the same stature among their peers by sexual conquests. The effect of these pressures is to raise the male's demand for sex and to decrease the female's supply of it (to say, S_2 and D_2 in Figure 7–4). At a zero price, there will then exist a shortage of sex to men since only Q_3 sex will be supplied by females and Q_4 will be demanded.

The upward sloping supply curve of female sex indicates that women are willing to offer a larger quantity of sex than Q_3 if the price (not necessarily in money form) is raised above zero. As indicated by the demand curve, D_2, men are willing to pay as much as P_2 for an additional sexual experience. We might anticipate, therefore, that nonmoney payments in any number of forms (security, dining out, and so forth) will be offered. The result will be that the quantity of sex will expand toward Q_2. Beyond Q_2 the side payment required by the women to bring forth an additional unit of sex is greater than what the men are willing to pay for the experience. (To see this clearly, the reader should ask how much the men would be willing to pay for an additional unit of sex at Q_1 and how much the women would charge for the unit.)

The market for sex continues to change along with individual values toward sex. The supply of sex by women is expanding. The availability of contraceptives is reducing the potential pregnancy cost of intercourse to women. Virginity is no longer as important to many, and more and more the message is getting out that women are capable of enjoying sex! Abortions are becoming more common, cheaper, and more acceptable. Assuming that these changes in cost and values have no effect on the demand side of the market, we can conclude that the quantity of sexual activity will increase and the price or nonmoney payment made to women can fall.[4] We are frankly uncertain about what is happening to the demand for sex by men. If the demand rises, but by less than the supply increases, the same general predictions as the ones above would follow; the price, however, would not fall as much, but the quantity of sexual activity would rise by more than in the case above. (What may be the consequence of a drop in the men's demand for sex?)

We have been speaking in terms of generalities, and, of course, an oversupply of sex for some women does not hold for all women. For some women—for example, the not-so-pretty and the old—there can be a shortage of sex, and they may have to make the nonmoney payments to obtain the desired quantity of sex.[5] In fact, if we individualize the market, we can postulate that what the woman may view as her "standards" may really be a mirror image of her relative market position—that is, because a woman is beautiful she can maintain higher standards than the woman who is less endowed and who has no offsetting differences.

PROSTITUTION

Why does prostitution exist? Once the existence of the cost of sexual intercourse and of the positive equilibrium price in Figure 7–4 are recognized, the question is easily answered. The price of prostitution, even though it may be $100, can be much lower than the cost the man (woman) would have to bear in order to obtain the same pleasure from other, more legitimate sources.[6] The man can pay the $100, and by doing so he does not have to spend the time that may be required to seduce the nonprostitute. He does not have to send her flowers or other gifts and, more important, does not have to become involved emotionally or otherwise. He can satisfy his needs and leave anonymously.

Another reason why a man may seek the services of a prostitute is that the quality of the service can be higher. The prostitute is a professional; she may not only have had more experience than the conventional sex partner, but she can prorate the cost of "training" and improving the quality of her service over a larger number of sexual experiences. The investment cost per "trick" can be trivial if she operates in large quantities.

Legalizing prostitution can have several predictable effects. First, since the penalties for being caught soliciting buyers will be eliminated, the cost of

---

[4]It is possible that the price will become negative. This would mean a reversal of roles: the women would be paying the men.

[5]From some points of view, such women may be viewed as deviates. However, such a designation may be inappropriate. These women can be behaving, in a sense, like everyone else; the only difference is the location of their equilibrium in the social market.

[6]On the other hand, by adding in the cost of VD or AIDS, we can understand why some men do not engage prostitutes. For some, $100 plus the cost of contracting various diseases can be a greater cost than the possible benefits (and lower than the benefits to others).

searching for buyers (streetwalkers have to keep on the move) will be substantially reduced. The supply of prostitutes should increase. This should result in a larger quantity of output. The quality of the product should also rise, bringing about in part a reduction in the threat of venereal diseases or AIDS. Houses of prostitution would be able to justify more expenditures on medical checkups for the prostitutes since the quantity of their business would reflect their reputation for cleanliness, just as in the case of Holiday Inns.

Furthermore, if we assume that the price or nonmoney payment charged for sex is competitively determined in the normal sex markets, the existence of clean, legalized prostitutes means a larger number of competitors for nonprostitutes, including wives. Legalization of prostitution should, where nonmoney payments are charged, reduce the nonmoney payments. Wives, or women in general, may be against legalized prostitution because of moral convictions; our analysis indicates, in addition, that they may (or should) be opposed to its legalization on the grounds that it can reduce their competitive position. In a similar vein, prostitutes probably do not look upon the changing values of women in general with much favor. To the degree that the price of nonprostitutes goes down, the price that the prostitute can charge must fall.

SEX AND LOVE

Our analysis has proceeded as if sex can be completely divorced from love. Obviously, it cannot always be, and this impression must be corrected. However, there is very little economics can say about love because love is an experience almost impossible to define or conceptualize. About all we can say is that love (whatever it is) and sex go together in many people's minds in much the same way as hotdogs and hotdog buns or razors and razor blades. Love and sex are viewed by many as complementary goods. This does not mean that the relationship between sex and love is exactly the same as the relationship of other complementary goods. We only mean to assert that a connection is drawn between the two, that the degree of love that exists will affect the demand for sex and, possibly, vice versa. Our assumptions concerning the normal slope of the supply and demand for sex can still hold; the demand can still be downward sloping and the supply can be upward sloping. The existence of the connection (although imperfect) between sex and love can determine the positions of the curves (and, possibly, their elasticities to a degree). A person's demand for sex can influence demand for a loving relationship, and the intensity of one's love for another can affect demand for sex.

Generally speaking, the common requirement among women that sex be coupled with a feeling of love is a statement that their supply curve of sex is further back toward the vertical axis than it would be if the requirements did not exist. However, as a group, they can still be expected to respond positively to an increase in nonmoney payments as we have been using the term.

Admittedly, there are women and men who adopt the decision rule that they will not engage in sex unless they are married or have established a strong bond with someone else. They, in effect, rationally choose to ignore costs and benefits and changes in costs and benefits. Even though such people exist (and they may be quite large in number), the downward sloping demand curve and upward sloping supply curve hold so long as there are people who do weight in their consumption decisions the costs and benefits of sexual experiences.

CONCLUDING COMMENTS

In this chapter we have tried to show how economic concepts and tools of analysis can be used to discuss people's sexual behavior. We have argued that men and women have downward sloping demand curves and upward sloping supply curves for various kinds of sexual experiences. This means that the quantity of sex supplied and demanded by men and women is affected by the explicit or implicit price that must be borne. In discussing sexual behavior in this way, we have been able to demonstrate a part of the logic—to the extent that it has any logic—people follow in pursuing sexual experiences. We have been able to draw several reasonable conclusions.

However, the reader should be careful not to assume that we have said more than we have. We have said nothing about how sexual preferences are formed, and we submit that much sexual activity is actually more related to preference formation than it is to the process of making choices founded on preferences already known. This chapter reveals the limited usefulness of economic analysis, its strengths and weaknesses. Reflections on our own experiences suggest many instances in which the analysis is and is not applicable.

QUESTIONS TO PONDER

1. To what extent and in what ways is sex different from other goods people produce in the home or buy in the store. What makes sex different in many people's mind? intensity

2. People often require that long-term commitments be made before they become involved in sexual activity. Why? What is the purpose of the commitment?

3. A new strain of venereal disease has been discovered that is not readily cured with the usual drug, penicillin. What effect will this discovery have on sexual activity of the population? decrease, cost up

4. What impact has AIDS had on sexual activity? On the relative amount of sexual activity among homosexuals and among heterosexuals?

CHAPTER 8

Exploitation of Affection

The strength of most personal relationships is founded, to a significant degree, on the affection one person has for another.[1] This is particularly true of the relationship between a man and a woman. The relationship works for two reasons. First, each person is concerned about the welfare of the other and is willing to do things for him or her. In this sense the relationship is largely charitable in nature; each person is both a donor of *gifts*, broadly defined as any form of charitable expression, and a recipient of such expressions from the other.

Second, both persons understand that there is a need for implicitly defined limits to their own behavior and the behavior of the other person. These limits form the basis of the unwritten social contract between the two. Each person may then proceed in his or her behavior, responding to the needs of the other, in the trust that the contract is being obeyed. This latter presumption makes possible behavior on the part of either person that is inconsistent with the agreed-on contract, implicit as it may be. It permits one party to, in a sense, exploit the other.

We intend to explain the logic behind this statement in the few pages that follow. We discuss the problem of exploitation after a chapter on sex because most of what is said has a direct application to man-woman relationships. We stress, however, that the argument is really very general in nature and can be applied to the personal relationship between parent and child and between close friends. The analysis provides an explanation of the breakdown in many personal relationships, and in general, why friends and loved ones can be "used." First, we briefly review the argument for what we call *charitable exploitation*.[2]

THE AFFECTION MODEL

The basic proposition underlying the charitable exploitation argument is that the donor of the gifts receives utility from giving to the recipient. This

---

[1]As we intend to discuss in considerable detail throughout the book, such relationships can also be founded on individual private interests that have nothing to do with affection. However, in this chapter we want to focus on the affection aspect of the relationship.

[2]This chapter is based on a short article by Wilson E. Schmidt, "Charitable Exploitation," *Public Choice* 10 (Spring 1969), pp. 103–4.

implies that he or she has a downward sloping demand curve for making gifts. Also, the rational donor will *freely choose* gifts until the marginal benefits of doing so are equal to the marginal costs. We give *gifts* a very broad meaning here. As is conventionally thought, a gift can be in the form of money or a material object, for example, a box of candy. However, it can be the time one person spends doing something for someone else, and this can simply mean the time spent listening to another person. A gift can also be allowing the other person to listen to a record of his or her choice, scratching another's back, or providing him or her with sexual experience of one form or another.

In Figure 8–1 we have placed marginal costs and benefits on the vertical axis and the quantity of the gift (which may be any single gift or a gift that represents a combination of gifts) on the horizontal axis. If we assume that the donor's demand curve (D_l) is downward sloping and, for simplification, that the marginal cost of units of the gifts is constant at P_1 in Figure 8–1, then

FIGURE 8–1

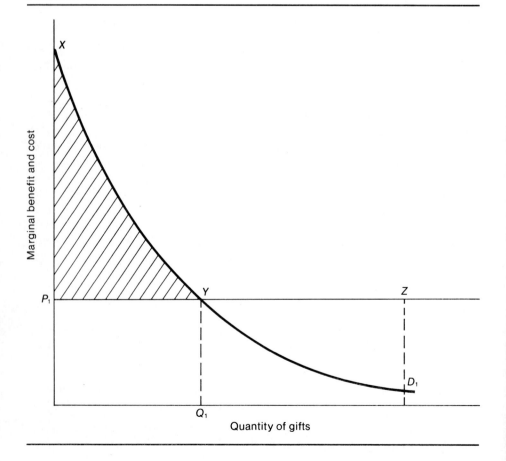

we can conclude that the donor will choose on his or her own to make gifts up to point Y or a quantity of Q_1. At Y the marginal cost is equal to the marginal benefits.

Notice that it is only for the last unit—the Q_1th unit—that the marginal costs and benefits are equal. Up to that point, the marginal benefits to the donor, as indicated by the demand curve, are greater than the marginal cost of each unit of the gift. As we have explained in Chapter 1, the cost of something is the value of that which is forgone. This means that the individual donor is getting more value in making each unit of the gift up to Q_1 than he or she could have gotten from the use of his or her resources in their best alternative. This excess value, referred to as *surplus value* or *consumer surplus* by economists, can be described by the striped area (P_1XY) in the graph. In simple language, when we do one thing we often say that we are better off in some sense; in terms of our graph we would say that the donor is better off to extent of the striped area.[3]

Given the extent of the consumer surplus indicated by the striped area P_1XY, the recipient, if he or she is the only recipient (or if all recipients act collusively), can force the donor to increase the gifts beyond Y by merely refusing to accept anything unless the donor abides by the recipient's wishes, which is getting more units of the gift. The recipient says in so many subtle words, "Either give me more than Q_1, or I will accept nothing at all." Notice that we have not said that the recipient threatens overt harm to the donor, but only threatens not to accept anything unless the donor gives more. The recipient in effect presents to the donor what is often called an "all-or-nothing deal" (which, in our graphical illustration, amounts to a "more-than-Q_1-or-nothing deal").

If the recipient is able to pose the deal subtly, without the donor actually detecting the scheme in mind, the donor is presented with a choice problem. If he or she refuses to give more, then he or she must give nothing, which means that he or she must give up the consumer surplus that would have been received by giving Q_1 units of the gifts. If he or she gives more, the marginal cost of each unit, P_1, will be greater than the marginal benefits of each additional unit (indicated by points on the demand curve below Y). There is what we might call a *negative surplus value* attached to these additional units beyond Q_1. As a result, the donor's total satisfaction level will be lowered by giving more.

We can postulate that if the negative surplus value is greater than the striped area in the graph, the donor will be better off by not giving anything at all. If the negative surplus value (the triangular area beyond Y) is less than the striped consumer surplus area, the donor will be better off by extending his gifts.

---

[3]In more detailed terms, the total value that the donor receives from making Q_1 gifts is equal to $0XYQ_1$. The total cost is equal to $0P_1YQ_1$. The difference between the total costs and total benefits is equal to P_1XY, or the striped area, which we have called consumer surplus.

This means that the recipient's ability to extract additional units of the gift, and in that sense exploit the donor, is not limitless. If at point Z in the graph the negative surplus value (area YZD_1) is just equal to the surplus value (P_1XY), then the smart (maximizing) recipient will ask for an amount of gifts equal to something just short of point Z. In this way, the recipient will insure that the negative surplus value is less than the consumer surplus and that therefore the donor will give more. If the recipient asks for more than Z, the negative surplus value is greater than the consumer surplus, and the donor will be better off by not giving anything. If the recipient asks for Z, the donor will be *indifferent* to continuing the gift giving and may, on some whim, stop giving.

Therefore, the closer the recipient tries to come to Z, the more risk he or she must assume that he or she has misjudged the charitable feelings of the donor, and may end up getting nothing. Remember, it is not likely that the recipient will be able to make the calculations that are implied here with a great deal of precision and certainty.

Two points need to be stressed. The first is that the ability of the recipient to extract a larger quantity of gifts depends on the number of alternative recipients of the gifts, that is, the number of what we might call competitors for the gift. If the recipient is one of many possible equal recipients and attempts to impose the all-or-nothing deal considered here, the donor can turn to someone else and in the end receive the full (or almost full) extent of the consumer surplus. The donor need not go beyond Y in Figure 8–1. The demand curve in Figure 8–1 is, in this case, the demand for giving in general and is not the demand for giving to any one individual.[4] If, on the other hand, the recipient is, in essence, a monopolist, the donor must in this circumstance either accept the deal or turn to buying goods that yield less satisfaction.

Second, exploitation of the donor will occur only to the extent that the recipient is unconcerned about the welfare of the donor. If the recipient "cares" about the donor, then the recipient will be worse off to the extent that donor loses his or her consumer surplus. By exploiting the donor, the recipient reduces the donor's welfare and consequently his or her own welfare.

ROMANTIC RELATIONSHIPS

The late Virginia Tech economist Wilson Schmidt, who formulated the foregoing argument, suggested that the argument can be useful in understanding the behavior of welfare recipients under the conditions prevailing during the late 1960s and early 1970s. At the time, many welfare recipients were demonstrating against the welfare offices around the country, "demanding" larger checks. One might reason that the recipients were in effect threat-

---

[4]The donor's demand for making gifts to any one of the possible recipients under highly competitive conditions (that is, a large number of alternative recipients) will be essentially horizontal.

ening the government with the disruption of the welfare system. In such event, the government would have been unable to make the "charitable" payments. Schmidt suggested that the protesting welfare recipients could have understood our argument to this point in an intuitive sense, recognizing that there may have been some consumer surplus that could be drawn out of the government bureaucrats and those who are in favor of giving to the poor.

We believe that the argument on charitable exploitation has a much broader application than was originally conceived and is, perhaps even more readily applicable to personal relationships. To show this we turn to romantic relationships between men and women. A romantic relationship is, almost by definition, a charitable one in the sense that the man's utility is related to the utility level of the woman and vice versa. The relationship is built on the presumption that this is the case, to some degree; as a result, a certain amount of trust develops concerning the intentions of the other party.

In a romantic relationship, the woman or man has a demand for giving in any number of dimensions. However, she or he will choose to freely give only so much, and that will be Y in our example, Figure 8–1. In the case of the woman, she may be willing to give Y because she feels confident in the man's feelings toward her. However, if she has been deceived, she can be exploited because of the existence of her consumer surplus. The man can drain the surplus value out of the woman in any number of ways. He can, to a limited degree, generally abuse her. He can make her go places and do things that she would not freely choose to do, and he can make her put up with quirks in his own behavior that he may find costly to change. In this sense he can make her go further in giving in to him than she would otherwise choose to go.

If, however, he pushes too hard—that is, asks her to go beyond Z—he will be dropped. The irony of this line of analysis may be that the woman may still "love" the man, but she drops him because he has asked for too much. All of this can also be placed in the context of the woman exploiting the man, which occurs perhaps as frequently as the man exploiting the woman. It is interesting to note that women's liberation has attempted to eliminate many economic and social barriers that interfere with women getting out of the home. The liberation movement has, in effect, been trying to increase the alternatives women have to the conventional marriage situation. Our analysis suggests that to the extent that women's liberation is successful, husbands will be less able to exploit their wives. To the extent that husbands have exploited their wives in the past and do not change their behavior, we would expect the divorce rate to rise because of women's liberation. (Can you explain why in terms of Figure 8–1 ?)

SEXUAL EXPLOITATION

The reader may sense that all of what we have said here can be readily applied to the physical sexual relationship between a woman and a man. There may be activities in which a woman (or man) may freely choose to engage because they may give her direct pleasure or, more important for our purposes, may contribute to the pleasure of the man she is dating. Because of the woman's value system, however, and because there may be psychic costs associated with many forms of sexual activities, there are limits to the number of times in which she may *freely* engage in sexual activity (that is, make the gift).

Because of the surplus value, the man, if he wishes and if he is her only boyfriend, can make the woman go further than she would freely choose to go. He can extract the surplus either in terms of an increased rate of specific acceptable activities (such as petting) or can draw the surplus out in the form of an activity in which the woman may not *freely* choose to engage (such as intercourse). This does not mean necessarily that the man can force the woman to have sexual intercourse, because the size of the consumer surplus may not be great enough to push her to that point. But, it does suggest that regardless of the level or kind of activity the woman chooses, the man can, in a sense and under the condition that he is a monopolist with respect to the woman's affection, exploit the woman to some degree. Regardless of how far she chooses to go, he can induce her to go further, if the all-or-nothing deal is appropriately posed.

On the other hand, if the man is only one of many possible dates for the woman—that is, the relationship has not been permanently established—the all-or-nothing deal cannot work as effectively. In the event the man tries to make the woman go further than she desires, she can merely turn to one of her other possible dates and retain the full consumer surplus from giving to the opposite sex. In this event, she has bargaining power.

The typical male may intuitively sense the essence of the foregoing discussion and realize that he can obtain more of what he wants if he is "the only one" as far as the woman is concerned. This line of analysis may explain why the man may refrain from trying anything on the first few dates. On the first few dates, he may intuitively understand that he is one of a number of candidates for the charitable affections of the woman, and if he attempts anything physical, she can turn to someone else to whom she may at that point receive equal pleasure in the sense we have been using the term and can ultimately receive the full extent of the consumer surplus from giving. By waiting and putting on his "best manners," he effectively may be able to eliminate the competition in the mind of the woman, and, by the delay, more accurately assess the size of the woman's consumer surplus. He may also be investing the time for the purpose of increasing the woman's charitable demand for him, in which case she will of her own accord go further. Finally, on those first few dates he may be attempting to determine what would be the most appropriate way of presenting the all-or-nothing deal. The reader must remember that if the deal is not carefully posed verbally, by facial expression, or otherwise, the woman's preferences for giving to the man can be damaged, implying a reduction in her demand for him. In other words, a deal clumsily made can reduce the woman's demand to the point that her demand curve intersects the vertical axis at P_1 or below P_1. In such case she will decide to give nothing.

Many women do trade sex for other goods, such as security, and the issue was covered in some detail in the preceding chapter. This, however, is not what is meant by *sexual exploitation* here; by the term we mean one party forcing the other party to go further sexually than he or she would freely choose to go. Many readers may believe—by thinking in terms of the over-sexed, male stereotype—that if women do in fact find it necessary to make men go further sexually than they would freely choose to go, it is of interest only as a peculiarity of the special relationships between nymphomaniacs and highly religious men.

The possibility of the female sexually exploiting the male becomes much more plausible if the male stereotype is set aside and if specific circumstances are considered. First, it should be realized that men can bear a cost by engaging in, say, intercourse; they may be liable for a share of the cost of an abortion and, if abortion is not an acceptable out, a share of child support, or they may be forced, because of personal values, into marrying someone who under other circumstances they would not choose. The existence of such costs and the possibility that once the woman is aroused, she may not want to stop short of intercourse, may partially explain why the woman may have to say, or subtly indicate, that "if you don't go all the way, then you may do nothing at all." Because of the male's surplus value from engaging in petting or from stimulating the woman, he may go all the way because by doing so he will be better off than he would be if he were not allowed to touch. (He could be even better off if he could touch without assuming the risk of pregnancy.)

Second, a married man may want to establish a rather impermanent, now-and-then relationship with some woman other than his wife. He gets pleasure out of doing things for her, but he still does not want the relationship to seriously encroach on his family life. The woman may require that he see her more often—engage in sexual relations more frequently—than he would freely choose. He may consent, again, because of the surplus value acquired from the first few units of the relationship consumed.

Lastly, one party may need to resort to sexual exploitation when his or her appetite for sex differs from the appetite of the other party. In any continuing relationship, it is quite possible that there will be many times when the female's appetite is greater than the appetite of the male. In such a circumstance, the female may find it necessary to exploit the male; and before closing, it should, perhaps be noted that male foreplay may be one means by which the women have sexually exploited the men. They in effect say, "Either you arouse me, or I will not be interested in anything you have in mind."

CONCLUDING COMMENTS

By suggesting that the woman (or man) can be exploited if she (he) has a monopolist for a boyfriend (girlfriend), we have been saying, in effect, that exploitation can more likely occur if the relationship is a well-established, permanent one; that is, if the woman and man are "going steady" or are engaged. We submit that the analysis supports many of the fears of parents in seeing their teenage son or daughter becoming tied down into a permanent relationship. In concluding, we emphasize that the analysis indicates what the man (woman) can do, not what he (or she) will do. What either does is, again, dependent on their consideration of the other's welfare. If one person loves another or cares about his or her welfare, then exploitation affects the other's welfare and, therefore, his or her own welfare. It follows that exploitation is most likely to occur when feelings of love or caring are not fully reciprocal; that is, when the party that wishes to do the exploiting does not care (to the same degree) about the other person. As we said at the beginning, the argument in this chapter is also applicable to basic friendships.

QUESTIONS TO PONDER

1. Does the argument in the chapter suggest an explanation as to how children (and college students) can exploit their parents—that is, get more from their parents than their parents would freely choose to give?

2. Does the analysis suggest an explanation as to why an only child may more likely be "spoiled" than children who have several sisters and brothers?

3. Explain divorce in terms of Figure 8–1.

CHAPTER 9

Dying: The Most Economical Way to Go!

It is only human for one to feel sympathetic toward the person who dies with everything going wrong; a malfunctioning liver, arteriosclerosis, a defective kidney, ulcers, respiratory problems, and waning eyesight. However, such a tumultuous exit may indicate that the individual involved has more thoroughly enjoyed life than the person who dies with only a failing heart and everything else in perfect order. If this is the case, the sympathy may be misplaced.

The fact that all of one's organs are malfunctioning at the time of death may indicate that one has fully utilized his or her organic capital assets in the pursuit of utility. The person who dies with a perfect liver may have forgone a number of drinks during the course of his life that could have contributed significantly to his own welfare: a liver in good order is useless if the heart goes first.

If a person is truly interested in maximizing his well-being (which is the natural assumption of economists), he should treat his bodily organs in the same manner he treats monetary wealth. "You can't take it (them) with you" is just as applicable to organs as it is to a bank account. A person should have a bank balance at death if he intentionally plans to bequeath it to someone (an act, the anticipation of which may give pleasure before death) or if he miscalculates the time of his death. The ideal exit is to die with a zero bank balance (above that which is planned) and with no surplus capacity in bodily organs (above that which is planned).[1]

---

[1] The planned surplus capacity in bodily organs would be affected by religious values, belief in reincarnation, and desire to bequeath one's bodily organs to help others. In attempting to maximize his well-being, a person, of course, does not have perfect information as to how his organs interact with each other; his ignorance, however, only affects the degree to which he is able to achieve his goals. Further, he will very likely, but not necessarily, build the strength of those organs that will have a positive effect in extending the life of other organs.

Such utility-maximizing behavior may go a long way toward explaining why elderly people as a group go to the dentist less frequently than others or why the prisoner on death row may be unmoved by government reports that smoking can cause cancer. Doctors do not, however, seem to fully appreciate this truth about human behavior. Most advice by doctors and most medical research is directed toward maximizing the lifespan of each and every bodily organ. Very little research is directed, it appears, toward ascertaining how a person should treat his organs (in order to maximize his utility during this life), given the lifespan of the limiting one (whatever it is.) In this vein, a redirection of much medical research is called for because many medical expenditures (and much abstinence) may be unwarranted.

The economist's advice is that a person should so employ his human and nonhuman resources that the world ends for him not with a whimper but with a bang.[2]

QUESTIONS TO PONDER

1. Do people behave the way the authors suggest they do? If you believe they do, can you give additional examples of how people attempt to employ rationally their organic capital assets? If you believe they do not, how do they behave? Why do they behave the way that you suggest? Is the problem one of a lack of appropriate information?

2. What effect will religious values have on the behavior of people with regard to their bodily organs? (Before answering the question specify the religious values on which you will base your answer.)

3. Suppose we introduce the possibility of an individual selling his organs before he dies. Will such a system work? What are the problems involved? Will such a system affect people's behavior?

4. Suppose that the amount of suffering one has to endure on his or her deathbed is greater when everything goes wrong than it is when only one organ has failed. Will knowledge of this affect a person's behavior? Suppose the opposite were the case. How would a person's behavior be different?

5. Bodily organs are interrelated. What does this fact do to the maximizing behavior of individuals? Is the maximizing behavior of individuals with regard to their bodily organs substantially different from the maximizing behavior of business firms that use several interrelated resources in the production process?

---

[2]In making this statement, the economist is implicitly suggesting that T. S. Eliot was probably misguided when he wrote: "This is the way the world ends/Not with a bang but a whimper."

PART THREE

The New World of Markets

CHAPTER 10

Markets and More Markets

In this chapter we consider several problems that will allow us to demonstrate how supply and demand curves can be employed to understand social issues and to predict directional movements in market price and quantity of a good purchased. Supply and demand analysis does not tell us all we may like to understand about the market—for example, how much price and quantity change—but it can indicate general tendencies and, to that extent, can help clarify issues that may otherwise remain obscure.

WHY COAL PRODUCERS LOVE OPEC

When the 13 countries that made up the Organization of Petroleum Exporting Countries (OPEC) restricted output and forced up the world price of oil way back in 1973, coal producers in this country and elsewhere smiled. The action of OPEC enabled them to achieve windfall profits they would not otherwise have had. Reference to simple supply and demand curves can illustrate why this was the case and why coal producers continue to be pleased when OPEC seeks once again to restrict the production of oil in their member countries.

Increases in the price of oil cause energy consumers, acting rationally, to seek substitutes for oil. This is a restatement of the law of demand that we studied in Chapter 1. Coal is a particularly good substitute because many electric utility plants are equipped to burn either oil or coal, depending on which is the cheaper at the time. Therefore, as a consequence of OPEC's actions, the demand for coal increased. In terms of Figure 10–1, the demand curve shifts from D_1 to D_2 to reflect the increase in demand. At the original market price for coal, P_1, a shortage develops which embodies the necessary ingredients for an upward movement in market price. The price in this example rises to P_2. As the price rises, production becomes more profitable and producers can justify incurring the higher marginal costs of production.

Because of OPEC's actions, the profit of the coal industry increased. The coal industry's revenues, before oil prices increased, are equal to the then current price of P_1 times the quantity sold, Q_1, which in the figure is equal to the area OP_1aQ_1. After the increase in the price of coal, the revenues of the

FIGURE 10–1

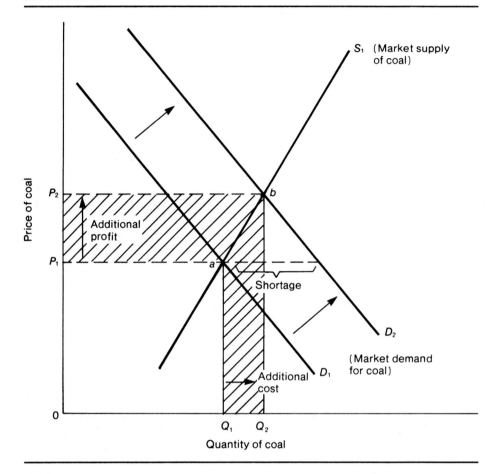

coal industry expand to the higher price, P_2, times the higher quantity Q_2, or the area OP_2bQ_2. The increase in revenues is indicated by the ell-shaped, striped area on the graph ($P_1P_2bQ_2Q_1a$). The supply curve tells us the marginal cost of each additional unit of coal produced; therefore, the total cost of expanding production from Q_1 to Q_2 is the portion of that shaded area that is under the supply curve (Q_1abQ_2). The additional profit, which is the additional revenue minus the additional cost, is that portion of the shaded area that is not underneath the supply curve (P_2baP_1). It is this additional profit that caused coal producers to smile when OPEC made its announced price increases.

There are several energy substitutes for oil, and the foregoing analysis applies just as readily to those other substitutes as it does to coal. OPEC's actions, for example, served the purpose of making wind and solar energy more attractive to energy consumers and, because higher prices can be charged, more profitable to investors. As the price of gasoline rose, reflecting higher oil prices, people began looking for alternative ways of accomplishing the things that could be accomplished with a gasoline engine. There was an explosion in the demand for bicycles; their prices rose and the quantity sold expanded considerably. As producers caught up with the dramatic increase in demand, we also experienced an expected drop in the price of bicycles. In these ways, the increase in OPEC prices sets in motion a whole series of actions that gradually eat into the energy market over which the Middle East countries may think they have more influence than they actually do.

Because of the interconnection of markets, economists are prone to take a cynical look at almost all policy areas. In 1987, when the United States was seeking to protect oil tankers from Kuwait in the Persian Gulf from attack from Iran, one economist wondered aloud, "I wonder if it really was Iran mining the waters off Kuwait. Could it not be one of the multinational oil companies?" While no oil company may have played a role, the economist's comments cannot be totally ignored by foreign policy officials. It just might be that some devious, and profit-maximizing, oil company was in fact doing the mining. The threat of a reduction in the supply of Middle Eastern oil during 1987 sent the world price of oil—and the prices of oil company stocks—sharply upward.

A MARKET FOR BODILY ORGANS?

An individual has legally recognized property rights to his (or her) body and the parts of it. He can therefore do many things with his body and his organs; he can build them up through exercise and diet, or mistreat them through lack of care or through overuse of drugs. He can give them away or even destroy them. (Suicide is not illegal, although it used to be. In general, today only attempted suicide is illegal!)

However, there is one thing people cannot do with their body parts, which is sell them. Senator Albert Gore (D. Tenn.), a 1987 Democratic presidential contender, has made certain of that. Senator Gore was instrumental in passing a federal law that outlaws the sale of bodily organs to transplant recipients. If laws allowed free commerce in bodily organs, much of the medical profession would resist such sales on ethical grounds. One spokesperson for a kidney transplant center has commented that it "without question would never even consider such a proposal [purchase or sale of a kidney]. Such a thing might open up a whole new concept that is abhorrent."[1] A doctor in northern Virginia announced in the early 1980s that he intended to go into

---

[1] As quoted in Marvin R. Brams, "Property Rights in the Human Body: New Dimensions of Individual Choice and Freedom." Paper presented at the Atlantic Economic Society Conference, Washington, D.C., September 1975.

TABLE 10–1   Number of Organ-Transplant Operations for Selected Years

	1986	1985	1981
Kidney transplants	8,800	7,695	4,885
Heart transplants	1,368	719	62
Liver transplants	924	602	26

SOURCE: United Network for Organ Sharing, Health Care Financing Administration, National Center for Health Services Research, as reported in Alan L. Otten, "Growing Demand for Organ Transplants Spurs Efforts to Expand Pool of Donors," *The Wall Street Journal* (March 18, 1988), p. 29.

the business of tradable organs, acting as intermediary between transplant organ sellers and transplant organ buyers. The medical profession in the area expressed horror, and Senator Gore introduced in Congress his proposed ban on organ sales.

Even the suggestion of a market in bodily organs may be grossly shocking to some readers, and there is much that is unattractive about the idea to the authors. However, reflections on how a market system may affect the availability of transplantable organs may make the idea somewhat more palatable.

Table 10–1 portrays the growth in transplants of kidneys, hearts, and livers between 1981 and 1986.[2] In that time period, the number of kidney transplants increased by 80 percent. However, the number of heart transplants increased by 22 times and those of liver transplants increased by 36 times. Still, many transplant patients were left without the needed surgeries. In 1988, 12,500 Americans were awaiting kidney transplants, almost 500 were awaiting liver transplants, while more than 150 were on the waiting list for heart-lung transplants.

The quantity of any transplantable organ, such as a kidney, is presently dependent almost exclusively on the charity of potential donors, and charity in this area is not an insignificant motivational force; without it, many people would die.

However, many potential donors are reluctant to give to medical schools for training purposes or to people in need for reasons that may seem strange to others but are nonetheless very important to them. Some people object to donating their organs totally on religious grounds; others resist the idea of donating their organs for fear of going to their "eternal reward" with some of their "pieces" missing. (They may not have all their marbles, but they want to have their kidneys, lungs, livers, and corneas just in case they are needed.) Still others resist giving their bodies or parts of their bodies to medical

---

[2]Alan L. Otten, "Growing Demand for Organ Transplants Spurs Efforts to Expand Pool of Donors," *The Wall Street Journal* (March 18, 1988), p. 29.

schools because they recoil at the thought of medical students making jokes about them.

If the legal prohibition against sale of, say kidneys is lifted, the quantity of transplantable kidneys can be more than the quantity made available out of strictly charitable motives. People may experience some discomfort in having to give up a part of themselves to which they have become attached, but many—not all—can be persuaded at some price to donate their kidneys (for transplantation at death, if not before) to a worthy cause. One person in the late 1970s advertised in a newspaper his willingness to buy a kidney in good order for $3,000, and had 100 people calling, willing to sell.[3]

As the price rises, more and more people will overcome their hesitancy to give up one of their kidneys (either before or after death) and to offer it for sale. In short, there is likely to be some quantity of kidneys made available when the price is zero; this quantity, depicted by Q_1 in Figure 10–2, reflects people's altruism. From that point in the graph outward, the supply curve rises in a normal positive direction, illustrating that a larger quantity will be made available to buyers as the price rises.

The demand for kidneys is a function of several factors. It is related to the size of medical schools and their need for kidneys in research and instruction and to the number of people who experience kidney failure. Since kidney failures can be caused by a person's eating and drinking habits, these habits can also affect the demand for kidneys. Further, the demand for kidneys is related to known techniques for transplanting organs. As the techniques in this area are perfected, the willingness of doctors to operate will rise, increasing the demand for transplantable kidneys. The demand may be highly inelastic, as is the curve in Figure 10–2, but it should still exhibit the normal negative slopes of all other demand curves. As the price of a kidney rises, some people may be willing to stay with the then cheaper dialysis machine; others may be excluded from the market because of insufficient funds to buy at the higher prices.

Under a completely altruistic system, no serious problem arises as long as the demand for kidneys is no greater than D_1. With a supply equal to S_1, charitable donors are willing to give Q_1 kidneys, and that is all potential demanders want even at a zero price. In this case, equilibrium is at E_1 with a price of zero. In the real world such an outcome is likely to be a rare occurrence, if for no other reason than that the demanders and suppliers are two different groups of people and are in the market for largely different reasons.

One might reasonably expect the demand for kidneys to be so great relative to supply that at a zero price there will be a shortage of kidneys. This is the case when the demand in Figure 10–2 is positioned at D_2, the quantity demanded is Q_3, which is greater than the quantity being offered out of

---

[3]Brams, "Property Rights in the Human Body."

FIGURE 10–2

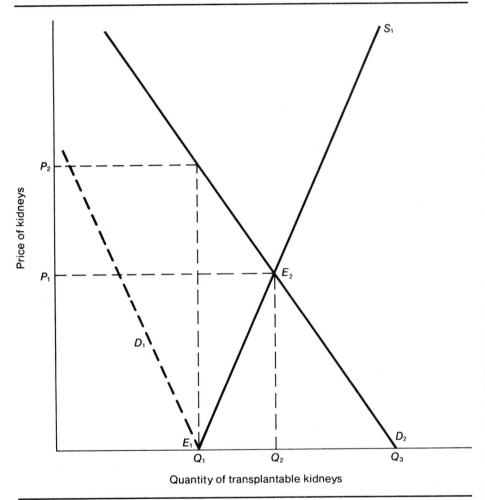

Quantity of transplantable kidneys

altruism, Q_1. Granted, it is possible that with campaigns to enlist new donors, the gap between supply and demand at zero price can be closed;[4] barring that, which we must point out can be an expensive process, the shortage means that many people will go without kidneys and, without any question, some will die.

---

[4]Transplant centers have also sought to relieve the shortage of organs by extending the number of hours an untransplanted organ may be kept before it is discarded and by increasing the maximum age of possible donors. However, the crackdown on drunk drivers has reduced highway deaths and therefore has reduced the availability of transplant organs. (Otten, "Growing Demand.")

If a free market in kidneys (or in any other organ) were allowed to function, the price of a kidney would rise toward the intersection of supply and demand, or P_1, which in real life can be several thousand dollars, if not tens of thousands. At present, the only viable alternative to a transplant for many patients is dialysis through a machine, which can cost upwards of $30,000 a year. The process can also be time consuming in terms of time on the machine and time in travel to and from the kidney center. Furthermore, the patient may have to relocate near a dialysis center and may have to endure all the anxiety that goes with waiting until the right donor comes along. Indeed, when the costs are totaled, one can see that many kidney patients may be willing to pay a handsome market price for a kidney not because it is an attractive or morally acceptable solution, but *because it is cheaper than the next best alternative.*

The prospects of individuals charging for "their God-given organs" is repulsive to many people because it will force some potential buyers out of the market. The people who take this position may simply have a strong ethical position that makes the sale or purchase of an organ "wrong"; they may also see that the quantity of organs demanded falls from Q_3 at zero price to Q_2 at P_1. Perhaps nothing can be said to many people who may be against the sale of kidneys that will cause them to change their minds, but there is one important point evident in the figure that should not be overlooked. At a price of P_1, the quantity of transplantable kidneys is greater than what is available under a completely altruistic system; people offer a total of Q_2 instead of Q_1. Because of the pricing system more people will have kidneys; fewer people will be strapped to a dialysis machine for the rest of their lives and fewer will die.

Clearly, the people who are willing to buy the kidneys, even at what may be considered a very high price, are made better off. The price they pay is evidence of the net benefit. The persons selling the kidneys are also better off, or at least, they expected to be when they sold the organ. If they give up their kidney while they are still alive, they run the risks associated with having only one kidney. Presumably, the price they receive compensates them for suffering those risks. The person who received payment for a kidney that he gives up on his death is compensated for the anxiety he may feel from knowing that he will be taken apart upon death.

Furthermore, doctors will have a greater variety of kidneys to choose from; and the greater variety can mean that doctors can more closely match the kidney to the recipient, reducing the possibility of rejection. The doctor will tend to receive a larger number of kidneys from live donors. Since experience indicates that the rejection rate is lower with kidneys from live donors than from cadavers, further reductions in the rejection rate can be achieved.

The market system is not without its difficulties in this area. As noted, some people in need of a kidney will be unable to buy one because of their limited financial resources. However, the introduction of a market for kidneys may reduce, but need not preclude, altruistic donations of kidneys. These donated kidneys can go to those people who have financial difficulties. In addition, such persons' financial problems can be solved in the same way that we now solve many other health-related problems of the poor, through charity and governmental aid. The market system has one redeeming feature, and that is the government and charitable groups will have more kidneys which they can buy and give to the poor.

In addition, it must be stressed that the creation of a working market in kidneys may not actually increase the financial burden to kidney patients. We say this for the following reason: Just because kidneys, which are very valuable, are given for use by donor, and just because no explicit price is placed on the kidney transplanted, it does not follow that the kidney has not been sold. The market value of the kidney may be included (disguised) in the prices charged by doctors and hospitals. The physicians' and hospitals' fees may be as high as they are partly because they can charge indirectly for the value of the organ (which may be one of several reasons physicians and hospitals resist the sale of organs).

Having recognized the prospects of the donated kidneys' being sold, we might ask for how much? In Figure 10–2, the donated quantity of kidneys could be sold for P_2 (assuming the demand is D_2), which is what would be charged in the event that the doctors and hospitals involved were out to maximize their take from the operations. This means that if the donated kidneys are actually sold to the patients (via increases in other bills) before the advent of a free market, then the advent of a free market in bodily organs would cause a drop (not an increase) in the price of the kidneys—from an implicit price of P_2 to an explicit price of P_1. If this line of reasoning were descriptive of the real world of organ transplants, any ban on explicit organ sales implies not only a restriction on the number of organs available, but also an inflated price for the organs that are transplanted. We cannot be sure that this would be the case, but economic reasoning warns us that we should at least consider these prospects before adopting a ban.

FROM BODILY ORGANS TO TENNIS COURTS

The principles developed in the preceding section relating to kidney transplants are readily applicable to the way most universities have allocated their facilities among students and faculty who want to use them. Consider the way tennis courts are allocated; this example can reveal both the advantages and the limitations of the market system as an allocator of scarce resources.

Typically, universities do not charge a price for the use of such facilities as tennis courts. This usually means that there is a shortage of tennis courts; more people want to use them during certain hours of the day than can use them. The courts are typically rationed on a first-come-first-serve basis. (Some may suggest that this amounts to "allocation by congestion.") Because of this system, many people take the time that is necessary to show up at the courts to see if one is open only to be turned away. Or they may have to waste time waiting until a court becomes available. Many others may like to play the sport, but do not play because they figure that the probability of a court's being open when they want it is too low to take the necessary trouble of trying to play. In any event, the cost of such a system to individuals can be extensive.

There are many ways by which the congestion can be reduced and the courts allocated among the competing "buyers," but we will concentrate on two: (1) the pricing system and (2) the sign-up system. When a price is charged, the number of people wanting to use the courts will diminish. Indeed, the price for different hours of the day can set a level whereby the number of people wanting to use the courts will equal the number of courts available. The number of courts available may not be affected by the revenues, since the sizes of athletic facilities are normally determined by legislative decisions in state capitals, but the price can serve the very useful function of rationing the courts among potential buyers. It can, thereby, save many people the cost of going to the athletic complex in search of a court and not being able to find one.

Still, we cannot overlook the problem that is created in any market for a good; that is, the market system discriminates against those with limited financial resources. However, so long as people have competing interests (i.e., want the same thing), discrimination (i.e., rationing) is necessary in one form or another.

Many students and faculty members even after considering the advantages of using price to ration the courts, may favor the first-come-first-serve system and would vote for it if a referendum were held on the matter; others may favor the pricing system. There are many reasons why opinions differ; however, the one we would like to highlight is the possible differences in the opportunity cost of students' and faculty's time. Those students and faculty who have a very low opportunity cost for their time—for example, they can earn only $4 an hour or be unemployed—may favor the first-come system. The cost to them in terms of the time wasted can easily be less than the equilibrium price that would be set in the market. On the other hand, a person whose time is very valuable—say one can earn $50 an hour—may gladly pay a rather high price to ensure that she will be able to get a court when wanted and to ensure that no time is wasted on futile trips going to and from the courts.

It is by no means certain that under a pricing system faculty will always outbid students for the tennis courts. First, there are probably a number of students on campus who make more at a part-time job than do faculty members at teaching. Further, even students who do not work while in school may be willing to pay a higher price than faculty members. One reason is that they enjoy the sport more. Another, possibly unnoticed, reason is that students, while in school, are "capitalists": They are investing in their future earning power, something that economists call "human capital." If they play tennis, they may reduce their future earning stream. In short, the opportunity cost of these students' time can exceed the opportunity cost of faculty members' time; in other cases, the opposite is true. The opportunity cost of one's time is largely a subjective matter; however, the market system permits such considerations to creep into the determination of how resources and goods, such as tennis courts, are allocated.

Alternatively, the congestion at the tennis courts can be reduced by sign-up sheets; players simply sign up for the times they wish to play. Although this system also has an element of first-come-first-serve in it, it does reduce the amount of time a person may have to wait for a court. This system may be used because it is simpler than the pricing system—it does not require that a cashier be present—and it is generally less costly to administer. Indeed, the pricing system may not yield sufficient revenues to cover the cost of administering it. Additionally, the sign-up system may be considered more equitable than the pricing system. People can register the intensity of their preferences in a pricing system; but they can also, perhaps with less precision, register the intensity of their preferences under a sign-up system by their willingness to get to the sign-up sheet first. Since price has little to do with the number of tennis courts a university has, it may, therefore, be understandable why the pricing system is rarely used to allocate tennis courts.

MARKETS AND THE ABORTION DILEMMA

The debating about abortion provides a ready-made issue for a political power struggle. Much is at stake: human life and individual choice. In contrast to the purpose of others, our purpose here is to sidestep the political fracas over abortion and consider how markets may provide partial, albeit imperfect, solutions to the abortion dilemma that can preserve both life and choice.

Heretofore, the public debate has been driven to rhetorical extremes on the presumption that the solution must be found solely through collective and political means. Accordingly, pro-life groups often characterize pro-abortionists as modern-day Hitlers, willing to set records in the slaughter of human life. Pro-choice advocates (who recoil at the pro-abortionist tag) frequently paint pro-lifers as religious fanatics willing to sacrifice individual freedom and dignity in their uncompromising, zealous quest to impose their morals on reluctant and imperfect mortals with real-world population and welfare problems.

The policy dilemma has been framed in equally stark terms: a virtual ban on abortions or a moral free-for-all in which mothers are licensed to kill their unborn babies almost at will. All the while, human embryos and fetuses continue to be discarded in the United States at a rate of more than a million a year.

The political solution commonly envisioned by moderates caught in the verbal crossfire is one in which each side gives a bit, meaning the abortion protagonists and antagonists accept the establishment of some legally defined date after conception at which *life* is presumed to begin. Pro-lifers need an alternative private remedy for what they see as an egregious social ill. Perhaps the political process will eventually reduce the period during which an abortion is legal from the current 24 weeks to, say 15 to 10 weeks. Realistically, this might be about all that can be expected from a pluralistic democracy composed of citizens with various perceptions of the beginning of human life. Still, pro-lifers will likely remain unsatisfied, interpreting such a compromise on life as a politically expedient death sentence for generations of unborn babies.

Two private remedies, both of which rely on markets, are becoming evident. The first remedy is already in place. The second is futuristic, relying on further development of fetus transplant technology.

The first remedy to the abortion dilemma has emerged from pro-life religious groups (especially fundamentalists) interested in saving what they consider to be the lives of fetuses, who are viewed as underdeveloped human beings. Without doubt, the favored solution of many religious groups is to dispense with abortions altogether. However, because of court rulings, the religious groups have reasoned that the best they can hope to accomplish is to reduce the number of aborted fetuses. To do this, Jerry Falwell, a nationally known Baptist minister and former leader of the "Moral Majority," initiated in the mid-1980s a fund-raising drive to finance homes across the country for pregnant women who might otherwise abort their fetuses. The homes would provide a comfortable setting in which pregnant women could avoid the financial and peer pressures to have abortions; the homes would also be places that would provide positive reinforcements to the women for having the babies, who could be adopted after birth.

Falwell has asked his followers to become "godparents," suggesting that each donate the necessary funds to cover the expenses of one pregnant woman who stays at one of the homes. In effect, he has asked pro-lifers to put their money where their hearts and beliefs are. At the same time, he has offered a market alternative to pregnant women: the facilities and care available at the homes would be offered in exchange for the women carrying their babies to term. Falwell imagines that if enough pro-lifers contribute to the homes, hundreds of thousands of fetuses will be saved—not a perfect solution to him (since hundreds of thousands might still die), but at least a second-best solution.

One can imagine that enterprising religious groups may, in the not-too-distant future, carry Falwell's idea one step further and begin to offer not only coverage of pregnancy and birth expenses but also some additional reward for not aborting the fetuses. All involved might find the idea of paying women to avoid abortion repulsive, but they might find continued abortions even more repulsive. Further, they may reason that the supply of avoided abortions is upward sloping, meaning they can save even more lives by increasing the reward from not aborting.

The second remedy may emerge from the fetus transplant technology being developed in animal science. For nearly two decades, animal scientists have been developing the capacity to transfer embryos from, for example, high quality cows, sheep, horses, and pigs to lower quality host females. Indeed, by giving a high-quality cow a fertility drug that causes her to "superovulate," and by transplanting the multiple embryos into an equal number of host cows, animal scientists have dramatically increased the reproductive capacity of high-quality cows. The transplant technology has been used to rebuild the stock of endangered species.

However, animal scientists have found that they can split embryos into two or even more parts and implant the parts in different host females with the result of identical twins, triplets, or quadruplets being born by different females. For example, a single horse embryo has been artificially split in laboratories and implanted in separate mares, which subsequently have given birth to identical twin colts. Zebra embryos have been carried to term by horses. The transplant technology may, of course, be adapted to humans with a great deal of difficulty but also with a great deal of promise.

The embryo and fetus transplant technology, while still in its infancy, should offer a great deal of hope to pro-lifers who must be terribly frustrated by their current inability to budge Congress on the abortion issue. The developing transplant technology may provide pro-lifers with another opportunity to put their money and even their bodies where their hearts and convictions are. Pro-life groups can start the search for a private solution to the political impasse on abortion by funding additional research on human embryo and fetus transplants.

Three areas of research (among many research needs) appear to be particularly important. First, doctors need to develop better and less costly means of detecting pregnancy at earlier dates and of extending the time period during which transplants can be successful. Currently, the optimum period for transplants in animals and humans is six to nine days after conception. Most women who may seek an abortion do not know they are pregnant for at least two weeks.

Second, successfully disengaging an implanted fetus from the uterus remains a particularly serious transplant obstacle. Third, nonsurgical methods of transplantation in women also need to be devised to reduce the costs of the procedures.

Once the transplant technology is developed—and there is every expectation that many of the important research questions can be answered—pro-life groups can establish clinics that will seek to match (and there will be matching problems) women seeking abortions with women wanting to have children (for whatever reason) or willing to save what would otherwise have been discarded embryos or fetuses.

Such clinics can specialize in encouraging pregnant women to carry their babies to term, at which time they would be kept or given up for adoption. Alternatively, as a solution short of sending pregnant women off to abortionists, these pro-life clinics can have the embryos and fetuses medically re-moved and transplanted into host mothers who, at term, may keep the babies or may give them up for adoption.

The expenses of both mothers can be covered in a variety of ways, in-cluding charges on the mothers involved or on the couples wanting to adopt or through contributions from people who share the clinics' central goal—the saving of human life. Such pro-life clinics can alter the number of babies saved by their generosity in covering the medical expenses of the mothers.

Granted, objections can be easily marshalled against the solution ten-dered here. Pro-life clinics are unlikely to eradicate all abortions; perhaps only a minor portion will be saved, mainly because of funding limitations and the matching legal problems involved. Not all transplants will take, and the preservation of human life will be tainted with money, as it is in so many other areas of medical science. Transplants may, in addition, encourage preg-nancies, since the pro-life clinics will likely represent a less objectionable means by which women can relieve themselves of unwanted pregnancies.

However, the objections to this admittedly imperfect transplant proposal must ultimately be assessed with reference to the status quo in which abor-tions abound. If life is truly priceless to pro-lifers, some marginal reduction in the current rate of fetus destruction—which would be accomplished by some, but not all, transplants—could only be construed by them as a social improvement. This would be especially true since the transplants would be voluntary and might be consistent with principles of individual choice. Re-gardless of whether you approve of these market methods of partially resolv-ing the abortion dilemma, we expect the methods will be hotly debated in the not-too-distant future.

INSIDER TRADING—AND NONTRADING!

In the late 1980s Ivan Boesky, a prominent New York stock trader, became known as the Wall Street equivalent of Ivan the Terrible. His crime: he dared to buy and sell stock basing his decisions on "inside information" (or infor-mation known mainly to corporation managers and officers and not generally available to the public). As a consequence, he was able to buy stock before it appreciated in response to public release of important corporate information. He supposedly made hundreds of millions of dollars by buying low and selling high. His only problem is that his dealings were against the law, since he had access to important information that had not yet been made public. As a result of his wrongdoing, the Securities and Exchange Commission levied a fine against him of about $100 million in 1986.

Should Boesky have been treated like a criminal for trying to make a buck? That question may appear to have an obvious answer. After all, Boesky did violate the law and, by his own admission, made huge profits. However, this obvious answer does not imply that economists agree that the law he violated should ever have been put on the books. Indeed, while businessmen and women generally support laws against insider trading, many (not all) economists who have considered the issue of insider trading dispute the value of laws against such activity. Some economists even argue that laws against insider trading have perverse effects—are inefficient, if not unfair.

Their arguments are developed along the following line: All stock (and bond) market trades are made with the intention of making a profit—by means of buying low and selling high. Hence, the buyers must assume they have information about the stocks they buy that is not known to all others in the market at the time of the trade. They base their trades on various sources of information, from "hot tips" to detailed research reports. The information they may use may be in the public domain, but it certainly is not equally available to all investors at more or less the same cost.

At best, laws against insider trading require an arbitrary demarcation between information that traders can use and information they cannot use. What is inside information is not always clear; therefore, what is against the law is not always clear. The difficulty of legal definitions may be largely solved by simply restricting the rights of corporate managers and officers (not just people who deal on the basis of inside information) to trade stocks that are in any way related to their work for their corporations.

As a consequence, economists who oppose insider-trading laws fear such laws deny corporations an important means of compensating their managers and officers. To that extent, the income of managers and officers may not be efficiently tied to their doing things that will produce greater profits for their companies—and their companies' stockholders. If managers and officers could trade on the basis of inside information, so the argument goes, managers and officers would have more incentive to make more money for their stockholders. In addition, by trading on inside information, managers and stockholders push the price of the stock in the right direction—up or down (depending on whether the inside information is good or bad news). Through changes in stock prices the inside information is made public (or, at the very least, people in the market have a greater incentive than otherwise to discover the reason for the stock price movement).

Still, proponents of insider-trading laws may reason that insider trading is unfair. In one important sense, insider trading may be deemed unfair. Managers and officers are provided an advantage in the purchase or sale of stock not given to everyone else. They know when, for example, the company is planning a merger, or has come upon a new invention, or discovered a new resource, or is about to be taken over by another firm. Indeed, stockholders may be induced by corporate officers to sell just prior to the announcement of the news and the appreciation of the stock. The stock market gain favors the corporate managers and officers, or so it is thought.

Looked at from the perspective of some economists, however, the claims about the unfairness of insider trading is, at the very least, open to question. The overall profitability of the company and the value of the stock to the stockholders need not be lessened by insider trading. Indeed, allowed insider trading may increase the value of the company stock. Because managers and officiers can be paid by way of allowed insider trading, companies will not have to pay their managers and officers as much in the form of salaries or any other form of compensation. The impact of insider trading on a company and its stockholders, therefore, probably depends on the relative efficiency of payment through salary, fringe benefits, stock options, bonuses, and capital gains (achieved through insider trading) and the tradeoffs that the companies have to make in securing the services of their managers and officers.[5]

It is doubtful that all firms will find that compensation through allowed insider trading to be equally desirable, which means that not all firms will want to permit insider trading. It stands to reason that in a diverse world some firms can be expected to permit insider trading while others can be expected to prohibit insider trading (for the same reason that they prohibit their managers and officers from selling off their office equipment). From this perspective, insider trading would be a criminal offense only if it violated a provision in the managers' and officers' employment contract. (In fact, Boesky may have been guilty of violation of laws against fraud and breach of contract, as well as the securities laws.)

Economists opposed to legislated (noncontractual) restrictions on insider trading also have worried that such laws imply an asymmetrical application of legal penalties. Specifically, only those insiders who buy stock based on nonpublic information are penalized. However, William Kelley, Clark Nardinelli, and Myles Wallace—three Clemson University economists—point out that insiders can profit from nontrading (or not buying and selling stock) based on nonpublic information, and the Clemson economists stress that insider nontrading may be a far larger problem than insider trading.[6] This is because many managers and officers have stock in their company and can always not sell their stock based on inside information. And, of course, everyone can potentially not buy stock based on inside information.

How does a manager or officer make money from not trading, you ask? The example provided by the Clemson economists is instructive:

> Consider the case of Ms. B., a highly placed corporate executive at ABD Inc. Ms. B has substantial holdings of ABD stock, and before a mid-morning meeting, she had planned to sell some of her holdings to take profits on a recent rise to $40 a share. At the meeting, she learns of a friendly takeover

---

[5]See Henry G. Manne, *Insider Trading and the Stock Market* (New York: Free Press, 1966). It needs to be noted that misuse of inside information by managers and officers is not necessarily costless in a world in which insider trading is legal. Managers and officers that misuse their authority can be penalized with reduced job opportunities and a lower future income stream.

[6]William A. Kelley, Jr., "The Plague of Insider Non-Trading," *The Wall Street Journal* (December 11, 1986), p 32. See also William A. Kelley, Jr., Clark Nardinelli, and Myles S. Wallace, "Regulation, Distortions, Insider Trading, and Insider Non-Trading" (Clemson, S.C.: Economics Department, Clemson University, July 1987).

bid from KNW Inc. at $60. Ms. B, acting on information not yet in the public domain, holds on to her stock after the meeting. Later, she sells out for $60, reaping a hefty profit from her earlier non-trade. Now, if she had purchased more shares in ABD prior to the public disclosure of the takeover, she would have violated existing codes. Although she did not violate any codes, by not going through with a planned sale, she clearly used inside information for personal gain.[7]

To make their point clear with a modicum of humor, the authors recommended that the Securities and Exchange Commission also regulate nontrading with no less dedication than it now regulates insider trading. Of course, the regulation of nontrading is hard to do, since it is difficult, if not impossible, to detect (and detectives need to detect) when people are *not doing something* based on nonpublic information. (Can you imagine how large the SEC would have to be in order to keep a watchful eye on people *not* buying and selling stock?) So long as insider nontrading is not regulated, the application of the law will continue to be discriminatory. Unfortunately, according to correspondence received from abroad, Italian politicians have taken the Clemson economists seriously and have proposed the banning of insider nontrading! Leave it to the Italians.

Why do people oppose insider trading? One reason has already been given: insider trading is perceived to be unfair. Another reason is ignorance or stupidity regarding the subtle consequences of insider-trading laws. Although economists are reluctant to lean on ignorance and stupidity as an explanation for any social phenomenon, it does not follow that people always understand the public policies they support (an observation most principles of economics teachers should appreciate).

Fortunately, there are probably other reasons, and economists are always worried that proposed restrictions are designed to benefit the people who recommend them at the expense of others. One possible private-interest explanation is that firms (or investment bankers) are not willing to incur the necessary cost of enforcing their own contractual prohibitions against insider trading. That is to say, for some (maybe most) firms, a contractual prohibition may be the most efficient means of compensating managers and officers, but the firms may still prefer to have someone else—the government—incur the cost of ensuring that insider trading does not occur.

Still another explanation may be that the managers and officers want to cartelize inside information, that is, make sure that the information is not leaked to the public by some independent insider. There is nothing in current security laws that prevents a company, acting in its own name, from trading on inside information. If the information cartel holds, it is altogether possible for the managers and officers to take the company private at a bargain price and then have the managers and officers divide up the spoils of change

---

[7]Kelley, "The Plague of Insider Non-Trading," p. 32.

known only through inside information. So long as the rules against insider trading are enforced, the "market" will never know what is afoot.

Of course, dominant stockholders within firms, who are officers or board directors and who may have considerable inside information, may want to see information kept within the firm. Dominant stockholders can ensure that the firm engages in insider trading in the name of the firm. The firm can buy the stock back from nondominant stockholders based on inside information, knowing that something is afoot that will substantially raise the profitability of the company. The benefit of the information is therefore internalized within the stock of the dominant stockholders. As opposed to all stockholders benefiting from the greater profitability, only the dominant stockholder will.[8]

We do not know if this is true. Economic theory only suggests what may be true. Therefore, such explanations must be treated as hypotheses, subject to empirical testing.

CONCLUDING COMMENTS

The market system is often criticized, and the criticisms are well known. Through the use of real-world examples, this chapter has been directed toward revealing a principal advantage of markets. The market system can perform the very valuable function of rationing scarce resources among all those who want them. It avoids the problems of congestion that will develop when no price is charged for the use of the resources, goods, and services. Further, the system allows people the opportunity to reveal their relative preferences for a good. In the process, the system can give rise to greater production of the traded goods at lower prices. These are the main lessons of this chapter.

QUESTIONS TO PONDER

1. It is possible that the federal government can reduce the sales of cocaine in three ways: (1) banning cocaine in American markets, (2) imposing tax on the sale of cocaine, and (3) paying cocaine producers not to grow the crops from which cocaine is extracted. What are the similarities and differences and pros and cons of these three control methods? Can you think of other control methods?

2. Given the arguments developed in this chapter for the sale of bodily organs, are you for or against a law that would ban such sales? What are your reasons? Is there any difference between the sale of blood and the sale of kidneys?

---

[8]These points are developed in Richard B. McKenzie and Clayton Hipp, "The Firm as Inside Trader" (Clemson, S.C.: Economics Department, Clemson University, March 1988).

3. "The nation's airports are overloaded with planes attempting to take off and land at several times during the day." Why do you think that is the case? What correction would you recommend?

4. Is it efficient to regulate insider trading at the same time that insider non-trading is left unregulated? Is it fair? What are the consequences of leaving the regulation of insider trading the way it is?

CHAPTER 11

The Minimum Wage: A New Perspective on an Old Policy[1]

By almost any national standard, many workers in the United States make abysmally low wages. Their wages are so low that it is understandable why many concerned citizens worry that these hard-working Americans are only marginally better off than unemployed workers. Even when workers earn the legislated minimum wage (set at $3.35 an hour in early 1988), they gross only $134 for a 40-hour week, an amount that is slightly less than $7,000 a year and slightly above the official poverty threshold for a single person.

If the minimum-wage worker has a nonworking spouse or children, then poverty must be a constant companion. Understandably, many of these minimum-wage workers may find little solace knowing that they are still fortunate to have a job that pays far more than many worse jobs in other countries around the world.

The apparent remedy for the low wages and poverty of many American workers is to boost the legislated minimum wage, especially now that the market value of the current minimum wage has been eroded by years of inflation. Indeed, according to supporters of an increase in the legislated minimum wage, "Policy makers should set the minimum wage at $4.33, because that is a level where only a few jobs are lost but where income and work-incentive effects are substantial."[2] It is also the level that would give the official minimum wage the same purchasing power it had in 1981, the last time it was raised.

In addition, a higher minimum wage would not materially affect the employment opportunities of those covered by the law. In the words of advocates of a higher minimum, "The Federal Minimum Wage Commission

---

[1]This chapter is reprinted with extensive revisions from Richard B. McKenzie, *The Fairness of Markets* (Lexington, Mass.: Lexington Books, 1987).

[2]Sar A. Levitan and Isaac Shapiro, "The Minimum Wage: A Sinking Floor," *New York Times,* January 16, 1986, p. 19. Senator Edward Kennedy proposed in early 1987 that the minimum wage be raised to $4.65 an hour by the first of 1990 and thereafter raised and held to 50 percent of the average hourly wage in the country. In early 1988 the Senate Labor Committee proposed to drop the indexing provision and raise the minimum wage to $5.05 per hour.

Study, appointed by President Jimmy Carter, estimated, in its 1981 report, that a 10 percent increase in that wage decreases teen-age employment by 1 percent, and concluded that the employment loss for adults is less than for youths."[3]

Clearly, a heart-wrenching ethical and fairness dilemma undergirds any political debate over legislated solutions to low wages for some Americans. The dilemma is not eased at all by economists' standard textbook argument that legislated minimum wages benefit some workers (those covered workers who retain their jobs) at the expense of others (those covered workers who lose their jobs or cannot find them) because fewer jobs are available.

Is it fair or ethical for government to institute such policies as minimum wages that knowingly will hurt some while helping others—that will redistribute income among some of the lowest income workers in the country? That is not an easy question to answer. From the perspective of conventional economic analysis, the question poses social trade-offs that must be politically debated and decided, and there is no particular reason to conclude that legislated minimum wages for the poor, blacks, women, or any other identified group are unfair or, for that matter, socially unwise policies. The question boils down to Whose welfare counts the most, that of those who retain their jobs or of those who lose? And How many people's employment can be sacrificed in the pursuit of improved welfare for others? Aside from declaring that they side with the welfare of some favored group (e.g., those who retain their jobs), economists appear to have no particularly useful expertise in providing an answer.

However, the trade-off presumed in this question is more theoretical than real. It is founded largely on conventional economic theory that is far more defective than generations of economists have been led to believe. If critical defects in conventional theory are corrected, as is done in this chapter, the perceived social trade-off in the minimum-wage debate nearly evaporates.[4] As a result, legislated wages are unfair because everyone (or practically everyone) affected by them is made worse off. It is counterproductive to promote policy based on fairness, let alone efficiency, if legislated minimum wages do not help low-income workers. The analysis that follows later in the chapter helps to explain why the employment effects of minimum-wage laws have been so inconsequential. Before we broach that subject, however, consider briefly the history of the minimum wage.

---

[3]Ibid.

[4]The qualification "nearly" is added simply because it is unrealistic to believe that a government policy would not benefit someone or some small group of affected workers. The point of the discussion in this chapter, which is that minimum wages do far more damage than is generally believed, still holds. That is to say, many of those people who are conventionally believed to be better off because they retain their jobs and because they receive higher money wages are made worse off by legislated minimum wages.

THE MINIMUM-WAGE RECORD

The first legal minimum wage, passed as a part of the Fair Labor Standards Act, went into effect in 1938. As shown in Table 11–1, the minimum wage in that year was $0.25 an hour. The following year the minimum went to $0.30, in 1945, to $0.40, not breaking $1.00 an hour until 1956. By 1968, the minimum wage had risen another 60 percent to $1.60 an hour; by 1981, the year of the last raise to date, the minimum wage had again more than doubled.[5] Throughout the five decades of its existence, the coverage of the minimum-wage law—meaning the number of people affected—has risen steadily.

However, since 1938, the purchasing power of the legal minimum wage has been affected as much by inflation as by legislative action, or more. As expected from Table 11–1, the value of the minimum wage in nominal money terms in Figure 11–1 rises in distinct steps throughout the period. What is most notable from Figure 11–1 is the long-term decline in the *real* or *constant (1986) dollar* minimum wage. This decline did not start in the 1980s, or with the advent of the Reagan administration. The real minimum wage peaked in 1968 at $5.04 an hour (1986 dollars). It then declined steadily to approximately $3.95 in 1973, only to rise again in 1974 and oscillate within a range of $4.45 to $4.16 until 1981. After 1981, it began another steady decline, reaching $3.35 an hour in 1986.

The political case for raising the minimum wage has been bolstered by a few simple facts of real deterioration in the minimum wage. The real minimum wage fell by more than a third (or $1.69 an hour) between 1968 and 1986, and 60 percent of the decrease of $1 an hour occurred between 1968 and 1981. In 1986 the real minimum wage was approximately the same as it was in 1950 and was only 43 percent above the real level of 1940.

TABLE 11–1   The Minimum Wage in History

1938	$0.25	1968	$1.60
1939	0.30	1974	2.00
1945	0.40	1975	2.10
1950	0.75	1976	2.30
1956	1.00	1978	2.65
1961	1.15	1979	2.90
1963	1.25	1980	3.10
1967	1.40	1981	3.35

SOURCE: U.S. Department of Labor.

[5]Actually, the last time a minimum-wage bill was considered by Congress was in 1977, when several scheduled annual increases in the minimum were passed.

FIGURE 11–1   The Rise and Fall of the Minimum Wage, in Current and Constant
(1986) Dollar Terms, 1938–1986

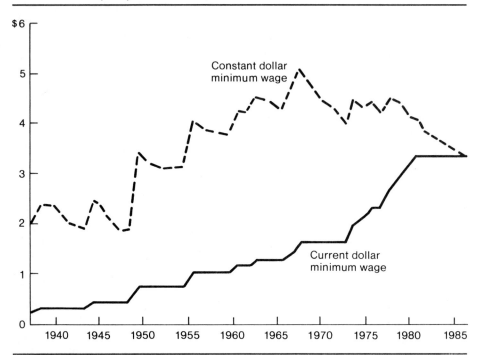

The decline in the minimum wage in the late 1970s and early 1980s might be attributed in part to the fact that the average hourly wages of all workers were decreasing, from a constant (1986) dollar high of $9.72 an hour in 1973 to $8.73 an hour in 1986.[6] However, the minimum wage fell slightly more rapidly. As a consequence, the minimum wage was 56 percent of average hourly earnings in 1968 and only 39 percent in 1986.[7]

Proposals made in 1987 to raise the minimum wage to $4.65 an hour by 1990 and to 50 percent of the average hourly earnings are, therefore, not drastic recommendations by historical standards. These proposals would only return the minimum wage, in relative terms, to levels first achieved in the early 1950s.

So, what is the problem? Why did the *New York Times* and the Reagan administration oppose what appears to be a relatively modest proposal in

---

[6]Just how much real hourly wages have fallen since 1973 is under considerable dispute. See Richard B. McKenzie, *"The Great U-Turn": Another Economic Myth or a New Economic Reality* (Washington D.C.: Joint Economic Committee, U.S. Congress, 1987).

[7]The minimum wage was also equal to 56 percent of average hourly earnings in 1950.

historical terms?[8] Is it that they are simply antiworkers? Antipoor? Many proponents appear to think so, arguing that they alone have the interests of low-income workers at heart. They appear to believe that the historical decline in the real minimum wage implies that the covered workers are worse off. This is a conclusion that is naturally but incorrectly drawn from misleading economic models of minimum-wage markets conventionally shared by analysts on both sides of the debate.

THE EFFECTS OF LEGISLATED WAGES: THE CONVENTIONAL ARGUMENT

There are many jokes about economists never reaching a conclusion or never agreeing on a matter—Harry Truman's search for a "one-arm economist" being one of the most familiar.[9] However, with regard to the effects of minimum-wage laws there is considerable agreement in the profession.[10] These laws are notorious for raising the wages of a subset of affected workers, reducing the job opportunities and wages of other workers, increasing the number of people searching for work, swelling the ranks of the unemployed, and causing inefficiency in the allocation of resources.

The predicted effects of minimum-wage laws have generally, but not universally, been supported by empirical studies. Finis Welch has written, "If there is a general theme to the empirical literature on the subject, it is that the simple theoretical predictions are confirmed. Almost every serious scholar of minimum wages would argue (on the basis of available evidence) that wage minimums have reduced employment for those who would otherwise earn low wages, particularly teenagers."[11]

---

[8]"The idea of using a minimum wage to overcome poverty is old, honorable—and fundamentally flawed. It's time to put this hoary debate behind us, and find a better way to improve the lives of people who work very hard for very little." "The Right Minimum Wage: $0.00," editorial, *New York Times*, January 14, 1987, p. 18.

[9]After hearing conflicting advice from his economic advisers, who frequently talked in terms of "on the one hand . . . but then on the other hand," President Truman is reported to have declared in a fit of exasperation, "What this country needs is a good one-arm economists."

[10]For a conventional textbook discussion of the employment and efficiency effects of minimum-wage laws, see Armen A. Alchian and William R. Allen, *University Economics* (Belmont, Cal.: Wadsworth Publishing Company, 1964), pp. 385–88. For a survey of the scholarly literature on the subject, including empirical assessments of theoretical predictions, see Finis Welch, *Minimum Wages: Issues and Evidence* (Washington, D.C.: American Enterprise Institute, 1978) and Keith B. Leffler, "Minimum Wages, Welfare, and Wealth Transfers," *Journal of Law and Economics* (October 1978), pp. 345–58. Leffler makes the interesting but perverse argument that the poor have a demand for minimum wages because of the positive effect that minimum wages have on welfare benefits.

[11]Finis Welch, "The Rising Impact of Minimum Wages," *Regulation*, November/December 1978, pp. 33–34.

The loss of employment opportunities is explained in three ways. First, some jobs do not produce sufficient market value per hour to cover the minimum wage some workers must be paid.[12] Second, there are some workers who do not have the necessary skills that would enable employers to make a profit by employing them at the minimum wage. Third, by raising the cost of labor, the minimum wage will cause a substitution of machines for workers.

However, for many persons who oppose the laws on ideological grounds, the long-run employment costs of minimum wages have been uncomfortably small, as revealed by real-world data. Economists have explained the small impact of the laws by noting, for example, that (1) the legislated minimum wage, after all, applies to only a small portion of the total labor market, (2) the demand for menial labor tends to be unresponsive to wage hikes, and (3) the minimum wage is typically not all that far removed from the true market wage for most of the covered workers.

THE MARKET FOR MENIAL WORKERS: IMPORTANT REVISIONS

The conventional line of analysis and policy proposals misses several important but relatively simple points. By its very nature, employment in any labor market is a complex phenomenon. Employment is based on a great variety of potential contract terms and a tremendous assortment of environmental conditions. The money wage rate paid workers is only one of many, many dimensions of work. To develop the analysis in its starkest terms, consider an unscrupulous employer who is interested in draining as much profit as possible from his (or her) workers, and who, therefore, pays his (or her) workers as little as possible.

Such a profit-maximizing employer will, before settling on a wage offer to workers, consider the entire work situation with an objective of minimizing costs and maximizing output. As is fully recognized in much highly sophisticated labor-market theory, the employer can be expected to seek a combination of capital (plant and machinery) and labor that results in the most profits. In addition, he or she will seek to adjust all of the implicit and explicit terms of the labor contract and the environmental conditions of the workplace to maximize the efficiency of labor, given the capital that is employed, and to minimize the *effective* total wage, including the money wage that may be paid on an hourly basis and the nonmonetary benefits of the workplace environment.[13]

---

[12]A part of the explanation is bound up in the *law of diminishing returns*, which mandates that beyond some point in hiring workers the additional output of additional workers will begin to decline. At some point additional workers will not produce enough market value to justify the minimum wage.

[13]Indeed, the profit-maximizing employers can be expected to adjust the conditions of work until the last dollar of cost incurred due to the adjustments is just equal to a dollar reduction

In less technical terms, an employer can effectively pay workers with dollars, with normal fringe benefits such as prepaid medical care, and with pleasant working conditions that may arise from the installation of air conditioning, noise abatement systems, or those informal musical programs broadcast throughout the workplace. The worker can also be effectively paid with the location convenience of the workplace, the courteousness of the management, the safety of the workplace, chances for on-the-job training, and the production demands of supervisors.

To achieve maximum efficiency and profits from a given expenditure level, the last dollar of cost incurred on, say air conditioning (or any other fringe benefit or condition of work) must reduce the money wage bill and/or raise company revenues by one dollar. If this marginal condition does not prevail, then the employer can either expand or cut his expenditures on said air conditioning and reduce his labor cost or he can increase his output with the same labor cost. The employer should, on the margin, be indifferent to spending an additional dollar on wages or an additional dollar on air conditioning or some other condition of work.

The employer's expenditures on different working conditions or fringe benefits will have different effects on supply of, and demand for, labor. Expenditures on, for example, company picnics may not affect worker productivity. However, since picnics can increase the supply of workers, such expenditures can be offset by a reduction in the company's money wage bill. The profit-maximizing employer will extend the expenditures on picnics up to the point that the last dollar of cost incurred will be just offset by a dollar reduction in the total wage bill that is due to an increase in the supply of labor.

Other changes in working conditions or fringe benefits can affect worker productivity. Worker productivity, for instance, can be increased by the introduction of air conditioning. The firm's expenditures on air conditioning or other work environment changes will be increased until the additional cost equals the additional revenue received by the improvement in productivity plus the reduction in the wage bill. Since each worker will be worth more in terms of output per worker-hour and receive less in money wages, the number of workers demanded should increase and the firm should be willing to hire more workers at any given wage rate.

When workers' productivity rises due to a change in the workplace or fringe benefits, the firm's supply of labor may increase or decrease, depending on how the change affects workers' job satisfaction (or dissatisfaction). If

---

in the money wage. Given the amount of capital employed and a competitive market, the firm's direct and indirect expenditures on labor (in a market free of government wage interference) can be expected to achieve maximum efficiency. The mathematics of the relationship between the prices of one factor input and other variable factor inputs is developed in C. E. Ferguson, *The Neoclassical Theory of Production and Distribution* (London: Cambridge University Press, 1969), chap. 6.

the work experience is made more satisfying, more workers should be willing to work for any given wage, that is, labor supply should increase. For similar reasons, the supply of labor should contract with workplace changes that reduce workers' job-related satisfaction. The important points to remember are that

- An increase in the labor supply can be expected to lead to a reduction in the wage rate paid.
- A decrease in the labor supply can be expected to lead to an increase in the wage rate paid.

This means that when the supply of labor increases, the cost of the change in workplace conditions can be offset by an increase in the productivity of labor or by a reduction in the wage that the firm would otherwise have to pay. Alternatively, the supply of workers may be reduced by the workplace change initiated by the employer. However, the change will still be made so long as it adds more to revenue than it adds to cost.

It is also possible the profit-maximizing employer could voluntarily (that is, without any government encouragement or requirement) make changes in the workplace that reduce the productivity of labor but increase the supply of labor. So long as the reduction in the value of worker productivity lost is less than the reduction in the wage bill, the change is profitable for the firm. Reducing the production demands on employees might also reduce productivity and the market value of workers to the employer. However, it might also increase the attractiveness of work—hence, the supply of labor—and therefore reduce the firm's wage bill.

The central point of the foregoing discussion is that, given all of the possible changes that can be made, the profit-maximizing employer will make those changes that enable him or her to minimize his or her labor cost and maximize profits. Indeed, firms in competitive markets will be forced to find a cost-minimizing combination of capital, labor, fringe benefits, and working conditions. If an employer in a competitive labor market does not achieve the cost-minimizing combination, he or she will be underpriced and the firm will be forced to contract its position or withdraw from the final product market.

THE IMPACT OF MINIMUM WAGES

Minimum-wage laws establish a legal floor for *money wages;* however, they do not suppress competitive pressures. These restrictions only cap the pressures in one of the multitude of competitive outlets, namely money wages. More to the point, they do not set a legal minimum for the *effective wage* (including the money and nonmoney benefits of employment) that is paid to workers.

The impact of mandating minimum wages depends on the ability of the employer to adjust the nonmoney conditions of work or fringe benefits in response to a required pay change. Conventional analysis of minimum-wage laws, embedded in economics textbooks, implicitly assumes that money wages are the only form of labor compensation. Hence, when the money wage is set at a legal minimum, employment falls by some amount given by the demand for labor.

Consider the impact of wages as presented in a standard supply and demand graph in Figure 11-2, which has the workers' wage rate on the vertical axis and the quantity of labor (or number of workers) on the horizontal axis. The demand-for-labor curve, labeled D_1, is downward sloping in accordance with the reasoned argument (implicit in the foregoing discussion) that employers will hire more workers if the wage is reduced. A decrease in the wage rate from a wage rate of, say W_m to W_o will lead to an increase in the

FIGURE 11-2   The Conventional View of Minimum Wage Laws

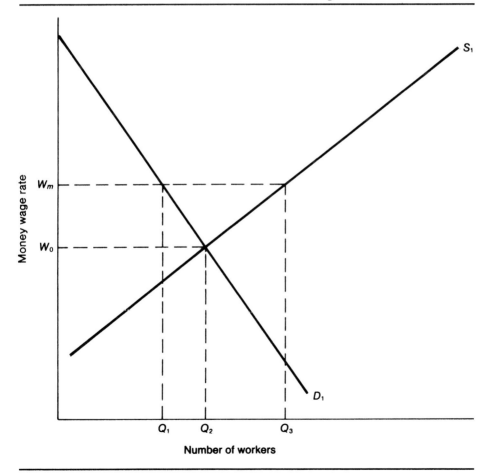

number of workers hired from Q_1 to Q_2. On the other hand, the supply of labor curve, labeled S_1, is upward sloping in accordance with the argument that more workers will be willing to work at higher wages than at lower wages. Therefore, an increase in the wage rate from, say W_o to W_m will lead to an increase in the number of workers willing to work from Q_2 to Q_3.

If an acceptable minimum wage is set at W_m in Figure 11–2, the quantity of labor demanded falls from Q_2 to Q_1 and the quantity of labor supplied expands from Q_2 to Q_3. According to the conventional view, a surplus of unemployed labor emerges in the market equal to $Q_3 - Q_1$. This is because there is no assumed way employers can react to that surplus of unemployed labor. From this line of analysis, the conclusion is drawn that the effective wage for those who retain their jobs rises up by the amount of the increase in their wage rate, the competitive market wage rate, W_o, minus the minimum wage, W_m. The people who lose their jobs are pushed into lower-paying labor markets or onto the roles of the unemployed. (Again, the unemployment can be conceptually measured by the distance between Q_1 and Q_3.)

This line of analysis may still be fully applicable to those few labor markets in which money is the only form of compensation and in which employers can do little or nothing to change the skill and production demands imposed on workers. In such cases, minimum-wage laws may still have the predicted effect, a labor-market surplus of unemployed menial workers caused by an above-market level of compensation.

However, the previous analysis does not consider the possibility that profit-maximizing competitive employers will adjust to the labor-market surplus created by the minimum-wage law.[14] It seems highly reasonable that employers who are capable of paying their workers wages that are "too low," because of, for example, antisocial attitudes or competitive pressures, are also quite capable of adjusting other conditions of work in response to the labor market surplus. Indeed, to keep cost-competitive, employers in competitive labor markets will have to adjust to the labor surplus by cutting labor costs in nonwage ways—for example, eliminating workplace picnics, reducing fringe

---

[14]Technically speaking, in the analysis that follows, the market demand for the labor curve is constructed, as is conventional, by appropriately summing the demand curves of individual firms. The firm's demand curve for labor is the locus of points obtained from shifts in the value of the marginal product curve, which in turn is due to changes in the variable factor inputs used in conjunction with labor. The market demand curve in the graphical analysis that follows is not, however, equivalent to the curve that represents the full marginal value of labor. The demand curve that is drawn in Figure 12–2 is the relationship between the money wage rate and the quantity of labor employed and is the net of the cost per unit of labor of improved working conditions and fringe benefits that equals, on the margin, the value of labor to firms in the market. The demand curve described in Figure 12–2, as a function of the money wage, is lower than the true demand curve for labor and is a function of the cost of the fringe benefits that are provided.

benefits, or increasing production demands.[15] Employers in such labor markets can be expected to reduce their labor costs in nonmoney ways until they are no longer confronted by a surplus—that is, until their labor markets clear once again.[16] That being said, the labor market effects of employers' nonmoney adjustments made in response to a wage minimum can be discussed briefly in terms of two general cases.

Case I: Changes in Fringe Benefits that Do Not Affect Labor Productivity

Employers can be expected to respond to a minimum-wage law by cutting or eliminating those fringe benefits and conditions of work, like workplace parties, that increase the supply of labor but do not materially affect labor productivity. By reducing such nonmoney benefits of employment, the labor costs are reduced from what they would otherwise have been and nothing is lost in the way of reduced labor productivity.

Continuation of such nonmoney benefits as affect the supply is made uneconomical by the money-wage minimum; they no longer pay for themselves in terms of lower wage rates. Furthermore, employers in highly competitive final products markets must adjust such work conditions to remain competitive and to survive. Otherwise, other firms will lower their labor costs (by contracting or by eliminating fringe benefits) and force the employers who retain their fringe benefits and continue to pay the higher minimum-wage rate out of their final product markets.

Because of the changes in the work conditions, the supply curve of labor (the position of which is partially determined by working conditions and fringe benefits) can be expected to shift upward. The effects of such a supply shift are shown in Figure 11–3, which incorporates the supply and demand curves of the preceding figure.

The vertical shift in the supply curve will be equal to labor's dollar evaluation, on the margin, of the adjustments made in employment conditions.

---

[15]Clearly, many minimum-wage jobs do not carry standard fringe benefits, such as life and medical insurance and retirement plans. However, most do offer fringes in the form of the conditions in the work environment, attitudes of the bosses, breaks, frequency and promptness of pay, variety of work, uniforms, use of company tools and supplies, meals and drinks, and precautions against accidents. These fringes are subject to withdrawal when minimum wages are mandated.

[16]More precisely, the labor markets should, after adjustments, clear more or less to the same extent as they did before the minimum-wage law was imposed. Of course, employers are not directly concerned with ensuring that their labor market clears. They are, however, interested in minimizing their labor costs, a motivation that drives them to adjust the conditions of work until the market clears. The point is that if the employer is confronted by more workers than he or she needs, he or she can offer less or demand more until the surplus is eliminated.

FIGURE 11–3   The Revised View of Minimum Wage Laws

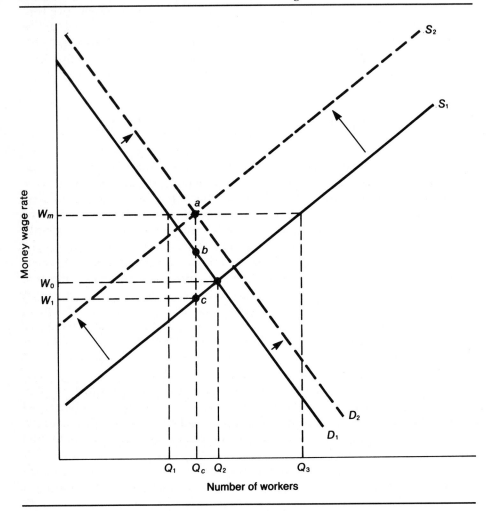

The demand curve for labor will shift upward to the right, reflecting the reduced expenditure per unit of labor on fringe benefits.[17]

As before, fringe benefits are provided so long as their cost to the firm per unit of labor is less than the reduced wage rate—so long as labor's evaluation of the fringe benefits lost is greater than the firms' costs. Therefore, the

---

[17]Remember that the demand-for-labor curve is the net of fringe benefits. A reduction in fringe benefits will thereby increase employer's willingness to pay higher wages, which explains the increase in (or shift outward of) the demand for labor.

vertical, upward shift in the supply curve will be greater than the vertical, upward shift in the demand curve. In Figure 11–3, the vertical shift in the supply curve is ac, and the vertical shift in the demand curve is less, ab.[18] It is important to note that the market clears, however, at the minimum wage because of secondary market adjustments in fringe benefits. But it is equally important to see that the market clears at a lower employment level, Q_c instead of Q_2.

In other words, the surplus of labor that conventional analysis suggests exists in face of a minimum-wage law is eliminated by the shifts in the curves. However, labor is worse off because of the wage floor and adjustments in fringe benefits. After the vertical distance between the two supply curves, ac (which, again, is labor's dollar evaluation of the fringe benefits lost because of the minimum wage) is subtracted from the minimum wage W_m, the effective wage paid labor is reduced to W_1, or by $W_m - W_1$. In short, when labor is paid in many forms, a minimum wage reduces, not increases, the effective payment going to affected workers.

Conventional analysis suggests that a minimum wage of W_m will cause employment opportunities for labor to fall to Q_1. The adjustments that employers make to nonmoney conditions of work cause employment opportunities to fall by less, to only Q_c in Figure 11–3.[19]

Case II: Changes in Fringe Benefits that Affect Labor Productivity

Because of the surplus that emerges when money wages are set at a legal minimum, employers can increase the production demands that are placed on their workers. The result can be an increase in the productivity of labor; hence, the demand curve for labor can rise. Workers who have to deal with the labor surplus must either accept the new demands placed on them or retire from the market. The supply curve falls by the workers' evaluation in money terms of the greater production demands.

The graphical analysis is the same as in the preceding case. The demand for labor, as a function of the wage rate, shifts upward, reflecting the greater productivity of labor. The supply curve contracts by the workers' marginal

---

[18]If the vertical distance of the shift in the supply curve were not greater than the vertical distance of the shift in the demand curve, then the change in fringe benefits would have been made even in the absence of the minimum wage.

[19]Indeed, if employers had an infinite number of ways to adjust nonmoney conditions of work, and the market money wage were a small part of total labor payment, the minimum wage would not significantly affect employment opportunities. When employers have an infinite or even a very large number of ways to pay labor, a change in the money wage by law will not significantly affect the payment options open to employers and the ability of the employers to pay the effective market wage.

evaluation of the higher production demands. The employment opportunities for labor can be expected to fall on balance because:

- the minimum wage law increases the cost of labor relative to other variable resources and induces some substitution of other factors for labor and
- the law increases the overall cost of production and reduces the quantity of the final product sold.

If more of other factors of production are employed in lieu of labor, then a lower output can be achieved only with less labor. However, the lower employment level will, as before, be accompanied by a reduction in the effective wage going to labor.

Employers can also react to the higher wage minimum by making changes in workplace conditions, such as air conditioning, which complements labor in production and which, if reduced in use, can lower the productivity of labor.[20] Firms will make such adjustments so long as the change in the money wage rate is greater than the dollar value of the change in labor productivity. These changes will cause the supply curve of labor to shift until it intersects the demand curve at the minimum wage rate. The effective wage and employment opportunities are then reduced as before.

DIFFERENCES IN PERSPECTIVE

This analysis conflicts with conventional textbook treatment of minimum wages in several important respects. First, conventional analysis holds that the effective wage rate increases for some workers, declines for others. As noted, this is because of the implicit assumption that an increase in the minimum-wage rate is equivalent to an increase in the effective wage rate. Our analysis, however, leads to the conclusion that the effective wage rate of *all* workers, including those who retain their jobs in spite of wage minimums, decreases; they are worse off to the extent that employers have the opportunity to adjust working conditions and fringe benefits. For that reason, minimum wages appear patently unfair to those who are covered by them (even by the standards of many of those who promote legislated wage minimums).

Second, conventional analysis predicts that the market does not clear. At any wage above the competitive wage levels, there will supposedly be an "army of unemployed" equal to the difference between the quantity supplied

---

[20]It should be noted that the employer must be careful in cutting back on some fringe benefits like air conditioning. A reduction in air conditioning for workers affected by minimum wage laws can adversely affect higher-paid workers, forcing the firm to raise the wages of the workers who are paid more than the minimum wage. However, this qualification does not affect the thrust of the argument, which is that the employer will make adjustments that are made economical by a legal wage floor.

and the quantity demanded ($Q_3 - Q_1$). From this perspective, some people who want jobs at the higher minimum wage will lose them. The analysis suggests that people who stop work because of the minimum wage do so because they do not want their jobs at the induced lower effective wage rate.

Third, standard textbook treatment of minimum-wage laws suggests that measured unemployment from the imposition of wage controls should be in the range of Q_1 to Q_3. (Actual job losses should be the difference between Q_1 and Q_2.) Recognition of the various adjustments employers can make in response to any surplus of *labor* that develops leads to the conclusion that actual job losses may be quite small[21]; how small depends on the variety of adjustments that employers can make to fringe benefits (nonwage conditions of employment) and the productivity of alternative ways of paying labor, and on the amount of time employers have to adjust to the wage law.[22] From the perspective of this new way of looking at the impact of minimum-wage laws, it is not at all surprising that researchers have found that minimum wage laws have decreased employment opportunities little. This is because they have had, on balance, little downward effect on the effective wage paid covered workers.

Fourth, the standard view of minimum wages assumes that unemployment arises because the number of workers willing to work expands (i.e., workers move up the market supply curve, S_1 in the figures). However, the exact opposite occurs in this new view: the number of workers willing to work falls (i.e., workers move down their supply curve). This is because their effective wage falls. It is also because many, but not necessarily all, of the affected workers have better alternatives in other labor markets, one of which is the market for contraband and other criminal activities.

Minimum-wage laws, in short, make many criminal activities *relatively* profitable by making money-wage deals below the mandated minimum wage illegal. Since minimum wages are likely to lead to a marginal increase in the educational and experience requirements of prospective employees, they will tend to encourage differentially the less-advantaged workers into criminal activities.

Regardless of its initial adverse impact on employment opportunities of the covered workers, the magnitude of the effect of any *real* minimum wage

---

[21]Of course, dispute remains over how small is small, and empirical studies vary in their assessment of the estimated impact of the laws. James Ragan estimated that the minimum wage in existence in 1972 resulted in lost employment for approximately 320,000 teenagers. The youth unemployment rate would have been, in the absence of the minimum-wage law, 3.8 percentage points lower than it was. See James F. Ragan, Jr., "Minimum Wage Legislation and the Youth Labor Market" (St. Louis, Mo.: Center for the Study of American Business, Washington University, 1976).

[22]As indicated in a foregoing footnote, if there were an infinite number of adjustments that employers could make in the nonwage conditions of employment, then an increase in the minimum would, on the margin, have no impact on the effective wage and employment levels. In this extreme case, there would be no loss in labor productivity.

should decrease with time. This is because with the passage of time, employers will discover a growing number of ways to circumvent the laws. In addition, competitive pressures will grow, encouraging more and more employers to find ways of cutting their workers' effective wages.

Fifth, conventional analysis reveals that higher minimum wages place many people (especially those who provide a second family income at the minimum wage) in higher marginal tax brackets. However, the higher tax payments only reduce the net benefit received by those who retain their jobs.

The revisions in the analysis presented here suggest that minimum wages not only throw people into higher tax brackets but also increase the money portion, and hence taxable income portion of their effective wage rate. This means that the *effective* marginal tax rate for people covered by the legal minimum wage is greater than specified in the tax schedules. The after-tax effective income is actually reduced by more than the drop in the effective wage rate; therefore, when the decrease in effective income is recognized, the total marginal tax rate resulting from all explicit and implicit taxes extracted from affected workers can be greater than 100 percent, which hardly seems in accord with the dictates of a progressive tax rate structure.[23]

MAKING WORKERS WORSE OFF: THE EMPIRICAL EVIDENCE

While still controversial, this new perspective on the adverse effects of minimum-wage laws is supported by a growing body of research.

   • Writing in the *American Economic Review*, Masanori Hashimoto found that under the 1967 minimum-wage hike, workers gained 32 cents

---

[23]Finally, it should be noted that textbooks conventionally demonstrate that in monopsonistic labor markets a minimum wage that is imposed at any level between the monopsony wage and the wage at the intersection of the marginal-cost-of-labor curve and the demand-for-labor curve will result in an expansion of employment. Further, it is argued that for any employment level between the monopsony and competitive employment levels, two minimum wage levels will result in the same level of employment. However, if the monopsonistic employer can adjust the nonmoney wage benefits of employment, then the analysis of monopsony markets needs to be revised in two respects. First, as in the competitive model, the supply of labor will tend to contract by more than the demand curve expands. An increase in the minimum wage will, therefore, result in a reduction in nonmoney wages, a decrease in the effective monopsony wage, and a decrease in the employment level. Second, a higher minimum wage will always provide employers with a greater incentive to make nonmoney wage adjustments and will lead to a greater decrease in demand for labor than a lower minimum wage. Therefore, two minimum wage levels cannot result in the same employment levels: the higher minimum wage will always cause a greater reduction in employment opportunities than a lower minimum wage. In summary, the employment effect of minimum wages will tend to be in the same direction in both competitive and monopsonistic labor markets.

in money income but lost 41 cents per hour in training—a net loss of 9 cents an hour in full-income compensation.[24]

• Linda Leighton and Jacob Mincer, in one study, and Belton Fleisher, in another study, came to a similar conclusion: increases in the minimum wage reduce on-the-job training—and, as a result, dampen growth in the real long-run income of covered workers.[25]

• Walter Wessels found that the minimum wages caused retail establishments in New York to increase work demands. In response to a minimum-wage increase, only 714 of the surveyed stores cut back store hours, but 4827 stores reduced the number of workers and/or their employees' hours worked. Thus, in most stores, fewer workers were given fewer hours to do the same work as before.[26]

• The research of Belton Fleisher, William Alpert, and L. F. Dunn shows that minimum-wage increases lead to large reductions in fringe benefits and to worsening working conditions.[27] For example, in the just-mentioned New York study, many stores reduced commission payments, eliminated year-end bonuses, and decreased paid vacation and sick leave. In his study, Professor Alpert found that for every 1 percent increase in the minimum wage, restaurants reduce shift premiums by 3.6 percent, severance pay by 6.9 percent, and sick pay by 3.4 percent.

• If the minimum wage does *not* cause employers to make substantial reductions in nonmoney benefits, then increases in the minimum wage should cause (1) an increase in the labor-force participation rates of covered workers (because workers would be moving up their supply-of-labor curves), (2) a reduction in the rate at which covered workers quit their jobs (because their jobs would then be more attractive), and (3) a significant increase in prices of production processes heavily dependent on covered minimum-wage workers. However, Wessels found little empirical support for such conclusions drawn from conventional theory. Indeed, in general, he found that minimum-wage increases had

---

[24]Masanori Hashimoto, "Minimum Wage Effect on Training to the Job," *American Economic Review* 70 (December 1982), pp. 1070–87.

[25]Linda Leighton and Jacob Mincer, "Effects of Minimum Wages on Human Capital Formation," in *The Economics of Legal Minimum Wages*, ed. Simon Rothenberg (Washington, D.C.: American Enterprise Institute, 1981).

[26]Walter J. Wessels, "Minimum Wages: Are Workers Really Better Off?" (Paper prepared for presentation at a conference on minimum wages, Washington, D.C., National Chamber Foundation, July 29, 1987).

[27]Belton M. Fleisher, *Minimum Wage Regulation in Retail Trade* (Washington, D.C.: American Enterprise Institute, 1981); William T. Alpert, "The Effects of the Minimum Wage on the Fringe Benefits of Restaurant Workers" (Paper, Lehigh University, Bethlehem, Pa., 1983).; and L. F. Dunn, "Nonpecuniary Job Preferences and Welfare Losses among Migrant Agriculture Workers," *American Journal of Agriculture Economics* 67 (May 1985), pp. 257–65.

the exact opposite effect: (1) participation rates went down, (2) quit rates went up, and (3) prices did not rise appreciably—findings consistent only with the view that minimum-wage increases make workers worse off.[28] With regard to quit rates, Wessels writes,

> I could find no industry which had a significant decrease in their quit rates. Two industries had a significant increase in their quit rates. . . . These results are only consistent with a lower full compensation. I also found that quit rates went up more in those industries with the average lowest wage. This shows that the more minimum wages forces employers to raise wages, the more full compensation is reduced. I also found that in the long-run, several industries experienced a significantly large increase in the quit rate: a result only possible if minimum wages reduce full compensation.[29]

Given the findings of various studies done by himself and other researchers, Wessels maintains that it is reasonable to deduce that every 10 percent increase in the hourly minimum wage will make workers 2 percent worse off.[30] This means that an increase in the minimum of $1.30 (equal to the 1987 Congressional proposal) could, on balance, make the covered workers worse off to the tune of 26 cents per hour.

THE POLITICS OF MINIMUM WAGES

Until the advent of the Reagan presidency, minimum-wage laws have enjoyed broad-based political support. The broad-based political support for minimum-wage legislation has been explained with reference to the contrast between, on the one hand, the concentration of the benefits in a relatively small group of affected workers who, in spite of legal minimums, retain their jobs and, on the other hand, the dispersion of the costs among a relatively large group of consumers who are burdened with higher prices for the goods and services they buy.[31] Also, a cost is incurred by some workers who must accept lower wages or unemployment.

The analysis developed here makes the political support for minimum wages somewhat perplexing. This is because it suggests that in the long run all, or practically all, workers in the covered markets are made worse off. Hence, the political support from workers in the targeted markets must stem from the expected *short-run* benefits of wage minimums. However, the long-

---

[28]Wessels, "Minimum Wages: Are Workers Really Better Off?"

[29]Ibid., p. 13.

[30]Ibid., p. 15.

[31]F. G. Stendle, "The Appeal of Minimum Wage Laws and the Invisible Hand in Government," *Public Choice* (Spring 1973), pp. 133–36; William R. Keech, "More on the Vote Winning and Vote Losing Qualities of Minimum Wage Laws," *Public Choice,* Spring 1977, pp. 133–37.

run costs incurred by many workers from legal minimum-money-wage rates that are held permanently above the market-clearing wage will exceed the short-run gains and will diminish seriously the number of people who support the legislation. Indeed, the analysis developed in this chapter suggests that many of the affected workers who may be fully informed about the consequences of minimum wages are likely to be political opponents of the legislation.

The political support for minimum-wage laws must, it would appear, emanate to a large extent from groups other than those in the targeted markets. These beneficiaries may include workers in labor markets that are not covered by the legal minimum and that, as a result of the legal minimums, experience an increase in their employment opportunities. On these grounds, active political support by unions for minimum wage laws can be appreciated. Further, producers of capital equipment who experience an increase in the demand for their products should also be supporters of minimum-wage laws.

Still, the extensive support that minimum-wage laws enjoy in many countries is difficult to explain, especially when it is recognized that all, or almost all, affected workers may be made worse off as a consequence of the law and that the employed workers must pay unemployment compensation to the affected workers who decide not to work at the prevailing *effective* wage. Perhaps, those persons who are covered by the legislation attribute the increase in their money wage rate to the "humanitarian concerns" of their political leaders and blame decreases in their nonmoney employment benefits on their employers.

Because of the myriad forces operating in the marketplace, affected employees may not be able to make the connection between the increases in their money wage rate and the decreases in their nonmoney employment benefits. Making such a connection may be particularly difficult when nonmoney benefits of employment are on the increase and when rises in the minimum wage only restrict the increase.

Perhaps the most powerful (but theoretically unsettling) explanation for the political acceptance of wage minimums is that people who support them are simply ignorant of their effects. Economists do not seem to have fully understood the market consequences of the laws. In fact, conventional supply and demand analysis of wage minimums may have misled many politicians into believing that such laws are an effective way of helping one segment of their constituency at the expense of another, smaller segment.[32]

---

[32]As an aside, regardless of the reason the government sees fit to control money wages, it is interesting to note that the minimum-wage laws may be one of several factors that induced federal and state governments to attempt to control, through regulatory agencies, the health, noise, and safety conditions of work.

CONCLUDING COMMENTS

The standard analysis of minimum-wage legislation was, perhaps, quite applicable to labor markets for menial labor when it was first developed, a time in which the money wage probably represented a substantially larger portion of the effective wage than it now does. And, as noted, the conventional analysis may still be fully applicable to the limited number of jobs for which money wages is the only form of compensation and for which changes in skill and production demands are impractical. However, times have changed: nonmoney benefits of employment loom much more prominent in workers' compensation than they used to, and theory must accommodate these adjustments in labor compensation.

This is especially true since jobs have become more technical, requiring more on-the-job training. And training can be construed as a fringe benefit of employment. Such a benefit can, because of minimum-wage laws, be less available to lower-income workers. With the surplus that emerges in response to minimum-wage laws, employers can increase the educational and training demands of their employees, requiring workers to secure the necessary education at a higher expense from off-the-job sources. The minimum-wage laws effectively bar workers from paying through wage reductions for on-the-job training. And this is the reason that Professor Richard Epstein argued that "a minimum wage of zero is far too high. This is because it would deny unskilled workers the right to pay for their on-the-job training and lead to their continued impoverishment."[33] It makes perfectly reasonable employment behavior uneconomical by effectively making it illegal.

The tax code and rising tax rates over time have, no doubt, been a major reason why a growing percentage of workers' compensation has come in nonmoney forms.[34] The adjustments in the relative share of nonmoney compensation in employment may have lessened the effectiveness of minimum wages as a redistributive policy tool. They have also increased their unfairness since they deny tax breaks and income to some of the lower-income workers in this economy.

The central lesson of conventional economic analysis of minimum-wage rates is that they promote inefficiency—that is, they reduce the nation's income pie subject to distribution among all citizens. The central lesson of this revised view of minimum-wage theory is that mandated minimum wages may even promote a degree of unfairness—that is, on balance, they reduce the portion of the income pie going to lower-income workers. Minimum-wage

---

[33]This is a paraphrase of comments made by Richard Epstein, University of Chicago law professor, in a political economy seminar at Washington University in St. Louis, January 23, 1986.

[34]Fringe benefits became a dramatically more important source of worker compensation during World War II when money wages were strictly controlled. Fringe benefits became a device for circumventing the *maximum*-wage controls.

laws can be opposed—as they should be opposed—because they have perverse effects.

There is, however, a much broader lesson to be learned from the nation's experience with minimum-wage laws: Well-intended controls of prices can have unintended but ultimately perverse consequences. This is because under such controls arrangements, markets are not controlled very effectively in their entirety (and cannot be controlled without the major problems encountered in centralized control systems). The pressures of competition still escape in some form, often to the detriment of those the controls are intended to help.

QUESTIONS TO PONDER

1. Who are most likely to lose their jobs as a consequence of a hike in the minimum wage?
2. Suppose Congress requires firms to provide health insurance for their employees. What will the effects of such laws be?
3. What would be the effects of a two-tier minimum-wage system, one in which workers over age 20 are paid more than workers under age 20?

CHAPTER 12

The Market for Pollution

The process by which a previously "free" natural resource enters a market—that is, the process by which scarcity is recognized, rights established, defined and guaranteed, and the market created—is not an easy one. For this reason, any market in air emission rights may be somewhat limited, perhaps for a considerable time, perhaps permanently. But the market for land is also limited. Owners of land may be required to follow performance standards and zoning ordinances. Excavation, mining, sewage, and waste disposal requirements further reduce the number of potential property rights that are subject to free market forces. Moreover, in some places land is owned by the state and leased for controlled uses. Still, there is a functioning market for land in which significant rights are freely traded.

Bruce Yandle[1]

Real estate agents provide a valuable economic service. They "make" a market for buyers and sellers for houses, land, and other real property; they in effect bring buyers and sellers together in order that efficient exchanges can be made. Although the agents are paid a commission for their services (which may be as high as 6 to 7 percent of the selling price), the buyers and sellers are presumably better off financially and in other ways by going to a real estate firm than by not going.

If the seller were not better off, why would the seller list property with the real estate agent? The seller presumably thinks the agent, with greater marketing ability and appeal to a wider market, can secure a price for the property that at least covers the agent's commission or can save the seller the time and expense of selling the property through word of mouth or ads in the local newspaper. The buyer is presumably better off by going through a real estate firm because he or she can save a considerable amount of time and trouble in searching the market for the type and style of house desired. Any extra price the buyer pays, because of the commission, can be construed as payment for the services provided by the real estate agent.

---

[1]Bruce Yandle, "The Emerging Market in Air Pollution Rights," *Regulation*, July/August 1978, p. 29.

The services of a real estate agent can be said to be economically beneficial partially because they arise voluntarily, as individuals seek to trade and maximize their own economic positions. The agent serves the economic function of reducing the cost of information search to buyers and sellers who happen to be in the market for property at the same time.

At times, the real estate agent may speculate in the market he or she creates. An agent may buy parcels of land, for example, at what he or she considers to be a low price, hold on to the land, and sell the land to someone else at a later date for a higher price. The agent's profit is the difference between the purchase price and the sale price (minus the interest that could have been earned had the agent put the money into a perfectly secure savings account and minus the risk cost of holding onto property that has a chance of going down as well as up). The agent in this case still provides an economically beneficial service: he or she moves property from someone who values it less (the person who sells in the current time period) to someone who values it more (the person who buys in the future time period). The trade between the buyer and the seller is intertemporal (covers a span of time), but both parties are still better off, else the trade would not occur.

Markets are efficient because the trades that are made within the markets are mutually beneficial, because the trades reallocate resources (or more properly, rights to resources) from less valuable to more productive uses. The result of free exchanges made in markets is an expansion of national products and income. Prices are important because they guide or direct resources into their relatively more valuable and productive uses and because they give people—buyers and sellers—the information they need to have to determine how and what they will produce and consume.

What does all this have to do with "pollution," a word used prominently in the title of this chapter? Through the Clean Air Act of 1970, Congress set national standards for ambient air quality (standards for the quality of air surrounding any given place). In doing that, Congress set standards for the amount of pollution that can be emitted into the atmosphere. It officially recognized air as an economic resource, which has alternative uses—for example, as a source of oxygen for living things, as a garbage disposal system (which is the function the air serves when smoke is emitted), and as a means of clear vision for watching a sunset.

By setting the pollution standards, Congress effectively established limited property rights to the atmosphere. Stated somewhat differently, although the intent of the standards was to reduce pollution, a goal that the standards will accomplish, Congress, through the Environmental Protection Agency (EPA), allocated to some producers the rights to emit certain limited amounts of pollutants into the air. Congress gave the polluters rights to pollute. It also allocated to the general public the rights to a certain level of air quality for breathing; these latter rights will be protected, presumably, by the EPA's enforcement of the pollution standards.

Land rights were once acquired by conquest and by first-come-first-served homestead programs in the eighteenth and nineteenth centuries as well as by purchase. Land is now bought and sold in real estate markets because it has alternative uses, and the market is seen as a reasonably efficient means of allocating, on a continuing basis, the land to more valuable and productive uses. Through the Clean Air Act people have acquired rights to air, which leads us to wonder: Should we not expect a market, similar to the one in land, to emerge to redistribute the rights that have been allocated to the air? Will the market in air rights that emerges contribute to expanding the national product and income in much the same way that the market for land rights does? Should we control any market in air or pollution rights that emerges? These are the questions with which this chapter is concerned. Before we can answer them, however, we must consider the initial state in which the air rights are distributed.

THE ECONOMIC BASIS OF POLLUTION

Not all pollution of the atmosphere is necessarily bad. The airways do have some absorptive capacity. They can absorb and or carry away some pollutants, such as sulfur dioxide, without the surrounding animal and plant life being affected or without the sensibilities of people being disturbed. This is, in other words, some level of discarding of waste that cannot be detected by anyone. Pollution becomes a problem only when there is too much waste being discarded at more or less the same time in the same places and when people prefer to use the atmosphere for some other, more valuable purpose.[2]

In past years, use of the atmosphere for disposal of waste has effectively been free to the user: the firm that dumps sulfur dioxide into the atmosphere has not had to pay for the privilege. It has not had to "buy" the air rights away from someone else. This is because the airways have been considered common (as opposed to private) property to be used by anyone at will. No one has had rights to the airways; therefore, no one has had the right to exclude anyone from use of the airways.

At a zero price—which does not reflect the opportunity value of the airways—polluters have used and abused the available resource; they have released in many areas so much sulfur dioxide that some people have, at certain times of the day, experienced eye irritation and have had to pay for medication, and other people have had to incur the cost of repainting their homes and business buildings. The people who have wanted to see a clear

---

[2]For additional discussion on the economic source of pollution, see Thomas D. Crocker and A. J. Rogers III, *Environmental Economics* (Hinsdale, Ill.: Dryden Press, 1971), chaps. 1–4; Hugh H. Macaulay and Bruce Yandle, *Environmental Use and the Market* (Lexington, Mass.: Lexington Books, 1977), chaps. 1–6.

(pollution-free) sunset have not been able to buy that right, even though they may have been willing to pay the polluters in total a sum sufficient to entice the polluters away from using the airways as a dumping ground. A market in air rights has not existed because the rights to the air have not been legally defined and, therefore, trades (which, of necessity, are trades in rights) could not occur.

There are probably many industrial and governmental polluters who care very little about society's welfare. They simply do not care if their actions harm or impose costs on others. However, when property is held in common there are probably many people who pollute but do not perceive that their emissions of pollutants are significantly harming others. They may rightfully reason that the amount of waste they, themselves, dump into the atmosphere is well within the tolerance level of the atmosphere and cannot be detected by other people. If they restrict their pollution, no one will materially benefit by their actions. The rational course of action: make full use of the atmosphere, which common property rights allow.

If all people within a given region follow the same logic and emit a small amount of pollutants, the result can be overuse of the atmosphere, a real environmental problem. The central problem of dealing with pollution is now evident; it is a problem of finding a way of getting people to curtail collectively their use of the airways, to restrict the total amount of pollutants being emitted into the airways in order that the atmosphere can be used for other, more valuable purposes. The task is one of bringing about the *optimum* level of pollution, which is another way of saying the task is one of achieving the optimum level of production of goods and services that people want. Seen this way, the problem of pollution corresponds to a problem of too few of the goods and services (including cleanliness) people want most.

In the area of environmental quantity, the government confronts two problems. First, there is the problem of determining what the optimum level of pollution is, which is a difficult task at best, given the deficiencies of the political system in determining people's relative values. Second, the government faces the problem of achieving whatever level of the pollution is established as the optimum. There are two basic ways by which the optimum level of pollution can be achieved: (1) direct regulation of the amount of pollutants that firms, homes, and governments can emit into the atmosphere, and (2) the distribution of pollution rights by some sort of governmental auctioning (pricing) system and allowing the rights to be traded at market changing prices.

As we will show in the next section, the selling of pollution rights is normally held by economists to be the more efficient means of controlling pollution. As we will see also, that conclusion holds only so long as the government does not allow pollution standards as rights to be sold in markets, which will very likely emerge when government attempts to regulate pollution directly.

EFFICIENCY IN POLLUTION REDUCTION

To evaluate the relative efficiency of the two methods of reducing pollution, consider an example of five firms that are emitting sulfur dioxide into the atmosphere of a given area and causing a pollution problem. Since the reduction of the pollution is an economic good that must be produced at a cost, assume that the marginal cost of cutting back on the units of sulfur dioxide emitted for each firm rises as successive units of sulfur are eliminated. Further, assume that the firms differ in the cost they must incur to curtail their discharge of sulfur dioxide. These assumptions are incorporated into the construction of Table 12–1 for firms A through E. The table shows that for firm A, for example, the cost it must incur to eliminate its discharge of the first unit of sulfur dioxide is $50; the cost of cutting out the next unit of sulfur dioxide is $100. And the marginal cost of reducing pollution for firm A, and all other firms, rises for each successive unit.

Although the table contains a hypothetical example, the structure of the table is reasonably descriptive of the conditions in most real-world pollution abatement problems. Real-world firms do not operate in exactly the same conditions as each other. They do not use exactly the same resources in production, and they differ in the technology they have available to reduce pollution. Whether firms are faced with the problem of producing actual goods and services for consumption by customers or the problem of producing clean air, they confront a technological fact of production processes: increasing marginal costs.

TABLE 12–1   Cost of Reducing Units of Sulfur Dioxide

	A	B	C	D	E
Cost of eliminating:					
First unit	$ 50	$ 100	$100	$ 300	$ 500
Second unit	100	300	200	500	1000
Third unit	200	900	300	700	1500
Set standard					
Fourth unit		400	2700	400	900	2000
Fifth unit		800	8100	500	1100	2500

Cost of reducing air pollution by set standards		Cost of reducing air pollution by price mechanism	
Cost to A of eliminating 3 units	$ 350	Cost to A of eliminating 4 units	$ 750
Cost to B of eliminating 3 units	1,300	Cost to B of eliminating 2 units	400
Cost to C of eliminating 3 units	600	Cost to C of eliminating 5 units	1,500
Cost to D of eliminating 3 units	1,500	Cost to D of eliminating 3 units	1,500
Cost to E of eliminating 3 units	3,000	Cost to E of eliminating 1 unit	500
Total cost	$6,750	Total cost	$4,650

Now, suppose the EPA determines that for the area in question the optimum level of pollution is 10 units of sulfur dioxide in the atmosphere. Suppose further that the EPA seeks to achieve the optimum level of pollution by prohibiting any firm from emitting more than 2 units of sulfur dioxide at the marginal costs that are specified. The total costs each firm must incur to achieve the set limit of 2 units of sulfur dioxide emitted are indicated in the lower half of the table. Firm *A*, for instance, must incur a relatively modest cost of $350 (derived by adding together $50, $100, and $200, the marginal costs of the first 3 units eliminated). The total cost incurred by all firms in the cleanup is $6,750 by the set-standard method.

As opposed to setting the standard that must be followed by each firm, the government can alternatively elect to control pollution by selling off 10 *rights* to *pollute*. These rights to pollute may be thought of as *tickets*, each of which gives the firm the right to dump a unit of waste into the atmosphere: the more tickets the firm purchases, the more sulfur dioxide the firm can emit into the airways—the more it can pollute—and the more cleanup costs the firm can avoid.

Although this proposal may not sound very attractive, remember that the government ultimately has control over how many tickets are sold initially—how much pollution occurs. It can achieve what it considers to be the optimum level of pollution by appropriately restricting the number of tickets it sells. Under either method—the set standards or the pricing system—the government keeps the level of pollution the same—10 units of sulfur dioxide in the area. Under the pricing system, however, the firms that want to avoid the cost of cleaning up the environment must bid for the tickets. The price will effectively rise until the quantity of rights, or tickets, demanded is exactly equal to 10.

The potential market for pollution rights can be illustrated by standard supply and demand curves in Figure 12–1. The supply curve in this case is determined by government policymakers, who establish the desired pollution level for the area. In this example, the supply of pollution rights is assumed to be invariant with the price, meaning that the supply curve in the graph must be a vertical straight line; as the price goes up, the number of pollution rights remains unchanged.

The demand for pollution rights, on the other hand, is derived from the costs that firms must incur in order to clean up the pollution they emit. As the price of pollution rights goes down, firms will individually and collectively demand a larger number of pollution rights. This is because the lower price on the pollution rights will mean that it will be cheaper for the firms to buy the pollution rights than to incur the cost of cleanup. The downward-sloping curve in Figure 12–1 fairly accurately describes the market demand curve for pollution rights; it is based on the figures in Table 12–1.

The market clearing price in the figure is approximately $750. (Actually, from the data contained in the table, the price can be anything between $700 and $800.) The market clearing price, or equilibrium price, is the price at

FIGURE 12-1

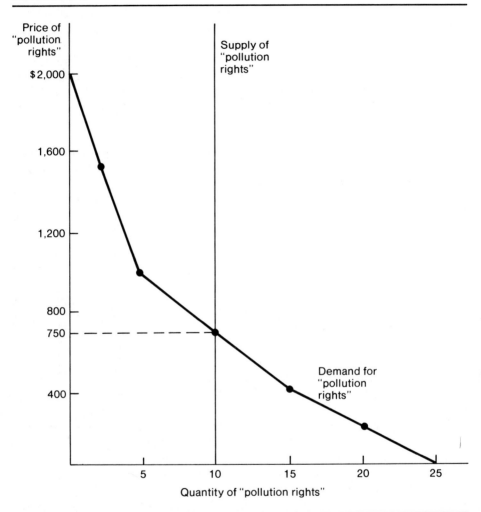

which the quantity of pollution rights demanded is exactly equal the number of rights made available for sale by the government. Who will buy those rights, who will clean up the pollution, and what is the cost of cleanup under the pricing system? Those are the questions that can now be addressed.

At a price of $750 per ticket, firm A is willing to buy one and only one ticket. This is because at that price it is cheaper for the firm to incur the cost of cleanup of its first 4 units (cleanup costs of those first 4 are $50, $100, $200, and $400) than to buy the tickets at $750 each. The firm is better off paying $750 for one ticket than incurring the $800 cost of cleaning up the fifth unit of pollution emitted. Through a similar line of reasoning, we can conclude that firm B will buy three tickets (clean up 2 units of pollution), firm C will buy no tickets, firm D will buy two tickets, and firm E will buy four tickets.

The economic cost of the cleanup must be measured by the value of the actual resources that go into the cleanup. Those values are approximated by the dollar expenditures of the various firms on the pollution cleanup, not the dollar expenditures on the tickets that give firms the right to pollute. The dollars spent on the tickets do not represent real resources; they represent only a transfer of purchasing power from the firms to the government, which sells the tickets.

Accordingly, the economic cost of reducing air pollution to 10 units is $750 for firm A, $400 for B, $1,500 each for C and D, and $500 for E. The total cost of the cleanup is $4,650, which, you may notice, is significantly below the cost of the cleanup when set standards are used ($6,750). In short, the pricing system is the more economical—that is, cost effective and technically efficient—means of achieving the socially desired (or government established) level of pollution. It is also the more economical way of achieving the socially desired level of goods and services. Indeed, because the cost of cleanup is lower for the pricing system, more goods and services can be produced when the pricing system is used than when the set-standard system is used.

This is the reasoning that leads economists to argue that if pollution is to be reduced, it should be reduced by selling rights to pollute (which implies the trading of pollution). Again, that method—and the wording used—may not sound very attractive; however, remember that when the government sets standards of pollution, it effectively gives away rights to pollute. Each of the firms in Table 12–1 is told, via the set standards that are announced, that it must reduce its sulfur dioxide by 3 units. By the same token, each of the firms is given the right to dump 2 units of sulfur dioxide into the atmosphere.

Any comparison of the two methods of pollution control, therefore, leads not only to the question of relative costs, but also to the question of whether or not the government should be in the business of giving away, free of charge, rights to the atmosphere, which has many different uses. Why should polluters be given those rights? Clearly, rights to pollute may be needed to continue production, but that is not an argument for giving away the rights. One can argue that land is needed in many processes, but that is not an argument for giving away, free of charge, rights to the public land in national forests. Use of the pricing system for distributing the pollution rights allows different potential users to bid for those rights, to express in a market setting the relative values that they place on having the rights to pollute. In this way, the rights can be allocated to the most valuable and productive uses.

THE EMERGENCE OF A MARKET FOR POLLUTION

Suppose the government decided to control pollution by way of set standards. Does it follow that the cost of cleanup will remain at the relatively high level discussed in the preceding section? Not necessarily. If the standards that are distributed can be traded among the producers, then not only can mutually beneficial trades be completed among the producers, but the cost of the cleanup can be lowered.

Notice in Table 12–1 that firm E under the set-standard control system must eliminate 3 units of sulfur dioxide. That firm has to incur marginal costs of $500, $1,000 and $1,500 for each successive unit eliminated; and it should be willing to pay something less than those amounts in order to acquire the right to emit units of sulfur dioxide. Further, notice also that firm A, under the set standard, has to incur the cost of cleaning up 3 units of pollution. However, like all the other firms, A can emit—has the right to emit—2 units of sulfur dioxide, and it costs A only $400 to eliminate the fourth unit of sulfur dioxide. A mutually beneficial trade can obviously be struck between A and E: E is willing to pay as much as $1,500 for the right to emit one additional unit of pollution, while A is willing to accept anything over $400 for the right that it holds (because of the standards that are set). If the price of a pollution right is set at, say, $750, then E gives up $750 for the emission right (for part of A's standard): but E does not have to incur the $1,500 cost of cleaning up that unit of pollution. E gains to the tune of $750 ($1,500 − $750). A, on the other hand, by giving up one of its rights, has to eliminate an additional unit of pollution; however, it received $750 from E and has to spend only $400 to eliminate the unit. Moreover, the cost of achieving the officially established optimum pollution level is reduced by $1,000 (which is equal to the $1,500 cost E would have incurred minus the $400 cost that A does incur).

Additional trades can be made. E finds it worthwhile to buy pollution rights from A and/or C. How many rights E buys depends, of course, on their price. Furthermore, B and D are willing to enter the bargaining process for rights that are effectively held by A and C. The competition in the emerging market causes the price to move toward the market clearing price of $750 depicted in Figure 12–1.

The end result of the emerging market is the distribution of rights that would have developed if the government had sold the rights at auction initially; and the total cost of achieving a pollution level of 10 units of sulfur dioxide is $4,650, a reduction of $2,100 from what it would have been if the market transactions had not developed. The only difference between the case in which standards are set and a market emerges and the case in which the government initially sells off the pollution rights is that under the former system the government does not receive any of the income transfer that results from the trades. The income transfer is reaped by firms A and C.[3]

---

[3]This way of distributing the spoils of pollution controls is either good or bad, depending on how you think the funds will be used by the firms (their workers and owners) and the government (its workers, taxpayers, and beneficiaries of government programs).

CONCLUDING COMMENTS

Should an emerging market in pollution rights be controlled? To the extent that rights to anything, land or pollution emissions, must be defined and guaranteed, the market for pollution rights must be supervised and controlled by government. In order to ensure that the officially established level of pollution is achieved on a continuing basis, the government must keep watch on the amount of pollution emitted into the atmosphere. (The government must ensure that the airways do not revert back to de facto common property by its failure to enforce the rights that are distributed.)

Beyond that, however, we have demonstrated that transfer of rights between buyers and sellers is beneficial to the parties and contributes to economic efficiency; the transfers reduce the cost of achieving the goals established by the government. Because fewer resources are involved in reducing pollution, more resources are available for the production of goods and services. Indeed, with exchanges allowed to occur, some of the resources that would have been used to achieve a given pollution level can be used to clean up the air further. Indeed, EPA is gradually loosening its controls on the trade of pollution rights and introducing other methods of more flexible pollution controls.[4]

Granted, trades in pollution rights mean that the rights distributed free by government will carry a market value. The persons or firms that obtained the rights will experience a wealth increase because of the market that emerges. The distribution of the wealth that occurs may, by some ethical code, be deemed unfair or unjust. The unfairness or injustice of the resulting wealth distribution is a consequence, it should be stressed, of the way in which the pollution rights were initially distributed, not a consequence of market exchanges. As we have pointed out in the chapter, there is no compelling economic reason for giving away rights to the air any more than for giving away farming rights to land in national forests. (Also, so long as the rights that are distributed can be resold, there is no compelling reason for not giving them away.) The point of the discussion is that the ethical question of the fairness of the wealth distribution must be dealt with prior to the distribution of the wealth. Given the initial distribution of rights—given its fairness or lack of fairness—economic analysis can show only that resources are saved, that the national income and output levels are raised, by free market exchanges in existing rights.

Without question, existing firms that are doing the polluting have an economic reason for favoring set-standards systems of pollution control: they are the ones likely to receive the free pollution rights when they are distrib-

---

[4]See Michael H. Levin, "Building a Better Bubble at EPA," *Regulation*, March/April 1985, pp. 32–42.

uted initially, and they are the ones that will then experience a wealth increase when market in pollution rights emerge.

QUESTIONS TO PONDER

1. People are able to buy land and hold it in an undeveloped state. They effectively bank land. Should firms that buy pollution rights be permitted to bank pollution rights? If firms do decide to bank pollution rights, will the banking contribute to economic efficiency?

2. "By allowing firms to trade their pollution rights, less pollution can be acquired at less cost; that is to say, the officially established pollution level can be 'tightened-up' with the same cost being imposed on society." Do you agree or disagree with that statement?

3. If businesses are permitted to sell pollution rights, would you expect brokers—that is, real estate agents—in pollution rights to emerge? Why? If they did emerge, would they contribute to the efficiency with which the officially established pollution level is achieved?

4. If pollution rights are traded, should the government impose a price ceiling on the pollution rights? Would such a control system contribute to the efficient allocation of resources?

5. What reasons can you give for expecting the market system to work less well in the allocation of pollution rights than in, say the allocation of cattle? Why might governments be reluctant to allow markets in pollution rights to emerge?

CHAPTER 13

Free To Lose: The Economic Value of Failure

Success is the professed goal of every economy, and the U.S. economy has had its successes. Those successes are vividly portrayed in statistical terms through the historical records of growth in gross national product, industrial production, employment, personal income, labor force participation —and in more human terms through the emancipation of many Americans from the grip of poverty and through the elevation of many others to riches.

But failures also are endemic to the U.S. economy. A continual flow of news reports on bankruptcies, plant closings, layoffs, stock market slumps, industrial accidents, financial losses, and persistent poverty makes the fact of pervasive failures indubitably clear. The failure of American firms to compete successfully with their foreign rivals, which concerns so many Washington politicians, is only one dimension of the problem of failure that pervades any market economy. After acknowledging the successes of the new-found capitalistic policies in contemporary China, Charles Krauthammer in a *Washington Post* column lamented that in the United States,

> however, many hands are wringing. They belong to steelworkers, farmers, and now, savings-and-loan depositors. The ravaged steel towns, the bankrupt farmers, the locked-out savers evoke Depression images. When seventy-one Ohio S & Ls were closed last week by order of the governor, pointed reference was made to the fact that this is the biggest bank closing since the thirties.[1]

In 1983 more than 31,000 commercial and industrial business failed in the United States. In 1985 the number of business failures was above 57,000 (one every 9 minutes). And the number of business failures during that year, and the previous two or three years, was up dramatically from the level of the 1970s.[2] Thousands of farms also went under each year in the mid-1980s,

---

[1] Charles Krauthammer, "One Cheer for Capitalism," in *Cutting Edges* (New York: Random House, 1985), p. 91 (reprinted from the *Washington Post*, March 22, 1985).

[2] These figures are based on a Dun & Bradstreet Corporation study reported in March 1986. The number of business failures was just over 52,000 in 1984. "Bankruptcies Increase 9.6%," *New York Times*, March 3, 1986, p. 31.

while tens of thousands more teetered on the brink of bankruptcy during each of the years.

However frequent they may be, business and farm failures represent only a minor fraction (less than 15 percent) of the bankruptcies filed annually in the country, which in 1985 totaled more than a third of a million. In the early 1980s bankruptcy filings were also substantially up, running at twice the pace experienced during the late 1960s and 1970s. Clearly, business failures during the first half of the 1980s were a serious problem that was getting worse.

The prevalence and consequences of economic failure can also be captured in the number of unemployed and dislocated workers. A rising trend in the number and percentage of American workers unemployed has emerged over the past two decades. Although the unemployment rate was falling in the mid-1980s, there were still more than 8 million Americans unemployed at the end of 1985. And the unemployment rate at the start of the recoveries during the 1969–1981 period was ebbing upward.[3]

Between 1981 and January 1986, 11.1 million Americans lost their jobs because of "a plant closing, an employer going out of business, [or] a layoff from which . . . (the worker in question) was not recalled."[4] Over five million of these workers had significant tenure (more than three years) at their jobs, causing them to be officially characterized as "dislocated."

For most of the dislocated workers, their employment troubles probably were not the direct consequence of their own individual actions; most were dislocated for reasons beyond their individual control. Most were, in other words, involuntarily unemployed, meaning most had clearly "failed" in a very real and personal sense in the complicated process of skill and job selection.[5]

---

[3]During the four recessions between 1969 and 1981, the following unemployment rates were measured at the cycle peaks:

Cycle Peak	Lowest Rate
Dec. 1969	3.4%
Nov. 1973	4.6%
Jan. 1980	5.6%
July 1981	7.2%

See Henry F. Meyer, "The Rising Natural Rate of Unemployment," *Wall Street Journal* (February 25, 1985), p. 1.

[4]An additional 2.3 million workers lost jobs for seasonal reasons or various other reasons that could not be easily classified. William J. Gainer, *Dislocated Workers: Extent of Closures, Layoffs, and the Public and Private Response,* GAO/HDR-86-116BR (Washington, D.C.: U.S. Government Printing Office, July 1986), p. 1.

[5]Failures that have important economic consequences are, of course, rampant throughout the U.S. social structure. In 1981, there were more than 100,000 deaths from accidents, nearly 21,000 suicides, 70,000 unwanted births, 1.2 million divorces, and almost a quarter of a

While flawed to one extent or another as descriptions of misguided economic decisions, all such statistics reported often in the daily press speak eloquently of the pervasiveness of individual and collective failures. Most such failures, however, have economic consequences, sometimes dire ones.

Unfortunately, it is all too easy to dwell on the dark side of the force of failure, that is, on the pain that people feel when faced with failures. Such pain is brought to life on the television screen when fired or laid-off workers, the homeless, foreclosed farmers, and airline crash victims are interviewed for the nightly news programs. The emotional appeal of these failures for governmental remedies is indeed intense and compelling, so much so that policymakers can hardly overlook them for both humanitarian and opportunistic political reasons. Confronted with the facts of failures, they are frequently driven to "do something," or they stall for time in the hope that the observed pain of these failures will fade with time.

Our purpose in this chapter is not to dispute the economic hardship and personal pain that is felt when failures occur. Nor is our purpose to suggest that all failures are deserved, just, or fair. Of course not. Rather we intend to balance public discussions of failures by recasting past arguments that lead to an important but frequently overlooked point: While failures may often be undeserved, unjust, and unfair, the system that spawns them may still be just and fair.[6] Nevertheless, democracies have a built-in political bias toward mitigating short-run failures and, in the process, creating long-run mischief. We make these points by first observing that many failures not only have a rational foundation but are often, but not always, expected by economic agents, private citizens and consumers, private investors, and government policymakers.

So while failures are avoided wherever and whenever possible, many failures remain unavoidable and often accompany successes. Indeed, failures often inspire future successes. In other words, contrary to what is suggested in the media and public policy debates, failures cannot be reasonably isolated from successes. This bright side of the force of economic failure—which attributes some economic value to economic failure—is the central concern of this chapter.

---

million court cases brought before the U.S. district courts (the vast majority of which involved disputes over contracts and property). Only about a third of high school graduates that year went on to college, and a mere 30 percent of the 18-year-olds four years earlier graduated from college in 1981. In 1984, 435 congressional candidates and 35 senatorial candidates lost their elections, and consumers bought millions of products that were defective, unsafe, or unusable. In 1985, a streak of unprecedented airline crashes claimed the lives of more than 2,000 passengers.

[6]While their arguments may not have been cast in justice or fairness terms, Joseph Schumpeter and Frank Knight have articulated many of the points repeated and recast here. See Joseph A. Schumpeter, *Capitalism, Socialism, and Democracy,* 2nd ed. (New York: Harper and Brothers Publishers, 1947) and Frank H. Knight, *Risk, Uncertainty, and Profit* (Chicago: University of Chicago Press, 1971).

THE ECONOMY OF FAILURE

To imagine any advantage at all to observed failures, it must be understood that failures arise because of the basic human condition of scarcity, because of the human search for rational results and greater rewards, and because of the capitalistic system. These sources of failures are considered in turn.

The Failures of Scarcity

Economists have long noted that because people's wants far outstrip their ability to produce, choices involving the allocation of resources are unavoidable. That point, while patently obvious, is fundamental because it acknowledges that not all goods and services can be produced. Nor is it reasonable to expect that all goods currently produced will continue to be produced. Some producers will fail to secure the necessary resources to start production. Others, already in production, will fail to retain the resources they have. In other words, choice and the necessity of allocation make failures absolutely certain, absolutely unavoidable. However, it cannot be forgotten that while some firms fail (those that do not obtain or cannot retain the limited resources), others will succeed.

The pervasiveness of scarcity ensures the pervasiveness of failure. This is because of the pervasiveness of success, that is, the ability of some to secure resources and, at the same time, deny resources to others. Firms fold, plants close, and workers are unemployed because strategic resources are reallocated to other more successful firms, plants, and workers. Indeed, the failures of some increase the probability of success for those remaining in the market. The failures cause (1) a release of resources that can then be employed (at possibly lower resource prices) by the remaining competitors and (2) a reduction in the supply of goods and services produced that can then be sold at higher prices, thus on more profitable terms.

The growth in the number of business failures during the early 1980s is, without question, partially a product of the twin recessions, spawned in large measure by government policies meant to reduce inflation. However, many failures were also spurred by the emergence of new firms and the expansion of established ones. There has been, for example, substantial growth in new incorporations, although the number of new incorporations, admittedly, is only a rough measure of the emergence of new businesses.[7] In the mid-1980s, there were twice as many new corporations as there were in 1970.

The businesses that emerged in the 1970s and 1980s caused the failures of others by driving up the price of resources to the point where some firms

---

[7]Many businesses arise that are never incorporated and many new incorporations are established businesses. Also, many companies are incorporated for legal and tax reasons, not to produce a new good or service.

were no longer competitive.[8] The textile and apparel industries, centered primarily in the Carolinas, have been racked by plant closings and layoffs for the past decade. Part of the problem for those industries has been the expansion of other kinds of industries in the Carolinas that has forced up labor prices paid by the textile and apparel firms. In addition, textile firms have become more productive with the introduction of new technology, putting downward pressures on textile and apparel prices. Textile firms have failed, in other words, because they have been unable to compete with their more productive domestic counterparts.

Relative Performance and Failures

The economic source of failure cannot, in a world of scarcity, be a matter of absolute performance levels. The firms that fold may be well organized, the plants that close may be very efficient and the workers unemployed may be quite productive in what they do. They can still fail because others are even better organized, more efficient, and more productive—and this is not an altogether unwelcome (or unexpected) result. The fundamental goal of every economy is presumably to overcome scarcity, and the process of failure is driven by people's efforts to get the most possible from the available resources.

Policymakers often lament the impact of foreign imports on domestic production, and relate the imports to plant closures and unemployment. For example, textile and apparel trade restrictions have been proposed on the proposition that expanding imports caused the closing of as many as 250 textile and apparel plants between 1980 and 1985, robbing American textile and apparel workers in the United States of hundreds of thousands of jobs.[9] The unemployment and plant-closing problem faced by the textile industry is presumed to have been created solely by imports (made competitive by low wages paid foreign workers).

In fact, economists have long argued that the direction of trade (what is imported and exported) is predicated on *comparative,* not absolute, cost advantages. While the textile and apparel industries blame foreigners, the industries probably have failed in their competition with other domestic producers for control over the available and limited resources in the domestic economy. As stressed in every introductory economics course, however, other American producers are in effect the competitive culprit because they are *relatively* more cost effective in production than are the textile and apparel industries

---

[8]We can anticipate also that an increase in the number of business failures will accompany, with a lag, an increase in the number of business formations, because of the lack of experience of the businesses that emerge.

[9]U.S. Congress, Senate, "Textile and Apparel Trade and Enforcement Act of 1985," S. 680 (February 26, 1985).

(or any other industry that has difficulty with foreign imports). They are more successful in capturing the country's comparative advantage in production and in being able to export (and not face import competition).[10]

To see this point with greater clarity, consider the following hypothetical data on the production capability of the United States and Hong Kong in textiles and beef:

	Textiles	Beef
United States	100	50
Hong Kong	40	10

The United States is more productive than Hong Kong in both textiles and beef. (In a given amount of time, the United States can produce 100 units of textiles while Hong Kong can produce only 40. Similarly, the United States can produce 50 units of beef, while Hong Kong can produce only 10.) However, the United States has a relatively greater production advantage—a comparative advantage—in the production of beef. It is five times as productive as Hong Kong in beef but only two and a half times as productive in textiles. If the United States specializes in beef and trades beef for textiles with Hong Kong, the trade can be mutually beneficial to both countries.[11]

However, note that the United States will be importing textiles—and domestic textile producers will have to compete with textile producers from Hong Kong. Note also that they are having to face the foreign competition not because they may have done something wrong, but because the beef industry has developed the comparative advantage (at the expense of the textile industry). If the U.S. beef industry were not quite so productive—say could produce only 20 units of beef in the given time period, then the textile industry would have the comparative advantage (the textile industry would then be the relatively more productive industry when compared to Hong Kong), and the beef industry would have to face competition from Hong Kong.

---

[10]Actually, the textile and apparel industries' sales have continued to expand, although irregularly, over the past two decades. However, the thrust of the argument still holds: the textile industry has failed to capture the country's comparative advantage on the margin of production.

[11]To see why trade can be mutually beneficial, note that the United States has to give up two units of textiles when it produces a unit of beef to export to Hong Kong. (These figures are obtained by dividing 100 units of textiles by 50 units of beef.) It would be willing to trade so long as it can get more than two units of textiles for a unit of beef. Fortunately, Hong Kong can produce as many as four units of textiles if it gives up a unit of beef. (These figures are obtained by dividing 40 units of textiles by 10 units of beef.) Hong Kong would find trade beneficial if it could give up fewer than four units of textiles in trade for a unit of beef. If the countries trade three units of textiles for a unit of beef, both can gain. Understand? Go through what we have said one more time—but this time, do it very slowly.

Information and Failures

The process of failure is greatly aggravated by the scarcity of one critically important resource that ties economic activity over time together: information on what consumers and other producers want and on how, where, and when they want what they do.

The information problem is made more complex—and more subject to the constraints of scarcity—by a lack of the amounts and kinds of information that can be useful in achieving successes and avoiding failures. Regrettably, such information is not readily accessible. Information on the availability of resources (for example, labor) is widely scattered among thousands, if not millions, of people and must somehow be induced from its holders. It is influenced by the amount of resources applied to gathering information, meaning that the amount and quality of the information flow will depend much on its cost. And even that kind of information is not always readily available in usable form.

To say the absence of adequate information is a source of failures is to state the obvious, but it is such obvious points that are often overlooked when policymakers consider remedies for failures, especially remedies that themselves fail to address the information problem. The information problem may not always be correctable simply because it is the result of scarcity. Public policy "solutions" may accomplish nothing more than a reallocation of resources—a redistribution of successes and failures. Indeed, changing people's incentives to provide and acquire information may aggravate the problem of failure.

Much has been made of the information problem in a market economy. The central criticism is that the multitude of market participants have only limited information, that is, their own individual plans, which are not coordinated with the plans of all others in the market. In effect, the "left hand in the market does not know what the right hand is doing." The housing industry, for example, goes through cycles of booms and busts because individual contractors, who are uncertain of each other's plans, overbuild, which causes precipitous price drops, bankruptcies, and contractor failures.

Many critics presume that centralizing the decision-making process will solve the information problem. Central planning of production may solve some information problems for example, how much is planned—but it can run headlong into other information problems, such as exactly how many resources (hours of work and energy expended) are available to individual producers.

The proposed solution is plagued by the limited capacity of planners to gather and assimilate manageable, available information. One of the great virtues (if we can call it that) of markets is that they divide responsibility for obtaining and handling information among a host of market participants, especially information that can minimize the chance of failures. Centrally directed economic activity can impose superhuman demand on the limited capacity of the planners to handle information. Increases in the complexity of production processes that may emerge with the integration of the world economy and with technological development only increase demands that would be imposed on planners.[12]

Risk, Uncertainty, and Rational Failures

Information deficiencies ultimately translate into problems of risk and uncertainty about future economic events, which also spell failures. Risk, which is grounded in probability, means that some ventures will not go as planned. That is to say, risk is a statement about the distribution of successes and failures over a series of ventures. For example, 7 out of 10 restaurants will fail. The missing information is about exactly which ventures will succeed and which will fail. The information is missing because of its cost or simply the cost of acting on the available information.

Uncertainty, on the other hand, amounts to a lack of information about the distribution of how ventures will turn out, meaning as successes or failures. Uncertainty is simply unsureness about what to expect and, as such, represents less information than exists with risk. Uncertainty emerges because of lack of experience and the difficulty of obtaining the requisite information on the probability of successes or failures. The cost of information no doubt plays a role in establishing the degree of uncertainty.

Risk and uncertainty ensure failures. Not everything can turn out right. Eliminating failure in the face of risk and uncertainty would be counterproductive because the costs of doing so would be higher than the costs endured through the failures. In other words, firms will fold, plants will close, and workers will be unemployed, not necessary because of anything wrong they may have done. Even though everything may be done correctly, justly, and fairly, or as correctly and justly and fairly as is economically reasonable, risk and uncertainty mitigate against the success of all firms, plants, and workers.[13]

---

[12]The limited capacity of planners to handle the necessary information required in efforts to centrally direct an economy, or a major sector of it, has been a life-long theme of F. A. Hayek, who once wrote prophetically, "The more men know, the smaller the share of that knowledge becomes that any one mind can absorb. The more civilized we become, the more relatively ignorant must each individual be of the facts on which the workings of his civilizaion depends. The very division of knowledge increases the necessary ignorance of the individual of most of this knowledge." F. A. Hayek, *The Constitution of Liberty* (Chicago: University of Chicago Press, 1960), p. 26.

[13]Granted, many failures in risky or uncertain endeavors (and the attendant costs) may be avoidable. We can only reason that they will be avoided, unless the costs of doing so are too great. If that is not the case, then we can only inquire as to why cost-effective avoidance of failures is not undertaken.

The most raw form of risk and uncertainty implies that many failures are planned and expected—that is, are no less founded in rational tests than are production and consumption decisions, which do not always match expectations. Less than perfectly suitable goods and services are produced because the benefits of improving them would not be worth the cost. Plants close because the cost of preventing their closing through acquiring more market information and other efforts aimed at ensuring against closure would be greater than the costs associated with their closure. Failures may be bad, which no one can deny; but a reduction of failures, especially if legislated, can be even worse because such a solution could increase the costs endured and decrease the net income received by people.

In a limited but analytically meaningful sense, failures ironically are sought to increase income (through production cost reductions). Failure can be looked upon as one of many costs of doing business. And if the rational firm were truly interested in maximizing profits, it would simply extend its operations to cover progressively more risky ventures until the additional income received no longer exceeded the additional costs incurred from failures and the use of all resources.[14]

In each instance of failure, there is an economic cost, of course; and as with any other cost, the cost of failure would preferably be reduced, if not totally avoided. However, most failures are not isolated ventures, but are part and parcel of a whole complex of ventures, all of which combined have some risk and uncertainty of not working out as planned. Risky and uncertain ventures typically carry the greatest rewards, partially to overcome the costs associated with failures and partially to compensate for people's natural or learned inclination to avoid risky and uncertain outcomes. (In the jargon of economists, many people are *risk averse*.) If an outcome is more risky and uncertain, the reward tends to be greater.

To accommodate risk and uncertainty, and to increase income, people protect themselves through the purchase of insurance policies and through self-insurance. They play the field—that is, play the probabilities—and expect greater returns in the process.

The paradigm analogy is the stock market investor who understands that the purchase of stocks entails risk and uncertainty along with the prospect of rewards. The investor typically assembles a number of different stocks in a portfolio, understanding that one or more of his or her purchases occasionally, perhaps even frequently, will not meet profit expectations. The investor evaluates the selections by how the entire portfolio does *on balance*. In this

---

[14]This statement is nothing more than an application of the general principle that firms should extend production level until the marginal (or additional) cost from expanded production equals marginal (or additional) revenue received from extended production. In the process of accepting more risk in the search of profits, in other words, firms will inevitably encounter failures.

sense, failure is planned, expected, and even sought. To ensure that no stock ever fails probably is a prescription for minimizing the return on the portfolio of stocks. However, because expected income is increased through the development of a portfolio of stocks, the investor is better able to buy stock—better able to suffer failures and more likely to suffer a greater number of failures.

Firm managers and workers typically deal with risk and uncertainty through what amounts to portfolios of activities. Firms produce several products and run several plants knowing that some products will fail in the market or that several plants will have to be closed. In effect, they rationally develop portfolios of products and plants and rationally plan for failures, although they simultaneously will do what they can (or what is economically reasonable) to avoid failures, termination of product lines, and plant closings. By developing portfolios, they expect to increase their production incomes *on balance*. Their ability to spread their risks and increase their incomes means more products will be developed and more plants opened. But it also means a greater number of failures, although the failure rate may be reduced through greater experience with more products and plants and through a greater capacity to absorb the costs of avoiding failure.

Workers and consumers also engage in portfolio management. Workers often develop a variety of skills (or keep their skills general, applicable to many different work environments) and engage in a variety of activities, one of which is a job. They understand that through time and over the course of a number of activities and jobs, they will at times fail—become unemployed or find their skills and abilities of less value than planned. Many consumers also buy appliances that they know are not "top of the line" and will occasionally fail, but they buy what they do in anticipation that their portfolios will yield them a greater net return than if they bought more expensive appliances with a lower chance of failure. The important point is that in spite of the failures, consumers and workers manage their portfolios with the intent of raising their incomes.

Learning from Failures

It is all too easy to think solely of failure as tragedy. After all, we do expend considerable energy seeking to avoid individual failures wherever and whenever possible.

Nothing could be further from the truth, for failures are highly instructive and necessarily productive. They help, perhaps more than successes, to outline the bounds of profitable and productive economic activity. Failures instruct those who fail on what they should not do the next time, if there is a next time; and, more important, they tell many others in the market what can be done wrong and what will have to be done to become or remain successful. They are, in other words, a critically important source of information. As such, they provide market participants with the necessary incentives and disincentives (instructions) on what people, acting independently of one another, should and should not do.

Past failures of many grocery stores have informed other stores that they could not remain content to offer only groceries but must expand to accommodate the demands of their customers for cosmetics, books, video tapes, prepared meals, and even restaurant services. The failures of computer companies have taught remaining computer companies that they cannot afford to hold back, for example, on the expansion of their computers' internal memory, to resist making them compatible with IBM computers, or to refuse to accommodate the needs of the business computer markets. From books and articles that are turned down by publishers, writers learn where and how they should direct their future writings.[15] From the rash of business failures of the first half of the decade, caused in part by superior and more aggressive Japanese firms, businesses in the United States have learned that they must rethink their management practices and investment strategies. The performance of the U.S. economy will likely show the feedback effects in improved growth during the 1990s, if not sooner.[16] (Students who fail the next test in this course will learn much from the experience, and many (but by no means all) can be expected to react to their failures.)

Failures are a part of an organic process that has both a past and a present, as are successes. "[S]ince we are dealing with an organic process," Professor Schumpeter reminds us, "an analysis of what happens in any particular part of it—say in an individual concern or industry—may indeed clarify details of mechanism but is inconclusive beyond that. . . . It must be seen in its role in the perennial gale of creative destruction; it cannot be understood irrespective of it or, in fact, on the hypothesis that there is a perennial lull."[17]

Risk Management through a Market Economy

Arguments for a market economy abound, and the conventional case for the market on grounds of efficiency and individual freedom has been devel-

---

[15]As an aside, it may be useful to note that professors generally find their acceptance rate on articles submitted to journals going up as their career progresses. One explanation is that the professors improve their research and writing skills. Another, perhaps more important, explanation is that the professors know better from their "turndowns" what should not be written and where manuscripts should and should not be submitted.

[16]For a review of the ways U.S. businesses have adapted to their new competitive environment, see Murray L. Weidenbaum, Richard E. Cook, and Richard E. Burr, *Learning to Compete: The Feedback Effects of the Non-Linear Economy* (St. Louis: Center for the Study of American Business, Washington University in St. Louis, 1986).

[17]Schumpeter, *Capitalism, Socialism, and Democracy*, p. 84.

oped in some detail elsewhere.[18] We need only note here that the logic of risk and portfolio management can also be applied to entire economies. The ultimate goal of societies is welfare improvement through human endeavors. In framing any economy, we know that not everyone has the capacity—the willingness as well as the ability—to succeed, to find welfare-enhancing (profitable) opportunities through alertness and innovation. We understand the risk of failure, but we also understand that we do not know exactly who will fail and who will succeed.

The market system is a grand portfolio of people that is devised for determining the critically important missing information on people's capacity to succeed *and* fail. One justification for the market system (but hardly the only justification) is that over time—and over the course of many people and circumstances—the vast majority of people's welfare will on balance be enhanced through combinations of individual successes and failures.[19] A critically important force in minimizing failures is the pricing system, which contributes to welfare by providing people with necessary market information and by coordinating people's individual activities. Markets tend to economize on failures.

THE JUSTICE OF FAILURE

Clearly, not all failures are just or fair. Some failures are the consequence of violations of contracts. Banks have failed because employees have embezzled funds. Real estate deals have failed because contractors did not build buildings as they said they would. And manufacturing plants have folded because supplies have not been delivered as promised, or strategic employees did not fulfill their contracts. The injustice of these instances of failures are interesting because they represent behavior that violates "rules to which one has given prior consent."[20]

However, many failures may be just in the sense that no previously agreed-upon rules have been violated. All contracts may have been honored; all rules, obeyed. The firms failed simply as a consequence of problems associated with scarcity, namely risk and uncertainty. Indeed, the failures may have been anticipated, and no loss of income may have resulted.

Individual instances of failure, isolated from successes, may appear to be unjust or unfair, but this does not mean that the system that spawned the

---

[18]The most prominent of the defenders of the market economy is Milton Friedman. See his and Rose Friedman's book *Free to Choose* (New York: Avon Books, 1981). One of the authors has made the case for the market economy in Richard B. McKenzie, *Bound to Be Free* (Stanford, Cal.: Hoover Institution Books, 1982).

[19]This theme is developed in Richard B. McKenzie, *The Fairness of Markets: The Search for Justice in a Free Society* (Lexington, Mass.: Lexington Books, 1987), chap. 9.

[20]The concept of justice employed has been developed in Geoffrey Brennan and James M. Buchanan, *The Reason of Rules: Constitutional Political Economy* (New York: Cambridge University Press, 1985), especially chap. 7.

failures is unjust or unfair. Again, no previously agreed-upon rules may have been violated. In addition, the failures may mirror an increase in income for those who experience the failures. People may be hurt by their own failures, but they can be helped by their other successes and by the failures and successes of others that result in improved goods and services. The result can be income greater from a system that allows failure than from one that deliberately attempts to contain them. The prospect of greater income, in spite of the prospect of failures, can be the impetus for the consent of those who operate within the system.

Still, not everyone is likely to gain from a market system that permits unchecked failures. There will be those who fail at everything or practically everything and end up as "net losers" from the system. The question of whether net losers should be helped by public means is a difficult question, one that cannot be fully treated here.[21] The net losers may have implicitly or explicitly agreed to the system, and they may simply have been unfortunate or unlucky.

On the other hand, there is no reason why the participants might not have agreed to a system that allowed for compensation be paid to the net losers just to ensure that no one is made worse off from the operation of the system. The compensation could be extracted from the greater incomes of those who, on balance, gain from the system.[22] If it were, it is hard to see how the system could be viewed as unjust.

THE SAMARITAN'S DILEMMA

Those who seem to object frequently to public efforts to help the businesses that go bankrupt, farmers whose farms are sold at auction and workers whose plants close are viewed as unable to empathize with the economic difficulty, if not misery, encountered by others. Differences on public policy arise because some people do not really care about the fates of others, while others do care. However, differences on what should be done to remedy failures arises even among those who care. This is because of the ever-present Samaritan's dilemma that will likely remain a central component of public welfare discussion: Should those in need be helped by public means? The answer is not nearly so obvious as might be presumed.

If public aid had no consequence beyond relief of failures, the debate would not be nearly so intense as it often is. However, as with failures, relief also has consequences. It can encourage the very problem that is the object of

---

[21]McKenzie, *The Fairness of Markets,* chap. 9.

[22]The taxes imposed on those who gain on balance from the system could be less than the increase in their incomes from operation of the system, meaning that everyone's position could, after transfers, improve. The inherent difficulty of granting government transfer authority to help the net losers is that it might be exploited by net gainers, a point that is developed in McKenzie, *The Fairness of Markets,* chap. 9.

the public remedy. Relief can make failures more palatable and, thereby, more likely. It can, in other words, reduce the tendency of a market economy to economize on failures and to learn from them. When this point is recognized, it does not follow that those who object to public remedies necessarily object to helping others. Objectors can be concerned about those future groups who will suffer from failures that are encouraged by policies adopted today.[23]

CONCLUDING COMMENTS

In the Charlotte, North Carolina, airport, there is a wall poster that sums up in a very few words a theme of this chapter: "No one ever accomplished anything without risking something." The same thought is aptly captured by the old adage, "Nothing ventured, nothing gained." That simple point is all too frequently forgotten in public discussions of policies that are myopically concerned with observed failures in our economy.

To those who understand the message on the airport wall, it comes as no surprise that the more dynamic, venturesome, and growth oriented a market economy is, the more it will be fraught with failures. This simple understanding is what caused Marx to praise capitalism.[24] It is also what Joseph Schumpeter meant when he characterized capitalism as "a process of Creative Destruction" and when he suggested that the long-run performance of any economy often depends on the economy's not fully utilizing its possibilities at every point in time—that is, on its being willing and able to endure passing failures and resist the temptation to prevent failures and the distress they individually cause.[25] It was also that simple understanding that *Washington Post* columnist Charles Krauthammer must have had in mind when continuing his commentary on the bad economic news of the early 1980s:

> These disasters are the product not of capitalism's failure but of its success. In 1984 the American economy grew faster than at any time since 1951. The paradox of capitalism is that it is most successful when most dynamic, and when most dynamic, it is most destructive. . . . It is the first system in history to lift the mass of men out of economic misery. But to keep the engine going,

---

[23]One of the more interesting, and frequently overlooked, analytical issues surrounding public relief efforts is whether or not democracy encourages too much or too little aid. Geoffrey Brennan and James Buchanan contend that democracy has a built-in bias toward too much aid, because people acting in their public role as voters would be more likely to provide more aid than they would in their private dealings. This is because people as voters will have a small probability of having to cope with the consequences of decisions made currently. See Brennan and Buchanan, *The Reason of Rules*, pp. 75–81.

[24]See M. M. Bober, *Karl Marx's Interpretation of History* (New York: W. W. Norton, 1965), especially pp. 18–19.

[25]Schumpeter, *Capitalism, Socialism, and Democracy*, p. 83.

it randomly visits misery on selected groups. Instead of searching for villains, it might be more humane for the rest of society, which benefits from that mighty engine, to devote some of its vast surplus to cushioning the fall of its victims.[26]

QUESTIONS TO PONDER

1. How can economic failure contribute to economic efficiency?
2. Is failure fair? When is it and when is it not?
3. What would be the consequences of attempts to eliminate failure from the economic system?
4. Explain how highly efficient firms can fail in markets.
5. Do people seek failures?

---

[26]Krauthammer, "One Cheer for Capitalism," pp. 91–92.

CHAPTER 14

The Fairness of Markets

Markets have been praised throughout history for their effectiveness in getting things done, but they have also been damned for their lack of fairness. Karl Marx's evaluation of the fairness of markets, crucial to his overall assessment of capitalism, is well known. While he admired the ability of markets to increase a country's productive capacity, Marx fervently maintained that the market system is unfair simply because workers are paid only a fraction of the value of the goods and services they produce in the labor market.[1] Their surplus value, which emerges as profit for capitalists, represents the extent of worker exploitation. This perceived unfairness will lead to worker revolutions and, inevitably, to the collapse of capitalism; communism will emerge through creation of a socialist state, or so Marx asserted.

However, criticism of the fairness or justice of markets has not been limited to the Marxian tradition. Even the late Frank Knight, University of Chicago economist and ardent supporter of markets, once noted that our ability to earn an income is "based upon a complex mixture of inheritance, luck, and effort, probably in that order of importance."[2] Unfortunately, Knight contended, only effort, not circumstances, has any "ethical validity." He reasoned that the moral merit of what people earn must have some minimum connection to the work people do.

UCLA economist Armen Alchian, another well-known market advocate, fully acknowledges that he does not know how the social worthiness—or the

---

[1]At the same time he condemned market capitalism, Marx could not avoid acknowledging capitalism's accomplishments: "The bourgeoisie and the capitalist system they control, during its role of scarce one hundred years, has created more massive and more colossal productive forces than have all preceding generations together." Karl Marx, *The Communist Manifesto* (Chicago: Henry Regnery Co., 1954), p. 23.

[2]Frank H. Knight, *The Ethics of Competition* (Chicago: University of Chicago Press, 1935), p. 56. Knight does not always appear to be consistent in his ranking of luck, effort, and inheritance in determining the income distribution. He writes in another context, "From an ethical point of view it would be more significant to analyze income into three sources of free choice or effort, inheritance, and luck. And the greatest of these is luck!" Frank H. Knight, *Freedom and Reform* (Port Washington, N.Y.: Kennikat Press, 1969), p. 10. Perhaps Knight would reconcile the two states (the one in *The Ethics of Competition* and the one in *Freedom and Reform*) by acknowledging the importance of luck in inheritance. The important point is the relatively low ranking of effort in the Knightian view of determinants of people's income levels.

fairness and justice—of market pay rates could possibly be established. After all, as entrenched microeconomic theory suggests, even in "perfectly" competitive markets (which is the best conceivable set of market conditions), workers earn a wage that approximates their "marginal product" (or additional contribution to their employer's output). However, the relative and absolute sizes of the various marginal products of workers and, therefore, their wage rates are greatly affected by the actual social system in which they happen to make their marginal contribution.

Following Alchian, we might reasonably deduce that few in the United States would earn an amount even close to what they receive had they been born anywhere else on the globe. In other words, if most Americans had lived anywhere else (except in a few industrial countries in the world), the overwhelming majority would probably be paupers.[3]

The late Arthur Okun has echoed Knight's and Alchian's concern about the questionable fairness of market-determined incomes. Okun, a Brookings Institution senior fellow, observed that workers' incomes are generally dependent on four identifiable factors:

1. Their inborn abilities and talents.

2. Their acquired skills and talents.

3. Their willingness to expend effort.

4. The market conditions for the services they provide and the services provided by others.[4]

In Okun's view, it is hard to see how any of these factors would necessarily produce fairness in the income distribution. In most essential respects, in spite of a substantially different philosophical and policy predilection toward the market system, Okun concurred with Marx, Knight, and Alchian.

However, Okun said that even the ethical validity of worker effort is a questionable basis for determining the fairness of market wages. This is the case because effort also is predicated on the circumstances of the workers (which includes their acquired skills and innate talents, the market conditions they confront, and their genetic and social birthrights)—largely, though not totally, outside direct control of workers. In short, worker effort is not greatly dependent on what workers, by themselves, do. At best, Okun maintained, the fairness of the income distribution is a matter of "personal judgment"; at worst, "incomes that match productivity have no ethical appeal. Equality in the distribution of income (allowing for voluntary leisure as a

---

[3]Comments made by Armen Alchian in a lecture delivered at Clemson University during a conference sponsored by the Liberty Fund, Inc. (July 1985).
[4]Arthur M. Okun, *Equality and Efficiency: The Big Tradeoff* (Washington: Brookings Institution, 1975), pp. 40-47.

form of income) as well as in the distribution of rights would be my *ethical preference.*"[5]

Obviously, the fairness of markets remains a contentious issue. By reflecting on consequences of markets (for example, income distribution), markets are, for some, difficult to justify on any grounds, much less on grounds of fairness. It is not easy to justify the income of professional football standout Herschel Walker—an annual income easily in excess of $1 million. It is equally difficult to justify nurses' salaries, which are often less than the salaries of beauticians. Because it is such a difficult problem, fairness has been a topic that economists have traditionally sought to avoid (or to discard as irrelevant).

Nevertheless, the purpose of this chapter is to reconsider the fairness of markets: more precisely, to question whether something meaningful cannot be said about the fairness of markets that draws on economic methods. At the same time, our purpose is to give insight into the matter—to say more about markets than just repeat the refrain that "markets are efficient and cost effective." Implicitly, the chapter seeks to determine if there are any grounds for arguing that market incomes that match marginal productivity have some ethical appeal or validity, contrary to the admonition of Alchian, Knight, and Okun, as well as Marx. In making such a determination, a blend of the contractarian perspectives of James Buchanan and John Rawls will be employed with necessary variation.[6] Unfortunately, as you can imagine, the topic of the chapter requires that the discussion deal with philosophy, but we hope you will find the discussion productive—even if you do not accept all we say.

The central conclusion accepts the conventional conclusion of economic analysis, which is that markets yield results; markets produce goods and services and distribute income very efficiently. This is what economic systems are supposed to do. On the other hand, in this chapter we conclude that because we have only limited information about what these results are (given the subjectivity of outputs and incomes), markets must be, to an important degree, evaluated as a process. Our evaluation must be in terms of how market results are achieved (which may be called *fairness*), not exclusively in terms of what is achieved (the conventional domain of economic *efficiency*).[7]

---

[5]Ibid., p. 47.

[6]See James M. Buchanan, *The Limits of Liberty: Between Anarchy and Leviathan* (Chicago: University of Chicago Press, 1975); and John Rawls, *A Theory of Justice* (Cambridge, Mass.: Belknap Press of Harvard University Press, 1971). The differences in perspective will be explored briefly in footnote 11.

[7]This means that market supporters and detractors alike must concede that the market as a *system* must be judged by criteria other than efficiency alone, because efficiency itself is a value-laden concept and is defined as outcomes internal to the actual *market system*. We really do not know, to any meaningful degree, what efficiency is—other than to describe it as that which emerges from trades within the established system of permitted exchanges.

Our analysis helps explain why market advocates maintain their support for the system in spite of knowing little about the specifics of measured production and income distribution during any given, relatively short period of time.

THE NATURE OF MARKET EFFICIENCY

Evaluating the fairness of markets is not familiar ground for most economists. Conventional economic analysis overwhelmingly stresses the value of market efficiency as a social criterion (that is, how well markets allocate resources to satisfy the expectations and welfare of market participants as those participants assess their own welfare). The principles of fairness and justice, as well as ethical criteria, are virtually excluded from the debate.

Indeed, many economists imbued with the standard skills of their profession deny that *fairness* has any useful scientific or even philosophical meaning. As Judge Richard Posner has quipped, words like *fairness* and *justice* are "terms which have no content."[8]

Like beauty, fairness is presumed to be in the eyes of the beholder. Because fairness means so many different things to so many different people, discussions of the fairness of markets are empty—or without merit—because they are without agreement on what is being discussed. In addition, fairness represents values that can only be contested but not ever settled in any scientific sense. On the other hand, efficiency has a very precise meaning to economists and can be described mathematically and graphically. It is, therefore, a far less elusive theoretical construct than fairness, or so most economists seem to think.

However, as economists have long recognized, efficiency (or more precisely, allocative efficiency) is an economic concept dependent upon a given system—a specified set of people with identified preferences, property rights, and rules for exchanges. An efficient exchange is any voluntary shift in property rights to resources, goods, and services *within the established system* that improves the welfare of the traders as the traders themselves assess their own welfare. An efficient allocation of resources is one in which further trades cannot be made without damaging the welfare of one or more people.

Note that the concept of efficiency in exchange presumes that property rights and rules for exchange can be identified, since these rights and rules are the objective components of the process subject to enforcement. By definition of voluntary exchange (that undergirds the concept of efficient exchange), efficiency does not afford the external observer/economist room for judging ex ante what trades are efficient and thereby *should* take place (or can

---

[8]As quoted in *The Wall Street Journal,* August 4 , 1986, p. 1. Posner is a former University of Chicago law professor who used economics extensively in his legal research while a professor and continues to rely heavily on it in his court decisions.

even be expected to take place). Judgments about the efficiency of trades can only be known ex post, after the trades have been made, and then can be made only because the trades have been made voluntarily.

The external observer/economist can only hope to know *what* is subject to exchange, but he or she cannot know with any reasonable degree of precision how the potential market participants evaluate their rights and the rights of others. This is because the personal values of the market participants are subjective and individual (not subject to external assessment).

Even then, after trades have been observed, we, the external observer/economists, do not know as much as we might think. We often cannot be sure what has been traded, except by very close inspection of the trades, and such inspections must necessarily be limited to a relatively few trades. We may observe ex post that deer and beaver have been exchanged (to use Adam Smith's example), but any detached, external observer may know little of the exact rights to the deer and beaver that have been traded or the extraneous obligations and contingencies that have been explicitly or implicitly tied to the trade of the deer and beaver.[9]

We judge the exact rights that have been traded in only those relatively infrequent cases in which traded rights have become matters of legal dispute. At that point the social problem is much more one of judging the social legitimacy of the trades—identifying the rights that were traded and comparing those rights with the rights that are claimed and clarifying the extent to which the rules of trade were followed. (We implicitly make such comparisons when we identify crimes.) The social problem is not one of identifying the efficiency of the trades in dispute; rather it is one of assessing the ability of people to make the trades that *they*, the traders, think are efficient (by evaluating the extent to which property rights are defined and there exist barriers to entry and exit, for example). The efficiency of trades is judged by the participants, not the observers.

Assuming that the traders know what they are doing when they trade voluntarily, trade only rights that are legitimately claimed, and follow the rules of trade, we conclude that efficient trades are more or less fair trades as evaluated strictly by the traders. To say that trades are fair in some other more generalized social sense, we must have in mind some criterion other than that of the traders.

Governmental policies are deemed to add to or subtract from market efficiency by an assessment of the extent to which they encourage or obstruct freely negotiated trades. Tariffs are deemed inefficient simply because they obstruct mutually beneficial trades through arbitrary elevations in market

---

[9]As economics Nobel laureate F. A. Hayek has repeatedly reminded the profession, through market theory we can begin to appreciate the "patterns of market outcomes," but not the "concrete content of those patterns." The distinction between the patterns of outcomes and concrete content of outcomes is central to F. A. Hayek, *The Constitution of Liberty* (Chicago: University of Chicago Press, 1960).

price. Pollution is inefficient to the extent that trades are obstructed through failure to define property rights, which, in turn, result in an underpricing of environmental resources to some users and overpricing to other users.

The pattern of incomes that are generated in a market economy must be equally efficient, since they represent claims to the goods and services that are produced through the complex network of mutually beneficial trades in the economy. But, again, the efficiency of the incomes can only be determined ex post and assessed internal to the system. This is true because the participants in the complex of market trades are the ones who understand what their incomes are. The external observer may think he or she can measure in dollar terms the income and distribution (for example, through surveys of household and individual incomes). However, such surveys may reveal grossly inadequate assessments of the true or real income distribution because they are not likely to consider the various forms of nonmoney incomes, not the least important of which may be leisure.

Clearly, it is hard to conclude that the plumber who did not go to college and who works from eight to five six days a week is better or worse off than the English professor who makes a much lower income but who may do little more than meet his twelve-hour weekly class schedule. The nonmoney income of the English professor may or may not make up for the money income differential between himself or herself and the plumber (or any other worker). We frankly cannot say which is happier, only that they may both be worse off if they had been forced, from the point of high school graduation, to switch places.

In addition, such assessments of the relative social worthiness of the plumber-professor (measured) income differential requires that the observer know more about the lives of the plumber and English professor than can generally be known in the abstract. Such assessments require that the observer actually become a plumber and an English professor, which is to say that the observer must become what he or she did not choose to become, and for good reason. Even if it were possible for the observer to assume the place of the plumber or professor, it seems altogether reasonable to conclude that the variety of income circumstances is so great that a full understanding of the true *total* income distribution emerging in the economy (after allowing for nonmonetary benefits, to expand on Okun's suggestion) is impossible. In short, our ability to evaluate the worthiness of the actual distribution, in efficiency *or* fairness terms, is ultimately checked by our inability to comprehend various circumstances under which people earn their incomes.

This is not to say that external judgments about relative welfare cannot be made—judgments based on measured money incomes, more or less. They *are* made. However, it does appear reasonable to demand that the money income differential be rather substantial before the differential can be taken as a clear indicator of relative welfare. The real world in which some people have standards of living that are greatly depressed demands that we make evaluations of relative welfare. However, the subjectivity and individuality of income, spawning complexity in evaluation, mandate the exercise of considerable caution.

THE MEANING OF FAIRNESS

Clearly, what is known about the accomplishments of any economic system cannot be ignored in any evaluation of the system, but the critical point of the preceding section is that we must recognize the limitations of knowledge of specific outcomes that are generated by any economic *system*. External observers can never know as much about what an economic system does accomplish as the economist's concept of efficiency, used as a central criterion, requires. The concept of efficiency, as revealed in market outcomes, implies a level of knowledge that far exceeds the ability of people to know.

Since consequences of markets, as revealed by actual output levels and combinations of goods and services and the income distribution are largely unknown, it would appear that an economic system must be appraised, not only by the extent and distribution of market freedom and power, but also by the standards of systems analysis, which are not dissimilar to the standards used to evaluate parlor or field games. Those standards might go by the name of *fairness*.

Admittedly, markets are not fully analogous to parlor or field games, but we can understand much about how markets can or should be evaluated by reflecting on the way we normally evaluate games. Games can be assessed in terms of how much interest and excitement they give participants and spectators; and markets have a great deal of entertainment value as a game to be played with facility. But, they can also be appraised in terms of their fairness. And the standards of a "fair game," which implies meaningful constraints on what game is played and how the game is played, may be viewed as threefold:

• First, the rules of the game (or system for play) must be generally agreeable to people who are reasonably informed about their implications for the play of the game.

Any appeal for the *fairness* of a game must be founded on the presumption that people know what the rules for play are, which requires a degree of education about the rules and tolerable stability in the rules.

Rules that are generally agreeable are likely to be nondiscriminatory. This means that they can be generalized to all similarly situated individuals and groups. It also means that they are applied in a nondiscriminatory manner, to all similarly situated people.

• Second, the game is not rigged; the rules of play are not designed to ensure that *particular* people or groups will be the winners and others will be losers.

This standard of a fair game means that the rules of the game are not chosen or changed in the middle of the play of the game simply to ensure that particular people win. People are treated equally with respect to the rules of play. A fair game does not necessarily mean that all participants have an equal chance to be winners (certainly this is not the case in Monopoly and football), but only that the rules themselves are not selected intentionally to affect the odds of winning for identified individual participants, given whatever abilities these participants bring to the game.[10]

• Third, participants play by the rules to which they have explicitly or implicitly given their consent.

Cheating is unfair play.

Given these standards, the fairness of markets becomes a matter of "fair rules" and "fair play."[11] Notice that fair rules are established by general consent of reasonably well informed rule makers whose personal interests do not guide the selection of the rules. Notice also that a fair game is not judged by the fact that there are winners and losers. Having winners and losers may be a prime objective of the game, which is true, for example, of Monopoly and football games. A game of Monopoly is generally considered fair so long as the players agree to the rules of play, the game is not rigged, and the players adhere to the rules that were known before play of the game begins. A perfectly fair game, which will always remain an elusive goal, would be one in which consent to the rules is virtually unanimous, the rules are totally unre-

---

[10]At our conceptual level of analysis, there is no particularly pressing reason to restrict the population giving consent to the existing generation. Indeed, if the rules under consideration are to be judged fairly, then it would appear to be important to consider the views of all generations, current and future, just to ensure that the current generation does not rig the game.

In most essential respects, the concept of fairness in this paper is identical to the concept of fairness in the writings of James Buchanan in *The Limits of Liberty* and John Rawls in *A Theory of Justice.* These two authors talk of justice as "just rules" in much the same way that this paper talks of fairness as "fair rules." The main difference in perspective emerges in the scope of agreement over generations of people. In general, Buchanan seeks agreement among the existing population of informed people for the conceptual foundation of justice. Rawls seeks agreement of people (presumably, the existing population) who are behind the "veil of ignorance." This paper seeks agreement among tolerably informed people over the course of generations of people where all have equal rights of participation in initial decisions over rules.

[11]Our notion of fairness is similar to Geoffrey Brennan and James Buchanan's notion of "just conduct": "It is useful to make . . . a distinction between the notion of 'just conduct,' on the one hand, and the notion of 'just rules,' on the other. The former involves justice *within* rules. . . . The latter involves justice *among* rules. . . . Just conduct consists of behavior that does not violate rules which one has given prior consent. The role of consent involves . . . the proposition that agreement, either implicit or explicit, is required to legitimize rules. Rules, so legitimized, then become the reference point against which the justice of an individual's behavior can be assessed." Geoffrey Brennan and James M. Buchanan, *The Reason of Rules: Constitutional Political Economy* (New York: Cambridge University Press, 1985), pp. 97–98.

lated to the particular skills and abilities of the rule maker–participants, and the rules are strictly obeyed.[12]

An unfair game means that the players have not, to a meaningful degree, given their consent to the rules that are enforced, that they do not understand the rules of play, that the game is rigged to produce particular winners and losers, or that the players do not overtly or covertly stick to the rules.

Clearly, *fairness* has other meanings; however, its meaning identified here is appealing because it is not altogether unfamiliar. Several universities (including Clemson University, Southern Methodist University, and the University of Nebraska) have been charged with playing unfair football games by paying their athletes more than allowed by the National Collegiate Athletic Association (NCAA). The charge of unfairness is understandable. By their membership in the NCAA, universities agree, albeit implicitly, to the rules forbidding payments. The offending universities violated those rules. (More will be said about the NCAA in Chapter 24.)

When the initial votes were tallied in the spring of 1986, former Philippine President Ferdinand Marcos was viewed as having unfairly "won" the election against now President Corazon Aquino. Marcos agreed to conventional democratic procedures, which explicitly preclude vote buying and require accurate counts of votes actually cast. Then he proceeded to subvert the election process by paying voters, counting for himself votes that were never cast, and destroying votes for Aquino that were cast.

IN DEFENSE OF MARKETS

Any defense of the fairness of markets cannot be construed necessarily as a defense of the status quo in the economic system, which may in fact be highly dependent on markets. This must be the case because the system, as currently constructed, may violate the standards of fairness outlined above. There are various institutional rules—including the tax code, the way the justice system metes out decisions, and the way governmental regulatory and expenditure decisions are made—that effectively rig the game to ensure that particular people (or firms) "win." The opportunity of people to play the "market game" is often restricted because markets are not fully open to some potential players. Those potential players, understandably, hold their support of the market system in reserve.

Nonetheless, the economic system in existence may be more fair than the system that is proposed through reforms. The reforms may themselves rep-

---

[12]Unanimity in the selection of rules might appear to be the ideal standard. However, unanimity is not only unrealistic, but also not ideal. This is because unanimity gives each rule maker considerable veto power and, therefore, can result in a stalemate of the rule-making process as each rule maker seeks to exploit his or her veto power to ensure that the rules operate to his or her advantage. "Proximate unanimity" is all that can be sought in achieving general consent.

resent additional violations of standards of fairness. Defenders of markets may talk totally in terms of the inefficiency of the proposed reforms, but such arguments may actually represent claims that the standards of fairness are violated by these reforms. Legislated wages are often found objectionable on the grounds that they make some workers winners at the expense of others. Tariffs and quotas are found objectionable also because they tend to be imposed in a discriminatory manner and because the industry groups seeking the protection from imports would not be interested in generalizing the protection to all other similarly situated groups.[13]

Constant intrusions of all kinds lead to instability of the rules of market play and make the game arguably unfair because general consent may be lost in the process of special-interest intrusions and because people are no longer able to remain tolerably informed about what the rules of play really are. The federal tax code in existence at the start of 1986 was deemed unfair largely because it was so complicated that virtually no one, including tax attorneys and Internal Revenue Service agents, understood what the rules were. (Tax reform in 1986 apparently made these problems worse.)

MARKETS: FREE, OPEN, AND FAIR

The concept of free and open markets, as an idealized economic system that should be sought even if it cannot be realized, can be defended on fairness grounds. The reasons emerge from our view of fairness as fair rules and fair play, as outlined in the preceding section.

First, markets are advocated on the grounds that they spur economic growth by efficiently allocating resources and providing people with substantial long-run incentives to work, save, and invest.

As indicated above, conceptual discussions on consent require that the views of future generations be considered on par with the views of the current generation. If markets are as efficient and growth oriented as economists maintain, then it would seem that markets would achieve consent from an overwhelming majority of the informed citizens, especially if future generations are considered. Future generations that stand to gain from economic growth would be inclined to favor an efficient growth-oriented market economy. Because of their sheer number, future generations would represent an overwhelming majority coalition against governmental intrusions into markets that might favor current generation at the expense of economic growth.

Second, because free and open markets are designed to maximize, within reasonable bounds, opportunities to participate meaningfully in economic

---

[13]Protectionists may not be interested in generalizing these industry protections on the grounds that they will then be worse off. They will benefit from the protection in their market but suffer from the protection in other markets. This argument is developed in Richard B. McKenzie, "Free Trade versus Fair Trade: The Justice of Protectionism" (St. Louis: Center for the Study of American Business, Washington University, 1986).

decisions, free and open markets are developed to expand the realm of consent for the economic system.

Free and open markets, however, do not mean that all potential market participants will avail themselves equally of the market opportunities or that everyone will benefit equally from the existing opportunities. Genuine opportunities must be just that, *opportunities* that can be exploited *or* rejected. To the extent that potential market participants can determine that their welfare will be improved *on balance* from the interplay of people taking advantage of opportunities, including cost effective production and mutually beneficial and competitively priced trades, the prospects of general consent, while not ensured, is certainly expanded.[14]

Third, although there will be winners and even losers in markets, the system (as conceptualized) is not rigged to ensure that particular identifiable people or groups are winners and losers. At least, the idealized market economy is certainly not advocated (at least by the authors of this book) on grounds of picking particular winners and losers.

Measured by their salaries, some market participants, such as William Perry, tackle for the Chicago Bears professional football team, may be substantial winners in a U.S. market economy. However, Perry's exorbitant income may be considered fair simply because, when the rules were developed and accepted, no one (including Perry) could have imagined that in the mid-1980s someone six feet two, weighing more than 330 pounds would be worth the income that he draws from playing a sport and selling hamburgers (which he does through ads for McDonald's restaurants).

Viewed from the perspective of fairness as fair rules and fair play, there is every reason to question Okun's claim that Perry's income might not have "ethical appeal" solely because it only reflects Perry's marginal productivity. His income can certainly have ethical appeal to the extent that the rules were not rigged intentionally in his favor and that he did not violate any of the agreed-upon rules.

Perry's "luck" in his place of birth and in the draw of genes that made him the "Refrigerator" (Perry's nickname), would appear to make his income all the more fair, contrary to what Knight and Okun maintain. Perry's luck means that the system could not have been rigged to his benefit. Anyone else could have been equally lucky. As opposed to being an undesirable characteristic of the market process, a measure of luck may be a highly attractive feature of the market system, just as luck in the draw of the cards, spin of the wheel, and toss of the coins is an attractive feature of other games.[15]

---

[14]From this perspective, economists' conventional discussions of the welfare effects of markets, including their efficiency through market competition among self-interested people, can be seen as part and parcel of the normative effort to expand general consent for markets, not a positive statement of just what competitive markets do.

[15]Indeed, elements of chance are intentionally added to many games (for example poker and "Wheel of Fortune," a television game show) simply to ensure their fairness.

Fourth, in a market economy systematic enforcement of property rights is crucial not because they protect the bourgeoisie but because they represent nondiscriminatory enforcement of agreed-upon rules of market play.

Calls for enforcement of property and contract rights that often accompany discussion of the market economy are nothing more than appeals to live by the rules of the market process, not to protect the wealth of identified people (or at least this is what we think is generally the case in philosophical discussions). To call for the protection of the rights of capitalists alone would clearly be an appeal to unfair play of the market process.

Fifth, strict restraints on government in a market economy are advocated not so much to retard government per se as to retard the ability of people (especially the politically and economically powerful) to change the rules of market play. The rules are changed to ensure that opportunities are made less equal and that they, the rule changers, are winners (or that they win more handsomely than otherwise).

Opening government to special interest legislation—or legislation that is not generally applicable to all—is bound to lead to unfairness of the system. This is true because people (again, especially the politically and economically powerful) can be expected to exploit the newfound powers of government to help themselves while hurting others.

WELFARE AND MARKETS

Economists and social philosophers interested in the efficiency of the social system have generally deduced that the role of government should be more or less very small, limited to the "minimal state." The creation and maintenance of a fair market system does not imply the retention of limited government, or even the minimal state, in the sense that there is little for government to do. To create a fair market system, government would likely be assigned many major tasks.

First and foremost, significant police powers for government would be necessary in order to ensure strict nondiscriminatory enforcement of the rules of the market system that achieve general consent. A market is impossible without rules, and all incentives to cheat on the rules (to free ride), which can be expected to expand with the size and scope of markets, must be dampened.

In addition to simply defining and maintaining property rights, the police powers may have to be used to make sure the rules of fair play are followed. The specific costs and benefits related to the enforcement of the rules in particular circumstances may not be relevant in all cases. The rules may have to be enforced because they promote fairness in play of the market process. Rules are rules, adopted because of their social worthiness over the course of time and in particular circumstances and are only valuable to the extent that they are enforced consistently and in a nondiscriminatory manner.

Second, and equally important, a welfare state of some limited size would appear to be necessary to achieve general consent. During any given period of time, markets will produce winners and losers, primarily because markets are partially designed to encourage people to adjust to a plethora of market forces, including changes in consumer preferences and production technologies.

When productivity in agriculture increases, some farmers are hurt. When the demand for jeans declines, denim producers close plants and textile workers suffer. However, the existence of such losses does not mean that the farmers and textile workers lose from the market *system.* This is true because they can be expected to gain from the many adjustments made by all others in the system that result in improved products sold at lower prices and that lead to greater employment and income opportunities for farmers and textile workers. A critical component of the case for markets is that the overwhelming majority of people will be gainers *on balance* from the operation of the market system. (This is a central point in the preceding chapter on economic failure.)

Still, because of the sheer number of people and events covered by the market system, some people will lose *on balance* from the market system. Such people, "net losers," must be of special concern to ensure general consent for the system—and thus its fairness. People who anticipate being net losers can be expected to object to the rules of the market system that they believe will make them net losers, perhaps through no fault of their own. Some *limited* amount of compensatory payment for net losers, welfare, may be required to expand to reasonable levels the general consent for the system.

However, to the extent that the welfare state is designed to improve the well-being of net losers, the size of the welfare state must also be strictly contained. As noted, the power of the state to transfer and compensate can be expected to be exploited by the "net gainers," who by definition are in a better position to exploit the state's welfare powers, all to the further detriment of the net losers. In short, the welfare state must be created and strictly contained, in the interest both of enlisting and maintaining the support of the net losers.[16]

Third, fairness in markets means that people must know the rules and must give general consent to them. People must have meaningful opportunities to learn the rules and to acquire the capacity to participate in markets, which means that the state may have substantial responsibilities for education and training programs. People who are not told how to play the game of Monopoly or do not know how to count money can be expected to question the fairness of play, especially when Monopoly is "the only game in town."

---

[16]This theme is developed in Richard B. McKenzie, "The Conservative Case for the Contained Welfare State" (St. Louis: Center for the Study of American Business, Washington University, 1986).

By definition, the broad structure of the economy is the only game in town.

Fourth, general consent and the adherence to rules may require a governmentally organized watch for the emergence of political and economic power centers, in both the public and private sectors. Economic and political power centers define the potential to change the rules of play and, for that matter, to violate the rules of play with impunity. The need to scrutinize monopolistic power in government, business, and labor is driven by the need also to ensure general consent to the rules, ultimately limited to countervail against concentrated economic and political power. Markets are designed to disperse power, and they may be expected to work tolerably well *so long as that power remains dispersed.* Markets may not be so efficient or even fair if that fundamental condition is not met.

CONCLUDING COMMENTS

The purpose of this chapter has been ambitious, to comment on the fairness of markets without stepping totally outside economic analysis. Much that has been said will be familiar to economists (who may also find many points with which they can disagree). Traditional points of economic inquiry have been crucial to the discussion. For example, we have assumed that people are tolerably rational in the sense that they know what they want and are willing to pursue their wants, within constraints, if given the freedom to do so.

While we have argued that we may never be able to know very much about the actual content of efficient outcomes in markets, we have presumed efficiency in the allocation of resources as a pattern of outcomes. We have assumed that within given resource and preference constraints, people will be able to imagine in general terms the improvements in their welfare that can come from the operation of markets. That may be an unreasonable demand on people in the real world, but the important issue in our discussion is whether markets can be justified in abstract conceptual terms, not in the real-world discussions of actual consent. To justify markets in an abstract discussion, all we need to do is to question how people would evaluate markets *if* they were reasonably well informed about how they operate.

However, we have also argued that the fairness of markets entails much more than the efficiency of them. Fairness entails fair rules, which implies general consent, and fair play, which implies that people uphold their agreements. Seen in this light, the case for markets, made in terms of fairness and efficiency, must be an appeal to the reasonableness of consent as a social criterion for the establishment of any economic system.

Consent as a criterion is defective in many respects, not the least of which is that motives for giving consent may not always be the most noble. Nonetheless, consent to rules has one important attribute: such agreement goes to the core of the social problem, finding institutional arrangements (rules) by which people can live together in tolerable harmony. Giving consent to the system is a necessary first step in achieving social harmony, or so it would seem to us. At the same time, consent requires that market advocates seriously reconsider just how small government can be in a market economy. A fair market system is not likely to mean that government will be anything close to "minimal."

QUESTIONS TO PONDER

1. Consider several newspaper articles that deal with the distribution of income. How is *fairness* defined (implicitly or explicitly) in the articles? How does the conception of fairness discussed in this chapter different from the conceptions found in the articles?

2. What does freedom of opportunity have to do with fairness of income outcomes?

3. "Free trade is unfair. We need protection from foreign competition to 'level the playing field' and to make international trade more fair." How do you react to that statement? Is protected trade fair trade?

PART FOUR

The New World of Crime and Dishonesty

CHAPTER 15

Law, Crime, and Punishment

Primitive human beings probably had few formal laws. In fact, they may have had no formal laws at all. Today, however, wherever you go in the world formal laws abound, and many of these laws in one place have many things in common with those in other places. In the United States, Russia, Chile, and China, murder, burglary, and theft are all illegal. In all four of these countries, when the laws are broken, a police system and a court apparatus deal with the crimes.

Needless to say, legal codes differ. In the United States, you are more or less free to say anything you wish, but this is emphatically not true in the other three countries listed above. Buying something with the intent of re-selling it at an increased price is illegal in both China and Russia, while the same act is perfectly legal in the United States and Chile. At the same time, New Jersey has outlawed self-service gas stations, meaning pumping your own gas in that state carries a penalty.

Just the fact that something is illegal does not mean that people act legally. There are two basic questions about the law that are of particular interest to economists. The first is why certain forms of behavior are illegal, and the second is why people behave legally (or illegally) as much as they do.

THE ECONOMICS OF THE LAW

The fact that laws differ from country to country is not particularly sur-prising; but the fact that the laws of many countries are similar in a number of basic characteristics is striking. Why do we find burglary illegal practically everywhere? One answer of course, is that it is immoral. We do not quarrel with this particular answer, but we would like to point out that there are good, practical—even economic—reasons for making burglary, theft, and murder illegal. Since this is a book on economics, we are going to deal with these practical reasons, not the moral issues. However, moral principles will not detract from our discussion.

In order to understand the economic underpinnings of laws, consider the relatively simple case of burglary. We start with an obvious observation. In burglary one person (the burglar) gains, and one person (the victim) loses. The victim obviously objects to the burglary. Furthermore, as a practical matter, the injury to the victim (in terms of the market value of the stolen property) is likely to be greater than the gain to the burglar. This is because the victim characteristically has acquired the property that is stolen for his or her own use, while the burglar normally steals it in order to sell it. The use value of the object to the rightful owner is apt to be greater than the sale value to the burglar.

Although it is normally true that the fence value of stolen property is less than its use value, it is not inevitable. In exceptional cases, the burglar may put a higher value on what is stolen than the original owner does. Still, the burglary amounts to a pure transfer of wealth with one person benefiting and another losing, and not everyone is always opposed to all such transfers. Robin Hood has been praised by generations of readers for having taken from the rich in order to give to the poor. During the New Left political movement in the United States in the late 1960s and early 1970s, "ripping off" the system was held up as a positively virtuous act by a fairly large number of people. However, the members of the New Left spoke only of theft from the system, not theft from their own members.

Some might argue that burglary poses no great problem to society. If burglary were perfectly legal, everyone would engage in it and no one would suffer any great loss. What A stole from us, we would steal from C, who in turn would steal it from A—or so it might be thought.

However, a critical point would have been overlooked. Suppose that you have some property. In order to retain it, you either have to guard it yourself (and this may not be sufficient if the burglars come in groups) or strengthen your house so that people cannot break in. Clearly, strengthening your house can be a difficult and expensive business, but if burglary were legal, people would provide themselves with far more protection against burglary than they do now. They would have better locks, stronger doors, grills on the windows, and so forth. They would also, no doubt, spend a fair amount of time guarding their property, and this would cut into their time applied to productive activity.

People's living standard would fall as they expended more resources protecting all that they have earned. With more resources devoted to protecting against theft, fewer resources would be available for satisfying consumer wants. Furthermore, the return on their productive work would be lower because they would have to calculate that in a world of legalized theft, a greater part of their earnings would in fact be stolen from time to time.

Those individuals in society who consider burglary a suitable occupation would devote more of their time and attention to stealing their neighbors' property. This means that a segment of the labor force would be involved in acquiring good burglar tools and skills. Of course, if people make their houses more burglar proof, burglars will react by improving their tools and skills. And the improved tools and skills of the burglar will mean that people will have to fortify their houses even more. Once again, resources are diverted from productive activity to uses that effectively cancel each other out.

When we buy a new lock for our doors, we injure the burglar by making it harder to break into our house. Similarly, when the burglar buys some new burglar tools, the gain he or she makes from them is accompanied by a loss to us: The tools make it easier for the burglar to get our property, and that, of course, is an injury to us. Thus, with no laws, the escalated plundering and protective behaviors will inflict severe costs (referred to as externalities) on everyone, and total production will fall. Certain individuals may not do too badly by such a modus operandi, but clearly, society as a whole loses.

THE COSTS OF CRIME

In the preceding section, we were concerned mainly with justifying on economic grounds laws of any kind. For the rest of the chapter, we seek to develop more thoroughly the economic model of criminal behavior. As you will see, this model leads to conclusions about how criminals should be treated in order to solve those social problems considered to be criminal.

Costs to the Criminal

As was subsumed in all that has been said so far in this chapter, crime is an economic as well as a sociological and psychological problem. There are definite benefits (at least to the criminal) and costs associated with criminal activity. Criminals can possibly increase their lifetime income even though at times they may be imprisoned. They can reduce the number of hours worked per week and, perhaps, improve their working conditions. In addition, criminals can, within some socioeconomic groups, raise their status among their peers by committing crimes and even by serving time.

To obtain these benefits, criminals must incur the costs of developing the right skills (unless they want to run the risk of bungling the job), acquiring necessary tools such as guns and explosives, and making the contacts that may be necessary to pull off the job. In the narcotics business, criminals must invest in raw materials, storage facilities, and processing and transportation equipment. Criminals, like other business people, may have to meet a payroll, which may include sales and administrative personnel. In the business of shylocking, the accumulation of financial assets is important. Prostitutes may have to incur the costs of physical abuse and medical treatment.

If criminals are specialists in armed robbery or burglary, they must spend the time required (which implies opportunity cost) to case the site of the crime, to wait for the opportune moment, to pull off the crime itself, to fence the stolen goods, and to stay under cover until things have cooled. If caught, they have the additional costs of legal help (unless a court-appointed lawyer is secured). If convicted, they must forgo the income they could have earned while incarcerated; and because of their records, they can suffer a reduction in earning ability after being released. There may also be, for some, the psychic cost of having done something wrong and the loss of respect within the family and community structure. (Consider the cases of former President Richard Nixon and former Vice President Spiro Agnew.)

The cost to the individual of committing his or her own crimes can be viewed as rising as the general level of criminal activity rises. As the crime rate rises, the public can be reasonably expected (beyond some threshold) to respond by applying more resources to crime prevention, making it more difficult (more costly) for the criminal to commit crimes. In addition, one might expect all criminals to commit those crimes first that will yield the largest amount of booty per resource expenditure, meaning the lower-cost crimes. This implies that to extend the level of criminal activities, criminals will have to seek out lower-cost alternatives or more lucrative opportunities. Like all other production processes, one might also expect criminal activity to be subject to the law of diminishing returns. (Why?)

Costs to the Victim

The victim of a robbery or burglary will suffer the loss of the stolen property, and possibly, bodily and mental injury, implying medical bills and loss of income. In the case of rape, the victim may be subjected not only to an extreme amount of violence but also to community gossip; and even though she may be innocent of any wrongdoing, her reputation can be damaged. This may be particularly true if the victim takes the rapist to court. The defense attorney, in an effort to make the strongest possible case for his client, may parade any possibly questionable relationships in the victim's past before the press and community, distorting them wherever possible. The cost of legal fees and time spent in lawyers' offices and the court can be (for her and other victims of other crimes) a substantial portion of the total cost borne. It is because of such cost, no doubt, that many crimes go unreported. In the case of murder, the victims may be, in addition to the one murdered, the family and friends who lose income and friendship.

Costs to Society

The total cost of crimes extends far beyond those directly involved in the crime itself. Nonvictims must, in an attempt to avoid being victims, incur the costs of locks, burglar alarm systems, outside lights, and the many other devices used to make crime more costly to prospective criminals. The nonvictim may also have to incur the cost required to avoid high crime areas.

Crime will also impose higher taxes on victims and nonvictims alike since police protection and judicial, penal, and (to a limited extent) rehabilitation systems are not likely to be avoided. Society may also experience a loss of social interaction. Because of fear of being sexually molested, children are taught not to speak to strangers and, above all, not to get in their cars. Women may avoid speaking to or walking on the same side of a street with men they do not know. Since police officers are given a considerable amount of discretionary power over whom to stop, search, and arrest, crime can impose on the general population a "liberty tax." Finally, people shopping in stores often go out of their way to ensure that they do not give the impression that they are shoplifting.

RATIONALITY AND CRIME

The societal problem of crime can be described and analyzed with the model of rational behavior developed in Chapter 1. This model will help us understand the limits of criminal behavior.

The Rational Criminal

To the degree that crime involves benefits and costs, crime can be a rational act, and the amount of crime actually committed can be determined in the same manner as is the amount of any other activity. The only difference may be that crime involves behavior that is against the law.

Like any other group, criminals can weigh off the benefits and costs and can choose the combination that maximizes their own utility; they will maximize their utility if they commit those crimes for which the additional benefits exceed the additional costs.

Because of the cost of crime, the amount of crime committed can fall far short of the amount that can, technically speaking, be committed. This would be true even if we ignore or dismiss the costs of being caught and punished. For example, suppose that the benefits of committing a particular crime, such as robbery, for a prospective criminal are illustrated by the downward sloping demand curve in Figure 15–1. (Why is the demand downward sloping?) (In this graph the quantity of crimes is on the horizontal axis and the marginal costs and benefits are on the vertical axis.) Suppose, also, that we consider only nonpunishment costs such as raw materials, labor, and equipment. Further, assume that the supply curve (or marginal cost curve, S_1) in Figure 15–1 is upward sloping.

As indicated by the graph, there are benefits to committing additional crimes until Q_1 have been committed; beyond Q_1, the additional benefits to further criminal activity become negative. However, at Q_1 the cost of committing the last crime (MC_1) is far greater than the additional benefits, which, at that level of activity, are zero. The criminal, if he is operating at Q_1, can increase his personal satisfaction by reducing the number of crimes committed. If he reduces the number of crimes all the way back to Q_2, the marginal benefits from the last crime would then exceed the cost, in which event it follows that he could improve his utility by increasing the number of crimes. Needless to say by now, the rational criminal can maximize his utility by committing up to Q_3 crimes, at which point the additional benefits are equal to the additional costs.

FIGURE 15–1

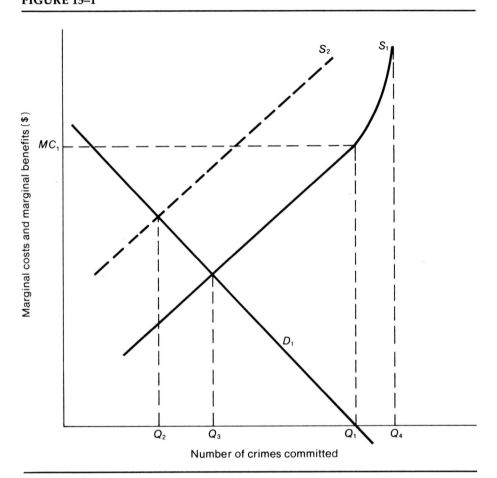

The analysis can be extended to include the total market for crime by adding horizontally the individuals' demands and supplies. The total community crime level would then be established at the intersection of the market demand and market supply curves.

There are three important points that can be drawn from the graphical analysis and that should be given particular attention. The first point is that the number of crimes committed by the rational criminal will not be equal to the maximum, which for our purposes can be defined as Q_1, where the demand curve intersects the horizontal axis, or Q_4, where the supply curve becomes essentially vertical.

The second point that needs to be emphasized is that, given the demand for crime, the number of crimes perpetrated is dependent on the cost. If punishment is introduced into the analysis and the type of punishment employed represents an increase in cost to the criminal, the supply curve will decrease (that is, move upward and to the left) to, say, S_2. As a result, the number of crimes the criminal will choose to commit will be lowered. One can also suggest that anything that reduces the cost of crime, such as reduction in the cost of handguns or an increase in the leniency of the courts, can increase the supply of crime and thereby the number of crimes actually committed. This would also be the case if society became more tolerant of or sympathetic toward criminals. (Why?)

The third point is that although one can observe that a large number of crimes are committed, such as Q_2 in Figure 15–1, one cannot conclude that the severity of punishment has no effect on criminal activity. If the difference between S_1 and S_2 represents the cost imposed on the criminal by the penal system, then one can deduce that the penal system has deterred Q_3–Q_2 crimes. In other words, the effectiveness of a penal system can be judged by how many crimes are committed. However, a more appropriate indication of the effectiveness of punishment, or any other policy that increases the cost of crime to the criminal, is how many crimes are never committed because of that punishment (but would have been committed in the absence of the punishment). This, we believe, is a point police readily see but one that other concerned individuals who count the number of crimes often overlook.

If the booty from committing crimes increases while the cost remains constant, one could also predict from our model that the demand for crime would rise to the upper right as in Figure 15–2. The number of crimes committed, we predict, would go up.

The Irrational Criminal

There is a common notion among lay and professional criminologists and sociologists that certain criminals who commit certain types of crime do not behave rationally: they do not weigh off the benefits and costs of their actions. We will treat this controversial issue in greater detail in the next chapter. At this point, however, we want to assure the reader that we concede the point that there are "sick" criminals, just as we would concede the issue if anyone ever suggested that there are sick plumbers, business people, and professors.

To the extent that sick criminals do not measure the consequences of their actions, their demand curves for crime are vertical. However, this does not mean that the demand for the crime in general is not downward. The market demand curve will still be downward sloping so long as there are rational criminals in the market. The existence of the irrational criminal just moves the market demand curve for crime out to the right and does not change the slope. The supply of crimes will also increase since there are more criminals.

For example, suppose that there are rational and irrational criminals in the market and the market demand for crime by rational criminals is equal to

FIGURE 15–2

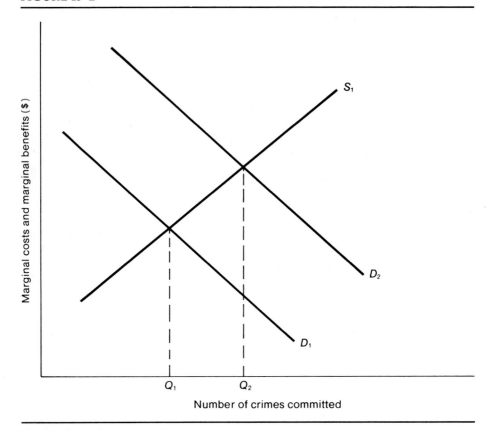

D_1 in Figure 15–3. If, for purposes of illustration, there are Q_1 crimes committed by irrational criminals, then the total market demand and supply curves
would be at D_2 and S_2. The total number of crimes committed would then be
Q_2, that is, Q_1 by irrational criminals and $Q_2 - Q_1$ committed by rational
criminals.

The reader should recognize that so long as the market demand for crime
is downward sloping, the changes in the cost of crime as discussed above
should lead to changes in the number of crimes committed by the rational
criminals. Since the irrational criminals, by definition, do not consider costs
in their behavioral decisions, one should not expect their level of crime to be
affected. However, the important point is that the total market response to
punishment should be in the same direction as predicted for rational criminals. (The percentage change in the amount of crime would not be as great.
This means that the introduction of irrational criminals reduces the elasticity
of demand for crime.)

FIGURE 15–3   The Revised View of Minimum Wage Laws

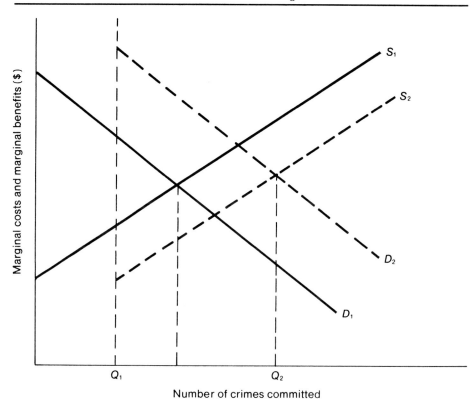

THE ECONOMICS OF BEING A NONVICTIM

Victims of crimes suffer, and in that sense, people can benefit by actively avoiding crimes. For certain types of crimes, such as aggravated assault, the benefits of crime avoidance can be considerable; for other types, such as having a potted petunia plant stolen from one's backyard, the benefits can be very slight mainly because the value of the stolen property can be very low.

In any event, people have a demand for crime avoidance, which implies a demand for locks and other devices and means of thwarting crimes. Furthermore, if nonvictims are rational, their demand for crime avoidance is downward sloping, as it is for everything else they value.

As illustrated in Figure 15–4, this means that a person will avoid more crimes the cheaper it is to do so. If the price (which must be imputed from the cost of equipment and time) of avoiding a particular crime is P_1, the number of crimes avoided will be Q_1. More pointedly, people will do only so much to reduce the risk of crimes being committed against them.

FIGURE 15–4

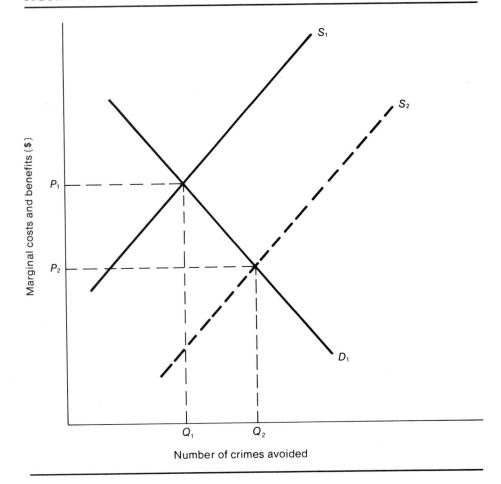

This means, of course, that they will "permit," in a sense, some crimes to be committed. Granted, if there were no cost involved in crime avoidance, everyone would prefer never being a victim to being one at times. However, if people did everything necessary to avoid ever being a victim, the cost (including time cost) of avoiding certain types or crimes, such as petty larceny or even burglary, could, over the long run, be greater than what they would have lost had they been less cautious and been at times a victim.

To put the problem in a little different perspective, would you expect someone to spend $100,000 to avoid being robbed of $75,000? This is an extreme example, but do people not address similar questions when they consider taking measures to avoid crimes?

Clearly, people do limit the number and quality of locks on their doors; college professors (the authors included) generally have locks on their doors that they know can be picked by any reasonably good thief. In fact, one of the authors is inclined to leave his office door wide open when he is out on errands or in class. One reason is that any prospective thief will have to pass by a secretary and can be observed by others who may be close by. Another reason is simply that he calculates that there really is not all that much in his office to steal and that, quite honestly, he generally figures the value of his time spent locking his door, searching for his keys, and unlocking the door can, over the long run, far exceed the value of the property likely to be stolen. You can be assured, however, that when he has an expensive laptop computer sitting on his desk, he closes and locks his door upon leaving. (Is his behavior inconsistent?)

Many people do not put bars on their windows; the major cost here is likely to be the deterioration of the outward appearance of their homes. People are also willing to walk in some areas at some times well aware that the probability of being mugged is above zero. Admittedly when the probability is quite high, such as may be the case in New York's Central Park at midnight, they may be willing to forgo their walks. However, just because people may not be willing to walk in Central Park, one cannot conclude that they are unwilling to assume any risk or take any chance of becoming a victim. If individuals tried to avoid ever being a victim of crime, we are convinced that they would lead a very dull life! In other words, rational behavior on the part of potential victims can make the criminal's work a little easier than otherwise.

Given the above discussion and Figure 15–4, it follows that if the cost of avoiding crime falls, the supply of crime avoidance will expand downward and to the right, resulting in an increased number of crimes avoided—that is, a person will buy more locks or take more time to avoid being caught in a threatening situation. Again, it should be stressed that given the cost reduction, the rational person will do only so much to avoid crimes.

It also follows that if the benefits from crime avoidance increase, the individual will expend more effort and money in an attempt to avoid crimes. This increase in demand, as illustrated in Figure 15–5, can be the result of an increase in the value of that which could be stolen, or perhaps an increase in a person's assessment of the worth of her own physical condition or life. A person who may be depressed and care very little about living can hardly be expected to divert many resources to avoid being killed. In addition, the increase in demand can result from an increase in the probability of being a victim; in such a circumstance it is reasonable to expect a person to be willing to pay a higher price for crime avoidance.

Notice that in all of these cases, the increase in the cost of avoiding crimes curtails the number of crimes that the individual will attempt to avoid. In our graph, if the price of crime avoidance had remained at P_1, the quantity of crimes avoided would have been Q_3; however, because the price of crime avoidance rises to P_2, the number of crimes avoided is Q_2. This quantity is higher than the original number Q_1, but still is not as great as it would have been had the price remained at P_1.

FIGURE 15–5

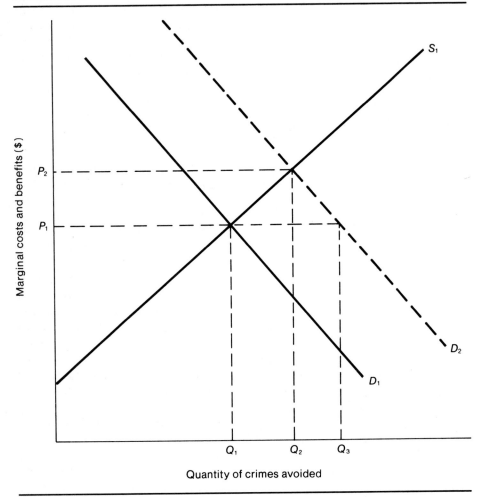

Quantity of crimes avoided

POLICE PROTECTION

The individual citizen, not the police, is society's first line of defense against crime. The citizen may be an amateur, undisciplined, and untrained in modern police techniques, but she does have one thing going for her and that is her own private interest in protecting those things that to her are valuable. If it were not for such motivation, we can be assured that the work of the criminal would be greatly eased. Police can contribute to crime control, but one should understand that, in urban areas today, there are only about two police officers for every 1,000 residents.

From this perspective, police protection and law enforcement should be viewed as a supplement to the basic protection people provide for themselves.

Generally speaking (but not always), the services of police are provided by local government, and this is done for two basic reasons. First, it may be more efficient to provide the additional protection through some collective organization. As opposed to having every store owner check to ensure that his doors are locked after closing hours, the duty can be assigned to a police officer on that beat. A great deal of traveling time can be saved. Such services need not be provided publicly and often are not. Shopping centers, for example, do provide their own security guards; in a sense they are selling police protection along with the floor space.

Second, police protection is not always the type of service that can be bought and sold in the market on a customer-by-customer basis. There are activities for which the police could conceivably charge in much the same way as Coca-Cola does for its drinks. This might be where the service is specifically intended to benefit one particular individual (or group) and the service can be withheld unless the individual pays the prescribed fee. An example might be a police officer's retrieval of stolen property for a particular individual; if the individual does not pay for the service, the service can be withheld.

On the other hand, the benefits of police activity can be spread quite generally across the community. The presence of the police can provide an additional threat to all criminals operating in the community, and the police can contribute to the removal of criminals from the community by making crime less profitable or putting them behind bars. In such cases, all members of the community benefit (albeit in varying degrees) since the risk of becoming a victim is lowered. In addition, the community can, because of the police presence, reduce their own private actions intended to thwart crime.

If such generalized benefits are provided, then all members of the community must share in those benefits. The police can deny some benefits to some people by denying them some services, as discussed above, but they cannot deny to anyone those benefits that pervade the entire community. Consequently, it may be extremely difficult (if not impossible) for the police to charge for the generalized benefits.

If a resident benefits regardless of whether or not he pays, then it is understandable why he may refuse to pay on a voluntary basis. For one thing, he can figure that he can get the protection free if it is provided. Second, he may reason that the amount he would be willing to contribute to the "police fund" may be so small in relation to what is needed that any contribution he makes will neither determine whether the police protection is provided nor significantly influence the amount of protection he receives. Therefore, police protection must be financed by some extramarket means—that is, by taxation.

The members of the community may gladly consent to some additional taxation because they know there are benefits to be reaped from police services; and without the intervention of government, meaning taxation, police protection may not be provided. This can be particularly true in the larger communities where social pressure is impotent. By voting for the additional taxes, not only may the individual acquire the very slight benefits from the taxes he himself pays, but he can also benefit from the taxes paid by others.

There are limits, however, to the amount of police protection acceptable to a voting public, mainly because, as we have seen elsewhere in this chapter, there are costs involved. As the level of protection is increased, taxes must be raised and people will have to give up other things, such as ice cream and clothes, which they value. As tax rates are raised, we can reasonably assume that there will be more and more people who will find that the benefits received from the additional protection will be less than the additional costs they must incur in the form of taxes. At some point, there will be a sufficient number of votes to defeat any proposal to expand police activities further.

The reader should recognize that by restricting the size of the police departments, the voting public is limiting the number of crimes that will be prevented. They are also allowing, in a sense, some crimes to be committed. The voting public may not like to have crime in their midst, but at the same time they may not want to see their taxes increased either. We personally see very little chance of the public's ever voting to wipe out all crime, even if it were possible. Doing so would be prohibitively expensive.

Having only limited resources with which to prevent and investigate more crimes than they can handle, the police themselves must make certain economic decisions. They must decide whether their resources should be applied in residential or in business areas or whether they should attempt to prevent or investigate burglaries, murders, or rapes. If they apply their resources in preventing burglaries, then they must allow other crimes, such as speeding violations and murders, to occur or go unsolved.

In recent times, the local police departments have been required to enforce price (or rent) controls and a host of other business regulations that have been mandated by the federal, state, and local governments. Having used their resources in this way, they cannot use them to solve other crimes. This is one aspect of government controls that is not readily appreciated by the public who may favor controls.

TWO PERSPECTIVES ON CRIME: THE ECONOMIST VERSUS THE SOCIOLOGIST

The editors of the *Washington Post* are against private ownership of guns and devote part of the paper's editorial content to denouncing it. As part of this campaign years ago, they found a professional robber in Washington and interviewed him quite extensively. Under guarantee of anonymity, he was— as far as we can tell—very frank and explained fairly accurately his motives and modus operandi. His special field was armed robbery, and he was apparently making a very good income from it.

He was vaguely unhappy about his occupation because he realized it was risky, but as he said, "I want to go to barber school, but I know there's not that kind of money in barbering." In general, he calculated the risks with care: "Now I know if I's gonna rob somethin' it ought to be big, because I'm gonna get the same time. I stay in the District where the police is too busy. . . . It's too risky in Prince Georges." He read the paper daily "for crime. . . . I want to know how much people out there are gittin' and who's gettin' what kind of time."

Thus, this young criminal explains his own behavior largely in terms of calculations of profits and risk of cost. It is notable that the *Washington Post* reporter seemed to pay little attention to this aspect of the matter, although he reported verbatim lengthy statements made by the criminal. The crimes in the article are blamed on the environment. The article begins by pointing out that the criminal came from a poor family background, but it devotes far more attention to the simple fact that guns are readily available in Washington, D.C., than to any other aspect of the environment.

Further, there seems to be no evidence that the reporter thought of the ready availability of guns in Washington as merely a reduction in the cost of criminal activity. The reporter regarded these environmental factors as direct causes of crime rather than as changes in technological conditions that may conceivably lead profit-seeking individuals to choose a life of crime. We got the impression reading the article—albeit we must read between the lines for this—that the reporter felt that the statements the criminal made about the risks and profits were evidence of his having had a bad environment, rather than statements about the cost-benefit calculations that led him to continue his life of crime.

It is possible that we are misrepresenting the reporter's attitude by imputing to him values and positions we find in the *Washington Post* and, indeed, in a very large part of all modern discussions of crime. The conventional wisdom in this field holds that criminals are either sick persons who require treatment or are the result of environmental deprivation (which seems to amount to much the same thing operationally), and that the possibility of punishment—which plays such a large part in this criminal's calculation—actually is unimportant in determining whether a person does or does not commit any crime. It is argued that people commit crimes not because they see an opportunity for profit, but because they are somehow socially deformed.

Further, it is thought that the way to deal with this problem is to change the basic environment so that no person is deformed by the environment or to rehabilitate the criminal once captured. This is one of two dominant hypotheses about criminal activity.

The other hypothesis, the one that immediately occurs to any economist, is that criminals are simply people who take opportunities for profit by violating the law. Under this hypothesis, changing the costs of crime—that is, increasing the likelihood of being put in prison, lengthening the period of imprisonment, or making prisons less pleasant—would tend to reduce the amount of crime. As discussed, the reasoning is simply that the criminals' demand for crime, like their demands for other more normal goods and activities, is downward sloping: the greater the cost or price, the lower the quantity demanded. Rehabilitation for such criminals would be relatively pointless, since the individual is not sick.[1] He is simply behaving rationally.

People with economic training are apt to take the latter of these two hypotheses as true and those with sociological training, the former. Until recently, in any event, sociologists were inclined to dismiss the economic view of crime:

> This misplaced faith in punishment may rest upon the unrealistic assumption that people consciously decide whether to be criminal—that they consider a criminal career, rationally balance its dangers against its rewards, and arrive at a decision based upon such pleasure-pain calculations. It supposedly follows that if the pain element is increased by severe punishment, people will turn from crime to righteousness. A little reflection reveals the absurdity of this notion.[2]

The problem, however, is basically one for empirical research. Before turning to a discussion of the empirical research that has been done in the field, we should like to clarify the two hypotheses a little bit, to explain the difficulties of testing the difference between them. The economic hypothesis holds that crime would tend to occur whenever the cost would fall below the receipts. The costs, in a very straightforward and simple way, would be the energy and equipment put into the actual crime (usually quite small) plus the expected value of punishment, which in our society is apt to be imprisonment.

From the sociological standpoint, these two variables would appear to be largely irrelevant. Indeed, we have never been able to understand how people who believe in the conventional wisdom favor imprisonment at all.[3]

The costs and benefits, however, are to some extent affected by environmental variables in which the sociologists are interested. First, a poor person is probably less injured by being put in jail than the wealthy person. Thus, one would anticipate that the poor would count the cost of imprisonment as being lower than would the wealthy. Hence, other things being equal, opportunities for crime that would attract the poor person would appear to be

---

[1] Our prisons, in point of fact, devote practically no effort to rehabilitation. This is probably wise since those experiments in rehabilitation that have been undertaken seem to show that we do not know how to do it. See Robert Martinson, "What Works?—Questions and Answers about Prison Reform," *Public Interest* 35 (Spring 1974), pp. 22–54.

[2] P. B. Horton and G. R. Leslie, *The Sociology of Social Problems* (New York: Appleton-Century-Crofts, 1960), p. 155.

[3] Indeed, some of them have drawn the logical conclusion from their reasoning and *are* opposed to imprisonment. This opinion, however, is more apt to turn up in private conversation than in print. For one example in print, see *Nation,* September 27, 1971, pp. 258–59.

unprofitable from the standpoint of the wealthy person. Second, the size of the booty would be of interest. Large concentrations of wealth would attract potential criminals who would not be interested in small quantities.

These two factors, taken together, would indicate that wide disparity in income might increase crime. A wide disparity of income means that there are some people in the community for whom imprisonment has a low cost and some targets for crime that would pay off very well. Both poverty and disparity of income might increase the crime rate under either the sociological or the economic explanation.

Last, life in the larger city may reduce the cost of crime as opposed to life in a smaller city. The reasons may be that crime targets are located more closely together and that there is a lower degree of social interaction (implying lower social costs). Ethnic groups may be more willing to protect their own, and, in general, it is harder for police to catch criminals in large cities.

It will be observed that we have listed a number of variables (which the sociologist might consider as causes of crime) as factors that affect the cost and benefit and that therefore may be viewed somewhat indirectly as a cause of crime. This might appear to make the test of the two hypotheses difficult, and indeed it would, were it not for the fact that there are some remaining variables. If we believe that criminals are sick and are not deterred by threat of punishment, then we would predict that changes in the rate of punishment would have no effect on the crime rate. From the economic viewpoint, we would predict that such changes would have an effect on the crime rate. Both the sociologist and the economist would expect the same outcome if statistical tests were made of the first several factors; but when it came to the effect of imprisonment upon the crime rate, there would be a clear difference in the expected result.

Even if the punishment has a statistically significant impact on the amount of crime, strictly speaking, we cannot conclude that the economic hypothesis has been proven. In a strict sense, no hypothesis can ever be *proven* with statistics. Statistics can only fail to *disprove* it. In addition, a much weaker hypothesis that people respond to cost, whether sick or well, would lead to the same result as what we have referred to as the economic hypothesis. Indeed, Gary Becker (an economist) and his students have always used this simpler hypothesis quite explicitly.

Most of the research we discuss below, then, goes to the question of whether or not punishment deters crime but does not directly relate to the rationality or sickness of the criminal. This is, however, enough. If punishment deters crime, then the sociological approach falls to the ground, and much of the advice given to governments by sociologists over the past 50 years is clearly wrong. Indeed, such advice might well be one of the major reasons for the rising crime rate.

Before going on to the question of whether punishment deters crime, it is necessary to make a brief digression on the type of punishment to be used.

At the moment, there are only two forms of punishment in general use in the United States, fines and imprisonment. Of these two, fines are clearly superior because of the immense deadweight loss involved in imprisonment. Not only is output largely lost because very little useful work is performed by prisoners, but the cost of imprisonment, which must be borne by society, is very substantial.

Unfortunately, a large percentage of all criminals cannot pay fines large enough so that we would be able to regard them as having the same deterrent effect of, let us say, 10 years in prison. Under the circumstances, we are driven back on imprisonment; but we should be more than willing to explore other possible alternatives. Prevention of crime by such things as better locks, more careful police patrols, and so forth is one way of reducing the crime rate. To some degree, in any event, it is cheaper than the imprisonment threat. Rehabilitation of criminals would be desirable if we only knew how to do it.

DOES PUNISHMENT DETER CRIME?

Until the 1970s, almost all of the empirical work on whether punishment deters crime was done by sociologists.[4] In practice, however, this work was both scanty and technically rather poor. Further, the small number of tests that had been undertaken mainly dealt with the death penalty. It is not necessarily true that if the death penalty did not deter murder, then imprisonment would not deter burglary.

Testing the deterrent effect of the death penalty on murder is rather difficult because, in the United States where most of the research has been done, death sentences have always been relatively rare. Even in the 1930s, murderers had only about one chance in 60 of being executed, whereas their chance of going to prison for a long period of time was 20 to 30 times as great. Under the circumstances, changes in the frequency of the death penalty would tend to be less significant by a wide margin than other variants in punishment policy.

The difficulty in assessing the effect of punishment on crime rates is that many forces in the criminal environment are often changing at the same time. Some of these forces might encourage crimes; others might discourage crime. There are modern statistical techniques that permit taking a number of factors into account at the same time. The most common technique involves statistical methods that fall under the rubric of *multiple regression analysis.* These early studies of the death penalty, however, used simpler and less effective methods of statistical analysis. In part, this is no criticism of the sociologists, for many of these studies were performed before large computers were available. It is notable, however, that the studies were not repeated with

---

[4]For a survey of the early sociological research, see Hugo Adam Bedau, *The Death Penalty in America,* rev. ed. (Garden City, N.Y.: Doubleday, 1967).

more modern methods by the sociologists until the economists entered the debate.

Even with the most modern methods, however, the results are poor with respect to the death penalty. The problem is simply that the death penalty has always been too rare to provide an adequate number of observations. The first economic study on the subject by Isaac Ehrlich showed that each execution prevented somewhere around eight murders.[5] More recently, critics have run a number of additional studies partly using additional data and partly questioning Ehrlich's methods. At the moment, we think an honest statement would be that the matter is in doubt. As economists, we tend to think that the death penalty would indeed reduce the frequency of murder, but that is a theoretical rather than an empirical statement.

However, the problem is an extremely theoretical one. Data in crime are almost incredibly bad, even for murder. Still, we can see little evidence that the sociologists have tried to apply really suitable methods to the problem. These inadequate tests of the deterrent effect of the death penalty were, however, until recently the only empirical investigations that had been undertaken on the deterrent effect of punishment. In spite of the fact that this evidence was extremely weak, sociologists and criminologists continued to say that it had been demonstrated that punishment had no deterrent effect.

The widely popular view that criminals are sick is based not on a few poor empirical studies but on zero empirical studies. Some criminals are indeed mentally ill, and they are customarily segregated from the other criminals during the trial process. Thus, most states maintain facilities for the criminally insane as well as for ordinary criminals. There seems to be, however, absolutely no evidence that criminals who are in the ordinary prisons are more likely to be insane than people outside or that the sickness they do have has much to do with their crimes.

In addition, if statistical investigations deal exclusively with criminals who are in prisons and who are, by definition, failures at their jobs, one can easily get a distorted picture. If we attempted to judge the intelligence and sanity of the business community as a whole by primarily observing the business people who go bankrupt, without question we would likely develop a distorted picture of the business community.

What, then, have the criminologist and sociologist investigated? The answer is the environmental background of the criminal. As we have pointed out, people from poor backgrounds are apt to have a lower cost of crime; hence, even under the economic explanation, we would anticipate that they would commit more crimes. Studies of this sort, then, do not differentiate between the two basic hypotheses, and such studies have dominated the work on the determinants of crime by sociologists and criminologists. Indeed,

---

[5]Isaac Ehrlich, "The Deterrent Effect of Capital Punishment: A Question of Life and Death," *American Economic Review* 65 (June 1975), pp. 397–417.

until very recently, those economists who turned their attention to crime simply accepted the dominant opinion of sociology and criminology and repeated the sociologists' studies, albeit with somewhat different methodology.[6]

Once economists began working on crime, however, it was inevitable that they would begin to investigate the possibility that crimes—like everything else—are affected by price. The deterrence theory of punishment is, after all, simply a special version of the general economic principle that raising the price of something will reduce the amount purchased.[7] The first serious empirical research by an economist to test this proposition was undertaken by Arleen Smigel Leibowitz under the direction of Gary Becker.[8] Presumably the basic research design was his, and it set the standard and style for the bulk of empirical research that we shall discuss.

For certain types of crime, Arleen Leibowitz ran a multiple regression routine in which the crime rate by state was a dependent variable and the punishment was the independent variable. She found a pronounced deterrent effect. The technical excellence of this study, together with the conflict between it and the conventional wisdom, set off an immense flood of further research. The research started slowly but, as time went by, it became a torrent. Having addressed all the basic issues, the economic research on crime began to dwindle in the 1980s.[9]

All of these studies of which we are aware have indicated that punishment does deter crime. The studies have been carried on in the United States, in Canada, in England, and in Germany. International comparison, although a little dubious, seems to show the same results. Students in search of new data have turned to local rather than national figures and have compared counties in various states rather than the states as a whole. On the whole, the data have become overwhelmingly favorable for the deterrence hypothesis.

Indeed, the more recent studies have normally accepted the deterrence hypothesis and investigated something else, with deterrence appearing in

---

[6]See, for example, Belton M. Fleisher, *The Economics of Delinquency* (New York: Quadrangle/ New York Times, 1966).

[7]For earlier and more rigorous discussions of the economic approach to crime, see Gary S. Becker, "Crime and Punishment: An Economic Approach," *Journal of Political Economy* 76 (March/April 1968), pp. 169–217; and Gordon Tullock, "The Welfare Costs of Monopolies, Tariffs, and Theft," *Western Economic Journal* 5 (June 1967), pp. 224–32. The latter refers to the deterrent effects of punishment only in passing.

[8]Arleen Smigel Leibowitz, "Does Crime Pay: An Economic Analysis" (A.M. thesis, Columbia University, 1965).

[9]In the first edition of *The New World of Economics*, we had a fairly lengthy discussion of this empirical research, together with a bibliography. We decided to leave that out here simply because the volume of evidence is now so overwhelming in favor of the economic hypothesis that merely listing it would take up too much space. The reader may turn to the first edition: Richard McKenzie and Gordon Tullock, *The New World of Economics* (Homewood, Ill.: Richard D. Irwin, 1975), pp. 153–55.

their equations not as the primary hypothesis but as a variable included to reduce what otherwise might be noise. In this way, the research continues to test deterrence, even though that is not the major objective of the researcher. Return to the use of the death penalty for murder by a number of states in the 1980s may be objectionable on a number of grounds. It will, however, provide researchers with much needed data on the deterrence impact of capital punishment.

CONCLUDING COMMENTS

Ideas influence the real world. The fact that most specialists in the study of crime have believed, written, and taught that punishment does not deter crime has had an effect on public policy. Legislatures have been more reluctant to appropriate money for prisons than they otherwise would have been; judges have tended to feel that imprisonment has little effect on crime and hence, at the intellectual level in any event, were less willing to put people in jail for long periods of time.

Further, the shortage of prisons so induced has made it impossible to keep people in jail for long periods of time for serious crimes. As a result, halfway houses (which are very inexpensive), parole, and probation have been resorted to on a very large scale, and this has sharply reduced the cost of crime. The reduced cost of crime leads in turn to a rise in the crime rate, which leads to further clogging of facilities and hence further reduction in the cost of crime. The rising crime rate in the United States to a very considerable extent may be blamed on our intellectual community.

QUESTIONS TO PONDER

1. Jeremy Bentham referred to the English common law as *dog law*. He pointed out that dog trainers sometimes simply punish a dog every time it does something they want it to refrain from doing. With time, the dog learns not to do the act that brings the punishment. Do you think this is a fair description of our law? Do you think it is true of other legal codes also? Do you think it is a good or bad thing?

2. Many of the people who allege that punishment does not deter crime seem to make exceptions for violations of the antitrust law and tax evasion. Is this consistent?

3. Good performance in school is usually rewarded with good grades and poor performance is penalized with bad grades. Even sociologists, who argue that punishment does not control people's behavior, use this method of grading their students. Is this consistent with their basic position?

4. If government increases the scope of its regulation of business, what is likely to happen to the crime rate? (Consider the effect on violations of the

business regulations, of laws against theft and personal injury, and of laws against tax evasion.) Why?

5. Executions of murderers escalated in the mid-1980s. Explain the effect on the crimes rate of the rise in executions, from the economic and the sociological perspectives. Is it possible to accept the economic perspective on capital punishment and, at the same time, to be against capital punishment?

- crime rate for major crimes will go down
- cost, death → too much

CHAPTER 16

Cheating and Lying

Criminal behavior can be, partially at least, explained and predicted by economic principles. That is the central message of Chapter 15. However, there is much behavior that is not criminal in the sense that any law has been broken but that may be equally reprehensible because social and institutional rules, not always enforced by government, are broken. This chapter is mainly concerned with two frequent ways social rules are broken by most of us, cheating and lying. Our purpose is to apply the economic principles developed in the last preceding chapters and to better understand the economic conditions that promote or retard cheating and lying.

THE ECONOMICS OF CHEATING

Cheating is a continual problem in all educational institutions. Exactly how much cheating is likely to go on across a university campus is unclear, but we do have several very interesting studies.

Charles Tittle and Alan Rowe, both sociologists, designed a study to determine the influence that moral appeal and threat of sanction had on the amount of cheating that went on in their classes.[1] To do this, they gave weekly quizzes to their students; the instructors took the quizzes, graded them without marking the papers, and then, at the next class meeting, returned them to the students for them to grade. Without any appeal being made to the students that they were on their honor to grade them correctly, the students in one test group took 31 percent of all opportunities to cheat. The other test group took 41 percent of all opportunities.

Next the instructors made an appeal to the students' sense of morality in grading the papers, and the instructors concluded that "emphasizing the moral principle involved in grading the quizzes was also ineffectual. A moral appeal had no effect whatsoever in reducing the incidence of cheating."[2] In fact, in one of the test groups, the amount of cheating went up substantially after the appeal was made.

---

[1]Charles R. Tittle and Alan R. Rowe, "Fear and the Student Cheater," *Change*, April 1974, pp. 47–48.
[2]Ibid., p. 47.

Finally the instructors threatened to spot-check the quizzes for cheating, and the amount of cheating fell sharply from the 41 percent range to 13 percent in one class and from 43 percent to 32 percent in the other. They also concluded from the study that the instructor who had a reputation of being "lovable and understanding" had the greater amount of cheating in his class, and they found that "Those who were most in need of points were willing to take greater risks (that is, cheated more). This is consistent with the theory that the greater the utility of an act, the greater the potential punishment required to deter it. And perhaps it shows the futility of a moral appeal in a social context where all individuals are not successful."[3]

One of the authors, McKenzie, replicated the above study in a somewhat different form and, in this case, for a slightly different purpose. He wanted to see how many students would cheat on a test which the students were told would not be considered in their grades. He gave his introductory economics classes a test on the first day of the term. He had their answer sheets photocopied and the copies graded by a graduate student. During the next class session, his secretary gave back the original answer sheets and called out the correct answers. Later, by comparing the copy and the original answer sheet, it was found that 15 percent of the students cheated, and this was on a quiz that had no bearing on the students' grades.

As a point of interest, one student was rather ingenious in the way in which he cheated. In taking the test, he had left the last eight answers blank; when he was given a chance to correct his own, he filled in the answers. Because he apparently did not want it to appear too obvious what he had done, he intentionally missed three of them and marked them wrong like all the others that he had missed!

The findings of these two studies provide educational insights unrecognized before the studies were undertaken. Several decades ago, Hartshorne and May undertook a study of several thousand children in the fourth through eighth grades.[4] Their study, which has not been seriously disputed, is considered a classic within the psychology profession.

One of their tests was to give the students a set of examinations in which the students could cheat with ease but the instructor would always know that they had cheated. Approximately 97 percent of the students cheated at least once. The Hartshorne and May conclusion is striking: "No one is honest or dishonest by 'nature.' "[5]

Less dramatically, Nicolaus Tideman invented a statistical method of determining how many times a particular type of cheating occurs. The type of cheating considered, copying the paper from the person sitting next to you

---

[3]Ibid., p. 48.
[4]Hugh Hartshorne and Mark May, *Studies on the Nature of Character: Studies on Deceit* (New York: Macmillan, 1930).
[5]Ibid., p. 412.

on a multiple choice examination, can be detected by a complicated computer analysis of the examination papers. Tideman's studies showed the number of cheaters in various classes as low as zero or as high as 20 percent.

The problem of cheating, then, is a relatively common one. However, the economist is typically interested in asking two other questions. What is the gain and loss from cheating? Who, if anyone, gets hurt?

Consider Pete, a student who is worried about his grade in a given course and thinks it would be possible to cheat. The gain if he does cheat is, of course, the improvement in grade he can expect from cheating times the probability that he will get away with it. This is true regardless of how much he learns in the course. How well he has studied is, of course, relevant to how much his grade will improve. If he will get an A anyway, why cheat?

The cost of cheating is, first, that the cheater's conscience may bother him. If Pete has been taught that cheating is a bad thing (and it must be remembered that this is not true of everyone), then there is some positive cost to him for violating his own ethical rule. For some people, this cost is so high that they would never violate the rule against cheating, no matter what the benefits they could expect. For other people it is so low that they would violate it any time they saw a chance.

President Carter's principal press spokesman, Jody Powell, was expelled from the Air Force Academy for cheating. Senator Edward Kennedy was expelled from Harvard for cheating on a Spanish test and being caught. Presumably at the time he hired a classmate to take the exam for him, he thought the chances of being caught were low. But, surely he realized there was some chance of being caught and took the prospects into account.

A student contemplating cheating, then, will compare the benefit with the cost. The moral issue is real but not the only one. A very immoral student may decide that the risk is too great, and a student of more than average morality may be tempted by a very good chance under circumstances where the benefit is very great and the chance of being caught is very low.

Who is injured by cheating? Most students tend to think of it as a game with the teacher, but the teacher is, in fact, not hurt particularly by a student cheating. It is true that most teachers disapprove of cheating and tend to feel that they have been made a fool of when students succeed in cheating, but it does not really injure them.

The people who are injured are the other students. In saying this, however, it should be kept in mind that the injury caused by one student's cheating is spread over a number of other students, so that the injury to any one from a single student's cheating is so small as to be almost invisible. Only if a considerable number of students cheat is the injury to any individual student serious.

Suppose a teacher in a class of 100 normally grades on a curve—that is, she gives the top 20 an A, the next 40 a B, the next 30 a C, and the bottom 10 are flunked. One of the students who normally flunks is successful in cheating and therefore gets an A. This means that one of the noncheating students who otherwise would have received an A gets a B, one who otherwise would have gotten a B gets a C, and one of the ones who otherwise would have gotten a C flunks. In this case, the injury is concentrated in three specific people, but it is hard to tell in advance which three students they will be. Thus, at the time the student contemplated cheating, the potential injury was spread out because no one knew who would be the lowest A, the lowest B, or C, and so on.

Curve grading of this sort is not, of course, the only way of grading, and many professors use absolute standards. That is to say, they have a fixed numerical scale for settling the grades of their students. How many of the different grades are given depends upon how many students make scores within the given grade ranges.

Suppose, for example, that there were 50 questions on the test and the professor intended to give an A to those who got 45 or more correct, B to those who got 37 or more correct, and C to those who got 30 or more correct. The cheater moves himself from 20 correct and a flunking grade to 47 correct and an A. This does not make any other single person flunk, but it does mean that there are more As and fewer Fs than there would be otherwise. Hence, cheating marginally depreciates the value of the As and Bs and makes the pain of flunking somewhat greater than it would be otherwise.

It is an intriguing, indeed paradoxical, characteristic of this reasoning that the cheater injures other people who cheat just as much as those who do not. Let us return to our original example where the teacher is grading on a curve, and suppose that Pete has succeeded in raising his grade by cheating so that he is the 20th student in the series and has an A. Another student now cheats and gets a higher grade, with the result that Pete is moved down to a B. Of course, the students who have not cheated are injured by both of these students' cheating, so they are doubly injured. However, it remains true that any student who cheats is to some extent injured by other students who cheat.

The discussion of cheating has assumed that students are injured by receiving low grades and benefit by receiving high grades. This is not absolutely certain, and there are people who maintain that the entire grading system is unimportant. Surely the individual who does not care what grade she receives is not injured by having his grade lowered because other people have cheated. However, the student who hopes that her grades will help her get a fellowship for graduate study or a good job is injured by cheating. Note that she is also injured if the cheating simply increases the number of As, rather than moving anybody down in grade, because this means that As are regarded as less valuable by future employers or future graduate schools.

Looked at from the standpoint of society as a whole, cheating reduces the information content of grades. If there is a good deal of cheating, then the grading system does not give very much information as to the quality of students. Hence, it is harder for employers to make decisions about whom to hire, to whom to give graduate fellowships, and so forth. The size of this cost depends on how good the grades are as a predictor of later success, and, unfortunately, we do not have very much data on that issue. Nevertheless, there must be at least some cost.

Rather ironically, we have come to the conclusion that the students should be strongly in favor of rules against cheating, at least insofar as these rules are enforced against other people. An unscrupulous student should favor a rule that prevents other people from cheating while permitting her to do so.

Unfortunately, rules of this sort are not likely to be acceptable. In general, we have to choose between institutions that make cheating difficult for everyone and institutions that make cheating easy for everyone. For most students, the former set of institutions will have a net payoff because the gains they may make from cheating, even ignoring the possible conscience problems of cheating, will be less than the loss they will suffer from other people's cheating. From the standpoint of professors, there is little cost either way. It is the students who should be opposed to cheating.

At the same time, penalties for cheating are likely to be necessary. Even though *all* students may favor a rule that forbids cheating, many a student will have a private incentive to cheat and improve his or her grade. If cheating is prevalent, many students who would not otherwise consider cheating may have to cheat just to protect their class standing. This problem is particularly acute in classes in which the professors scale their grades. (Can you explain why?) However, the problem of cheating for self-protection is not absent when the scale is fixed. As noted earlier, students who might not otherwise cheat may feel compelled to cheat because given grades are depreciated by rampant cheating. Penalties for cheating can be viewed as a necessary means of reducing the cheating of others and, thereby, decreasing the incentive they have to cheat for defensive reasons. Professors may see the penalties as a means of diverting student energies from finding ways of cheating to finding ways of learning the course material.

THE ECONOMICS OF LYING

Cheating is special form of dishonesty that is not infrequently observed. Lying, however, is probably far more prevalent, simply because of the breadth of opportunities for people to lie.

Beginning with simple lying, an individual who is thinking of telling a lie once again has the problem of conscience. One of the costs he must face if he is to tell a lie is the moral cost. As we have said before, for some people this is a very large cost and for some people it is a very small cost. In addition to that cost, there is the possibility that he will be caught telling a lie, and this must be multiplied by whatever injury he will suffer from being caught. Since we are talking about simple lying, this injury may constitute nothing more (or less) than a loss of reputation for honesty. If you are once caught telling a lie, people are likely to think you will tell lies in the future; hence, you may have greater difficulty getting them to accept your word, even when you are telling the truth. To the economist, "greater difficulty" translates into greater cost.

For example, a sales representative who sells gadgets door-to-door has little need to be concerned with the "reputation cost" of lying. It is unlikely that he or she will return to the same home again. If the buyers find out that the gadget is not what it was said to be, there will be little cost inflicted on the sales representative. On the other hand, someone who sells to the same people again and again, particularly if the product is valuable enough so that the buyers give careful thought to transactions, can lose immensely from lying.

For example, take the vice president of a large steel company who has the duty of acting as principal sales representative to General Motors, Ford, and Chrysler. The cost to her of losing the confidence of her customers is so great that she would be a fool to lie to them.

This is particularly so since they will be experts and likely to catch the lies that are tried. In any event, the buyers will have an opportunity to make a very thorough test of her product if they buy it. In the real world, repeated sales arrangements are often based on such a high degree of honesty that the sales representative will rarely make an effort to sell a product if a competitor has one that is clearly more suitable to the purchasers' needs. The central point is that the more frequent the contact between two parties—buyer and seller—the more unlikely that lying would be expected.

Most cases of purchase and sale are intermediate between the two cases just mentioned, the door-to-door salesperson and the steel vice president. The manufacturer of canned goods had better have a satisfactory product if he wants to stay in business; but exact truth on the label is not all that important because the purchaser probably does not read it.

The benefits from lying are a little more complicated. Presumably the reasons for telling a lie are varied. People may want to influence someone to do something they would not do if they are told the truth. The door-to-door sales representative, for example, if he or she accurately described the product, might sell very few units of the product. On the other hand, by a suitably colorful sales pitch, he or she may make quite a nice living. The benefit from the lie, then, is the profit (whatever it is) from influencing the victim's behavior.

For example, suppose that if the sales representative correctly describes the object, he or she has a 1-in-10 chance of selling it. Assume that a suitable lie increases the chances to 50–50. Assume further that the commission on the sale is $5. If the sales representative lies, he or she moves from a 1-in-10 chance of making $5.00, which is worth $0.50, to a 50–50 chance, worth $2.50, and the payoff on the lie is then $2.00.

But this is the gross benefit. Obviously the potential liar has to subtract from the expected gross benefits the possible cost of the lie. Ignoring possible legal penalties, this cost, as we said above, is the reduction in credibility. For the door-to-door sales representative, this may have substantially zero value; hence he or she can say that a $2 profit was made by telling a lie. For our vice president in charge of sales for a major steel company, on the other hand, the payoff to him from completing a sale by telling a lie might be $100,000 or so, but the cost to him of being detected in a lie might be $2 or $3 million in reduction of lifetime earnings.

The fact that people may tell lies, of course, has an effect on the behavior not only of potential liars but of the people who will hear the lie. Most spouses who stay home are properly skeptical of door-to-door salesmen selling complicated devices. On the other hand, most purchasing agents who deal in large sums of money are so convinced of the honesty of the sales vice presidents with whom they talk that they may actually use them as sources of technical information.

All of this, of course, depends on the fact that the people to whom a potential liar might make a dishonest statement try to estimate his truthfulness. The individual who hears a statement by someone else will put resources into determining whether or not it is true. In some cases, he may have great respect for the person making the statement or he may realize that the person making the statement has no particular motive to tell a lie. Hence, he would put high credence on the statement and not do a great deal of individual investigation. This is, of course, the reason that having a reputation for truth as opposed to a reputation for lying is valuable to people in business or, indeed, in any walk of life.

Consider, then, the situation that confronts Judy, a saleswoman, dealing with a potential customer. If Judy is known to be honest, the customer will invest fewer resources in checking her statements. In consequence, the cost of the sale will be lower. This honesty on Judy's part generates a net and perfectly genuine social gain for the joint society of the two of them: part of this value goes to Judy and part to the customer. Thus, social institutions that improve the reliability of information can have a positive payoff.

Note that this argument has nothing to do with morals, although it is in accord with the received moral code. There are simply economies to be gained if all statements made are truthful. These economies partly have the effect of reducing the resources invested in checking the accuracy of statements and partly in reducing errors made because false statements are believed. No matter how many resources we invest in checking the truth or falsity of someone else's statements, we will be fooled occasionally if he or she tells enough lies. There is a further saving in the reduction of sales effort by the sales people.

One way of investing resources to prevent lying is simply refusing to believe the word of someone whom you have caught lying in the past. This superficially appears to be costless but it is not because it means that you disregard many statements that are true. Hence, there is the cost of obtaining the same information from someone else or remaining ignorant. The problem at hand is almost a game. The more skeptical we are of things you say, the more resources you will have to invest to convince us and the more resources we will invest in checking what you have to say. Further, the chance exists that we will disbelieve you when you are telling the truth. Under the circumstances, there is a net social loss from our belief that you may be lying.

There is, of course, an optimal amount of resources for us to invest in checking your statements, given that we have some idea of how likely it is that you are lying. Knowing the resources we will invest in checking your statements, there is an appropriate amount of resources you should invest in "improving" your lie.

For example, you may generate false data, misinterpret true data, improve the attractiveness of your statements by various means, and generally respond to our skepticism by resource investment. This resource investment, of course, should lead to more resource investment by us in detecting possible lies. It is not sensible, however, for the potential victim of the lie to invest an infinite amount of resources into reducing the likelihood that he will believe an untrue statement. In this case, the cost of further information should be offset against the benefit from the reduction in the likelihood that we will be fooled. Similarly, the potential liar should not invest an infinite amount of resources in making his lie believable because, here again, the potential resources do cost something and should be employed only if the potential gain is greater than the cost.

LYING IN POLITICS

A very important situation in which lying occurs in most governments—democracies or dictatorships—is politics. The average person has a very low opinion of the honesty of politicians, and this opinion is completely justified. The basic problem is that the voter has very little motive to check up on the statements of the politician; hence, politicians can get away with a good deal of dishonesty.

The reason why the voter has little to gain by checking up on the honesty of a politician comes essentially from the fact that the individual voter has very little effect on the outcome of an election. If we devote a good deal of resources to determining that one of the two candidates is lying and vote against him, in the presidential elections this has less than a 1-in-10-million chance of having any effect on the outcome. Under the circumstances, we are not even likely to remember very accurately what the politician has promised.

There are complicating factors that make lying in politics even more likely. A man running for Congress who promises to do his best to get Blacksburg, Virginia (which is in the Appalachian Mountains), converted into a deep-water port by a massive and expensive government dredging program may in fact do his best, but Blacksburg may never become a port because he is only one congressman. Thus, we cannot tell whether he kept his promise or did not. Further, it is certain that conditions will change between the time the man is elected to office and the time he has an opportunity to act on one of his promises. Whether the change is such that the voters would agree that he should not carry out his promise is, once again, a matter for dispute.

There is one area in which politicians are well advised to keep their promises, but unfortunately this is no great benefit for the functioning of our democratic system: If a member of Congress makes a promise concerning some matter of great moment to a few constituents, then it is likely that the constituents will be very well informed on whether their representative makes a real effort. Since the matter is of great interest to them, they will try to be informed on what the representative did for them in Washington. In general, they are apt to punish or reward him or her in the future according to whether the promise is carried out. Thus, this is the kind of promise politicians try to keep.

Unfortunately, this type of special-interest activity does not make the political system function well, and, indeed politicians may be simultaneously making public statements against some program and privately telling a small group of people that they will back it. In many cases, this is the optimal course of action for a suitably unscrupulous person. (Do we not observe this kind of special-interest legislation?)

Under the circumstances, it is unlikely that people attracted into politics are those who have very strong moral objections to lying. In many cases, of course, they do not consciously think of themselves as lying; they just are not very careful in examining their own motives. It is very easy to convince oneself that whatever is good for oneself is good for the country. Politicians probably do this a great deal and, hence, do not consciously feel that they have done anything immoral.

Political lies are one area in which we have great difficulty making use of the government to control lying. The government, by definition, is in control of politicians, and the politicians are more likely to make use of the political process to injure their opponents than to seek absolute truth. In consequence, most democratic societies have very little in the way of controls on lying by politicians. Politicians, of course, take advantage of this. Granted the possibilities for the government in power to use any legal process that punishes telling political lies as a means of punishing political opponents, we can see why laws against political lying are rare. Unfortunately, this means that the politicians are even freer in telling lies than they would be if we changed the institutions.

In the United States at the moment, the freedom politicians have to tell lies is partially offset by the fact that it is fairly safe to tell lies about politicians too. The laws of libel and slander have been adjusted by the Supreme Court recently so that it is almost impossible for politicians to sue a person who has maligned them. There are special circumstances in which such a suit is possible, but they are extremely narrow, and most statements anyone might choose to make, either in print, on TV, or simply in conversation, are perfectly safe no matter how untrue they are. Unfortunately, although this may even things up with respect to the politicians, it does not mean that public communication on political matters is particularly honest.

CONCLUDING COMMENTS

In sum, then, lying and cheating, like most other human behavior, have positive payoffs, and they have costs. They also have moral implications, and for many people, these moral implications are more important than the economic calculation. Unfortunately, there are also many people for whom the economic calculation is the controlling one. Any set of social institutions for controlling lying or cheating should be based on firm recognition of that fact.

QUESTIONS TO PONDER

1. Would you expect small children to cheat more or less than college students? Why? *– less, they are more easily scared – less benefits, more costs*
2. Generally speaking, colleges can be divided into two categories, one using the honor system and another in which there is supervision to make cheating at least hard. In some cases the honor system fails, and there is a great deal of cheating; but in other cases it has been successful. How would you account for this? *– nice teacher, cheat – taken advantage of – easier to cheat*
3. How do you account for the fact that students usually object to procedures that will make cheating harder?
4. Explain in economic terms why professors often require medical excuses before make-up tests are given.

PART FIVE

The New World of Political Economy

CHAPTER 17

Public Choice Economics

This chapter is about *public choice economics*. The title itself implies that our interests extend far beyond the workings of the market system, which was the focal point of chapters already covered. The central concern is the public sector. More to the point, the chapter is about how choices are made in the public sector. A central question undergirding much of the discussion in conventional economic discussions of the public sector is, "Given the objective of economic efficiency, what are the optimum government policies?" Little is said about how government policy is derived or why governments follow the policy courses that they do.

In this chapter, we make a major shift in our analytical interest. The main concern of public choice economics is with analyzing the functioning of government itself—that is, the process by which government decisions are made and carried out. Instead of suggesting what the government should do to achieve efficient (or equitable) outcomes, the interest of public choice economists is to comment on how democracies with different rules can be expected to result in public choices. In short, public choice economics addresses the question of why the government operates the way it does.

Even though our topic is essentially political, our analytical techniques remain economic in nature. This means that we continue to assume that people in the political realm operate with an eye extensively toward the private costs and benefits of their actions. Our reasons for taking this approach are quite simple. First, our primary purpose is to understand how government works, and this requires that we examine participants in the political process as they are, not as we think they should be. People will vote to obtain those things that they think they want. Indeed, the secret ballot affirms and protects that right, and we do not wish to propose changing that right. Further, although we may like them to behave differently, politicians will espouse programs and platforms that reflect their own private interests, one of which presumably is being elected and reelected.

Second, voters and consumers are the same people. John Doe makes purchases and he votes; he is the same man in the supermarket as he is in the voting booth. In both capacities, he can express his public and charitable concerns; however, in both capacities he also has his own private interests and will behave on the basis of those interests. To the extent that people make cost-benefit calculations of the kind we have discussed in all areas of behavior, the economic model of individual behavior in the marketplace is transferable to discussions of the political process.

We see in this chapter that economic analysis can yield very valuable insights into the workings and limitations of the democratic system as a means of allocating scarce resources. However, we cannot hope to cover a field as diverse as public choice economics in the course of a few pages. We therefore offer only a sample of the insights public choice economists have achieved over the past three to four decades. Specifically, we consider how the Founding Fathers (several of whom were in many ways the first American public choice theorists) viewed government, how two-party and three-party political systems operate, and how logrolling (vote trading) affects political outcomes. The following two chapters take up the related issues of rent seeking and constitutional economics.

DEMOCRACY AND SOCIAL CONTROL

The framers of the Constitution of the United States fully recognized the need for government and for restrictions that government imposes on individual freedoms. John Jay in *The Federalist* wrote,

> Nothing is more certain than the indispensible necessity of government; and it is equally undeniable, that whenever and however it is instituted, the people must cede to it some of their natural rights, in order to vest it with requisite powers (to carry out its assigned responsibilities).[1]

The reason for government is implied in James Madison's often repeated statement, "But what is government, but the greatest of all reflections on human nature? If men were angels, no government would be necessary."[2] Having recognized the need for government, the founding fathers were equally (if not more) concerned with controlling government. Madison continues:

> If angels were to govern men, neither external nor internal controls on government would be necessary. In framing a government, which is to be administered by men, the great difficulty lies in this: You must first enable the government to control the governed; and in the next place, oblige it to control itself.[3]

---

[1]John Jay, "The Dangers of Foreign Force and Influence Threatening the United States," *The Federalist*, No. 2. A modern edition is available in paperback: (New York: Washington Square Press, 1964, originally published 1787–88), pp. 5–6.

[2]James Madison, "The Social Foundations of Political Freedom," *The Federalist*, No. 51 (New York: Washington Square Press, 1964), p. 122.

[3]Ibid., pp. 122–23.

The framers of the Constitution defined a role for government; at the same time, however they defined, by way of the First Amendment, certain basic rights that would not be subject to infringement by conventional political processes and simple-majority vote: "Congress shall make no law respecting an establishment of religion, or prohibiting the free exercise thereof; or abridging the freedom of speech, or of the press; or the right of the people peaceably to assemble, and to petition the Government for a redress of grievances." They felt that these basic rights were too important to allow them to become the subject of normal political maneuvering; in other words, the potential cost of political infringement on these rights was too great. The First Amendment represents a set of rights for individuals; along with other provisions of the Constitution, it also represents a means of control on government.

Observers of the political process often look upon the political decision-making process incorporated in the Constitution as a means of facilitating the operation and extension of government. However, having recognized the need for government in a limited number of areas, the framers of the Constitution were intent upon establishing a "political obstacle course" that would restrict the scope of government. This is a major reason for the division of power between the state governments and the federal government, for the two houses of Congress, and for the veto power of the president. Further, by extending to people the right of the vote, their interest was in dispersing the decision-making power among a great many people and increasing the difficulty by which a majority of people can unite and impose their will on the minority through government. Madison, again wrote in *The Federalist*:

> It is of great importance in a republic, not only to guard the society against the oppression of its rulers; but to guard one part of the society against the injustices of the other part. . . . [By way of the Federal republic] the society itself will be broken into so many parts, interests, and classes of citizens, that the rights of individuals, or of the minority, will be in little danger from interested combinations of the majority. In a free government, the security of civil rights must be the same as that for religious rights. It consists in the one case in the multiplicity of interests, and in the other, in the multiplicity of sects.[4]

Clearly, the democratic system that was established was intended to be a mechanism for the social control of government; its purpose was to permit maximum attainment of individual freedom. Further, so long as the government remained relatively small the democratic system would be a reasonably effective control on government. The framers were concerned that growth in government would lead to a breakdown in the controlling power of democratic processes. They feared that a large government would mean that rep-

---

[4]Ibid., p. 125.

resentatives would begin to pursue their own interests, and not those of their constituencies, and that bureaucracies would become large, unwieldy and detached from the controlling influence of the Congress and the voting public.

Still within the bounds of the constitutional framework, the democratic system that was devised is a means by which politicians, in their competitive efforts to be elected, will seek to represent the interest of their constituencies on issues that are within the purview of government. How a two-party system does this and how economics can be used to answer that question is the subject of the next section.

THE PRACTICAL POLITICS OF A TWO-PARTY SYSTEM

Elections are held for the purpose of determining the winners of political campaigns; and winning candidates (or issues, when they are up for public consideration) in a two-party democratic system, such as the one that dominates United States politics, are typically middle-of-the-roaders. They tend to represent the views of the very large group of voters who are neither staunch liberals not staunch conservatives; winning candidates usually have moderate views or political positions. Further, there is generally little difference between the candidates of the Republican and Democratic parties. Indeed, a major slogan of George Wallace, who ran for president as a candidate of the American party in 1968 and 1972, was that "There is not a dime's worth of difference between the two of them," meaning his Republican and Democratic opponents.

To see the reason why this tends to be the case, consider Figure 17–1, which shows all possible political positions on a liberal-conservative continuum. Given that the continuum is all-inclusive, there is some position on the horizontal axis that represents the favored political position of each potential voter. The bell-shaped curve indicates the distribution of voters along the political spectrum. There are a few voters out on the wings of the distribution; however, most voters are assumed to be clustered in the center. Actually, the distribution of voters can vary from that indicated on the graph. On the other hand, the distribution that we show seems reasonable, and a change in the shape of the distribution will not affect our analysis.

Assuming that the candidates of the two parties are intent on winning the election, and assuming that voters will vote for that person who most closely approximates their own preferred political position, politicians will not choose political positions out in the wings of the distribution. To see why, suppose that the Republican candidate chooses a platform that establishes a political position at R'. The Democratic candidate can easily win the election by setting his political position slightly to the left of the Republican's position, for example, at D'. The Republican will take all the votes to her right, which as indicated by the curve, are very few, and may take roughly half the votes between R' and D'. However, the Democrat will take all the votes to his left, since he comes closer to their preferred political position than does the

FIGURE 17–1

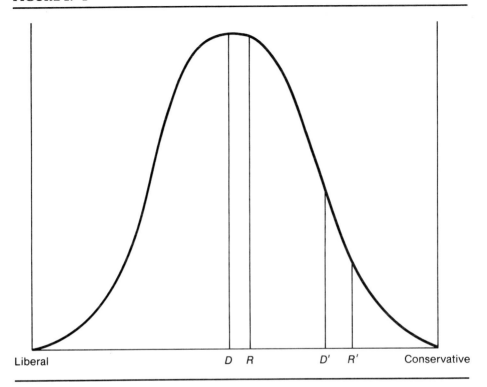

Liberal   D   R   D'   R'   Conservative

Republican; he will also take roughly half the votes between D'and R'. Clearly the Democrat will have an overwhelming majority.

The smart politician will choose a position near the middle of the distribution in order to avoid being outmaneuvered by his or her opposition, as above, and ending up losing the election. The opposing candidate must also go to the middle. Otherwise, he or she will lose the election. For instance, suppose that the Republican develops a political platform that puts her at R and the Democrat remains at D'. The Republican will then take all the votes in the left-hand side of the distribution and roughly half the votes between R and D'. She will have more than the necessary simple majority needed to beat her Democratic opponent.

In short in order to contemplate victory or to avoid being beaten in a two-party system, both parties will tend to choose political positions that are close to one another and in the middle of the distribution. Their positions must be sufficiently distinct that they can claim that they are in fact a different party to many voters; but still they must be sufficiently close that they will minimize the number of voters that are in between them.

Many people often criticize politicians for taking similar stands on issues. Their criticism is understandable, since there are many people to the left and the right of the political positions of the major candidates; they would no doubt like to see candidates who more closely represent their own views. However, the analysis of this section suggests that the competition between candidates for votes will lead them to take positions that are in the middle of the distribution and similar to the opponents'. The candidates are in a classic "prisoner's dilemma." If the two candidates are ideologically far apart, each can increase the number of votes received (or the probability of winning) by moving closer to the other candidate. Each must also consider the prospect of the other candidate's moving closer and making his or her defeat more likely.

Like everyone else, politicians can make mistakes and can misinterpret the political positions of voters. This is so simply because the distribution of voters represented in Figure 17–1 is not known with perfection before an election; politicians must do what they can to determine where the distribution of voters is and to develop their campaigns on that basis. At times, politicians will misread the public's political sentiment and will be defeated because of their mistake.

For example, when the political campaign starts, the Democrat may believe, but not know, that the distribution of voters is skewed to the left, as is the curve labeled A in Figure 17–2. Consequently, he will take a political position at D', thinking that it is in the middle of the distribution. On the other hand, the Republican candidate may believe that the distribution is skewed to the right, as is the curve labeled B, and therefore may establish a political position at R'. However, the true distribution may be the symmetrical bell-shaped curve labeled C in the graph. Since the Democrat is closer to the center of the "true" distribution, the Democrat wins.

Over the course of several elections and with the aid of opinion polls, politicians will learn from their mistakes and will discover, in an imperfect way, what the actual distribution is. They will then move toward the center of the distribution and represent the views of the people in that middle—the so-called *median voter group*. Those in the median voter group will, in a two-party system, tend to have a government that is very much in accord with their preferences. However, other people, particularly those who are in the extreme wings of the distribution, will be continually frustrated by the gap they observe between what they think government should do and what the government actually does.

This relatively simple model of the two-party political process surely does not explain all elections, but it is useful to note how close so many presidential elections are, for example, the Kennedy/Nixon election of 1960, the Nixon/Humphrey election of 1968, the Carter/Ford election of 1976, and the Reagan/Carter election of 1980. When elections have not been close— such as the Johnson/Goldwater election in 1964 and the Nixon/McGovern election in 1972—the parties appear to have corrected their political positioning. We can imagine that given their massive defeat in 1984 in the Reagan/ Mondale election, the Democrats will undertake corrective action in 1988

FIGURE 17–2

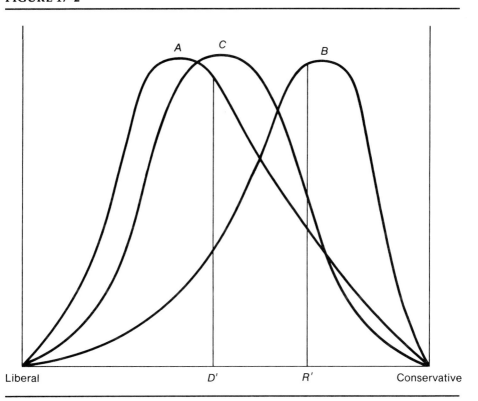

Liberal   D'   R'   Conservative

with the selection of a candidate who is politically distinct from Walter Mondale.[5]

Often many people are upset because government tends to favor the preferences of the average person; but, fortunately, or unfortunately, this is what a two-party democratic system tends to do: rational politicians, pushed by political competition, will move toward the center of the road in order to maximize their chances of getting elected.

[5]The median voter model of political behavior described in Figure 17–1 has been found to be very useful in sophisticated statistical studies in predicting government policies toward such public concerns as the absolute size of school budgets and conservation programs. See R. Barlow, "Efficiency Aspects of Local School Expenditures," *Journal of Political Economy* 78 (September/October 1968), pp. 1028–40; J. Barr and O. Davis, "An Elementary Political and Economic Theory of the Expenditures of Local Governments," *Southern Economic Journal* 33 (October 1966), pp. 149–65, T. C. Bergstrom and R. D. Goodman, "Private Demands for Public Goods," *American Economic Review* 63 (June 1973), pp. 280–96; T. Borcherdig and R. Deacon, "The Demand for the Services of Non-Federal Governments," *American Economic Review* 62 (December 1972), pp. 891–901.

A MORE COMPLEX POLITICAL MODEL: MORE PARTIES AND ISSUES

From the analysis in the section above, we can conclude that skillful politicians will adopt political positions close to the preferences of the median voter. However, you should understand that the model we employed was very simple, involving only one issue and two parties. Indeed, the conclusion we have just restated applies only to a two-party system. In this section we introduce complications to our model and show that in a three-party election that involves two issues, the candidates will, if they start with political positions that are closely similar on two issues, move apart. We cannot say just how far apart candidates will be in a three-party election, but we do not expect them to be as close as two candidates will be in an election involving only two parties.

To illustrate, consider Figure 17–3. In this figure we show two possible issues, expenditures on police and on fire fighters, on which the three candidates, X, Y, and Z, can take a political stand. The possible expenditures on police are on the horizontal axis, and the possible expenditures on fire fighters are on the vertical axis. Assume that voters are evenly distributed within the figure, that the three candidates take very similar positions initially at X, Y, and Z in the center of the graph, and that this means they divide the votes among themselves. Candidate X takes all the votes bounded by the area O*abc*, candidate Y takes all the votes in the area bounded by the area *bcdef*, and candidate Z takes all the votes in the area bounded by *abfg*. They divide the votes in this way simply because the voters in those respective areas are closer to the candidate in the area than they are to either of the others. Notice that at their initial positions each candidate has an incentive to move away from the center of the figure; this is because each candidate can, by moving away, increase his or her vote total and thereby increase his or her chances of winning the election.

If, for example, candidate X moves away from the center to a position like X', he or she may lose some votes in the center of the distribution. This is because some of the people who would have voted for the candidate at X now find their political position closer to one of the other candidates. On the other hand, by moving away from the center, candidate X takes a political position that is now closer to the positions of voters who were initially closer to Y and Z. The graph illustrates that by moving away candidate X gains more votes than he loses. The people who will now vote for X are in the area bounded by O*hid*. Notice that the total area that X adds to his or her political support (striped areas) is greater than the area that X loses (shaded area). Similarly, Y and Z have an incentive to move away from the center: they know that by doing so they can increase their chances of being elected and offset the gains that would otherwise have been made by candidate X. Conse-

FIGURE 17–3

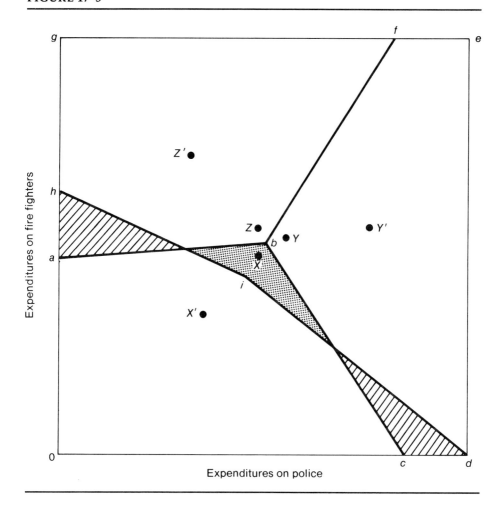

quently, we might anticipate that the three candidates will end up at political positions something like X', Y', and Z'.

Thus, in a two-party system, one anticipates that the parties would be very close together and, in a system of three or more parties, there would be considerable differences between them. This is what we observe in the real world. In those European countries in which there are more than two parties, the differences between the parties are usually considerably greater than in the two-party system.

One thing can be said for certain about a system of three or more parties: it requires a great deal more skill on the part of the party leaders, and mistakes are much easier to make. In a two-party system, there is a simple operational rule for the politician: go find out what the other party is doing and take a position very close to it in the popular direction. With a three-party system, there is no such rule. Difficult decisions must be made, and frequent errors are to be expected.

LOGROLLING AS A FORM OF POLITICAL EXCHANGE

The word *logrolling* is an unusual word. Its meaning, however, is really very simple; logrolling is vote trading. One member of Congress, for example, will agree to vote for something that another member wants in return for his or her vote on another issue. Logrolling is also very common in any democratic political system; indeed, in most democracies it dominates the policy selection process, although it is frequently concealed from public view. In this section we consider the advantages and disadvantages of logrolling as a form of *political market activity*.

Implicit and Explicit Logrolling

Logrolling is usually classified as either explicit or implicit. Either can be a clearly defined trade of votes by two politicians, in which case it is *explicit logrolling*, or it can be implied by the way the legislation is proposed, in which case it is *implicit logrolling*. For instance, measures that different politicians favor can be incorporated in one piece of congressional legislation and voted on at one time. Each member voting for the whole legislative package has voted for the measure or measures especially favored by the others as well as for the measure he especially favors. Therefore, although difficult to detect, an exchange of votes has effectively taken place.

Regardless of whether it is implicit or explicit, logrolling occurs because most laws have differential effect: they affect some people more than others. A proposed change in the laws would have more effect on some citizens than on others. Even changes in the criminal law usually have differential effects in a society. Under the circumstances, logrolling is not obviously undesirable in all cases.

Suppose that all governmental acts are decided upon by direct majority vote. Further, suppose that there is a project that would benefit some city, say Denver, very greatly and that would have a relatively modest cost to the national taxpayers. The total benefit received by people in Denver may exceed the cost of the project. However, if the project were paid for by a national tax, the proposal to federally fund the project would most assuredly lose in the absence of logrolling. There can be many other projects in other areas of the country that would suffer a similar fate if implicit or explicit logrolling were forbidden. To illustrate the problems more carefully, we can consider cases of logrolling.

Implicit Logrolling: The Interstate Highway System.   In Congress logrolling is fairly open and aboveboard. It is true that the bulk of the negotiations take place in committees, cloakrooms, and congressional offices, but there is no particular secret as to what is going on. Suppose, then, that we are back in the 1950s and President Eisenhower has decided that an interstate highway system should be built in order to improve the ease of automobile travel. It is to be paid for (as indeed it was) by those who drive on the interstates and those who do not.

Under these circumstances, any given community can be better off if it has one of the interstates running through it or around it, but it must also pay for interstates built in other parts of the country. One would anticipate, then, that the congressional delegation from Utah would, on the whole, be in favor of interstates in Utah and, to some extent those outside; but, generally speaking, the representatives would not be interested in taxing the inhabitants of Utah to build interstates in Oklahoma. This problem was met by Eisenhower by implicit logrolling. He made up a package of interstates so designed that it benefits a majority of constituencies. The individual member of Congress, instead of having to make up his or her own bargains with people, could look at the whole collection and decide whether he or she would vote for it. Note that this does not in any real sense eliminate logrolling; it simply obscures it. At any rate, the interstate highway system passed as a package. Presidential candidates also try to get elected through developing the same type of package in the form of their platforms and position papers.

In a way, the clearest example of implicit logrolling will be found in some referenda on local improvements in the United States. Sometimes these referenda involve a large project of one sort or another. The voters in, say Montgomery County, Virginia, may vote down a proposal for a new courthouse, if offered by itself for a vote. Often, however, the referendum proposal is a collection of different projects that have no great relation to each other except that it is thought that, if they are all grouped together, a majority of the population will favor them, whereas there would be a majority against any individual one. This kind of referendum is frequently used in school financing.

Explicit Logrolling: An Oceanographic Laboratory.   Explicit logrolling is more visible but also a little more complicated to develop. Suppose that the congressional delegation from Mississippi is interested in having the National Oceanographic Laboratory moved to southern Mississippi (where, in fact, it is now located). It goes to the delegation from Nevada and offers to support some irrigation projects there in return for its support for Mississippi. It also approaches, let us say the delegation from Oregon, which is interested in a flood control project in Oregon, and agrees to vote for that in return for support. By making a number of such trades with Texas, New York, and some other states, eventually the Mississippi delegation gets a majority of members willing to push for the establishment of the oceanographic laboratory in Mississippi. Other states are engaged in soliciting by similar methods, and we may find that the flood control project in Oregon and the irrigation project in Nevada will go through.

Note that there is no reason in this type of logrolling why the coalition that votes for the oceanographic laboratory in Mississippi should be the same coalition of states as that which voted for the irrigation project in Nevada. Mississippi will vote for the irrigation project in Nevada because that is the trade, but Nevada probably has at least some states in its winning coalition that are different from the states backing Mississippi.

When Is Logrolling Desirable?

If logrolling can clearly create benefits for the society, it can also cause harm. Consider a very simple society of nine voters who confront a large collection of measures, each of which will be paid for by a tax of $1 per head and each of which will confer benefits exclusively upon one of the nine. Policy A, for example, will cost a total of $9 in the form of a $1 tax on each voter, but it will confer upon voter A a benefit worth $15. Clearly, we would, on the whole, prefer that projects like this go through, although we might object to its distributional consequences. Normally, we would anticipate that the voters, if confronted with only this bill, would vote eight to one against it; but with logrolling, assuming there were similar projects for other voters, it would get through as part of a package. The end product could be an improvement in the state of society.

Consider another project which, like our first one, involves a cost of $1 to each of our nine citizens and confers upon voter A a benefit of only $2. Here there is a net cost of $7 to society as a whole. We would not want this bill to get through. As a matter of fact, it would not get through under logrolling because the voter could not afford to vote for four other bills, each of which would cost him $1 apiece, in return for four other people voting for his bill. This would lead to a loss for him of $3 net; hence he or she would not attempt to logroll the issue through.

So far, logrolling has worked very well; unfortunately, there is an intermediate class of issues where it can work to the detriment of the country as a whole. Suppose that the return to voter A of a bill (which, once again, cost $1 apiece to every one of the nine taxpayers) is $7. He would be willing to trade a favorable vote on four other issues for four votes on his or her issue. This would net $2 on the entire deal. Society as a whole, however, would have been paying $9 for something which was worth only $7. In this case logrolling reduces the efficiency of government.

DECENTRALIZATION AND COMPETITIVE GOVERNMENTS

The power that an individual producer has over the customer is dependent on the number of competitors he or she confronts, that is, the number of close and viable substitute goods and services the customers can turn to. A producer who is the only producer of a good with no close substitutes—who is a monopolist—can raise the price of a product with little concern that the customers will move to other producers. On the other hand, a producer who is one of a number of producers of a good knows that any attempt on his or her part to independently raise the price (or lower the quality) of the product will cause the customers to move not only to distant products, but also to other producers of the same or a very similar product. Also such a producer knows that any price increase will result in a sharp reduction in the quantity of the good that will be sold. Further, to avoid being undersold the individual producer must do what is possible to keep production costs down as low as possible. In these ways, competition constrains the behavior of private producers; it keeps the price down and production efficiency up from what they would be in the absence of competition.

These are basic points that are central to the theory of market power. They are also points that the framers of the Constitution had in mind when they set up the American system of government—or more precisely, system of governments. James Madison wrote,

> The accumulation of all powers . . . in the same hands, whether of one, a few, or many, and whether hereditary, self-appointed, or elective, must justly be pronounced the very definition of tyranny.[6]

Recognizing the control that a division of powers and responsibilities among different governmental units (like states, counties, and towns) would have on government, Madison also wrote,

> In a single republic, all the power surrendered by the people is submitted to the adminstration of single government; and the usurpations are guarded against by a division of the government into distinct and separate departments. In the compound republic of America, the power surrendered by the people is first divided between two distinct governments and then the portion allotted to each subdivided among distinct and separate departments. Hence a double security arises to the rights of people. The different governments will control each other, at the same times each will be controlled by itself.[7]

In short, the framers of the Constitution intended to establish a system of competing governments. Under this system, governments will be controlled by people's votes and people's ability to move among governments. If one governmental unit, like a city, raises its "tax price" for the services it renders (or attempts to lower the quality of those services), people can move to other, competing governmental units. The government that raises its tax price will lose a portion of its tax base. Granted, many people are resistant to moving

---

[6]James Madison, "The Social Foundations," p. 124.
[7]Ibid., pp. 124–25.

because of an independent tax increase; consequently, governments, even in the republican system that was established, do have a measure of monopoly power. However, the founding fathers were attempting to introduce at least a modest amount of competitive control into their system of government.[8]

There are several good arguments often heard for extending the scope of any governmental unit to cover the responsibilities that are held by several units. For instance, it is frequently argued that local governments, especially those in metropolitan areas, should consolidate so that their garbage, road, and sewage services can be offered on a large scale or on a lower-cost basis. In other words, there are economies of scale in the provision of governmental services, just as there are in many private industries. Further, the benefits of services offered in one governmental unit are often external to that unit; they spill over into jurisdictions of surrounding governments. The government that provides the benefits is unable to tax the people outside its jurisdiction for the benefits they receive. For example, people who work in downtown Chicago but live outside the city benefit from the garbage pickup and road maintenance that are paid for by the city of Chicago; the beneficiaries do not have to bear their share of the tax costs of the services. By consolidating several governmental units into one large unit, the benefits are internalized; the people who benefit are taxed.

Consolidation of governmental activities, however, can be a mixed blessing. James Madison would be very much concerned that consolidation movements will tend to reduce the benefits of competitive governments and will, therefore, increase the control that any one government has over its residents. Larger governmental units will reduce the number and variety of alternative government forms that are open to people, and they will increase the cost that individuals will have to incur in moving to an alternative governmental form. Consolidation, in other words, can increase the monopoly power of any government. If we can assume that politicians and government employees are interested only in pursuing the public interest, no harm may be done by consolidation. However, if the people who run governments have private interests of their own, a government with greater monopolistic power can be used as a means by which they can pursue their private interests. Although the potential for greater efficiency may exist through consolidation of governments, the actual efficiency of government may be reduced as the cost of the larger government is raised, the quantity of services provided is reduced, and the efficiency benefits of government are absorbed by politicians and bureaucrats in terms of high salaries, better working conditions, and less work. The available data, indeed, suggest that there is a direct relationship between the

---

[8]For an extended discussion of this thesis, see Robert L. Bish and Vincent Ostrom, *Understanding Urban Government: Metropolitan Reform Reconsidered* (Washington, D.C.: American Enterprise Institute for Public Policy Research, 1973); and Vincent Ostrom, *The Political Theory of a Compound Republic: A Reconstruction of the Logical Foundations of American Democracy as Presented by The Federalist* (Blacksburg, Va.: Center for the Study of Public Choice, 1971).

size of governmental units and the cost of their services.[9] The data are not conclusive, but the data and the competitive-government argument indicate that proposals to consolidate governmental units or such special programs as welfare services should be examined very carefully. Together they raise the question of whether we should expect behavior from people in the public sector any different from what we expect from private entrepreneurs in private markets.

CONCLUDING COMMENTS

In this chapter we have applied the cost-benefits analysis used in our discussion of private markets to politics; in this way we have developed elementary economic models of problems of democracy. The picture of politicians that we have drawn indicates that each one is attempting to be elected and not necessarily attempting to maximize the public interest. Public choice economists think that is realistic and that, in particular, politicians who are attempting to get elected are more likely to be elected than politicians who disregard that goal.

Barry Goldwater, George McGovern, and Walter Mondale, the respective 1964, 1972, and 1984 losing presidential candidates have demonstrated the fate of politicians who have strong policy ideals and who attempt to persuade the voters of the truth of these ideals. (Enoch Powell is a British example.) Although all three have been able to get a good deal of national attention, not one has risen to the goal he sought.

This chapter may have impressed you as a criticism of democracy. This is the way it impresses us, too. Public choice economists, however, argue that democracy depends upon a set of politicians who make actual decisions, but the system attempts to control these politicians by making their continued employment subject to the will of the voters. The political maneuvering of a politician in search of votes will tend to reflect his or her accurate or distorted distribution of information. To say that this is, as it is, a weakness of democracy is not to say that some other form of government is better. Indeed, the common nondemocratic form of government—the dictatorship—has immense defects of its own.

QUESTIONS TO PONDER

1. In their studies of politics, many people have assumed that the aim of politicians has been to maximize achievement of those goals that are in the public interest. In this chapter, the authors have assumed that politi-

---

[9]For a short review of several studies, see Bish and Ostrom, *Understanding Urban Government*, chaps. 4 and 6. For more details on the underlying argument, see Delores T. Martin and Richard B. McKenzie, "Bureaucratic Profits, Migration Costs, and the Consolidation of Local Governments," *Public Choice* 23 (Fall 1975), pp. 95–100.

cians aim to maximize their private interest. What does the change in the assumption at this basic theoretical level do to the case for government? To the likely acceptable scope of government?

2. Assuming that the objective of government is not to give people what they want, what is it? Discuss your suggestions with your classmates and see if there is much agreement. Why do you suppose that this assumption—that the objective of government is not simply to give people what they want—has been so widely made?

3. If politicians did not adopt political positions near the position held by the median voter, would the political process be improved?

4. As a student you face certain required courses and certain elective courses. Do you put as much time and energy into finding out in advance about the quality and significance of the required courses as of the electives? Why? What does this have to do with the subject of this chapter?

5. Are voters very knowledgeable about the political positions of presidential candidates? Why or why not?

CHAPTER 18

The Rent-Seeking Society

Since the 1970s, economists have been hard at work reconsidering a number of issues that most of them thought had been settled long ago. These issues fall mainly in the areas of income redistribution and trade restrictions. This reconsideration has tended to use analytical tools that categorize the issues under the name *rent seeking*. The term suggests an investigation of rents paid on apartments, which is hardly what rent seeking is all about. Unfortunately, *rent seeking* is not a terribly good descriptive term, but once people begin using a word, it develops a life of its own, and it is probably true that rent seeking will continue to be the term used for this line of investigation.

As used by economists doing the writing in the field, rent seeking is generally thought of as the search for profits (what are called *monopoly rents*) through artificial, government-imposed controls on market activity. It is, therefore, the farmers' quest for extra profits through government price supports or the textile industry's search for extra profits through government tariffs and quotas on imported textile products. Whenever people or businesses look to government to boost their incomes above market-determined levels, some form of rent seeking is generally involved.

RENT SEEKING: THE BASIC MODEL

To begin our discussion, consider the old economic chestnut that transfers of income cost nothing to society. Conventionally, economists have held that a transfer of income from individual A to individual B did not involve the use of resources (except for the relatively trivial amount tied up in the exchange). Therefore, nothing of significance had to be forgone; little or no cost was incurred.

This point is made clearer with reference to Figure 18–1, which describes the various combinations of income (resources) for two people. In Figure 18–1, we have on the two axes the incomes of Mr. X and Ms. Y. Let us assume that the total resource in our little two-person society is $1,000. This $1,000 can be divided between them in any number of ways. Mr. X could have $1,000 and Ms. Y, nothing, or Ms. Y could have $1,000 and Mr. X, nothing, or there could be some intermediate division. The line *PP* represents the locus of all possible divisions of income, and point *A* represents a division of these resources between the two so that Mr. X has $700 and Ms. Y, $300.

FIGURE 18–1

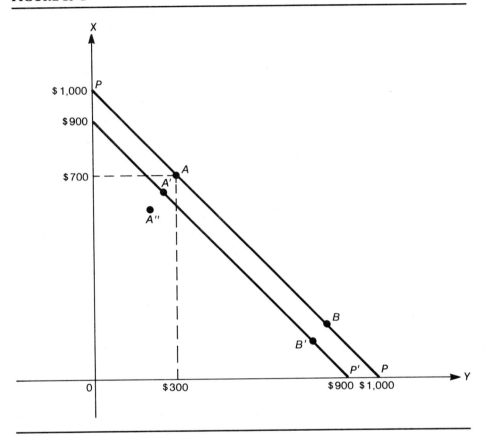

The standard economic discussion of this point would say that if we transfer some of Mr. X's wealth to Ms. Y, the result would be without cost, and we could end up on point *B* with Mr. X having $150 and Ms. Y, $850, but with society as a whole having as much (more or less) in total as it had before. Mr. X's loss is exactly the same as Ms. Y's gain; hence, there has been no social loss. This proposition is no doubt true if we believe that the transfer of the resource from Mr. X to Ms. Y was imposed by God with no cost.[1]

In the real world, however, transfers from one person to another do not simply appear out of the blue. They are normally the result of hard work and investment of resources by the person who will receive the transfer. Some-

---

[1]Even in this case it is not certainly true since it is conceivable that the transfer of wealth away from Mr. X may lead Mr. X to work less hard; hence, total social wealth may be lower. This point will be ignored throughout the rest of this chapter, not because it is unimportant, but simply because the chapter is on another topic.

times they are the result of investment of resources by some third person (Miss Z) who feels that redistributing funds from Mr. X to Ms. Y is desirable. The drive to force the transfer in income is what is called *rent seeking*.

Note that the transfer cannot be the result of the investment of resources by Mr. X because if Mr. X wishes to give the money to Ms. Y, then we do not have a situation in which social wealth remains unchanged—it actually increases. If Mr. X wants to give a gift to Ms. Y, then Mr. X is benefited by the gift and so is Ms. Y. The same sum of money does double duty. This last phenomenon might be called the *paradox of charity*. If you receive satisfaction out of giving something to someone else and the recipient obtains satisfaction out of receiving it, then the gift is, by ordinary measures, extremely productive. This is because the gift increases the utility of two people instead of only the one whose utility would be increased if, for example, Mr. X spent the money on himself. Societal welfare rises because of the voluntary income transfer.

However, if people have invested resources in obtaining the transfer of funds from Mr. X to Ms. Y (let us say they have gone to Washington lobbying at some cost), then the amount of resources that would be divided between Mr. X and Ms. Y after this expenditure is not PP, but some lesser amount, say $900, as shown by the line $P'P'$. Ms. Y will not get $850 (85% of $1,000) but less, for example, $765 (85% of $900), as shown at the point B'. Of course, the cost of lobbying or engaging in some other kind of political maneuvering in order to cause a transfer may be much smaller than our example implies. Nevertheless, although any individual lobbying activity is not expensive, the sum over society as a whole can be considerable. But more will be said on that topic below.

We must be cautious here, however, in drawing conclusions about the relative attractiveness (or social value) of points A and B'. It might be that point B' is in some sense a better location for division of the income in this little two-person society than point A. Perhaps Ms. Y is in fact more deserving than Mr. X. If this is so, then in a way society is better off after transfer than before, but it is not better off in the rather simple meaning that the clause *transfers have no social cost* normally conveys. Using the type of measurements the economist typically uses, the resources represented by $P'P'$ are less desirable than PP, albeit it is possible that point B' is superior by some standard to point A. This social gain, if there is such a gain, however, has been obtained at a cost and the move inward of the production frontier shows that cost.

Further, investment of resources by Ms. Y to obtain the transfer is not, in and of itself, enough to guarantee that the transfer will occur. The resources may be ineffectively employed in lobbying, in which case they may be wasted. In addition, the resources expended by Ms. Y on lobbying may not be all the resources devoted to rent seeking. It is likely that Mr. X will decide to lobby defensively also, which he may be willing to do because of the potential loss of income. The cost he must incur to avoid the transfer may be less than the expected loss in income if, indeed, the forced transfer occurs. The result of Mr. X's defensive lobbying may be that no transfer occurs, and the waste of the resources in the two lobbying activities (offensive and defensive lobbying) that counterbalance each other will put society a A' or even, if enough resources have been used, to point A''. In this case, by almost any standard, society has, on balance, been injured by the attempts to redistribute the income. This is so because point A' is decidedly inferior to point A. Everybody is worse off, in that less income is received.

Thus, transfers cost real resources even if they are successful, and if they are unsuccessful, their only effect may be a waste of resources, with the result that everyone is worse off. This conclusion was overlooked by economists for a long time, essentially because economists paid little attention to the details of government behavior. They would say, perfectly correctly according to the theory underlying their analysis, that if the government forcibly transfers money from, let us say the reader of this book to the two authors,[2] there would be no clear-cut social cost, because your loss would be the same as our gain.

The mistake in analysis involved an unbelievably simple oversight by generations of economists. The fact that we, the authors, would have to use resources to make the transfer possible and that you, the reader, would probably invest resources to defend yourself was overlooked. Thus, a good part of the real problem of transfers was overlooked, and the part that remained— that is, the part that they did concentrate on—was a portion in which there was no resource cost. However, before discussing further the problem of costly transfers through rent seeking, let us turn to another area in which somewhat the same kind of error has been made by traditional economics, the conventional treatment of monopoly rents (or profits).

THE RENTS OF MONOPOLIES

A monopolist has market power. By this we mean that the monopolist is sufficiently dominant in the market that it can choose to restrict production for the purpose of raising its price and profits above competitive levels. Competitors do not have the same kind of market power. If a competitor raises its prices by restricting production, then consumers will move their purchases to one of the other producers in the market or to one of the producers that can readily enter the market when any one firm tries to raise its price. The monopolist has monopoly power to the extent that other competitors do not exist and to the extent that other competitors are unable to enter the market.

In Figure 18–2, we show the diagram conventionally used to illustrate the cost of a monopoly. Temporarily we need not concern ourselves with the question of whether this monopoly is obtained privately by, let us say, merg-

---

[2]Obviously a meritorious transfer.

FIGURE 18–2

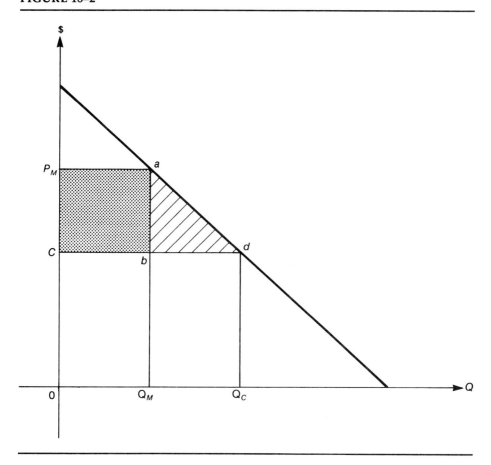

ing steel mills, or whether it is a result of some governmental regulation that prohibits import of foreign steel or prevents independent truckers from undercutting the prices being offered by chartered truckers.

In Figure 18–2, the price per unit of the monopolized product that is shown on the vertical axis and the quantity sold on the horizontal. To simplify the analysis, we assume that the monopolist's product can be produced at a constant marginal (and average) cost of C, as shown by the horizontal line. Under competitive conditions, the quantity Q_c would be produced at a price of C. (Quantity Q_c is the point at which the marginal benefit of the last unit of the good equals the marginal cost. Refer back to Chapter 1 if you fail to understand that competition would result in an output level of Q_c.)

Suppose that in its search for maximum profits, the monopolist does what all good monopolists do: equate marginal cost with marginal revenue. This means that the monopoly restricts production to Q_m, permitting it to raise its price to M. The traditional measure of the net welfare cost of restricted production by the monopolist is the striped triangle. Why is that the net welfare cost? The area under the demand curve between Q_c and Q_m, which represents the value of those units, exceeds the area under the supply curve, which represents their cost. The striped triangular area is the amount by which the benefits of Q_m to Q_c units exceeds the costs; it is the net loss from not having those units produced.

The dotted rectangular area, on the other hand, is the monopolist's profit. If the monopolist charges P_m for Q_m units sold, its revenues equal the box bounded by $0P_maQ_m$. Its costs are represented by the area under the supply curve up to Q_m units, or the area bounded by $0CbQ_m$. The shaded area is profit because it is the amount by which the revenue exceeds the costs of producing Q_m.

Economists have traditionally argued that profits are transferred from the customers who continue buying the good to the monopolist. The gains of the monopolist, it is argued, exactly counterbalance the losses of the customers represented by this rectangle. The profits do not evaporate, hence, are not a meaningful part of the social cost of monopoly. Nothing has to be given up, or so it is argued.

According to this conventional argument, the true loss is the striped area that represents the consumer surplus from quantity Q_c minus Q_m that the monopolist refuses to produce. It is, of course, true that the striped area is part of the cost of the monopoly, but the belief that the profit rectangle is not a cost is based on a failure to consider the process by which monopolies are organized.

Clearly, if large profits (rents) can be made by developing a monopoly, whether this involves private maneuvering or talking the government into unwise legislation, we expect people to invest resources in obtaining the monopolies and the profits that go with them. We expect them, in other words, to engage in rent seeking. Further, we expect them to invest resources up to the point where the return on the last dollar put into getting the monopoly or special restriction is equal to the return elsewhere. The result will then be that the resources invested in attempting to obtain the monopoly will be roughly equal to the present discounted value of the dotted rectangle.[3] Thus, the actual social cost is about the sum of the triangle *plus* rectangle. This cost estimate is much higher than conventional wisdom would have indicated. The error is the same as the error discussed above with respect to transfers: resources invested in obtaining the transfer or, in this case, the special privilege are ignored; hence, large social costs are understated.

---

[3]Note the word *roughly*. Actually the problem of exactly measuring the waste is quite complicated. See Gordon Tullock, "Efficient Rent Seeking," in *Towards a Theory of the Rent-Seeking Society*, ed. James M. Buchanan, Robert D. Tollison, and Gordon Tullock (College Station: Texas A & M Press, 1980), pp. 3–15. But the assumption that the rectangle represents the cost, although not precise, is a reasonably good one.

The size of these social costs has been roughly approximated by two studies carried out by Duke University's Anne Krueger.[4] She considered only one particular kind of special restriction: the requirement that people importing merchandise to India and Turkey obtain foreign-exchange licenses. In this case, the beneficiaries of the restrictions are not the importers or even the manufacturers who competed with imports, but the bureaucrats who handle the issuance of the licenses and take bribes. A monopoly is, in this case, created by the government for the benefit of its own employees rather than for the benefit of some outsider.

Professor Krueger found that in India 7 percent of the national income and in Turkey 15 percent was being wasted by these specific types of rent seeking. In both countries this was merely one example of many, and it seems likely that the total waste from all forms of rent seeking was much larger than these figures.

In order to fully understand this type of rent seeking, however, it is necessary to follow a rather complicated chain of reasoning. The central bank official who is bribed to give out foreign exchange licenses did not directly waste that bribe in rent seeking. He or she had already engaged in rent seeking in order to obtain this job as a bank official. It was the resources wasted in competition to obtain a job in which the official could take bribes that constitute the waste of rent seeking here. Many people had gone through Indian and Turkish colleges not with the intent of obtaining a training that would have value in later life, but simply because that was a requirement for obtaining a position to take bribes. Having graduated from college, the officials devoted a great deal of time and energy to maneuvering in devious political channels for the jobs. In general, this meant that they could not hold gainful employment at anything else for years on end. Of this large collection of people who invested so many years in political maneuvering, only a few lucky ones received the bribe-rich jobs. They were, of course, making a sizeable profit out of their special privileges.

What happened in this case was that a great many people, in essence, bought lottery tickets at a very high cost, let us say three years of their life devoted to political maneuvering. A few of them drew the lucky numbers. Those few, of course, did very well, but socially the total cost of the lottery may have been at least as great as, and very possibly larger than, the benefit that these people gained. It was like any other lottery in that all the people who buy the tickets pay, or typically more than pay, for the prize of the winner.

The conventional lottery, however, is a transfer that is entered into by its customers for what may be termed entertainment purposes. The cost of tickets partly goes to pay administrative cost, including profits. The investments

---

[4]Anne O. Krueger, "The Political Economy of the Rent-Seeking Society," *American Economic Review* 64 (June 1974), pp. 291–303.

by the people engaging in devious political maneuvers in hopes of being appointed to the agency that distributes foreign exchange licenses are a pure waste in the sense that no one receives any direct benefit from them. Indeed, one of the reasons for the backwardness of India and Turkey is that so many bright, well-educated people devote their time to this type of activity instead of to productive work.

RENT SEEKING THROUGH HISTORY

Looking back from the present, it seems quite astonishing that for so long the economists missed the point we are making. The two authors of this book can, however, testify that we, together with other economists, missed it for quite some time.[5] It would appear, however, that in a way the astonishment in the economic profession indicates that we don't read our own history as carefully as we should. Adam Smith discussed rent seeking in *The Wealth of Nations*, although not under the same rubric; and it was fairly well known by most of the economists in the early part of the nineteenth century. It gradually dropped out of the economic literature during the nineteenth century and has only recently been revived.

The intellectual history of rent-seeking discussions, however, roughly parallels the importance of rent seeking in society. In Adam Smith's time, rent seeking was an important activity in the leftover vestiges of mercantilism; hence he brought it into his famous book. In the late nineteenth century, it declined to a very low level with the advent of free trade, and most economists began to ignore the problem. Rent seeking is becoming important again in most western countries, and therefore, it is returning to the forefront of economic investigation. Consider the following examples of rent seeking in our recent history.

The Rent-Seeking Airlines

One prominent expression of rent seeking was in the airline industry. Now that the airlines have been deregulated for more than a decade, the rent seeking that went on in the airline industry may now be unknown to current readers. A lesson in regulatory history may, therefore, serve a useful purpose.

Until 1985, the Civil Aeronautics Board (CAB) regulated the airlines. From 1937 when the CAB was created with the intent of reducing the competitiveness of the airline industry until the late 1970s, the CAB ran a cartel for domestic American airlines and participated in the International Air Transport Association (IATA), which was an international cartel for international airlines. The airlines had lobbied for and obtained the CAB as one of

---

[5]The argument was first developed in modern times by Gordon Tullock, "The Welfare Costs of Monopolies, Tariffs, and Theft," *Western Economic Journal* 5 (June 1967), pp. 224–32.

the New Deal reforms and obviously got a reasonable return on their lobbying efforts. But in the process of getting the bill through Congress, they found it necessary to make deals with various special interests other than the airlines themselves.

To take a few examples from more recent times. Piedmont Airline was compelled for many years to fly in and out of Pulaski, Virginia (as well as other places) for the convenience of a very small number of people who wanted to fly from Pulaski to Washington or Atlanta. Because Pulaski is a small town, Piedmont lost money on this stop. Piedmont was also compelled to serve Chicago by way of Midway Airport (a small airport close to downtown Chicago) instead of by way of O'Hare International Airport (the major airport in the Chicago area). From Piedmont's standpoint, these were both significant costs, but their monopoly gains elsewhere from the CAB regulation made up for their losses.

On a more general level, the fee schedules were calculated in such a way that, in essence, people flying long distance were overcharged and people flying shorter distances undercharged. Further, the first-class passengers paid somewhat less than the cost of their rather luxurious quarters, while the tourist passengers paid somewhat more. The income transfer from tourist-class passenger to first-class passenger and from people flying long distances to people flying short distances may perhaps serve some social goal, but it is certainly an obscure one.

Politically these rules are not hard to explain. Small cities, the citizens of which normally take an airplane for a short distance rather than a long one, are spread through far more congressional districts than our major cities in which the long flights originate. First-class passengers are almost certainly on a per-capita basis more politically influential than tourists. Indeed, most senior government officials, including congressmen, travel first class. Under the circumstances, it is obvious why the airlines seeking support for their cartel would find it sensible to advocate these two special fare arrangements.

On a basic level, however, the cartel itself in the long run did not turn out to be particularly profitable, which was perhaps the political reason it turned out to be possible to break it up with the airline deregulation act passed in 1978. The CAB could set fares and routes, and after a while it set standards of service.[6] The space between the seats, for example, was regulated, and indeed now it is considerably smaller than it was in the late 1950s. Individual airlines were attracting passengers by moving their seats farther

---

[6]Originally, tourist-class travelers were served only sandwiches. This led to a long and undignified squabble as to what a sandwich was. On the North-Atlantic run, a number of airlines such as Swiss Air adopted the view that if there was a piece of bread somewhere on the plate, it was a sandwich. Of course, as anyone who has flown Swiss Air can imagine, the piece of bread was completely hidden under a pile of roast beef, liverwurst, salami, cheese, and so forth. The end of the squabble was the establishment of an agreed-upon standard for tourist meals, but these standards did not attempt to keep them at the sandwich level.

and farther apart and making it possible for them to be inclined at flatter and flatter angles. Eventually the seat was, to all intents and purposes, a bed. Although the individual airline did this to attract additional passengers and, hence, make money, it was obviously bad for the cartel as a whole, and the CAB came to the rescue of its members by forcing them to put the seats closer together.

However, the CAB does not have the power to limit the number of flights that any airline may make between two points. The airline can increase the number of passengers by providing a crowded schedule with the result that there are more passengers who find it convenient to fly American Airlines with a crowded schedule than, let us say, United with a sparse schedule. Since the prices that the CAB had set, together with the restrictions on the service, meant that the prices were considerably above what they would be without regulation, the airlines competed by putting more flights on with the result that the airplanes were often flying half empty.

This phenomenon of nonprice competition is familiar to economists, and it almost always follows when prices are set above cost and competition is permitted on any single dimension. Resources may be invested along that uncontrolled dimension until the full benefit of the cartel is exhausted. Instead of reducing the prices, service is increased. The result is that customers are worse off than they would be with lower prices, and the airline is not really benefited. Nonprice competition is very difficult for any cartel manager to avoid because there are so many ways to compete. In any event, this is what happened to the airlines. As a result, the reduction of the cartel restrictions actually permitted them to make better use of their aircraft and temporarily increase their profits.

Politically it is a little obscure why the CAB was not given the power to restrict the number of flights as well as controlling everything else about the airline business. Surely the cartel would have been more profitable if this had been so. It may be that in this case, the airline manufacturers were being "paid off" by an expanded demand for their product. If so, this would be a further case in which the cost of maintaining the monopoly has actually been dissipated in economic waste.

Rent Seeking at the Post Office

Another example of rent being dissipated in waste can be seen in the carriers for the U.S. Postal Service who are overpaid. The evidence that mail carriers are overpaid is simply that they are willing to take examinations and then wait for a long period of time, usually several years, before getting their jobs. If the pay was equivalent to just the opportunity costs of their work, they would not be willing to do this; hence there would not be long queues of people waiting for the postal appointment. It is, however, these long queues that make up the social waste.

Note that this system of hiring postal carriers is brought into equilibrium by the length of the delay. Suppose that the postal salary is extremely high. Under those circumstances, enough people would study for the exam and pass it so that the delay before appointment to a postal job would be very long indeed. With a lower postal pay but with pay that is still higher than that of equivalent nonpostal jobs, the delay they would be willing to take would be shorter. If the post office simply paid the same amount that such organizations as United Parcel Service pay, no one would be willing to wait in queue for a postal job, and so people would be hired almost immediately after taking their exam. It would also be necessary to see to it that the exam did not require any special preparation. The waste here is in the delay that the successful candidates must undergo before taking up their main career. The rent has, in this case, very neatly been consumed by waste.

Turn back to Figure 18–2. Assume that the actual cost of hiring a mail carrier is C, but the price is M. We have, of course, the small shaded rectangle as the loss that occurs from not hiring as many mail carriers as would be hired at C. The large rectangle is entirely consumed by preparing for the exam and then waiting for an appointment to the postal service.

Rent Seeking in Korea

Airlines and the U.S. Postal Service are merely two examples of rent seeking. Modern society and, for that matter, most societies in the world history before about 1800 provide many similar cases. If funds are transferred from X to Y, the transfer itself (and this is the element of truth in the conventional wisdom) does not have any social cost, but Y will put resources into attempting to get the transfer and X, to avoid it. The sum of these resources will normally be about the present discounted value of the transfer. The problem is a very general one and can have very great effects on the economy.

One of the authors of this book spent some time in the Orient. Specifically, he had one year under the Nationalist government of China, one year under the Communists, and about 18 months under President Rhee's government in Korea. In all three of these regimes, the principal way of getting ahead was to obtain some special government privilege. These privileges varied a good deal from society to society. In Communist China, for example, it was mainly getting a high-ranking government job. In Nationalist China and Korea, government jobs certainly were desirable, but there were also ways of getting rents if you were not a government employee. The advantages of achieving these special positions of power and privilege were and are great, and individuals invested great resources in attempting to achieve them. For one example, the most important businessman in Korea took a trip to the United States. In order to understand what follows, it must be said that this was right after the war in Korea and things were unsettled and depressed. President Rhee traveled, when he left his palace, in an elderly car

274 Chapter 18 The Rent-Seeking Society

called a Packard, which had originally been imported to Korea as the car of the American ambassador, who had since replaced it with a more modern car.

The prominent businessman returned to Korea not by air but on a freighter which docked in Inchon very close to Seoul. The freighter contained a great many things belonging to the businessman, and on the deck were two Buick automobiles, one blue and one green. The businessman was told by customs that substantially everything on it was banned for import (which meant that he would have to bribe the customs inspectors). He went immediately to Seoul, leaving his baggage behind, and called on President Rhee. He said that he had been perturbed at the president's driving around in the streets of Korea in this elderly Packard and therefore had brought back a Buick for the president to drive in; in fact, he brought back two Buicks, and the president could take his choice. He would use the other himself. The president then asked where the Buicks were, and the businessman said they were being held at customs but no doubt President Rhee could get them released. President Rhee immediately told the customs officer in Inchon to release the businessman's personal effects including the large items.

On the following day, the businessman turned up at the Korean White House with two cars, and President Rhee chose the blue one. The businessman not only improved his relations with President Rhee for various future transactions, but the cost of one Buick was no doubt much less than he would have had to pay the customs inspector to get the rest of his baggage through. It was an example of an intelligent man in a rent-seeking society taking action to minimize the rents he had to pay.

The point of this story is that activity like this is the thing that pays off most in societies in which rent seeking is common. Instead of seeking opportunities to cut costs and prices or produce commodities that people would like to have, the man who wants to get ahead in such a society will devote his attention primarily to trying to minimize the rents he has to pay other people and maximize the rents he receives. The private return is high in this area although there is not social return at all. Thus, immense resources in human capital are diverted from productive channels into areas where, although they benefit the individual, they have no social payoff.

Indeed, in most cases, the diversions of resources to rent seeking actually have negative social payoffs. Rents mainly are derived by putting restrictions on market activities. The net effect is that society is poorer after they are imposed than before. Thus, talking the government into giving up a monopoly on the sale of insurance on transpacific cargos not only means that great resources are diverted into an activity that will produce large rents, but also means that insurance itself will be produced monopolistically and, hence, with relatively inefficient market results.

Thus, if the steel industry succeeds in getting imports of steel reduced, this will not only mean a rent for the steel industry, it will mean that Americans will purchase their steel under less than competitive conditions with the result that there is a net loss there, too. Not only does the society bear the cost of the lobbying on the part of the steel industry together with a certain amount of counterlobbying on the part of steel consumers, but when the steel lobby wins, society is actually injured. Valuable resources are invested in causing injuries rather than in producing more wealth.

THE RETARDATION OF GROWTH

Whenever resources are wasted, economic growth is impaired. Hence, rent seeking can reduce economic growth over time. Consider the situation in England before about 1600. Suppose you want to make money selling soap. You could invent a new, improved kind of soap, invest in a cheaper way to making soap, or reduce your total cost as compared to your competitors by simply good organization and hard work. All of these would be ways of making money. There was, however, an alternative. You could get the king to give you a monopoly on selling soap in England.[7]

On the whole, the latter would be most profitable if one could obtain a monopoly; but not only did you have to talk the king into granting such a monopoly, you had to be certain he gave it to you and not to, let us say, the cousin of his mistress. Resources would be invested in these various ways of making soap out to the point where the marginal returns were equal. This would mean that there would be considerably less resources invested in improving soap or the technology for making it than there would be if the possibility of getting the king to give you a monopoly did not exist. Thus, we have the rent-seeking waste. Further, of course, if the king did give you a monopoly then the normal problems of monopoly, that is, higher cost and the loss of the conventional welfare triangle shown on Figure 18–2, would also occur. Thus, the possibility of investing resources in rent seeking would tend to retard economic development.

It seems likely that one of the basic reasons for the relatively slow development of the world before what is called the Industrial Revolution and its fairly rapid development in the nineteenth century was the fact that rent seeking was a major activity in most of the world during most of the history and became of relatively minor importance in England when the Industrial Revolution started in the eighteenth and nineteenth centuries. Certainly the situation observed in China and Korea was not conducive to growth. Investment in a factory or other capital installation for improving production was highly risky unless large resources had been invested in obtaining protection for that factory against rent seeking by officials. Thus, the actual cost of production was frequently half or more rent-avoidance activity of the sort described in connection with the Buick for President Rhee, and much of the

---

[7]The actual soap monopoly turned out not to be terribly profitable because it was very difficult to enforce.

higher management devoted their principal attention to this area. Production efficiency was a relatively minor interest.

University of Maryland economist Mancur Olson uses a variation of our rent-seeking model to explain "the rise and decline of nations" in a widely read book by that title.[8] Professor Olson begins with a full recognition that rent seeking has detrimental effects: It can divert resources from production of consumer and capital goods and can lead to government controls on the economy that throttle production and growth. When a nation is newly formed, Olson argues, it may go through a relatively blissful period of open trade, few government controls, little rent seeking, and high economic growth. (The United States may have passed through such a fortunate period in the seventeenth and eighteenth centuries.) However, as time passes, the interest groups are better able to organize their forces and develop political influence that leads to greater monopoly rents for their respective members but growing restrictions on the economy—and to slower economic growth. Hence, Professor Olson maintains that rent seeking (or the effects of rent seeking) go a long way toward explaining why more mature and stable economies often grow more slowly than they did when they were not so mature and stable, or more slowly than other less mature and, in the past, less stable economies. The more mature economies are shackled with more controls and more rent seeking (offensive and defensive).

Professor Olson maintains that his rent-seeking view of the world also helps explain why economies often grow more rapidly after a disruptive war or a natural disaster. The disruption breaks the strangle hold that the rent seekers have on the economy. As a consequence, trade is freer and growth is greater than before the disruption. He believes that his theory helps explain the miraculous revival of the Japanese and West German economies after World War II. The Allied Forces—in a manner of speaking—did those two countries a favor by breaking the established political influence that interests groups had on their respective economies.

In the Olson broad view of social and political history, political stability can be something of a mixed blessing. It ensures that resources are not devoted to coping with unstable economic environments. However, the stability itself provides ample opportunities for interest groups to gain government-backed controls over competitive forces in their markets through rent seeking.

CONCLUDING COMMENTS

Today, once again, one of the major ways of making money is to get the government to provide some kind of privilege. This special privilege may be

---

[8]Mancur Olson, *The Rise and Decline of Nations: Economic Growth, Stagflation, and Social Rigidities* (New Haven, Conn.: Yale University Press, 1982).

hiring you as a civil servant at more than what you can make elsewhere, restricting foreign imports of competing products, or prohibiting domestic competition, securing direct government grants, and so forth. The list is endless.

Measuring the exact amount of rent seeking is very difficult. The influence community, which is such an important part of the Washington life and which combines with the highly paid federal civil service to make the Washington suburbs one of the highest-income areas in the United States, is no doubt the source of considerable waste but is a tiny portion of the total cost of rent seeking. The plethora of expensive French restaurants that have sprung up in Washington illustrates the expense of rent seeking. But there are other and far more expensive ways of influencing the government. Lockheed once put a major defense plant in the constituency of the chairman of the House Armed Services Committee. This was, in all probability, not the best place to locate an aircraft plant, although as a matter of fact, it wasn't bad. Similarly, General Dynamics beat out Boeing in a contest to build a plane that eventually became the F-111—to a large extent because they had a factory in Texas and it was during the Johnson presidency. Since the F-111 turned out to be both very costly and poor, this was indeed an expensive form of rent seeking.

The forms in which rents are dissipated are more varied than the names on government agencies. Indeed, we suspect that growth in government responsibilities and rent seeking go hand in hand. One of the reasons members of Congress may favor the expansion of government is that the growth increases the demand for their services and incomes. Indirectly, they too are the beneficiaries of the rent seeking society.

QUESTIONS TO PONDER

1. Can you suggest any reason why rent seeking first became relatively uncommon in the English speaking world in the nineteenth century and now is becoming much more common?

2. Why is it that the authors say that the wasted resources from rent seeking may be equal to the monopoly profits (the shaded rectangle in Figure 18–2)?

3. Can you think of any methods of reducing the amount of rent seeking?

4. What are the advantages in monarchies of having the throne passed down to the firstborn child? What does such a rule have to do with the potential waste from rent seeking?

5. Identify forms of contemporary rent seeking by reading the morning newspaper. Can any of these forms be productive? Explain.

CHAPTER 19

Constitutional Economics

An important new subdiscipline is beginning to take shape in economics. The economists (along with political scientists and legal scholars) who work in this line of inquiry are mainly concerned with reconsidering the constitutional constraints on the fiscal, monetary, and regulatory powers of the federal government.

This subdiscipline has been rightfully dubbed *constitutional economics* (or, more pedantically, *constitutional political economy*). Following in the tradition of Thomas Jefferson, these economists tend to agree that every now and then people must reassess their institutions and, where appropriate, alter them for the common good, not by way of a continuous stream of ad hoc policies that emerge from the political process, but by way of fundamental adjustment to basic rules that underlie political institutions and markets. Their concern is with the long-run regulation *of* government, not regulation *by* government.

Accordingly, constitutional economics is fundamentally concerned with the framework for social processes: the structure of political and economic institutions, and their inter-relationships—all designed to allow people, individually and collectively, to pursue desired ends. The underlying theory of constitutional economics is a theory of the rules by which political and economic processes will be allowed to operate through long periods of time. This chapter is about how economists are inclined to evaluate rules for a democratically elected government. In this chapter we sample the insights these *constitutional economists* have to offer.

CONSTITUTIONAL ECONOMICS: BACKGROUND

Although the rubric may be new, constitutional economics is built on a solid foundation of scholarly work written by economists, political scientists, and philosophers. It has emerged out of the life-long work of eminent scholars such as Nobel laureates James Buchanan, Milton Friedman, and Friedrich Hayek. Milton and Rose Friedman's *Free to Choose*, which sets out constitutional reforms in its final chapter, has been the most widely read book that can be brought under the rubric of constitutional economics,[1] but academic

---

[1]Milton Friedman and Rose Friedman, *Free to Choose: A Personal Statement* (New York: Harcourt, Brace, Jovanovich, 1980).

economists are well aware of many other treatises that are concerned with constitutional economic issues (although the rubric may never be used in several of them).[2] President Ronald Reagan's first *Economic Report* indicates that concern for the economic implications of constitutional matters has penetrated the Executive Offices of the White House.[3]

In many important respects, however, all of the new work on constitutional economics is a throwback to the beginning of economics as a discipline. Even Adam Smith was concerned with the broad institutional framework for government, as well as with markets. He saw markets as constraints on governments—as realms within which governments should not be permitted to intrude. Why? The long-run "wealth of nations" was at stake. The wealth of nations could be fostered by a long-run hands-off policy adopted by government.

As were their intellectual forebears, the modern scholars behind constitutional economics are very serious in their attempts to shift professional attention away from short-run policy questions to long-term constitutional constraints on government. These constraints on government can be procedural or substantive in nature. The *procedural restrictions* limit the *ways* in which policy decisions can be made by the various branches of government; the *substantive restrictions* limit the *range* of issues that can be considered by the various branches.

The voting rule (or size of majority) used for determining when policies are adopted is probably the most widely recognized procedural rule; however, procedural rules can also specify when votes are taken, who is entitled to vote, and how the adopted policies are to be administered. The voting rule as a procedural restriction may appear to be a totally political problem. Nonetheless, the voting rule can determine the types and numbers of economic and social policies that are adopted and can, therefore, affect the nation's

---

[2]Anthony Downs, *An Economic Theory of Democracy* (New York: Harper and Row, 1957); F. A. Hayek, *The Constitution of Liberty* (Chicago: University of Chicago Press, 1960); Hayek, *Law, Legislation, and Liberty.* 3 vols. (Chicago: University of Chicago Press, 1977–79); James M. Buchanan and Gordon Tullock, *The Calculus of Consent: The Logical Foundations of Constitutional Democracy* (Ann Arbor, Mich.: University of Michigan Press, 1962); James M. Buchanan, *The Limits of Liberty: Between Anarchy and Leviathan* (Chicago: University of Chicago Press, 1975); James M. Buchanan and Geoffrey Brennan, *The Power to Tax: Analytical Foundations of a Fiscal Constitution* (New York: Cambridge University Press, 1980); Gordon Tullock, *Toward a Mathematics of Politics* (Ann Arbor, Mich.: University of Michigan Press, 1967); Robert Nozick, *Anarchy, State, and Utopia* (New York: Basic Books, 1974); Bernard H. Seigan, *Economic Liberties and the Constitution* (Chicago: University of Chicago Press, 1980); Terry Anderson and P. J. Hill, *The Birth of the Transfer Society* (Stanford, Cal.: Hoover Institution Press, 1980); Richard B. McKenzie, *Bound to Be Free* (Stanford, Cal.: Hoover Institution Press, 1982); and Dwight R. Lee and Richard B. McKenzie, *Regulating Government: A Preface to Constitutional Economics* (Lexington, Mass.: Lexington Books, 1987).

[3]Council of Economic Advisers, Executive Office of the President, *The Economic Report of the President* (Washington, D.C.: U.S. Government Printing Office, 1982), chap. 2.

production, employment, growth, inflation, and poverty rates as well as many other notable economic variables.

A substantive restriction can impose serious limits on what government can and cannot do in the economy. Rules that prohibit the government from taking private property without compensation (power of eminent domain) is an obvious economic constraint on government. However, First Amendment rights—freedom of speech and press—definitely affect the economic powers of government, because much business involving speech and press cannot (within strict boundaries) be controlled by government. Substantive rules can also cover operational constraints on how much the government can spend and tax (fiscal constraints), how much money the government can create (monetary constraints), and the extent to which government can regulate business or any other group (regulatory constraints).

The proposed balanced-budget, tax-limitation amendment to the Constitution (which, if ever enacted, would require the federal government to match its expenditures with tax revenue and to hold taxes to a given percentage of national income) is one of the most widely discussed fiscal constraints on the federal government.[4] The projected $150 billion to $200 billion budgetary deficits for years to come ensure that questions of how Congress can be forced or induced to balance the federal budget will remain the focus of public debate.

As you may imagine, given the continuing debate, there remain many unsettled normative and positive issues in the balanced-budget/tax-limitation debate. For their part, the positive question constitutional economists address in the debate is whether and how a balanced budget or tax-limitation requirement in the Constitution will actually work in practice. Will such devices actually constrain the democratic process? How will Congress try to get around the constitutional restrictions? What will such limitations do to income, employment, growth, and so on?

These are hardly trivial issues, but they are concerns that arise from even larger philosophical matters. We may all agree on the absolute necessity of government if individual freedom and economic security are to be secured and maintained. However, that point conceded, an important question that immediately arises is how to erect an institution—call it *government*—and proceed to anoint it with powers of coercion: give it the authority to tax, to transfer income, and to build police and military forces; and at the same time keep it contained, or corralled within desired bounds? How do we, in other words, control those who have been delegated the powers of control? That is the mammoth question that the Founding Fathers faced over two centuries ago; they literally sweated over it during the summer of 1787 in Philadelphia. The question will likely never go away.

---

[4]U.S. Senate, Committee on the Judiciary, 97th Congress, 1st session, "Report: Balanced-Budget, Tax-Limitation Constitutional Amendment" (No. 97–101; July 10, 1981).

THE CONSTITUTIONAL PERSPECTIVE:
A DIFFERENT WORLD VIEW

Obviously, constitutional economics is not economics as usual. It is concerned with predicting the efficiency of the economy, as is true of all economic analysis; however, the thrust of what is sought is social improvement; the search is for an appropriate institutional design for a society of free people. Although somewhat different from the conventional economic approach to economic and political issues, the analysis of all of these issues, grouped for convenience under the category of constitutional economics, is founded on premises of individual behavior that are readily accepted in standard economic analysis. Indeed, constitutional economists generally assume, as do other economists, that people are motivated by personal interests, many of which are completely selfish but others of which are altruistic. Constitutional economists' primary purpose is to apply this self-interest postulate to the political setting. In doing that they place the analysis of the political sphere on an equal footing with standard economic analysis of market behavior.

In generalizing our assumption about behavior, constitutional economists must break with much standard economic policy discussions but follow in the time-tested tradition of public choice economics (see Chapter 17). Typically, when economists observe market failures, they suggest corrective policies and then recommend that government apply these policies to improve the performance of the economy. This might be a satisfactory approach if, as is implicitly assumed, the only motivation of political decision makers were totally altruistic or totally consistent with economic efficiency for the economy as a whole.

Unfortunately, politicians have their own personal agendas (much like their counterparts in the private sector) that may or may not be consistent with the broader public interest. Given this, it no longer automatically follows that market failures call for corrective government actions. This may be true no matter how technically competent is the economic theory upon which the policy prescription is based. Political failures may be just as pervasive as market failures, and we should never allow ourselves to be blinded to the existence of the former in our concern over the latter.

Throughout much that is written in constitutional economics, one principle stands out: If we are to live together harmoniously, means must be found to convert our competing private interests into public gain. In the private sector, economists argue that competitive market processes tend to do just that: in seeking personal gain, the private entrepreneur is coaxed by competitive forces to provide what others want on improved terms, a serendipitous benefit to the public that may not have been a part of the entrepreneur's intentions.

Competitive politics that emerges from the drive of people to be elected and re-elected also helps to convert private interest into public gain, but constitutional economists (following in the tradition of public choice economics) are concerned that the political process, especially if left unbounded by substantive rules, has deficiencies. Democracy needs rules (for example, who may vote, how votes will be taken, and what can be voted on) in order to operate.

To answer the question of what the rules should be, a theory of government is needed, and much of constitutional economics is taken up in expounding alternative theories of government. Economists James Buchanan and Geoffrey Brennan argue that the search for appropriate constitutional bounds on government is a search for a social contract and should be approached much like the search for a building contract.[5] When we seek a builder for a house, we are naturally concerned with the reputation and integrity of prospective builders. However, in nailing down a contract, we effectively assume that the builder we have chosen is completely devoid of principle, totally concerned with making money, and perfectly willing to chisel on the agreement—to take us to the cleaners whenever and wherever he or she can. We assume the builder is the perfect *homo economicus*. We make this assumption in our contract discussions not so much because that is what we think of our builder, but because that is the type of behavior from which we seek contractual (and legal) protection.

Similarly, the image of government in constitutional economics is not always a pretty one; it is one of a self-serving Leviathan (or an overly rapacious government), fueled almost exclusively by totally self-serving political operatives. Constitutional economists start with this perception of government in part because those are the kinds of people that rules for government are designed to check. What constitutional economists often seek is a system of government in which, as F. A. Hayek has noted, "bad men can do the least harm," if they ever acquire the reins of power.

CONTAINING GOVERNMENT POWER

The ability of politicians to keep their spending within the bounds of their financial resources must be questioned. Fifty years of progressively growing tax receipts and mounting deficits perhaps may speak more plainly of the attractiveness of a fiscal constitution than all of the theoretical arguments combined. Much theory developed in constitutional economics supports the commonsense appraisal of government: The temptation for our political leaders to pad the pockets of some of their constituents at the expense of others is forever present. Constitutional rules are one means of restricting the powers of government.

Rules for government need not be written down. Indeed, the most effective constraints on government may have been natural in the sense they

---

[5]Buchanan and Brennan, *The Power to Tax*, chap. 1.

were technologically based or founded in deep, commonly acknowledged values. At one time, James Buchanan and Richard Wagner argue, before the Keynesian revolution in public-policy economics, the country had informally adopted the "balanced-budget norm," which, although unwritten, effectively forbade politicians from routinely spending more than government received from taxes.[6] Now, that norm has been extensively discarded with the blessings of a whole generation of Keynesian economists who saw, and still see, no harm, and often see much good, in budget deficits;[7] and politicians find it convenient to offer their constituencies benefits for which no direct taxes are collected.

According to Buchanan and Wagner, Keynesian economics may have made one crucial mistake: it assumed that if given good theory, then good people in power would put this theory into practice to do good. The historical record of what people in power will do must make us reconsider this view. Given a realistic view of the motivations of political decision makers, it becomes quickly apparent that the structure of political incentives is just as important to sound economic policy as the development of sound economic theory.

THE OPEN-ENDED POLITICAL SYSTEM

As evident in what we have already said, constitutional economists appear to be in agreement over one proposition: Without bounds on how much government can do in the economy, an open-ended political system will tend to do too much, that is, more than people would choose to have it do if all the decisions were made together as a package. A major problem with democracy is partially one of majority rule, a procedure that offers a simple majority of voters the right to acquire government services for its members by imposing an undue portion of the costs of government on the rest of the population.

Majority rule is replete with opportunities for special interests to exploit the rest of the population. Special interests, although they may represent a very small fraction of the voting population, tend to have political power disproportionate to their numbers. The benefits they receive from the government may be quite substantial. Therefore, they have reason to become and remain politically active, constantly promoting their special interests through their own political leaders.

On the other hand, constitutional economists maintain, the costs of the special-interest programs can be so diffused over the general population that no one outside the special interest has an incentive to incur the costs associated with political opposition; for any one average citizen loses little. The

---

[6]James M. Buchanan and Richard E. Wagner, *Democracy in Deficit* (New York: Academic Press, 1977).

[7]A basic tenet of Keynesian economics is that government can pull the economy out of recessions by running budgetary deficits.

result of the political process can be burdensome: a relatively small group of dairy farmers, for example, can have the government jack up the price of their products through production restrictions, all for the dairymen's benefit and to the detriment of consumers. The same can be said for the entry restrictions on trucking firms, the tariffs on imported textiles, the subsidies for university education and research, and the interest ceilings on savings accounts. The political imbalance between the latent general interests and the kinetic special interests can translate into an engorgement of the federal budget with special-interest programs, the sum total of which no one may like. Containing this presumed appetite for the taxpayers' dollars—by, for example, tying maximum tax collection to a fixed percentage of national income—is an important consideration in constitutional economics.

POLITICAL MYOPIA

Constitutional economists worry that an inherent inconsistency exists between the demands of an open-ended, unconstrained democracy and the needs of the economy. As presently constructed, the political system forces politicians to look to the near term and the next election and to seek what may be the quick-fix policy that usually inspires greater short-run federal spending and taxation. The result can be that government can actually be less effective in the long run in solving the country's economic and social problems.

These points can be made clear with the *Laffer curve* that describes the expected functional connection between tax *rates* and total tax *collections.* This concept is founded on the proposition that as tax rates go up initially, tax revenue may also rise—at least for some range of tax rate increases. However, beyond some point, a further tax rate increase may actually lower tax revenues, meaning the rate increase reduces the ability of government to accomplish its social objectives (whether they include building defense bases or helping the poor). Tax revenues go down because the high tax rates discourage people from working, saving, and investing, and encourage people to evade and avoid taxes. The resulting reduction in income that is subject to taxation can be so large that when the high tax rate is multiplied by the reduced income, tax revenues are lower than they would otherwise have been.

Why would any rational government choose tax rates so high that the country would suffer lower tax revenues, a circumstance that appears to be to no one's advantage?[8] Such a position means that workers are enduring

---

[8]James M. Buchanan and Dwight R. Lee, "Politics, Time, and the Laffer Curve," *Journal of Political Economy*, August 1982, pp. 816–19.

higher taxes and receiving lower incomes than they could receive if tax rates were lower. Similarly, government revenues are less than they could be at lower tax rates, meaning politicians have less to spend on constituencies than they could have if tax rates were lowered. Why? That is the question supply-side economists (including Arthur Laffer, originator of the Laffer Curve) never thought to pose.

Constitutional economists James Buchanan and Dwight Lee's answer to the puzzle stresses the inconsistency between the short-term horizons of political leaders and the long-term perspective of private investors. On the one hand, considerable time is required for current investment to pay off in terms of higher income growth (and higher tax revenue growth). On the other hand, politicians must evaluate their taxing and spending decisions in terms of elections two, four, or at most, six years away. These political leaders, who seek the funds to provide benefits to voting constituencies, may take advantage of people's inability to shift out of taxable income in the short run. Consequently, any increase in tax rate will in the short run lead to higher tax revenue. Again, tax revenues may fall because in the short run people do not have a chance to change their behavior—to reduce their capital stock or alter their skills and production capabilities. So, the higher tax rate times the slightly lower income level can still retain tax revenues higher than before the rate increase.

In the long run, however, the higher tax rate can translate into a contraction of the nation's capital stock and income, lowering the government's revenue below the maximum that could be achieved. That is to say, in the absence of constitutional fiscal constraints, the short-run proclivities of politicians may produce a perverse long-run result—lower tax revenues and expenditures than could have been achieved if tax rates had been kept at lower levels all along.

These points can be made with the aid of an actual Laffer curve drawn in Figure 19–1. Pressed by interest groups and the election cycle, politicians must be concerned with revenues in the short run, and they must therefore worry about their short-run Laffer curve. The short-run Laffer curve is represented in Figure 19–1 by the dashed line. That curve illustrates the basic proposition in the above discussion: Over some range of tax rates, from zero to R_2 in the figure, the government can raise its tax rates and collect more revenue. However, beyond R_2, further increases are counterproductive; revenues go down. This is so because at the high rates taxpayers have an incentive to learn how to escape their tax burden through tax avoidance and by taking their pleasures (income) in nontaxable forms (e.g., leisure).

In terms of Figure 19–1, Buchanan and Lee argue that short-run pressures can push members of Congress to the peak, identified by point A, of the short-run Laffer curve (again, the dashed curve that, given the politicians' time horizons, represents the only viable set of tax rate–tax revenue

FIGURE 19–1   Laffer Curve

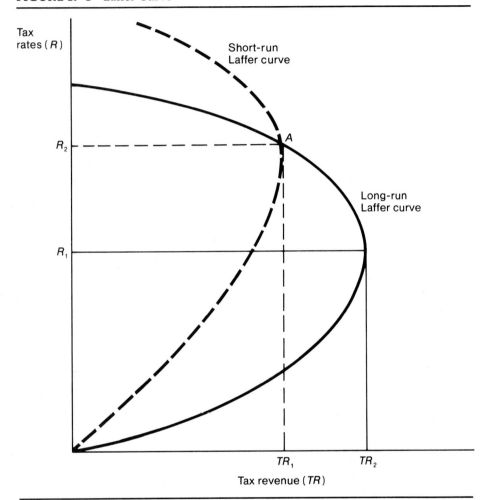

combinations open to them). However, that peak can be on the upper portion of the long-run Laffer curve, meaning that a rate cut could bring a revenue increase after a period of years or decades.

Once at point *A*, politicians are caught in a political bind. They can imagine that a tax rate reduction can increase government revenues—*but the increase will occur in the long-run* (after people have a chance to invest more in the nation's capital stock and thus increase national income). The politicians also see that a tax rate reduction will cut into current revenues, contract social programs, and increase the current budget deficits. The current politicians voting for such cuts will suffer the political consequences.[9] Any benefits from real reductions in current tax rates will be reaped by future politicians who will see government revenues rise with greater national income. What may be needed is an explicit constitutional rule that forbids tax rates from rising above R_1.

The need for constitutional rules for government may be better appreciated by placing them on an equal footing with our need for personal rules of behavior. In selecting rules that restrain our personal behavior, we fully acknowledge that such self-imposed restrictions will at times work against our private welfare, as it is perceived at any given moment. For example, we may adopt a rule against stealing, fully realizing that there will be instances in which stealing will be quite profitable (and the risk of being caught will be virtually nil). However, we adopt the rule of behavior because it makes sense in the long run over the course of a whole sequence of events, a few of which will be against our interests but most of which will further our interests. We adopt the rule because of what it does to our welfare *on balance.*

For similar reasons, in devising a social structure constitutional economists argue that countries must seek guiding principles. Without such transcending principles, we can become confused by a bewildering array of public policies that have no unifying theme—that are offered for legislative consideration by every conceivable interest group that believes its causes deserve special attention from government.

Constitutional provisions have long been recognized as necessary restraints on political myopia. They are also necessary constraints on the abuse of competitive politics. In 1981 Congress, at the urging of President Reagan, passed a comprehensive tax package that extended over a period of years. The package contained successive annual tax rate reductions for 1981 through 1984, after which tax rates would be indexed to inflation. This tax package implicitly recognized the long-term nature of investment decisions. Entrepreneurs invest today with an eye on after-tax returns for many years to come. Any hope the Reagan tax rate-reduction package had to revive the economy was as much dependent on future rate reductions as they were dependent on rate reductions in the year of the investment.

However, any expectation that the Reagan tax-cut package would stimulate the economy may have been nullified in part as one tax increase after another has been enacted and as one politician after another has threatened to repeal the future indexation of taxes. Constitutional economists worry that the threat of tax increases discourages investment currently because the in-

---

[9]Members of Congress who voted for the Reagan 1981 tax-cut package have, indeed, been chided for fiscal irresponsibility and insensitivity to the needs of the poor—because it lowered tax revenues from what they would otherwise have been and substantially increased budget deficits.

come from the investment will necessarily be earned in the future, and the future may hold higher tax rates. Constitutional (fiscal) constraints can offer a form of income security and can, therefore, produce income growth.

THE LIMITS OF POLITICS

Many constitutional economists hold to the view that the federal government cannot *fine-tune* the economy into a blissful state of low unemployment and low inflation rates. Unfortunately, they argue, government has tried in the past, and its efforts have run amok, making the problems of inflation, unemployment, and low productivity growth worse, not better. Economists have grossly oversold their talents, or so it is argued. Economists who have studied constitutional issues are concerned that economists in general simply do not know enough about the macroeconomy to engage in fine-tuning. Even if economists understood what they should do, there is considerable reason to question whether the political system, left to make frequent short-run policy decisions, would not pervert their efforts.[10]

In addition, there is the ever-present temptation to overtax the capacities of government to solve problems today even at the expense of greater problems in the future. This is because the current generation of voters have the controlling interest in the political process. They have the votes. Future generations do not have votes because many of them do not now exist. We should expect the current generation of voters to seek to distribute income from future generations of nonvoters, just as we expect current interest groups with disproportionate political power to use that power to redistribute income from other less politically powerful current groups.

CONSTITUTIONAL CONSTRAINTS
AS SELF-PROTECTION

Constitutional constraints on government may be seen as devices for protecting people from themselves. In an open-ended democracy, in which the government's powers are virtually unrestricted, businesses especially may be led by something approximating an "invisible hand" (also called an "invisible foot") to subvert market forces through the use of unchecked governmental powers.[11] This is because unchecked government powers can be seen by business as important exploitable resources in the pursuit of profits. As opposed to trying to outproduce and underprice their competitors, businesses may simply try to have government restrict the number and aggressiveness of their competitors.

---

[10]See Edward R. Tufte, *Political Control of the Economy* (Princeton, N.J.: Princeton University Press, 1978) for a convincing analysis of how the political system is used to further the short-run goals of the politicians.

[11]This theme is developed in McKenzie, *Bound to Be Free*, especially chap. 5.

Constitutional economists see much past and current government regulation in international trade, transportation, banking, agriculture, and a host of other markets as covert methods by which business lobbyists have reduced competition and increased the profits of the firms in their respective industries but have, at the same time, reduced economic growth.[12] Many budgetary expenditures are viewed in a similar light, as the visible ends of quid pro quos between politicians (who need campaign contributions and personal income) and business people (who seek government subsidies, bailouts, and contracts).[13]

Without constitutional constraints on government, *free enterprise,* as that term is commonly understood, contains the seeds of its own potential destruction. If business people do not seek government handouts, they run the risk of being replaced by someone who will attempt to turn a profit through the search for government subsidies or government protection from market forces. Business people must be able to tell their boards of directors that any investment they make in seeking government favors will be fruitless and a poor investment for the company; constitutional constraints on what government can do give business people that out.

Similarly, when pressured by firms and industries in search of a subsidy or some other favor, the president and the Congress need to be able to say their hands are constitutionally tied. Constitutional constraints are a potential means of tying their hands and thereby ensuring that resources are not diverted into unproductive lobbying efforts.

During the recessions of the early 1980s, lobbyists from a large number of industries that were pressed by the adverse economic conditions pressured the president to give them various kinds of bailouts. The savings and loan institutions wanted relief from the mortgages they held with very low interest rates; the housing industry went in search of interest subsidies on home mortgages; the automobile industry wanted tighter restrictions on imported automobiles. The president had to waste his time listening to the industries' predictions of gloom and doom because, unfortunately, he could have given them much of what they wanted—the power to bail out was present, and the industry leaders knew it.

Even in good times, the drive to make money through the manipulation of government persists. In the late 1980s, after more than five years of recovery, a host of industries continued to ask for protection from foreign imports.

---

[12]See George J. Stigler, *The Citizen and the State* (Chicago: University of Chicago Press, 1975); and Mancur Olson, *The Rise and Decline of Nations: Economic Growth, Stagflation, & Social Rigidities* (New Haven, Conn.: Yale University Press, 1982).

[13]Robert E. McCormick and Robert D. Tollison, *Politicians, Legislation, and the Economy* (Boston: Martinus Nijhoff Publishing, 1981); Thomas E. Borcherding, ed., *Budgets and Bureaucrats: The Sources of Governmental Growth* (Durham, N.C.: Duke University Press, 1977); and James M. Buchanan, Robert D. Tollison, and Gordon Tullock, eds., *Toward a Theory of the Rent-Seeking Society* (College Station, Tex: Texas A&M University Press, 1980).

By then, the employment, production, and profits of the textile industry were decidedly on the rebound from recession of years earlier. However, industry leaders continued to push for more protection. They reasoned that they could make even more profits if textile and apparel imports were further restricted.

THE FATE OF THE POOR

To constitutional economists, it is not at all clear that an open-ended welfare state can, on balance and in the long run, be expected to benefit the poor of the present and the future—those who are most politically and economically deprived.[14] Certainly, the poor have been the focus of many welfare programs, but by all estimates the total federal expenditures trickling down to those below the poverty line must account for a trivial portion of the total federal welfare budget.[15] The poor, on the other hand, pay their share of all government costs by way of social security taxes, sales taxes, excise taxes, corporate income taxes (passed on to consumers in the form of higher prices), property taxes (extracted by way of landlords in rental payments), and higher prices brought on by a plethora of government programs designed explicitly to transfer income from everyone else to some particular middle- or high-income group. Further, many of the poor have become wards of the state through generations of dependency on a welfare state that measures success more by dollars spent than by relief of poverty.[16]

Constitutional economists, as a group, are not necessarily any more cold-hearted than others who openly express concern for the poor and seek poverty relief. Indeed, they may fully acknowledge that an unfettered market economy may leave a significant number of people destitute. However, poverty relief does not flow automatically from wishful thinking, or even from legislative action.

Constitutional economics is a systems approach to the study of such social issues as poverty relief. As such, it recognizes that the poor are poor because they lack the necessary skills to earn a decent income in competitive markets.

Unfortunately, politics is also a competitive process that pays out rewards—rewards that are in part based on the skills of the participants in the political process. When the political process is open ended, that is, can concede to all claims for relief, regardless of the income status (or deservedness) of the claimants, it is certainly unclear that the poor should be expected, on balance and over the long run, to gain at the expense of the rich.[17]

[14]Morgan Reynolds and Eugene Smolensky, *Public Expenditures, Taxes, and the Distribution of Income* (New York: Academic Press, 1977).

[15]See Morton Paglin, *Poverty and In-Kind Transfers* (Stanford, Cal.: Hoover Institutional Press, 1980).

[16]George Gilder, *Wealth and Poverty* (New York: Basic Books, 1980).

[17]For the details on this line of argument, see Richard B. McKenzie, *The Fairness of Markets: A Search for Justice in a Free Society* (Lexington, Mass.: Lexington Books, 1987), chap. 9.

The poor's relative skills in manipulating the political process may be no greater—and may be lower—than their skills in manipulating the market process. We must wonder whether rich people who are unwilling to help the poor in the market process would be willing to concede their favored position in the political process. At least this line of argument suggests that some thought should be given to how the transfer authority of government can be restricted—so that the poor, on balance, will benefit from the welfare state.

The poor and their supporters (as well as any other identifiable interest group) might prefer a political system in which they alone benefit by transfer activity. The question is, however, whether the political system can be opened just enough so that the needs of the poor can be met by government without, at the same time, being exploited by every other group to the detriment of the poor. Some thought has been given to how the welfare state can exist within constitutional bounds.[18] An important proposal—that the welfare budget be constitutionally contained in terms of its size relative to national income—has been made in the hope of reducing the extent to which all political groups, rich as well as poor, exploit the political system for welfare transfers.[19]

REVISIONS IN PUBLIC FINANCE

The constitutional perspective has begun to raise questions even about the validity of widely held conclusions drawn from standard theory in public finance. For example, conventional public finance wisdom holds that if the distorting effects of excise taxes are to be minimized, then the federal government should be allowed to impose excise taxes on products with *inelastic* demands (that is, consumers do not respond very much to any price increase caused by the excise tax). Because consumer purchases do not fall very much with any given excise tax, any given tax revenue can be collected with a minimum of change in consumer purchases. (In technical terms, the deadweight welfare loss from the excise tax is minimized.)

However, this conventional line of argument is founded on the tenuous assumption that government intends only to collect a *given* amount of revenue, and will not use its market power to collect as much in taxes as possible.[20] If the analysis starts with the assumption that government is a potential Leviathan in its appetite for revenue, then giving it the power to tax *only* products with inelastic demands is license for the government to extort considerable income from consumers. Constitutional economists suggest that government should be restricted to taxing the exact opposite, products with *elastic* demands.

In a similar manner, many supporters of the flat-tax movement have argued that tax rates should be lowered (to encourage more work, saving, and

---

[18]See Hayek, *Law. Legislation, and Liberty,* vol. 3.

[19]Ibid.

[20]This line of argument is developed in Buchanan and Brennan, *The Power to Tax.*

investment) and the taxable income base broadened by eliminating exemptions and deductions in such a way that the government is able to collect the same amount of tax revenue. They argue that national income will rise and tax rates overall can be reduced. Constitutional economists, on the other hand, reason that any broadening of the tax base is tantamount to granting more monopoly power to government. This is the case because people would then be less able to escape income taxation. As a consequence, government can more readily raise its tax rates without fear of a reduction in the tax base and tax revenue. Constitutional economists predict that the flat tax movement will lead to higher tax rates over time.[21]

Drawing on conventional microeconomic theory, many economists have argued that the deregulation of many industries will lead to reduced monopoly power, lower prices, and greater production in the previously regulated industries. They reason that deregulation will mean less waste of resources—greater economic efficiency. However, they implicitly assume that once deregulated, the industries will remain deregulated. However, without constitutional constraints on the government regulatory (and reregulatory) authority, the deregulation may itself be a short episode between periods of regulation. The deregulation may cause significant adjustments in the economy, which may involve the waste of resources.[22]

For example, the trucking industry was deregulated starting in the late 1970s. Many firms went out of business, many terminals were closed, and many truckers lost their jobs. Those adjustments may have been deemed acceptable on the grounds that the costs would be more than covered with efficiency improvements over a period of years. However, if the trucking industry is soon reregulated, the deregulation movement may, in retrospect, be construed as a net welfare loss.

For similar reasons, an antiinflationary policy may be totally counterproductive in a world in which the monetary powers of government are not held in check.[23] Disinflation can be destructive, as was true of the period of disinflation in the early 1980s. After the Federal Reserve drastically reduced the rate of growth in the money stock to curb the inflation rate, beginning in the late 1970s, the economy went into a recession in 1980. Tens of thousands of factories closed down; millions of workers were unemployed. The idled resources were justified on the grounds that disinflation was an important national objective that would be paid for with the benefits of future price stability. However, without constitutional (monetary) restrictions on government, price stability may be short lived—not really worth the economic loss experienced during the recession.

---

[21]Ibid.
[22]Lee and McKenzie, *Regulating Government*, chap. 6.
[23]Ibid.

CONSTITUTIONAL SOLUTIONS

Conventional solutions to observed social problems often would have the government take action. Solutions for the failures of government to behave properly are sought in better theories of how the private sector works, in improved predictions of how people will respond to government actions, and in the election or appointment to government offices of better-informed and better-motivated people. While these efforts are worthy of much attention, constitutional economists seek solutions in other quarters—long-term rules for government action. Four approaches to containing the economic powers of government have emerged from constitutional economics and have received widespread attention:

1. Require the federal government to balance its budget.[24]
2. Limit the growth in federal expenditures by tying its tax collections to growth in national income.[25]
3. Deny the federal government the power of inflation taxation by holding the growth in the money stock to a rule, say 3 percent to 5 percent a year.[26]
4. Return as much fiscal power as possible to states and communities.[27]

This short list is not all-inclusive by any means. The discipline incorporates tentative theories on the relative revenue capacity of various tax rules, such as progressive and regressive income tax rate structures. Not everyone writing in constitutional economics is in agreement. The important component of the promotion of any paradigm is the honest search for workable

---

[24]One section of a proposed balanced-budget, tax-limitation amendment reads:

Prior to each fiscal year, the Congress shall adopt a statement of receipts and outlays for that year in which total outlays are no greater than total receipts. The Congress may amend such a statement provided revised outlays are no greater than revised receipts. Whenever three-fifths of the whole of the number of both Houses shall deem it necessary, Congress in such statement may provide for a specific excess of outlays over receipts by a vote directed solely to that subject. The Congress and the President shall ensure that actual outlays do not exceed the outlays set forth in such statement. U.S. Congress, Senate, Committee on the Judiciary, 97th Cong., 1st Sess., "Report: Balanced-Budget, Tax Limitation Constitutional Amendment," (No. 97-101; July 10, 1981), pp. 1 2.

[25]Another section of the proposed amendment reads:

Total receipts for any fiscal year set forth in the statement adopted pursuant to this article shall not increase by a rate greater than the rate of increase in national income in the last calendar year ending before such fiscal year, unless a majority of the whole of the number of both Houses of Congress shall have passed a bill directed solely to approving specific additional receipts and such bill has become law. Ibid.

[26]For additional constitutional remedies, see Friedman and Friedman, *Free to Choose*, chap. 10; Buchanan and Brennan, *The Power to Tax*.

[27]See Claude E. Barfield, *Rethinking Federalism: Block Grants and Federal, State, and Local Responsibilities* (Washington, D.C.: American Enterprise Institute, 1981).

solutions to perceived problems. The need for government and for some fiscal discretion for any established government is fully acknowledged. With these four proposed amendments, the federal government would retain a great deal of discretion. It could still decide how best to spend a huge sum of money, and it could still grow, provided the private sector grows. Indeed, the search of constitutional economists is partially taken up with ensuring that federal officials have proper incentives to work with the interest of the private sector in mind—with guaranteeing, to the extent possible, that government will no longer be able to impose its additional costs on the private sector by overt tax increases or covert *bracket creep* (through inflation), without first getting the consent of a significant majority (more than 50 percent) of both houses of Congress.

Accordingly, proposals have been made to relate inversely pay of members of Congress to actual deficits that are incurred: That is to say, the greater the actual budget deficits the lower the pay of congressmen the following year, an example of restricting incentives.[28] Similarly, proposals have been offered to tie the pay of the Board of Governors of the Federal Reserve System to the inflation rate: The greater the inflation rate, the lower the pay of board members.[29]

Constitutional amendments alone cannot be looked upon as a social panacea. Problems abound.[30] For example, proposed tax-limitation amendments are necessarily founded on some national accounting concept such as gross national product or national income used to advantage. Proposed balanced-budget amendments, for example, generally require the government to balance its budget on a planning basis, meaning unrealistic estimates of planned revenues and outlays can camouflage actual budget deficits.

Constitutional economists are not so naive as to believe that amendments inscribed on paper will supplant the need for an intellectual appreciation of a commitment to bounded government. Certainly, as John Maynard Keynes stressed, people in authority are ruled by little else than ideas,[31] and constitutional economists are foremost academics and scholars interested not so much in the day-to-day politics of balanced-budget and tax-limitation amendments as they are in the give-and-take in the competitive market of ideas.

Constitutional economists seek to understand, by way of abstract theory, what people in general would agree on if they were reasonably well informed

[28]Lee and McKenzie, *Regulating Government,* chap. 8.

[29]Morgan Reynolds, "Incentives versus Bad Money: Let's Try Indexing Salaries at the Board of Governors," *Pathfinder,* July/August 1981, p. 4.

[30]For a review of a number of the arguments for, and problems inherent in, constraints on the fiscal capacities of the federal government, see W. S. Moore and Rudolph G. Penner, eds., *The Constitution and the Budget: Are Constitutional Limits on Tax, Spending, and Budget Powers Desirable at the Federal Level?* (Washington, D.C.: American Enterprise Institute for Public Policy Research, 1980).

[31]John Maynard Keynes, *The General Theory of Employment, Interest, and Money* (New York: Harcourt, Brace, and World, 1936), p. 383.

on the alternatives. They seek to reverse the intellectual revolution they believe was brought about by Keynesian economics, which tended to focus public policy exclusively on the short run because, as Keynes is believed to have observed, "in the long run we will all be dead." To many constitutional economists, such an admonition reflects not only a degree of moral bankruptcy but also intellectual absurdity.

CONCLUDING COMMENTS

In the view of constitutional economists, government may very well have grown beyond the consent of the governed because democracy, left unconstrained, is an imperfect control system subjected to the influence of revolving special interest. The Founding Fathers recognized the need for auxiliary (constitutional) precautions. Constitutional economics seeks to offer advice on the economic consequences of proposed precautions. Coming up with advice is actually more difficult than it might first appear. Nevertheless, that does not mean economists cannot productively apply their methods in the full knowledge that constraints on government as an institutional framework are no less necessary than constraints on markets as an institutional framework.

QUESTIONS TO PONDER

1. Name provisions in the U.S. Constitution that affect economic activity.
2. Is there any reason for believing that the poor would be any better positioned in the political process than in the market process to improve their economic status.
3. Why are most political decisions made with a simple-majority vote? List the types of decisions that are not made by simple-majority vote. Why do these decisions require a super majority?
4. Are procedural rules dictating how the political process must work all that is necessary to control government? Why? or Why not?
5. Suppose the electorate is thinking of controlling the fiscal powers of government in one of two ways: (1) by holding tax revenues to a fixed percentage of national income or (2) by holding government expenditures to the same fixed percentage of national income. Which fiscal constraint would be most effective in controlling the growth of government (assuming that were the objective)?
6. If the government proposes to lower tax rates and expand the tax base (amount of taxable income) by eliminating exemptions in such a way that short-run tax revenues would be held constant, what would you expect to happen to the growth in future tax collections?

PART SIX

The New World
of Higher Education

CHAPTER 20

The University Economy

Typically, universities catch hell from their students. Students frequently complain about the quality of food; they deplore meaningless general education requirements and criticize professors who are more concerned with their research and professional standing outside the classroom than they are with the quality of their classrooms, and some tire easily of humbling themselves before the lords of the university, the administrators.

Students beef about poor or remote parking facilities or about regulations that prohibit cars on campus altogether. In years gone by, they have grumbled about and demonstrated against petty rules—such as dress codes, curfew hours, and sign-outs—that restricted their social conduct. More recently, the hot issue on some campuses has been whether or not coed suites within dormitories should be allowed—or even whether men and women students should be permitted to bunk together in the same dorm rooms.

On the other side of the desk, professors are not without their complaints. They bemoan what they sense has been a deterioration of academic standards. They are very concerned with what has come to be known as *grade inflation*, or the gradual increase in grades given to students. Now, more than ever, there is concern over pay raises not keeping up with the cost of living. As one professor recently complained at a faculty meeting, "I wish the administration would stop talking about 'annual raises'; I haven't had a real raise in years."

In this chapter we are not concerned with the legitimacy of student and faculty complaints. Nor will we spend much time evaluating the tactics employed by students or faculty to get what they want. We prefer to consider the more interesting question of why the university can operate the way it does. At the start, we readily admit that part of the basis for much student and faculty discontent may simply be an unbridled attempt on their part to get more and more for little or nothing. However, we think a fuller understanding of modern university operations requires some reflection on the institutional setting of the education process.

UNIVERSITY PRICING

The modern public university has one notable feature: It typically receives part of its funding from state appropriations and/or grants, endowments, and charitable contributions. The rest, generally less than 50 percent, comes from students (or their parents) in the form of tuition and fee payments.

At most of the better colleges and universities, there has traditionally been a shortage of openings for students; that is, more students have wanted to get in than could be admitted. The reason for past shortages, as we will show, can be traced to the way in which education has been financed. Many of the problems students have confronted in their college careers can also be laid at the feet of the state and federal government subsidies given to education. That may be a mouthful, but we intend to explain in detail. First, we need to lay out the framework for the analysis, which means the market for education.

In Figure 20–1, we have scaled the number of university openings (that is, the number of students that can be admitted) along the horizontal axis and the price (which amounts to the marginal value of education) along the vertical axis. The student demand for education, labeled D_1 is viewed as the horizontal summation of all students' individual demand curves. It is the market demand for education, and it is a function of anything that gives value to being an educated person, such as the inherent satisfaction from learning, the additional lifetime income the educated person can receive, and any change in social status that may be experienced by students and attributable to education. In the discussion, the demand is assumed to have its normal negative slope. (Is that a reasonable assumption?) This means that more people will want to enter college if the price falls.

The supply of education (how many openings will be offered at each price) is a function primarily of the number of faculty members and/or classroom seats available and of the teaching technology being employed; that is, the greater the number of faculty members employed and/or the greater the number of classrooms and seats, the greater the supply of university openings students can fill. Also, if television or large lecture rooms are used, then more students may be accommodated.

To give some realism to the model, the supply of education, S_1 in Figure 20–1, is assumed to be upward sloping but highly inelastic with respect to tuition and fee payments from students. We make this assumption recognizing that the number of students universities can admit is determined in large measure by decisions of state legislatures or, in the case of private institutions, charitable organizations. They are the ones who make appropriations for dormitories and classroom buildings. However, it seems reasonable to assume that schools can and do respond to a limited degree to changes in the price they can charge their students. Hence, the upward sloping curve.

If education were provided on a free-market basis, the market clearing price would be the price at which the supply and demand for education intersect in the graph. On the other hand, assuming that the legislature both subsidizes the students' education and limits the physical size of the university, the price charged students in the form of tuition and fees will be below

FIGURE 20–1

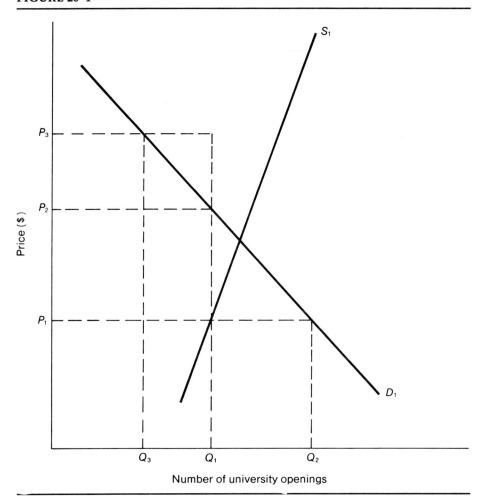

Number of university openings

the market clearing price—for example P_1. (For simplicity, we assume all universities charge the same price.) Note that at P_1, the number of student openings in universities will be Q_1; however, the number of students wanting to enter will be much greater, Q_2. In other words, given the supply and demand and price of education in this illustration, there is a shortage of openings for college students (Q_2-Q_1), and this, we believe, fairly accurately describes the situation of most reasonably good universities and colleges for the 1960s and 1980s, but not for the early years of the 1970s. (If this were not true, one must wonder how else we could have experienced a shortage.)

The existence of the shortage goes a long way toward explaining the behavior of universities. Because of the shortage, the available openings must be distributed among those who want to be admitted in some extra-market manner. Since there are more students knocking at the doors than can be admitted and since the students are not paying the full cost of their education, there is certainly little incentive for the university (when a shortage exists) to pay much attention to the wishes of the students. It is also clear why the criteria for admission has traditionally been on the basis of who the most intelligent students are and who are the best or most efficient learners. Not only do such standards permit the faculty to fashion students after their own idea of what an educated person should be, it may make life in general a little easier for the instructors. It is often much easier to teach an intelligent person than one who may not be so well endowed mentally. By saying it is easier to teach better students, we mean that professors can not only increase the better students' achievement levels but can also divert more of their time to nonteaching duties, for example, research and consulting.

Those students who want to go to college but who cannot get in represent a threat to those students who are admitted. If the admitted students do not conform to the requirements (standards) of the university or faculty, they can be replaced by those who would otherwise be a part of the shortage. Therefore, as opposed to accepting a total payment of P_1 from each student, the demands of the optimizing university can be raised. The effective price, meaning the money price plus the nonmonetary payments the university will charge, can in fact be raised to P_2 in our illustration. P_1 is paid by the students in the form of tuition and fees, and the rest, P_2-P_1, can be extracted from the students in any number of forms.

The university can impose general education requirements the student may not appreciate and can impose social regulations that are not liked. The university can also neglect the quality of the accommodations, such as food and dormitory facilities, and it can require students who want to drive cars on campus to park in a remote area. The professor can require more work than students will freely choose and can require that they learn material that is of little interest to the student but of considerable interest to the professor. If students do not like the way they are treated in or outside the classroom, they can be replaced or, less severely, penalized with low grades.

Notice that P_2 is the highest price that can be charged. If the university attempted to extract a higher money and nonmonetary price than P_2, for example, P_3, the number of students wanting to go to college would fall to Q_3. Given that Q_1 openings will be available, a surplus of openings (Q_1-Q_3) will exist; universities can anticipate a cutback in funds from students and state appropriations; and professors will be threatened with a possible loss of jobs and income.

In such a situation, what can we expect to happen? Being economists and university professors and recognizing that competition does exist among faculty members and universities, we would anticipate that the demands placed on students would fall back to P_2. This means that something would have to give, such as the extensiveness of general education requirements, the toughness of courses, the attitude of university personnel, the quality of food, and so on.[1] From this analysis, we may conclude that what professors and universities view as their standards may be primarily an expression of their market position and their ability to extract a nonmonetary price from students. It also follows that their ability to lay claim to standards and induce compliance from students is dependent in part on public subsidies; this is revealed in the gap between P_1 and P_2, and their ability must rise and fall with the difference. For example, suppose that the university raised the tuition and fee payment to something above P_1 and there is no offsetting increase in demand. The result would be, barring a change in supply and demand conditions, a reduction in the shortage and, more important for our present purposes, a reduction in the gap between P_2 and the price charged for tuition and fees. Here again, if something did not give, the number of students wanting to enter college would drop, and we would have the surplus problems discussed above. The anticipated results would be, as above, that the optimizing university would have to concede some of its demands in other areas of university life. Having to make such concessions is one possible constraint on universities' abilities to raise their tuition and fees.

If the university does not concede in areas such as rules governing social conduct and parking, then a reduction in demands may have to be realized in the area of expected academic performance. The reader may think professors have their standards and will maintain them at all costs, and we agree that there are professors who are like that. However, visualize for the moment a professor who may have a family to support and very few employment opportunities outside the university. Consider also that this professor may not have tenure. If there exists a surplus of university openings, such as Q_1–Q_3, then there will be unfilled seats in someone's classroom, portending a possible cutback in the number of faculty members needed. If the university cuts back on faculty, who would you guess would go first? Given the attention administrators pay to student-credit-hours generated by faculty and departments, it is quite likely that if a cut is made, it will be where the number of students in class is low.

Recognizing this prospect and remembering that faculty members are not all irrational when it comes to their own welfare, the individual faculty member can attract more students to his or her classes in two basic ways. He or she can attempt to change the nature of the course, improve its inherent value to the students, and increase the demand for the course. This option has the disadvantage of requiring more work on the part of the professor. The other basic way he or she can attract more students is by cutting back on

---

[1] An aloof attitude on the part of professors and administrators is one means of reducing the utility of education to students, and, to that extent, it is one means of extracting a nonmonetary price from students.

demands on students. In other words, the price to students of taking these courses can be reduced by lowering requirements or raising the grades students can expect to receive for any given level of achievement.

If one professor, by such methods, attracts more students, then other professors, who may not have originally been caught with an enrollment problem, may now be saddled with unfilled seats and the threat of losing their jobs. The result can be a competitive devaluation of academic standards and inflation of grades. This is not necessarily bad for the students, for remember that we originally said that professors may have been imposing on the students what they thought was important, and they may now be catering more to student desires. At the same time, we must recognize the possibility that the public (and parents) may have been subsidizing college education in order that the professors' will (which is thought to be more in the long-run interest of students and society) could be imposed. Because tuition and fee payments can influence the ability of professors to extract work from students, it is understandable why they may side with students in opposing higher tuition payments and in promoting government subsidization of education.

We can complicate the analysis a little by considering the effect of changes in demand and supply conditions. If the demand for college education increases while the supply remains constant, as described in Figure 20–2, the expected result is an increase in the shortage of openings from Q_2-Q_1 to Q_3-Q_1. Note also that the effective price universities can charge can go up from P_2 to P_3, meaning the universities can increase their tuition and fee payments or increase their demands in other areas of academic life or both. (Similar conclusions could be drawn if the supply increases but the demand increases by more than supply. Try showing this on a graph of your own.)

This situation of increasing demand (relative to supply) may have been reasonably descriptive of almost all universities in the late 1950s and much of the 1960s. (It is also descriptive of the market condition faced by many colleges and universities in the 1980s.) The value of a college education was definitely on the rise during that earlier period. In addition, incomes and the population of potential college students were increasing. In the 1950s and 1960s, the college diploma was generally considered a surefire ticket to the pie in the sky that all young people and parents dream about. All of these factors were increasing the demand for college education faster than openings could be made available.

In the late 1960s, however, the supply and demand conditions in the university education market began to change dramatically. The growth in the number of potential college students began to taper off, the college diploma became much more common and its prestige value began to drop, and surpluses of college graduates, especially in teaching fields and engineering, began to emerge—all of which led to a significant drop in the growth of

FIGURE 20–2

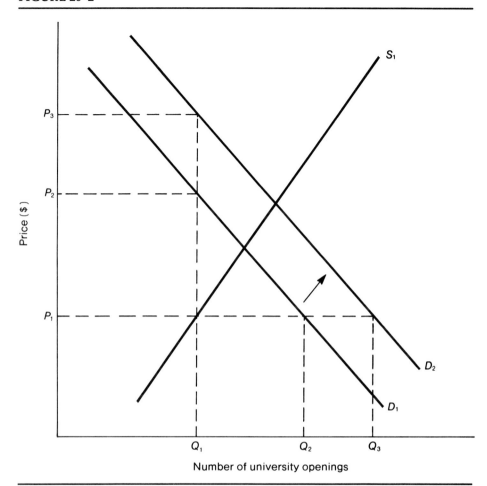

demand for college education and, in some states or areas, to an absolute drop in the demand.

On the supply side, state appropriations for classroom buildings and dormitories gained momentum; community colleges and technical schools began to proliferate. The result was that in many areas of the country the growth in the supply of student openings outstripped the growth in demand. Shortages of college and university openings at first fell and then later evaporated all together; surpluses of openings emerged on many campuses.

To illustrate the consequences of these changes, consider Figure 20–3. The initial supply and demand conditions are depicted by S_1 and D_1. We have increased the demand and supply curves to D_2 and S_2, but notice that the

FIGURE 20–3

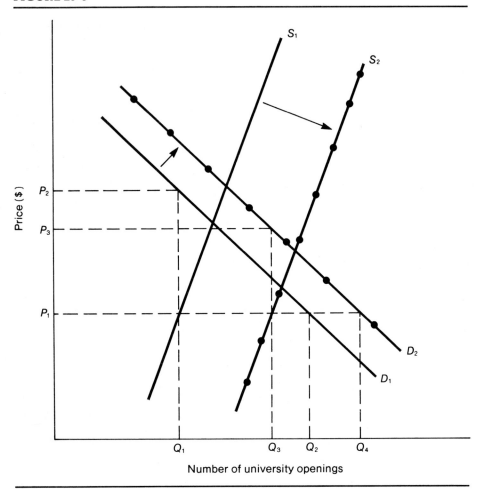

supply has been increased by more than demand (that is, supply has been moved further to the right). For purposes of simplicity only, we assume that tuition and fee charges remain constant.[2] The graph may appear on the surface to be a little confusing; but if you look at it carefully, you may see that the results of the changes are a reduction in the shortage from Q_2–Q_1 to Q_4–Q_3 and a reduction in the effective price universities can charge, from P_2 to P_3.

---

[2]We realize that tuition charges have gone up dramatically during the period with which we are concerned; however, such changes do not harm our conclusions. In fact, such changes, if introduced, would serve to reinforce our conclusions. Can you show why?

Given this latter reduction and the constant tuition price, the university or faculty must reduce their demands on students. We would predict that the changes that occurred in the educational market during the late 1960s would be reflected in one or more of the following areas: reduced social regulations, a relaxation of general education requirements and other restrictions on students' college programs, a change in the attitudes of administrators and professors toward students, and perhaps lower academic standards, however defined.

Interestingly enough, those of us who have been a part of university systems during the past two to three decades (which is true of both authors) have seen almost all of these changes come about. Especially in the late 1960s and early 1970s, colleges and universities began reducing their general education requirements, and some eliminated them altogether. Universities began turning more and more toward student evaluations of faculty and courses as a means of evaluating faculty performance and ensuring that faculty members pay more attention to the desires and feelings of students. Social rules, which used to be very stringent on the activity of women in particular have been abolished.[3] Students were given much more freedom in taking independent study courses and in designing their college programs to meet their own needs.

Grades began going up in the late 1960s and early 1970s—so much that on many campuses more than two thirds of all grades given were As and Bs. On many campuses, the dean's list became a joke to those who knew what had been happening. *Newsweek* magazine reported the following on grade inflation:

> In 1961, about half of the seniors at Harvard College graduated with honors; this month, when the class of '74 received their diplomas, degrees cum laude or better went to an astonishing 82 percent. The average University of Colorado student in 1964 maintained a grade-point average of 2.4 (out of a possible 4 points), but his counterpart today has a GPA of 2.82. Between 1962 and 1972, the University of North Carolina doubled the percentage of As it handed out. The average grade at the University of Wisconsin has soared

---

[3]As a side note, one of the authors has been associated with two schools that, when he was there, had very strict dress codes and sign-out requirements for women. For example, at one school women had to be in their dorms by 10:30 P.M. during the week and could not be gone from campus for more than four hours without signing out again. They also could not wear bermuda shorts on "front" campus. At another campus, women could not date men of another race without written permission from their parents. When students demonstrated against such rules in the early 1960s, the administration would respond by arguing that they were doing what they thought was right and in the best interest of the women students. At both schools, when enrollment problems began to appear, the rules were scrapped almost in toto. The justification given was that women in the middle and late 1960s were more mature and responsible than were their counterparts in earlier years. Such statements made good press releases, but few in the college communities took them very seriously.

from C-plus to B-plus in just nine years. And the dean's list at the University of Virginia included 53 percent of the student body last year—compared with 21 percent in 1965.[4]

In addition, one should realize that grades went up in the face of a downward drift in Student Achievement Test scores of entering freshmen. Employers, graduate schools, and organizations such as Phi Beta Kappa no longer looked upon high grades as clear evidence of superior ability. At one time, employers looked to colleges and universities that screened the bad students out and graduated the people who were markedly better than those who failed to make it through. In the 1970s, however, with rising grades and a growing uncertainty over what they meant, more and more employers were turning away from seeking college graduates and were turning toward training their own people. To the extent that these trends were evident, the value of the college degree deteriorated, reducing the demand for education further.

Before closing this section, we need to stress three points. First, we have discussed the problem of education in the context of an environment in which the shortage of openings has been reduced. In the late 1970s, many colleges and universities found that their demand was once again expanding more rapidly than their available openings for students. Indeed, the growth in the supply of openings was curtailed by many states partially because of deteriorating academic standards. The result was, once again, a tightening of academic standards in some places, especially in colleges of business where student demand became especially strong in the early and mid-1980s.

However, with a slowdown of growth in the number of college-age students in the late 1980s, and the possible reduction in college-age students in the 1990s, this recent trend may shortly be reversed and the shortage of openings again decrease. The problem of grade inflation and falling academic standards may once again return in the 1990s—unless, of course, controls are imposed on the supply of openings.

Second, we recognize that many of the changes that have occurred in education are in part the results of fundamental social changes in attitudes and preferences of people toward what education is and should be. We merely submit that the market has played a significant role in the development of educational policies and attitudes.

Third, the faculty of any given university could get together and could put restrictions on the grades any given faculty member could distribute to his students. However, such a move is likely to run headlong into the opposition of those who believe that such a policy would be a violation of academic freedom. In addition, if one university restricts its grades and others do not, the result can be a movement of students to other universities, jeopardizing jobs in the university that restricts faculty grades.

---

[4]"Grade Inflation," *Newsweek*, July 1, 1974, p. 49.

FACULTY SALARIES

Because of the tremendous growth in universities during the 1950s and 1960s, there was a corresponding increase in demand for faculty members. Salaries rose substantially and graduate schools geared up to satisfy the increasing demand for persons with doctorates. Because education appeared at the time to be a sound investment, many persons eagerly sought advanced degrees. The usefulness of the graduate programs that sprung up, however, was predicated on a strong growth in university systems; and when this growth began to level off, graduates continued to be pumped out. The eventual consequence of a system in which salaries could not be readily adjusted downward was a surplus of prospective faculty members. In the 1970s, many Ph.D.s, in the humanities especially, went begging for jobs and ended up selling hot dogs and driving trucks.

Although money wages of existing faculty members could not be easily reduced, salaries of beginning faculty members began to stabilize in the 1970s and, in some areas, to fall. In a situation in which more faculty members abound than can be hired, one might anticipate state legislatures and university administrations taking every opportunity to reduce the real income (that is, the purchasing power of money income) of the faculty members. As a result, pay raises in most states did not in the 1970s keep pace with inflation. (If legislatures had not permitted this to happen, they would have had a difficult time, perhaps, explaining the rather high salaries of faculty members to their constituencies.)

One might also expect universities to reduce the income of faculty members by putting greater demands on them. And so we had in the 1970s a growing trend toward eight-to-five days for faculty, whereas in the past they have been relatively free to come and go as they pleased. Administrations began imposing standardized evaluation on faculty and raising their demands in the areas of research, publications, and community and regional service. In the 1960s, tenure was offered to prospective faculty as a fringe benefit; in the 1970s, however, the probationary period before one can receive tenure was being lengthened. Faculty began slowly but gradually to lose the benefits of free parking and football tickets. All of these changes and cutbacks in graduate programs were working to reduce the surplus of Ph.D.s on the market. Of course, as expected, when in the 1980s the supply of faculty began to fall in many academic areas and when the demand for education began to rise once again, many (but not all) faculty began to recoup some of their income losses.

In the foregoing analysis, we have been discussing about the broad market for faculty. When the market is segmented by discipline, these generalizations do not always hold. They do appear to hold very well for professors in the humanities and education but not so well for professors of accounting and finance. Herein lie potential pitfalls for university administrators who may attempt to make sweeping rules for all faculty. If the administration dictates that all faculty raises are to be the same, the university may hold on to those faculty whose employment market is glutted, but they may lose, for example, their accountants whose market wage rate may have risen by more than the standardized salary increase. If the university does not pay the market wage to those accountants it has, it will then have to enter that same market they tried to ignore and hire other accountants at the going market wage, incurring in the process the cost of searching for replacements. If they refuse to incur those costs, their accounting program can suffer.

This is one aspect of market forces many administrators fail to appreciate. As an illustration, and as discussed above, some universities have put more reliance on student evaluations in determining salary increments. This may mean that the mean scores received by the different faculty members in different disciplines are ranked and raises are dispensed accordingly.

To reveal the inherent problems of such schemes, suppose that all of the accountants are basically "crummy" teachers in the eyes of their students but they are typical of others in the profession. (Believe it or not, some of our best friends are accountants!) In the college of business, let's suppose that they score relatively low among other faculty in the college; economists (being inherently superior in all aspects of university life!) score relatively high. The evaluation scheme of allocating raises on the basis of student evaluations would mean that the economists receive more than the accountants. However, suppose that the market for accountants is much tighter than the market for economists; the market wage of accountants would rise comparatively more. The market would dictate that the accountants receive a higher raise.

If the university or college employs student evaluations as a criterion for raises, what do you think would happen? You can rest assured that unless the accountants were bound to the school for nonmonetary reasons, the college of business would lose their accountants. The school would then have to enter the market to hire the accountants at the higher wage. The university could avoid all of the expense associated with faculty turnover by simply looking to market as a guide for adjusting salaries.

CONCLUDING COMMENTS

The reader should understand that the foregoing analysis does not necessarily reflect the way we think university students, administrators, and faculty should behave. As has been our goal throughout the book, we have only tried to explain why they have behaved the way they have and how they might be expected to behave, given changes in market conditions.

QUESTIONS TO PONDER

1. If the university increases its tuition and fees while the demand for and supply of educational openings remains constant, what will happen to educational standards, social regulations, and attitude of faculty and university officials?

2. Suppose that the demand for education switches from the humanities to business, everything else held constant. What will be the effects of the change on the academic standards in humanities and business?

3. Suppose that the salaries of college business graduates goes up relative to the salaries of other graduates, what will happen to academic standards in the colleges of business? Does your answer have anything to do with the supply response of universities?

4. Explain the following statement: "An increase in the state subsidy to higher education will directly and indirectly increase the welfare of faculty members."

5. Colleges and universities often set all fees and payments—room, board, and tuition—at a fixed level and then proceed to give many students (even a substantial majority) various amounts of scholarship assistance based on need (where need is often determined by the reported income levels of the students' parents). Why do they devise such a pricing system?

CHAPTER 21
Learning Economics

Psychologists and educators have been concerned with learning behavior for some time. We now know a good deal about the learning process, particularly among the lower-order animals; however, it is abundantly clear from experience that educators have a long way to go before much can be said about how students' learning within a classroom setting can be improved. The federal government and foundations such as the Ford and the Rockefeller have spent literally billions of dollars over the past several decades researching the learning and educational processes. Unfortunately, researchers have all too frequently concluded that there is no difference between their experimental and control groups—that nothing appears to work in the classroom.

For example, Robert Dubin and Thomas Taveggia found this to be so in their examination of 91 major studies of experiments that had evaluated different techniques, methods, and classroom conditions.[1] H. Kiesling concluded, "It is striking to note that such pay-parameter variables (as teacher experience and training) were seldom found to be related to pupil performance."[2] After a decade of actively funding projects to change education in the public schools, the Ford Foundation in the early 1970s concluded that very little that was done made much difference.

Where there has been a favorable difference between experimental and control groups, researchers have been very reluctant to suggest that their conclusions be generalized to other similar (but not identical) situations. Policymakers have readily questioned whether or not the small benefits achieved were worth the cost incurred.

The inability of educators and psychologists to demonstrate how learning in the classroom can be upgraded stems in part from the terribly complex nature of the classroom environment. In that environment, students are being constantly bombarded with thousands of bits of information (stimuli). And if one assumes that a change in the flow of any one type of information will actually have a material effect on student learning, he or she may rightfully be guilty of presumption.

---

[1]Robert Dubin and Thomas Taveggia, *The Teaching-Learning Paradox* (Eugene: University of Oregon, 1968).

[2]H. Kiesling, "Multivariate Analysis of Schools and Educational Policy" (Santa Monica, Cal.: The Rand Corporation, 1971). Darrell Lewis and Charles Orvis drew basically the same conclusions from their review of the literature in economic education, *Research in Economic Education: A Review, Bibliography, and Abstracts* (New York: Joint Council on Economic Education, 1971).

However, we feel that the failure of the educational establishment to explain the educational process may be more fundamental in origin—that is, it may be at least the result of the way the learning process is perceived by those who are doing the research. This can mean that the wrong questions have been asked and the evidence has been misinterpreted. We suggest that the economics of the learning process must be appreciated to interpret data gathered from the educational environment.

THE TRADITIONAL VIEW OF LEARNING

The dominant view of learning among educators and psychologists appears to be a very mechanistic one—and perhaps overly so. The subjects or students receive stimuli and respond accordingly. The task of the teacher is one of providing the right stimuli in order that the right response can be imprinted in the behavior of the students. In this way, the students learn by connecting stimulus and response.

From the perspective of traditional learning theories, it appears to us that the students do not have real choice in the sense that the theories allow them to choose in some rational manner from among viable options. This may be because students are not credited (from a theoretical point of view) with having a preference that is independent of the stimulus-response mechanism and that can operate on or alter that mechanism. They merely respond. Once the imprint—that is, the connection between stimulus and response—is made, students can be likened to a computer: The data can be typed in and a printout is received without any intervening creative thought process.

The main reason for this mechanistic approach to learning may be taken because the admission of active choices made on the parts of students and teachers can muddy the theoretical waters. One purpose of any social science, such as education or psychology, is to make predictions regarding human behavior and, more specifically for our purposes, the learning processes. If the choice is admitted to the discussion, then educators may fear that it is impossible to say anything about learning. That is to say, if choice is to be real choice, then it must be unpredictable. If choice is predictable, then one must wonder how it can be real choice. Seeing this conceptual roadblock, psychologists and educators may have tended to avoid the subject of choice altogether.

In these few pages, we want to show you how student and faculty choice can be introduced into the discussion of learning process.[3] The individual

---

[3]In this chapter we are at best able to outline certain broad themes in the economics of learning and conventional psychological theories. Robert Staaf deserves considerable credit here for originating and developing the economic approach to learning. For a more detailed and rigorous treatment of the economist's approach, the reader may want to see Richard B. McKenzie, *The Political Economy of the Educational Process* (Boston: Martinus Nijhoff Publishing, 1979).

student or instructor is not viewed as an academic robot, responding mechanistically to stimuli from the environment, past and present. We accord the individual a preference that is, to a degree, independent of environmental factors. The student or faculty member can therefore choose from a range of options or combinations of goods and services, which may include learning or education.

Our approach to learning is different from conventional views in one important respect. Educators, in an attempt to explain the learning process, are inclined to point to genetic and environmental conditions (such as sex, age, race, class size, and method of instruction) as causes of student learning behavior. Such factors are not unimportant. Nevertheless, in applying the economic approach to learning, we look to the choice calculus of the individuals as a primary explanatory factor and one that tends to be overlooked in more conventional studies. This is not to say that environmental and genetic conditions do not constrain the choice process. It is to say, however, that we may come upon unexpected insights into the educational process by taking a different tack.

THE RATIONAL STUDENT

We begin by assuming that students are rational in the conventional economic sense of the term. As discussed in Chapter 1, this means that students know what they want and attempt to maximize their satisfaction by consuming from a range of commodities that are available. Perhaps, the reader feels that an assumption of rationality is inappropriate in any discussion of education. A person can only make rational decisions among those alternatives that are known. By definition, what is to be learned is not known; and therefore, a person cannot make rational decisions regarding learning he or she knows little about.

The fact is that people make decisions that involve unknowns and uncertainties all the time. The decision to research involves what is yet to be found. People regularly buy cars and appliances (often used ones, at that) they know virtually nothing about. It is certainly questionable whether or not the public knows more about the costs and benefits of the cars they buy than they know about, say a course in economics before they enter the class.

Remember, students are not completely in the dark about the classes they sign up for; they do spend a significant amount of time attempting to acquire information about courses and professors they take. People make decisions on the basis of the information they have at hand and can rationally justify acquiring, and this goes for the decisions to learn.[4]

---

[4]A fruitful departure (but one that cannot be taken) would be to consider a question economists have pondered for years: When does a person stop acquiring information and make a decision? Remember that the acquisition of information itself can be a rational act. Aside from

At any rate, if you can accept our assumption, you may further recognize that rational students will fully allocate their resources—that is, time and material and monetary wealth—and will equate the ratios of the marginal utility of the goods they buy to their respective prices. (These points were covered in Chapter 1.) Including knowledge (k), which is the end product of the learning process as a good that can be consumed by the students, the marginal condition is:

$$MU_a/P_a = MU_k/P_k = \ldots = MU_n/P_n,$$

where MU denotes marginal utility, the subscript a can represent any good such as an apple, and subscript n can stand for any other good. P denotes price, which in the case of knowledge may mean the money and time expenditure required to obtain a unit of knowledge.

If the equality has not been attained and, for example, $MU_k/P_k > MU_a/P_a$, then the students have gotten more utility for the last \$1 (or resource) spent on knowledge than on apples. They can consequently increase their utility by shifting resources from apples to the acquisition of knowledge. In other words, if they are rational, we can expect them to choose to learn more and to continue to expand their knowledge until equality is attained among the ratios.

Here, knowledge has been treated as a composite good, whereas we know that it comes in many diverse forms. This means that the actual utility-maximizing condition is a little more complicated. Letting subscripts e, f, and h denote knowledge in the fields of economics, French, and history, the marginal condition becomes:

$$MU_a/P_a = MU_e/P_e = MU_f/P_f = MU_h/P_h = \ldots = MU_n/P_n.$$

If, instead, $MU_e/P_e > MU_f/P_f$, students can increase their utility by learning more economics and less French.

Another way of saying the same thing is that Paul Smith, a student, will purchase knowledge or any particular kind of knowledge up to the point that the marginal benefits equal the marginal costs. He will purchase only so much, and he will vary his consumption of any kind of knowledge, such as economics, not only with the price he himself pays (that is, the demand curve for economic literacy is downward sloping), but also with changes in the marginal utility and price of other goods.

For illustrative purposes, suppose that the marginal utility of apples (which, by the way, is totally outside of formal classroom setting) increases; this means that MU_a/P_a will become greater than MU_e/P_e. It would then be

this issue, one economist, Gary Becker, showed that even if people are irrational in at least one sense of the term, many of the deductions made from an assumption of rationality still hold. "Irrational Behavior and Economic Theory," *Journal of Political Economy* 70 (February 1962), pp. 1–13.

rational for Paul to consume more apples and less economic knowledge. If, on the other hand, P_e were to rise, it would be rational for Paul to spend less on economics and more on other goods, such as apples, or even more on other subjects. If he does not do this, assuming equality among the ratios before the price increase, MU_e/P_e will be less than the other ratios. (To test your understanding of what has been said, what would the student choose to do given the following changes: an increase in MU_e; a reduction in P_f; and an increase in P_a.)

A simple conclusion that deserves special note is that the amount of knowledge Paul acquires may not be the same the professor believes he should acquire; or in other terms, any disagreement between what Paul does in fact accomplish in class and what the professor expects him to accomplish may simply be due to a difference between what the professor perceives the benefits for him to be and what Paul perceives them to be.[5] Also, recognize that in our view of student behavior, Paul does not automatically respond to stimuli; rather, he is viewed as receiving information about relative costs and benefits about matters to be learned and about matters that are outside the educational environment, weighing this information in terms of his own preference, and then choosing an appropriate response. The extent of his response depends on what happens to the marginal utilities of the goods as more or less is consumed.

For example, going back to the situation in which $MU_e/P_e > MU_f/P_f$, we concluded that Paul would choose to learn more economics, but how much depends on the rate at which MU_e falls as more is consumed. If MU_e diminishes rapidly, he will learn less additional economics than if the MU diminished slowly. Keep in mind that he will increase his knowledge in economics until the ratios are equal. This leads to the point that a new classroom device or technique can, from a technical point of view, increase the ability of the student to learn economics. However, because of the cost involved and perceived benefits to the student, the student may choose to increase his understanding by less than what is technically possible.

To illustrate this last point with more precision, assume for simplicity that two subjects, French and economics, are open to Paul, that both subjects yield positive benefits, and that he has allocated a given amount of time to the study of these subjects.[6] In Figure 21–1, we have scaled his achievement in economics along the horizontal axis and achievement in French along the vertical axis.

---

[5]We also wish to point out that any disagreement could just as easily be due to the fact that the instructor and student do not evaluate the MUs of other goods as being the same. Can you explain why?

[6]Admittedly, as we have discussed, the amount of time available for educational purposes is not likely to be fixed. However, the assumption does simplify the discussion and does not detract from the limited argument we have in mind. Also see Robert J. Staaf, "Student Performance and Changes in Learning Technology in Required Courses," *Journal of Economic Education* 3 (spring 1972), pp. 124–29.

FIGURE 21–1

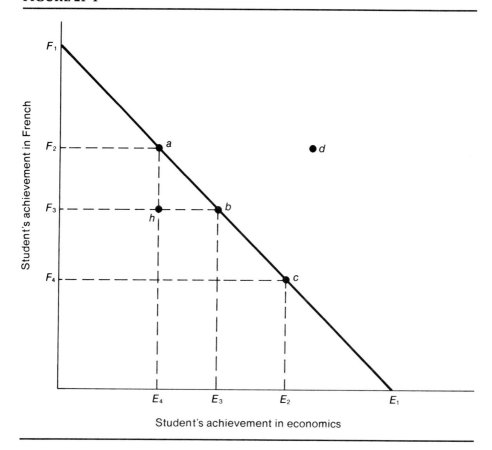

Student's achievement in economics

We do not know a great deal about Paul, but we do know that if he allocates all of his time to the study of economics, he can achieve only so much in that field.[7] We have arbitrarily selected E_1 in Figure 21–1 as that limit. We also know that if he chooses to achieve E_1 in economics, he will learn nothing in French. This, of course, assumes that learning French requires some time and that learning economics has nothing to do with learning French. The same can be said about his ability to learn French. If he devotes all of his time to the study of French, he can learn only so much; we have indicated this limit by F_1.

Alternatively, Paul can choose to divide his time between the study of French and economics in any number of ways, changing the relative achievement in the two subjects. By taking time away from the study of French and

---

[7]We recognize that some students come to a class with such a backlog of knowledge in a given subject area that they do not have to do anything to pass the course. Here again, we are attempting to concentrate on the typical student in the typical class.

applying it to the study of economics, he can increase his achievement in economics while giving up achievement in French (that is, the cost of achieving in economics). It is from this line of reasoning that we have drawn a line between F_1 and E_1. This line (or more properly, *transformation curve*) depicts the numerous combinations of French and economics achievement that can be produced by Paul. He can therefore choose to consume any combination along F_1E_1.

Although it does happen, it is doubtful that the typical student will choose either combination F_1 or E_1. Assuming that Paul must pass both courses, he cannot afford to have zero achievement in either field. Consequently, we would expect him to choose some interior combination, such as *a*, *b*, or *c*. Combination *d* is out of the range of possibilities; it requires the use of more resources than Paul has available for education. (For some other student, who may be more efficient at learning economics and French, *d* might be possible. Why?) If Paul chooses combination *h*, he will not be fully using his resources; he can have more achievement in French and/or economics. Therefore, any combination inside, and not on, F_1E_1 will not be chosen by the rational student. Hence, Paul's task is to sort through all combinations along F_1E_1 for the one combination that will maximize his own satisfaction. If he chooses *b*, it must be because it is preferred over *a* and *c*.

The task of the professor can be viewed as twofold. First, the professor of economics can attempt, by various persuasive techniques, to change the student's preferences toward economics. The result may be that the student prefers combination *c* over *b*. The student learns more economics, but notice that the greater achievement in economics in this case is at the expense of achievement in French. (The efforts, on the other hand, can induce the student to allocate more time to education, in which case the transformation curve will move out to the right.)

Second, the economics professor can attempt to increase the efficiency with which the student learns economics. If he accomplishes what he sets out to do, the student can achieve more in economics; the limit of the student's achievement can move, for example, from E_1 to E_2 in Figure 21–2. Assuming that the French professor does nothing to improve learning in his discipline, the student's transformation curve will, pivoting on F_1, move to F_1E_2.

The student can then choose any combination along this new curve. He can choose combination *r*; his achievement in economics increases while his achievement in French remains constant. On the other hand, the student can choose combination *s*, in which case his achievement in French would rise and his achievement in economics would remain constant. If we had put some leisure activity, such as golf, on the vertical axis instead of achievement in French, the result of the efficiency change in economics could have meant more rounds of golf for the student. The commonsense explanation for this is simply that since the student can now learn more economics in the same amount of time, he can reduce the amount of time spent studying economics, learn the same amount, and spend the extra time on some other activity such as golf or studying French.

FIGURE 21–2

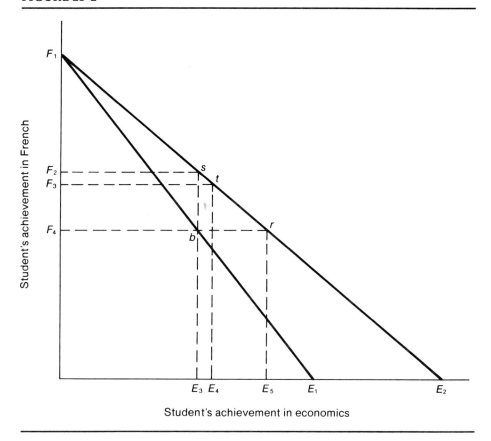

Student's achievement in economics

The student can also choose combination *t* in which case he increases his achievement in both subjects. However, in our example, the increase in economics is much smaller than the increase in French. This might be the expected result for the student who is a French major and is taking economics as a means of satisfying his general education requirement.

This analysis suggests a possible explanation for the outcomes of experiments conducted by educators that appear to have no impact. The researcher can have two classes of students. In one class, the instructor teaches the conventional way, and the mean student achievement may be measured at level E_3. In the other class, the instructor does something that is innovative and in effect moves the transformation curve out to F_1E_2. However, the instructor really does not know if, or how much, the curve has moved. Besides, she may not even think in terms of the students' transformation curves. All she does is measure their new mean achievement, which may be E_4.

Because the difference between E_3 and E_4 is quite small, the instructor may conclude that the experiment was a failure. While it is possible that what is done did not have any effect on learning efficiency (that is, the curve actually does not move), the failure of the instructor could have been the oversight of the increase in the student's achievement in French or the greater amount of time the student spends goofing off or out on dates. If the instructor had broadened her research and had considered the possibility that students may have been choosing to do something else, her conclusion may have been different. This is only a possibility—derived from economic analysis—but one that researchers in education should not pass by lightly.

Before leaving students' maximizing behavior, one additional, important point can be made. We have implicitly assumed that the marginal utility of knowledge, MU_k, is positive, which is in accord with the paradigm that there are benefits to education. Therefore, the student is willing to pay some price to acquire some finite amount of knowledge. However, some types of knowledge may have no perceivable benefits to the student. This may be descriptive of many of the courses included under general education requirements. In such a case, the student must be paid before he can be expected to bear freely the cost of learning the subject.

Of course, one way of paying the student is to impose a cost on him if he does not voluntarily learn the material. This can be done by making the course work a requirement for graduation or entry into a profession. The student can also be penalized with low grades, damaging his future income-earnings ability. If he takes the course work, he is permitted to obtain his degree. The degree then becomes the payment. Such tie-in sales can be made to the student as long as the price charged in the form of tuition and fee payments is below the market-clearing price.[8]

THE RATIONAL PROFESSOR

The professor can also be viewed as a rational human being and as facing a transformation curve. Consider Figure 21–3. In that graph, we have put the leisure time of the professor on the vertical axis. Assuming that the professor's field is economics, we have scaled the mean achievement of the professor's classes along the horizontal axis.

If the professor does nothing with her classes except walk into class, she will have only so much leisure time available for doing other things, such as playing golf or undertaking research. We have arbitrarily indicated this limit as L_1. On the other hand, she can use all of the time raising her students' understanding in economics. In this event, the students' mean achievement can rise to E_1.

Like the student, the professor can divide her time between leisure activity and academic activity (for the professor, increasing her students' achievement), in which case she will have open a number of leisure-achievement

---

[8]We force students to go to public schools. The element of compulsion suggests that the perceived benefits of education for those who actually have to be forced is not sufficient to cover the students' private cost of the education.

FIGURE 21–3

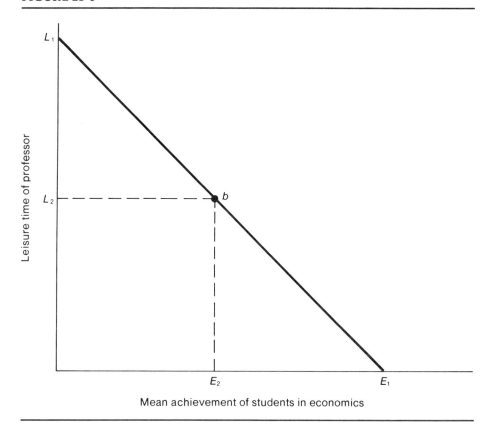

Mean achievement of students in economics

combinations, described on the graph by L_1E_1. Also like the student, the professor is faced with the problem of choosing the combination along L_1E_1 that will maximize her utility. Remember, the professor does have academic freedom, which gives her considerable leeway in deciding how she will use her time.

If she chooses combination b, the student's mean achievement level will be E_2. This implies that the students will, given their abilities and effort, learn only so much, and this is, in part, the result of the utility-maximizing behavior of the professor. If the professor had chosen to work harder, the students would have learned more, possibly as much as E_1. However, the professor would have had less leisure time available or less time for research, and she apparently, in this example, did not believe the additional achievement was worth the costs in terms of leisure time.

If we now introduce some innovative technique into the classroom that can improve the efficiency of the learning process, the professor's transformation curve will, pivoting on L_1, shift to L_1E_3 in Figure 21–4. The professor can now choose any combination along this curve. She can choose combina-

FIGURE 21-4

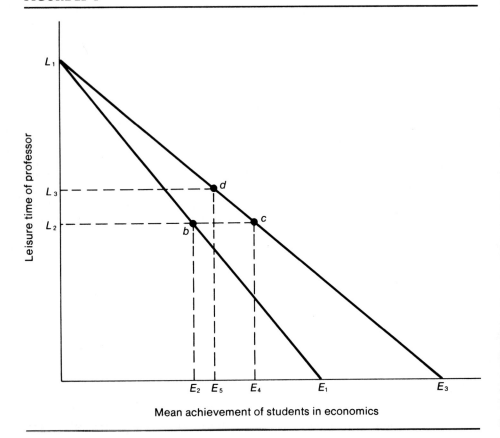

Mean achievement of students in economics

tion *c*, in which case the full benefits of the change in classroom efficiency is revealed in student achievement, which rises from E_2 to E_4.

On the other hand, the professor can trade some of the gains in learning efficiency for additional leisure time. She can choose combination *d*, or any other between *c* and L_1. If the combination chosen is *d*, the net increase in student achievement from the innovation is very slight. If this were a part of an experiment, the researcher might conclude that the innovation was ineffective. Recognizing the possible range of choices by students and by faculty, and recognizing that most educational experiments are undertaken in public schools and general education courses at the college level, it may be understandable why researchers so often may have found that their experiments have had little effect.

STUDENT EVALUATIONS

Increasingly, universities have turned to student evaluations as a means of evaluating faculty performance. However, the issue of whether student evaluations can be influenced by the grades the professor gives her students is unsettled. Allen Kelley, in a study in economic education, found a positive relationship between grades and student evaluations but concluded, "Providing students with high course grades does not appear to exert an important impact on evaluations."[9] Furthermore, he suggests that if the instructor had raised his quality point average from 2.27 to 3.50, the mean ratings for the course would have increased by only 2 to 3 percentage points. Conversely, Dennis Capozza, in another study in principles of economics, came to a dramatically different conclusion.

> The results indicate that every 10-percent increase in the amount learned reduces a professor's rating by half a point. On the other hand, if a professor's grades average 3.5 instead of 2.5, she improves her rating by one and a half points. Another way of expressing the relationship would be that if a professor wishes to receive a perfect rating of 1.0, then he should teach nothing and give at least two thirds of the class As.[10]

In this section, we will demonstrate what economic (choice) theory can contribute to our understanding of the subject.

On student evaluation forms, students are typically asked to respond to such questions as "What is your overall appraisal of the way in which your professor conducted the course?" The students are asked to rate the professor on a scale that may range from "far below average" to "far above average." At best, student evaluations reflect the degree to which the course and instructor agree with the student's preference for such factors as grades, leisure, course content, and, we might add, classroom entertainment. We can therefore reasonably assume that the higher the relative utility (or the lower the relative disutility)[11] the student acquires from attending class under one professor, the higher the relative evaluation of the instructor and course.[12]

Setting aside the multidimensional nature of student preference, assume for the time being that all professors, other than the one with which we are

---

[9]Allen C. Kelly, "Uses and Abuses of Course Evaluations as Measures of Educational Output," *Journal of Economic Education* 4 (fall 1972), p. 13.

[10]Dennis R. Capozza, "Student Evaluations, Grades and Learning in Economics," *Western Economic Journal* 11 (March 1973), p. 127. For other studies on the same subject, see V. M. Voeks and G. M. French, "Are Student Ratings of Teachers Affected by Grades?" *Journal of Higher Education* 31 (June 1960), pp. 330–34; Miriam Rodin and Burton Rodin, "Student Evaluation of Teachers," *Science* 177 (September 29, 1972), pp. 164–66; Alan Nichols and John C. Soper, "Economic Man in the Classroom," *Journal of Political Economy* 80 (September/October 1972), pp. 1169–73; and John C. Soper, "Soft Research on a Hard Subject; Student Evaluations Reconsidered," *Journal of Economic Education* 5 (fall 1973), pp. 22–26.

[11]The student can possibly dislike all of his instructors; but if asked to rate the instructors, he will give the one whom he dislikes least the highest rating.

[12]These statements seem reasonable to us because if the student is asked to give comparative ratings to different professors in different fields or different courses, he must be able to reduce the comparative problem to one common basis. We use the economist's concept of utility as that common denominator.

concerned, hold their grades constant and that the student is rational and views grades (or quality point average) and leisure time as goods from which he receives some utility. Assume also that higher grades (As and Bs) are preferred to lower grades and that leisure time (which can be used for anything inside or outside academic life) available to the student is limited to L_1 in Figure 21–5.

These assumptions appear to us to be reasonably descriptive of the typical student. Grades (or quality point averages) in an economics course are scaled along the horizontal axis.

Given the professor's standards and assuming the student has to work for his grades, we know that the student will have to forgo leisure time to raise his grades. Because other things may be important to him, we would not expect him to spend all of his time studying and attempting to raise his

FIGURE 21–5

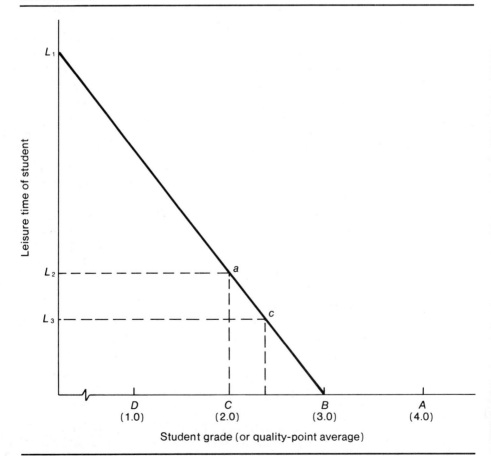

grade to the highest point possible, which in this case is B. The student may choose combination a, at which he makes a grade of C and has L_2 leisure time available for studying other subjects or going out on dates. (He uses the difference between L_1 and L_2 for studying economics.) The student may choose combination c—that is, he could have made a higher grade—however, since he did not, we must assume that the additional time spent studying $(L_3$-$L_2)$ was worth more to him than the marginal increase in his grade.[13]

The professor can change the grading structure in any number of ways, but to keep the discussion short and simple, we will focus attention on one way and assume that the professor will give the student the opportunity to make a higher grade for the same amount of effort. Furthermore, we assume that the professor eases up in such a way that the student's transformation curve between grades and leisure time shifts out in a parallel manner, from L_1B to L_1A in Figure 21–6.

Given the shift, the student has the opportunity to move from combination a (on L_1B) to any point on L_1A. He can move to b, in which case he will have a higher grade (B) and the same amount of leisure time. This means that his effort (L_1L_2) and achievement in the course should remain constant. On the other hand, the student could choose combination c; there he would end up with the same grade (C) but with more leisure time. If he chooses c, he will spend less time studying economics and presumably will achieve less.

Alternatively, the student can choose any combination between c and b and end the course with a higher grade and more leisure time. Since he can have more of both if he wishes, we must assume that from the student's point of view, he is better off and conclude that the professor's rating will rise because of reduced standards. How much, however, we cannot say. Even if the student chooses a combination like d, in which event he would have a higher grade but less leisure time, we would still expect the professor's rating to rise. The student can choose, say, combination e—that is, more of both— and in the event he chooses d, we must deduce that d is preferred to e. Since e is obviously preferred to a (because there is more of both at e), d must also be preferred to a. Therefore, the instructor's rating should be up at d. (This is a little tricky and you may want to reread this paragraph to ensure that you follow it.)

There are two points that fall out of the graph that need to be especially stressed. First, if the students as a group choose a combination like e, it means that the grade they receive under the new grading structure may rise by an insignificant amount; but the instructor's ratings will still be up. If a researcher correlates the grades that professors give with their student evaluations and never looks at what the student achieves in the course or what he

---

[13]A point worth mentioning at this juncture is that if a researcher observes several students making higher grades than others in the class, he cannot on a priori grounds expect their ratings of the instructor to be higher—for the simple reason that they may have worked harder to obtain their grades and are therefore no better off.

FIGURE 21–6

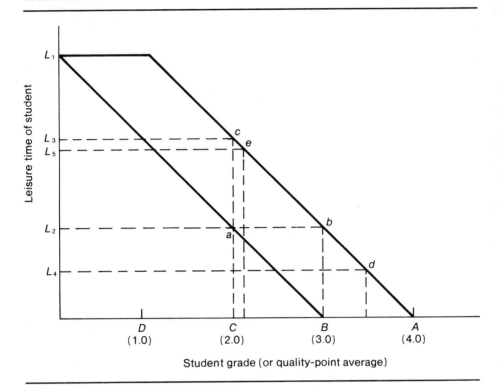

does with his leisure time, the researcher may find very little or no correlation. He may actually conclude that higher student ratings cannot be bought with changes in the grading structure. However, there are professors who in fact may be buying higher student ratings with an easing of their standards. The problem is that the researcher has failed to see that students are taking the benefits of the professors' lower standards in terms of more leisure.

Second, as noted above, it is possible for the student to choose a combination like *d* (less leisure and a higher grade). If he does, he will be studying and achieving more in the course; however, it is interesting to note that Capozza, in the study quoted in the first part of this section, found an inverse relationship between achievement and student evaluations, meaning that the students may be choosing combinations like *e* (more leisure). The suggested inverse relationship between achievement and student evaluations was also borne out in studies by Attiyeh and Lumsden[14] and by Rodin and Rodin.[15]

[14]Richard Attiyeh and Keith G. Lumsden, "Some Modern Myths in Teaching Economics: The U.K. Experience," *American Economic Review* 62 (May 1972), pp. 429–33.
[15]Rodin and Rodin, "Student Evaluation of Teachers."

Interestingly enough, most studies on the relationship between student ratings and grades have been, for the most part, undertaken in courses like principles of economics, which are required for one reason or another. In such courses most students may not want to be there in the first place; and under such conditions, if given the chance, they may move from a to, say e—that is, they may take the benefits of the higher grading structure in terms of more leisure time. If the course is one students want to take because they like the subject or because they believe the knowledge acquired can be used to bolster their income, then one may more likely find a strong positive relationship between achievement and student ratings of the professors.

REAL GRADE INFLATION

In the foregoing discussion, we explicitly assumed that other professors held their grades constant. However, if all professors inflate their grading structure, which tended to be the case in the 1970s, the value to the student of any absolute grade falls. This is because the student's own ranking among his classmates falls if he continues to receive the same grades while their grades go up. The student's utility from taking a course under a professor who does inflate should fall and so should the student's rating of the professor. Therefore, if student evaluations are used in determining salary increases, the professor who does not inflate can experience a drop in relative income. Also, if grade inflation is the general rule among professors, a professor may, to raise his rating relative to that of other professors, have to inflate grades relative to the general trend.

Testing any hypothesis regarding the impact of grade inflation on student ratings of professors and performance of students in the course is fraught with difficulties. Ideally, a given set of students should be taught a course under a given grading policy, and their ratings of the course and professor should be taken. They then should be given the same course with the only change being in the grading policy. The results of such an experiment would have meaning only if we could assume that in the process the students' preferences and opportunity sets are not changed, which is, of course, a totally unrealistic assumption.

In order to obtain some idea of the result of grade inflation, Paul Combs and one of the authors (McKenzie) took a second-best approach, which was to conduct a control group–experimental group study.[16] Combs taught two sections of the same introductory course in statistics, and McKenzie taught two sections of the same course in introductory economics. Combs and McKenzie each gave his two classes pretests and posttests, taught his two

---

[16]J. Paul Combs and Richard B. McKenzie, "The Empirical Effects of Grade Inflation on Student Evaluations and Performance" (Boone, N.C.: Economics Department, Appalachian State University, 1975).

sections similarly, as closely as possible, and gave the same tests during the course. The only difference in their instructional methods was their grading policy. Each designated one class as being the *easy class* and one as the *hard class*. In the case of Combs, the easy class was given partial credit for incomplete answers, but the hard class was not; the difference in the numerical grade on the last day of class was approximately one half of a letter grade. McKenzie, on the other hand, gave the same numerical scores on the tests of the two classes; the difference was that his grading scale was much lower for his easy class. That is, a *B* began at a lower numerical score for his easy class than for his hard class. The difference between the mean grades given in his two classes was a little over a full letter grade on the last day of class.

As we have hypothesized, Combs's mean student ratings were approximately 10 percent higher in his easy class than in his hard class. However, the students in his hard class had a greater improvement in their understanding of statistics; their improvement was approximately 10 percent greater. Since McKenzie had a much larger differential in his grading distribution in the two classes, one might expect a much larger differential in student ratings and performance, and this is exactly what was found. The students in McKenzie's easy class gave him a 25 percent higher mean rating than did the students in his hard class. On the other hand, the improvement in economic understanding of students in his hard class was 85 percent greater than for students in his easy class. In our preceding analysis, all we could possibly say is that we should have found an inverse relationship between student ratings and performance, given a difference in the grading structure. Frankly, we did not anticipate the difference to be so dramatic.[17]

CONCLUDING COMMENTS

At this point, the reader may believe that we look upon student evaluations of professors as a totally perverted device for evaluating teaching. On the contrary, we recognize that students can see good qualities in teachers. We believe that students can fairly accurately tell when a professor is pre-

---

[17]Upon more sophisticated regression analysis (for those who understand statistics), we standardized for a number of characteristics of the students, such as sex, age, race, marital status, quality point average, and so forth. We found in the McKenzie test, the dummy variable introduced to distinguish between the students in his hard and easy classes was statistically significant at 0.001 in the equation in which the professor ratings were used as the dependent variable and in which the differences in the student's performance on the pre- and posttest were used as the independent variable. This dummy variable was not significant in the analysis of Combs's results, but the sign of the variable was in the predicted direction. This suggests, but does not prove, that if Combs had increased the difference in his grading structures, the differences in ratings and performance would have been significant. The study also suggests that if student ratings had been used in ranking the faculty within the department for purposes of raises, Combs and McKenzie could have, assuming other faculty members held to their grading policy, raised their rankings and raises by inflating their grades.

pared for class and if she is sufficiently competent to teach the course. They can also make judgments about her treatment of themselves and other students. All of these judgments can be reflected in their rating of the professors they have.

The main point we have been trying to make in this section is that, given the quality of the professor, economic theory suggests that student evaluations can be distorted by the professor's grading structure. If two professors are equal in every other respect, we would predict that the professor with the higher grading structure (in the sense that we have used the term in this section) will tend to receive the higher student ratings. In a similar manner, if two professors are distinctly different in the eyes of the students, one being better than the other, our analysis suggests that the professor who would otherwise have the lower rating can (partially) offset the differential by easing up on his grades.[18]

QUESTIONS TO PONDER

1. Suppose that two professors increase the efficiency of the learning process in their classes at the same time but they increase the efficiency by different amounts (or percentages). What effect will such changes have on the choice behavior of the student with regard to the two courses and some other leisure time activity?

2. Do professors have an incentive to increase the efficiency of the learning processes in their classes? If they do, what is it? What other institutional changes can be made to increase this incentive?

3. Suppose a professor can inflate grades by changing the grading curves (see accompanying graphs). What effect do the changes have on the price or cost of a higher grade? In which case is the student most likely to choose to learn the most after the grading structure is inflated? Explain in terms of basic economic principles.

---

[18]For those who may be concerned with this study from a moralistic point of view, the authors of the study maintained a difference in their grading policy until the last lecture session at which the student ratings were taken. In the final analysis, the classes were graded on the same basis. In fact, because we realized that we had "framed" the students, the student grades were higher than they normally are in classes of the professors.

CHAPTER 22

Committees and Comment Pollution

Committees are an integral part of the internal governance of colleges and universities. They are typically delegated major responsibilities such as determining admissions standards, developing curricula, handing out awards, and making policy recommendations on such important matters as internal resources allocation, grading systems, tenure, and other faculty and student welfare measures.

Although one may like to think of the committee process as one in which learned men and women, through an in-depth evaluation of a problem area, make sound judgments, faculty members and administrators commonly characterize their committee meetings as dull, boring, and a monumental waste of time. They are also prone to suggest that what may appear to be informed judgments are often (though not always) nothing more than the personal expressions of members who throughout the committee sessions made little or no attempt to come to grips with the issues at hand (and it should be noted that, generally speaking, the larger the committee, the more common the complaints). If these criticisms are correct, not only may the university be employing its resources inefficiently through direct support of the committees themselves, but it may be operating on the basis of very poor judgments.

The purpose of the analysis in this chapter is not to suggest that all university committees operate, in some sense, badly but rather to develop an economic explanation as to why they so often operate as badly as they do. Specifically, we are concerned with why there is likely to be an excessive production of comments (or *comment pollution*) within many committee meetings (or why meetings may be long and dull), and why the judgments of the individual members may often (though not always) be uninformed, or why little effort may be made in studying the assigned task of the committee. Once the sources of the problems of the committee are recognized, remedies do emerge as is indicated below.

In developing the argument, we take the usual position that committee members—faculty, administrators, and students—are similar to their counterparts in other walks of life in that they weigh the costs and benefits of taking action, will take an action if the benefits exceed the costs, and will extend *production* of the activity up until the point at which the marginal private benefits of the action equal the marginal private costs. In a word, the committee member is rational.[1]

COMMENTS AS PUBLIC GOODS

A comment made by a committee member in a meeting is a public good (or perhaps as frequently as not, a public bad) in much the same sense as is police protection or industrial pollution. (What is a public good? A public bad?) Take, for example, the situation of the industrial polluter, considered in Chapter 13. When it fouls the air, it imposes a cost on persons who may live or work in the surrounding area: the people on the street may experience eye irritation, and the pollution may soil the clothes on the line. If the property rights to the air are left unassigned (as has been the case in the past), the polluter need not consider these external costs in its production decisions. Consequently, its private costs are less than the social costs of the industrial activity, and we can expect that production (and the emission of pollutants) will be extended beyond the social optimum.[2] It is only through the internalization of the external costs through user charges or taxes that an economically efficient output can be achieved.

In the case of the committee member's comment, once the comment is made, all members of the committee must hear it. There are external costs involved (as in the case of the industrial production), since people other than the one making the comment must, if they are present, spend the time to hear what is said. The private cost to the individual making the comment is mainly equal to the time he or she spends listening to himself or herself.[3] (There may be those who fear making a fool of themselves with their comments; however, we find that there are many in the universities who get a great deal of positive utility in making comments to any group. They enjoy

---

[1]The chapter is in part the application to a specific problem area of the general line of analysis that was developed in Chapters 5, 13, and 17.

[2]The social optimum is the output level at which the marginal social costs equals the marginal social benefits. The social costs include all costs incurred by those directly involved in a transaction and those who are not a party to the transaction but who are affected indirectly. It is the emission of particles beyond the point of social optimum that economists would call pollution. One Indian can urinate in the Hudson River (as many did for a long time) without affecting (in the sense that anyone is disturbed) the aesthetic beauty of the area or the quality of the water. The problem of pollution exists when all people start throwing their waste into the river at basically the same place and same time; that is, they go beyond the social optimum amount of waste disposal.

[3]Problem: several years ago people who were very concerned about the destruction of the environment gathered on what was then called *Earth Day* at the Washington Monument. After all the speeches on what human beings were doing to the world were over, they left, leaving the grounds covered with litter. Realizing that the mess was created by "concerned citizens," how could it happen? Would you as an economist have expected them to create the mess? Why?

sounding off before the committee in the same way that a musician likes to perform before an audience.)

The social costs, on the other hand, are equal to the summation of the opportunity cost incurred (or value of time spent) by all members of the committee listening to the comment, and it needs to be emphasized that the discrepancy between the private and social costs for a comment expands with the size of the committee. The rational committee member will extend the production of comments until the marginal private benefits equal the marginal private costs; and since the private costs are likely to be less than the social costs, we should expect there to be a natural tendency for committees to overproduce comments for the same reason that industries (when external costs are not internalized) can be expected to pollute.

A solution for efficient operation of a committee is for the chairperson to impose costs on members making comments—to the extent necessary to achieve equality between the private costs actually considered by each member and the costs to the committee as a whole. This may be easier said than done; however, recognition of the problem of inequality between private and social costs may suggest to the chairperson attitudes and devices that have the effect of raising the effective private cost of a comment to the individual.[4] Firmness would indeed be a desirable characteristic of any good chairperson, and such a tack may be easier for the chairperson to embrace if he or she understands that controlling the comments of individual members can be desired by all members.[5]

It may appear to be paradoxical, but it is still the case that even though each individual member may freely choose to pollute the committee with comments, he or she could still desire some form of collective (chairperson) control over the comments made by all committee members. The simple reason is that although his or her own freedom may be restricted, he or she does not have to endure the comment pollution generated by others.

---

[4]The individual who is concerned about the feelings of others may also include in her own calculations the additional factor that her comments may inconvenience others or may lower her stature in their eyes. This still does not mean that the assessed private costs of the individual making the comments are necessarily equal to the social costs as calculated by the other members of the committee and that the committee will necessarily work properly. There are committees that do in some sense work properly; however, our purpose here is to develop a model of committee behavior that will enable us to understand why so many committees do not. In addition, full inclusion of all "charitable feelings" in the choice calculus of the individual committee member makes the model so general that all predictive content is lost. Our assumption regarding the costs that are considered is similar to the assumption of profit maximization in more conventional economic discussions of the firm.

[5]We must hedge the issue at stake here since an economist has no particular expertise in suggesting what may actually constitute an increase in cost, barring the use of such things as taxing income or, what can amount to the same thing, charging for each comment made. The authors seriously doubt that such techniques would be an acceptable or necessarily efficient means of controlling a committee member's behavior.

THE JUDGMENT OF COMMITTEE MEMBERS

If Judy Sims, a doctoral candidate, were to select as her thesis topic "The Effectiveness of the Interest Equalization Tax Act from July 1963 through December 1964," she would no doubt undertake an exhaustive review of the relevant literature, make a point-by-point evaluation of the provisions of the act, collect mountains of data and evaluate them in different ways, and end up spending no less than nine months in concentrated study. If Ms. Sims was hired by a university and appointed to a committee whose function was to make recommendations on the internal allocation of university resources, most of her colleagues (given the typical committee organization) might indeed consider her to be a little unusual (if not queer) if she addressed the task of the committee with the same thoroughness with which she developed her doctoral thesis. She would probably get the same reaction even though the problems confronting the committee were considered by all to be more important than the subject of a doctoral thesis.

One obvious explanation for the disparity in the amount of effort expended on a thesis and on a committee task is that Ms. Sims must, once employed, divide her allegiance and work effort among the demands of her students, department chairperson, and professional activities: she simply may not have the time for committee work.[6] In addition, she may not have any particular personal interest in the problem facing the committee, whereas her doctoral research may have been personally gratifying, and many committee tasks, admittedly, require only that the committee members express their own preferences.

Our concern, however, is with those committees that do require study and preparation on the part of the members, yet the effort expended may never come close to being as much as is required. We seek explanations for the behaviors of committee members that have largely gone unrecognized by university officials but are no less important than those reasons frequently cited.

Committee work can be exceedingly costly to committee members. For example, Ms. Sims, if she does a good job studying the issue of internal resource allocation, can be expected to spend 5 to 10 hours a week for a period of a year or more trying to assess the scope of the problem at hand and evaluating current programs on campus. If she has no particular expertise in such areas—for example, she is in English or music—the magnitude of her task is considerably multiplied. This means she must forgo other activities that may have value to her. If she is inclined to operate within the

---

[6]Of course, the most desirable situations for *any* individual committee member would be for the chairperson to permit her completely free range in making comments while at the same time restricting the comments of the other members. We are suggesting in the text that the member would be willing to compromise this position to move away from a completely free and open committee session.

publish-or-perish world or if she consults a great deal, serious effort on the business of the committee can reduce her future income stream. If not that loss, or in addition, time spent on committee work can deny her rounds of golf or conversation with students or family. In short, in absence of compulsion, the decision to undertake committee work at any level is an economic (choice) problem for her.[7] Therefore, to understand her behavior, one must compare the costs with the benefits of committee work as perceived by Ms. Sims.

The cost of Ms. Sims's work potentially includes the value of the time spent on research, as indicated above, plus the time spent in committee meetings listening to others, relating what she has learned, attempting to synthesize the information the receives from others with that which she has collected, and attempting to convince others of the relative correctness of her own position. There are in essence two basic types of potential costs: (1) research costs and (2) costs associated with dealing with the committee members. Note that almost all costs are under the control of Ms. Sims, the exception being the minimum number of times she must attend meetings—and that many of the costs of dealing with the committee escalate exponentially with the size of the committee.

As suggested earlier, comment pollution and length of the meetings are likely to rise with the number of members: The more members, the more perspectives, and therefore, potentially more comments to be made. And when there are more members, there are more people to convince that any given position should be taken.[8] Again, there are more perspectives in the larger committees, which must be won over to a given position, if a position is to be taken; and therefore, the variety of tactics required to convince, to develop a winning coalition, is likely to be greater.

On the benefit side of Ms. Sims's choice ledger, one can distinguish between indirect and direct benefits of committee work. Indirect benefits may include such factors as the effect Ms. Sims's work on the committee will have on her own income, security, and prestige through the actions taken by the committee. In the case of the committee on internal resources allocation, Ms. Sims, through her effort, can possibly affect university policy and, therefore, the demands for her services as a teacher. The direct benefits may include the entertainment value (for want of better words) associated with being in on

---

[7]Although she may have no choice with regard to whether she is appointed to a particular committee, the committee member typically has a great deal of latitude in determining how many meetings she will attend, how well prepared she is for the meetings, and how attentive she is during the sessions.

[8]Because of the public-goods nature of comments made within committee meetings, the cost of persuasion is not likely to rise proportionately with the number of committee members. This does not mean, however, that the cost will not rise. One of the reasons for forming committees in the first place is to make comments public goods and therefore reduce the costs of forming a consensus among a number of people who may represent various aspects of campus life.

what is happening on campus, giving the impression that she is doing something, and having interesting conversations with people with whom she does not normally associate.

The amount of work she is willing to undertake depends on the perceived benefits from her action and how they compare with the cost of achieving those benefits. As we assumed in the beginning, Ms. Sims will undertake no work unless the benefits exceed the costs, or the payoff is positive. In many instances, the indirect benefits from committee work can be small for the individual member; the decisions made may have nothing to do with the member's own welfare (but may have a great deal to do with welfare of, say students).

In the event that the effects of the committee decisions are generalized over the entire faculty, the effect can be small for any one individual, and if so, she will make her decision on how much research to undertake on the basis of the individual benefits she receives and not on the basis of the total effects. Since the decisions of the committee are public goods themselves, the effort expended by each member can easily be suboptimal.[9] It is indeed apparent that one tends to observe greater effort expended by those committee members who are directly or indirectly affected substantially by the decisions of the committee.

As for the direct benefits, committee work, and particularly the quality factor, is given very little attention in the evaluation of faculty members. Student credit hours generated and research are by far the dominant considerations. Clearly, the typical department chairperson, who is primarily responsible for evaluation, may never do anything more than count the number of committees each member of his or her faculty is on. In fact, inquiry into the quality of the individual's committee work can be considered in many circles of academia a violation of commonly accepted professional ethics.[10] We do not mean to suggest that there is never any feedback but only that it may be so scant that it does not reflect the true effort of the committee member and may be too unreliable to use as a basis for evaluation. The other direct benefits (entertainment) may explain his attendance at meetings but tend to detract from his research effort.

Ms. Sims's work can also be related to committee size but in an inverse manner. The larger the committee, the smaller the perceived benefits from expended effort. In a large meeting of faculty—take, for example, a faculty meeting as an extreme case—the vote of an individual faculty member is one among many. The probability of her individual vote determining the outcome

---

[9]Gordon Tullock, "Public Decisions as Public Goods," *Journal of Political Economy* 79 (July/August 1971), pp. 913–18.

[10]It would be in the interest of the faculty member to employ some personal resources attempting to give the impression that she is working harder on her committees than she actually is. It may be rational for her to work harder at giving a false impression than on committee business.

of the meeting is rather small, and one may add also, the probability that what she does or says in the faculty meeting affects the outcome of the meeting is rather small (or smaller than for smaller committees). For smaller committee meetings, the probability goes up.

However, Ms. Sims will be rational and will still discount the benefits resulting from the committee actions by (1) the probability that her own vote will be affected by research (denoted as A; see below); (2) the probability that her position, determined by her own research, is the correct one (D); (3) the probability that her research will affect the outcome of the committee vote (E); and (4) the probability that the committee decision or vote will actually affect the individual committee members (F).[11] Even for the smaller committees, it might be deduced that these probabilities and corresponding discounts can be so low that the expected personal benefits, resulting from the research efforts, will have to be far greater than the expected costs, which can in themselves be quite large.

For example, assume that the following values are associated with the probabilities noted above: $A = 0.5$, $D = 0.75$, $E = 0.2$, and $F = 0.5$. (These values seem to us to be reasonably generous for purposes of illustration.) Ms. Sims will undertake the cost of research (C) if the discounted benefits (B) are greater than the costs or if $(ADEF)(B) - C > 0$. For this example, this means that the expected benefits would have to be greater than \$26.67 for each dollar value of research cost incurred [$\$26.67 = \$1/(ADEF) = \$1/(.5 \times .75 \times .2 \times .5)$].

Even if it were conceded that the probabilities are too low and should be adjusted upward, we should still find that the expected benefits will have to be several times the expected costs. In light of the analysis, it is quite understandable why many committee members, even in relatively small committees, do very little to become informed on the subject matter facing them.[12]

The foregoing analysis also suggests several general guidelines for committee organization:

1. University committees that are organized to study a problem for which there is no obvious answer should be kept small. From personal experience, the authors doubt that a committee with more than six members will actually study any problem before it. Larger committees should be reserved for those areas of university life for which study is not required or the mere expression of individual preferences toward an issue

---

[11]This last factor must be added since many committees are set up for the purpose of making recommendations and not for taking action directly. In such instances, it is not certain that what the committee recommends will actually be adopted as university policy.

[12]In a large faculty meeting, E would be much smaller than in the example above. If $E = 1/500$, the benefits would have to be greater than \$2,666 for each \$1.00 of cost. This would mean that to expect the committee members to incur \$1,000 worth of cost on committee work, one would have to expect \$2,666,000 worth of benefits. The obvious paradox is that a few people actually work as hard as they do.

is the underlying function of the committee. As is now virtually axiomatic within the study of groups, large groups should be used for reaction and not for action.

2. In the interest of reducing the cost of research to the individual committee member, the task of the committee should be segmented, and responsibility for research in the different areas should be delegated to the members. This means that if large committees are thought to be necessary (for some political purpose, for example) subcommittees should be organized, and clear lines of responsibility should be drawn and made known.[13] Since not all members will be studying the entire problem facing the committee, there is a cost embedded in this suggestion. However, if the entire problem is laid on the committee as a whole, the cost of a complete study of the whole problem can be too great for anyone to undertake any research. In addition, each committee member may attempt to become a free rider, meaning that no one does anything.

3. Before a committee is organized, there should be a high probability that the recommendations of the committee will be put into action. If an administrator frequently organizes committees and almost as frequently ignores their recommendations, this behavior will reduce the diligence with which the committees will tackle any problem that is assigned. In other words, it will reduce the probability that he or she can accept the recommendations of the committees that are appointed.

CONCLUDING COMMENTS

There have been two overriding conclusions that come out of the foregoing discussion. First, committee meetings are likely to be dull and boring because, given their typical organization, there is likely to be an overproduction of comments, and these comments are likely to be based on uninformed judgments. This goes for student, as well as faculty, committee meetings, and it is just as applicable to committee meetings that are wrestling with the question of what to do about industrial pollution as to those deciding how to reallocate faculty resources. If the reader has difficulty accepting this as a generality, then it is clear that he or she has not been on many committees.

Second, many of the problems universities have experienced in the past may be the result of the extensive use of committees and the general lack of concern over (or understanding of) the operations of a committee. A university may well be advised to be more selective in the use of committees, particularly the larger ones.

---

[13]An alternative would be for the committee to be given the authority to hire someone to undertake the research and draw up proposals the committee can approve or disapprove.

QUESTIONS TO PONDER

1. Do you find groups of which you are a member behaving in the same way as the committees described in this chapter?

2. What do you think should be done (if anything) about this problem of how committees operate? Why are committees organized in the first place?

3. Given our arguments about the operations of committees, devise arguments for supplanting many committee functions with administrator/dictators.

CHAPTER 23

The Emergence of Kickbacks in University Textbook Adoptions

University students generally believe that their professors make decisions on textbooks for their courses with considerable care. The adopted textbooks are often presumed to be the best available, given the interests and abilities of the professors and their students and the prices of competing texts.

However, many adoption decisions on university textbooks are made with little or no care. (You may think that was the case with this book!) In addition, to a growing extent, decisions are being influenced by what observers outside universities might call a form of bribery. In overt and covert forms, textbook publishers and authors are channeling kickbacks to individual professors or their departments. Although kickbacks in adoption decisions are not yet common, rewards for adopting the "right" text are also not unknown (or possibly not even uncommon). Kickbacks are now influencing more adoption decisions than earlier.

Explaining why adoption kickbacks are emerging is critical to understanding their efficiency or inefficiency and to devising constructive solutions, if solutions are deemed necessary. The economic consequences of kickbacks for textbook adoptions are not clear. After all, economists may view kickbacks to professors for adopting texts in the same light as payola to disc jockeys for playing records—that is, a mutually beneficial income transfer.[1]

THE ADOPTION DECISIONS

Clearly, many (if not most) textbook adoptions are made with the type of care envisioned by students.[2] Many professors do take a nontrivial amount of

---

[1]Since universities have done little or nothing to prevent kickbacks, critics might conclude the kickbacks are efficient. As Ronald Coase deduced in his analysis of payola in the record/broadcasting industry, "The lack of any serious effort on the part of the broadcasting industry in the 1950's to prevent payola suggests that there was a broad congruence of interest between operators of radio stations and disc jockeys." R. H. Coase, "Payola in Radio and Television Broadcasting," *Journal of Law and Economics*, October 1979, p. 308.

[2]An inherent problem in making generalizations about adoption decisions is that few, if any, reliable studies have been made on exactly how, or on what basis, textbooks are adopted.

time to read through parts (if not almost all) of a select number of competing textbooks, evaluating their pedagogy for ease of learning and their content for accuracy, cogency, and currency. Just as much attention if not more, may be given to the usefulness of the accompanying materials—for example, the study guide, test bank, overhead transparencies, and computer programs. Some professors are also truly concerned about the prices of required texts, choosing the lower-priced textbook package, everything else being equal.

However, just as clearly, a nonquantifiable but significant number of textbook adoptions are made by professors who give little thought to the texts they select. Textbooks may be chosen because others in the department are using them. Professors may also adopt their textbooks because they used an earlier edition, do not want to change lecture notes, like the sales representative, or for a variety of even less substantive reasons.

Indeed, textbook sales representatives frequently admit that for some professors the color, length, weight, and size of books weigh more heavily in adoption decisions than content and pedagogy. Publishers are intensely concerned that their final products pass the *flip test*, meaning that they are "bullet-proofed" against defects blatantly obvious to those professors who give adoptions decisions no more time than that required to flip through the entire book. In general, some sales representatives will also readily admit (off the record) that the overriding factor governing textbook decisions is the pervasive laziness about teaching among many faculty. Because the adoption process is so casual and the adopted texts are bought only by students, professors often have only a vague idea of the cost of the texts they adopt.

This casual attitude toward textbook adoptions is understandable for several reasons. First, the prices of required texts will rarely, if ever, affect professors' income and job tenure. At most universities student evaluations of professors (which can be affected by their course requirements, including the prices of their textbooks) are simply not taken very seriously.[3]

Second, in actual use, textbooks that in the past have been adopted and readopted by colleagues have, perhaps, stood the test of scrutiny of students and professors. Sometimes adoption decisions made in the past may be viewed as a reasonable and useful predictor of how students will react to a course in the future.

Third, many professors have found through experience, if not study, that regardless of how textbooks are chosen, the textbooks selected will have little

---

Publishers have frequently surveyed professors on the topics the professors want to see covered in textbooks, but even publishers tend to rely heavily on the judgments of their sales representatives for explanations of why textbooks have or have not been adopted.

[3]While student evaluations may also *not* be dismissed, the research and publication records of professors are typically far more important than student evaluations. Besides, the price of a university education is typically subsidized, meaning the student pays a below-market price. The subsidy can be partially absorbed in higher work demands on students and also by higher prices for required course materials. See Chapter 21.

or no detectable effect on student learning and attitude. Time spent on adoptions under such conditions may be largely a waste.

Fourth, most textbooks in any given subject area, especially introductory survey courses, tend to be intellectual clones of one another, differing more dramatically in terms of tone, format, color, and available auxiliary learning aids than in actual content. Path-breaking innovations in textbook content are relatively rare. Again, this is especially true at the introductory level. Textbooks tend to be similar because adoptions are often political, relying extensively on committee (or full department) decisions or on the ebb and flow of political power within departments.

When adoptions are made collectively, responsibility for the textbook is diffused and is thereby assumed by no one. In addition, time spent on the adoption decision may not affect the decision, in which case such effort can be viewed as a waste. Under such conditions, mistakes on textbook selections are likely to abound, and the pervasive existence of mistakes can further mask the lack of effort applied to adoption decisions. Faculty members can reason that it just does not pay to divert time to the adoption process from their "more important" research.

THE EMERGENCE OF CREATIVE KICKBACKS

Realizing the often frivolous and political dimensions of textbook adoption decisions is important also in understanding the emergence of what is likely to become a major political and economic (if not legal) problem in higher education: kickbacks, or bribery, or payola, going from publishers and authors to professors or their departments and favored collegiate interests.[4] While most university administrators, and some faculty members, are unaware that the kickback problem exists, the amounts of the kickbacks are escalating and the methods of disguising them, out of sight of administrators (who may, at times, intentionally look the other way), are becoming more creative. Growing numbers of professors are accepting kickbacks in one form or another.

Few publishers actually spend any time seeking to sell their books directly to students. This should be expected, given the typical university-institutional setting. While students pay for the books, professors (or their departments) adopt the books.

Textbook promotions—publisher to faculty—have traditionally involved nonprice competition with little or no attention given to the prices students

---

[4]An important persisting problem in adoption decisions, not considered in detail in this chapter, is the extent to which professors and administrators use adoption decisions as means of increasing the incomes of friends and colleagues. Faculty members have at times adopted the textbooks of their friends and colleagues for the express purpose of increasing their friends' and colleagues' income and currying return favors for themselves. The problem is especially questionable when administrators press their faculty members to adopt their own textbooks or those of their friends and colleagues with implied threats of retaliation if inappropriate adoption decisions are made.

will have to pay. The traditional and most widely used nonprice selling techniques include glossy brochures extolling the virtues of their books, complimentary copies of textbooks, and instructional aids that reduce the professor's teaching time.[5] The instructional aids may include test banks in books or on computer disks, overhead transparencies, and computer programs for determining and analyzing student performance. However, publishers have also sought to sell their books by giving cocktail parties for faculty attending association meetings, passing out calendars and pens embossed with the titles and authors of their textbooks, and arranging lunches for selected faculty with their sales representatives.

These sales methods may, at times, have caused raised eyebrows, but they have not been disturbing. After all, complimentary copies may be more or less necessary if textbooks are to be evaluated properly. Test banks may actually improve professors' tests, especially since the test banks may have been carefully edited by the publishers. And, admittedly, useful information about textbooks can be passed at cocktail parties and lunches, especially if sales representatives and authors are available for questions.

Over the past decade, however, nonprice competition in textbook markets has become more creative—and questionable. Sales representatives have provided faculty members in charge of large classes or on departmental adoption committees with textbooks for courses other than the ones taught. The "comp copies" have been provided in expectation that they would be sold in the used book market, which has become far more efficient over the past several years.[6]

At least one publisher has promoted one of its textbooks by including the names of adopters in a drawing for desktop computers. Several publishers have also given adopting departments grants for buying educational films and materials, athletic equipment, and computers. Money has also been contributed for departmental functions that would not normally be permitted under normal budget constraints.[7] For example,

---

[5]Of course, any feature of the textbook or auxiliary material that reduces the time professors must spend teaching their courses can be construed as an indirect increase in the professors' real incomes. Professors can use the extra time for consulting or for leisure activities or for writing publishable article that increase their competitive market salaries.

[6]Used book buyers are now frequently seen in the halls of professors' offices with specially constructed hand carts for carrying books—that is, complimentary copies—bought from professors with "cash on the spot," which has made the income received largely untraceable and nontaxable. Purchased complimentary copies are then sold from central distribution centers, along with used books bought from students, to university bookstores. The resale price ranges between two thirds and three quarters of the new-book price. The growing number of used-book buyers has, naturally, increased the prices professors have received for their unwanted books and, accordingly, increased the value of complimentary copies and the usefulness of this form of bribery.

[7]Generally, publishers are unconcerned with how the funds supplied for films or other classroom materials are used. The publishers' primary concern is with ensuring that the funds result in adoptions.

- A publisher gave a department at a northeastern university a $2,000 grant with no strings attached for adopting its textbook.
- Another publisher agreed to give a department in a southwestern university $1.25 for each of the publisher's books sold on campus.
- The athletic department in a small southern school received a treadmill after adopting department-wide a health and physical education textbook.

Publishers have also been known to be far more blatant in their efforts to influence adoptions—by making direct money payments to professors. However, publishers have sought to legitimize the payments with some appropriately constructed academic cover. For example, publishers have been known to pay professors of large classes for reviews of their books being considered for adoption, knowing that the professors really understand that the payments are actually intended to compensate for adoptions, not for critical or constructive comments. Under the guise of a "departmental enhancement policy," a publisher has agreed to reimburse professors or their departments up to fifty cents per copy for expenditures on an "approved" list of items. Of course, the approved items cover only "educational equipment and supplies," which may include personal computers bought by the departments for professors to use in their campus or home offices.[8] In other instances, the need for a ruse has been all but forgotten. Adopting professors have been sent checks.

It may be assumed that various forms of kickbacks in textbook adoptions decisions have emerged at the initiative of publishers, not professors. Nothing could be further from the truth. Experienced sales representatives will confess, off the record, that it is not uncommon for professors, who are potential adopters, to ask that they and their wives be taken out to dinner or to request additional complimentary copies of books. Other professors will initiate the kickback by recounting what other publishers are willing to do for their departments or for them personally, only to ask, "What are you willing to do for me?" Still other professors insist that their author friends or colleagues take them out to dinner, buy them drinks, or adopt their own books in return for their continued adoptions. Authors, no doubt, have yielded to the temptations presented them or have created additional enticements.

---

[8]Because of the growing prevalence of "allowance policies," one publisher that felt compelled to clarify its position regarding "media allowance policies" maintains that it will continue to offer products (film strips, slides, transparencies, computer software, etc.) to accompany their textbooks. However, the company "shall not offer any form of cash payment contingent on the selection of our texts." It added that it believes "that all of Higher education—bookseller, faculty, publisher, university—has the absolute responsibility of setting and maintaining ethical standards by which the future generations of our society can be guided." (Memorandum from the college sales department of a major textbook publisher, October 1, 1986; publisher's name withheld intentionally by the author.)

THE ECONOMIC FOUNDATIONS OF
ADOPTION KICKBACKS

In very general terms, publishers are willing to make side-payments for adoptions for one fundamental reason: they expect reimbursement from sales—more specifically, from sales revenue in excess of costs, including the editing, distribution, and kickback costs. Even though this statement says a great deal, it does not fully explain how the kickbacks can be profitable.

Kickbacks can be highly profitable (and thereby very tempting) because most of the costs of publication at the time textbooks are released are sunk costs, already captured in past expenditures for editors, reviewers, composition, and printing. For the most part, these costs cannot be reclaimed, regardless of how many books are sold. The marginal cost of printing and selling additional books (including the author royalties) is relatively modest, perhaps amounting to no more than 25 percent of the retail price in university bookstores. Additional adoptions, especially for a large number of books, can be highly profitable on the margin.

Kickbacks can also supplant other forms of advertising and entertainment expense and can speed up adoption decisions, reducing the publishers' cost for the time needed by their sales representatives to close adoption decisions. From the standpoint of the publisher, kickbacks ensure adoptions (given in previous years to competing textbooks) that could not be accomplished in any other way. Many professors are reluctant to change textbooks. Such a switch can significantly increase the amount of time required to prepare lectures. That increased time represents a cost to the professor in that it reduces his real income—because he has less time to spend in research, writing for publication, and consulting, which are significant supplements to his salary income.[9]

The kickbacks may be seen by publishers in the same way frequent-flyer points are seen by airlines, as private incentives focused directly on decision makers (professors) who have to bear a significant proportion of the cost of switching their textbook adoption. Some professors may see the kickbacks as compensation for the personal costs they incur through allocating more time to lecture preparation and less time to other activities that can increase their real income.

Publishers may know that kickbacks increase the price of textbooks. But student demand for courses is, in most instances, highly inelastic—meaning that the additional cost can be passed on to students in the form of higher prices with no appreciable sales reductions. Furthermore, professors accept-

---

[9]Coase notes that payola in broadcasting was opposed in the 1950s by the established singers, writers, and record companies, many of whom were witnessing a reduction in their market shares. Among the music writers leading the opposition to payola were Oscar Hammerstein, Richard Rodgers, Irving Berlin, and Burton Lane. Coase, "Payola in Radio and Television Broadcasting," pp. 312–15.

ing the kickbacks and adopting the textbooks may be unaware of the influence the kickbacks have on textbook prices.

Besides, the publisher may be caught in a competitive bind. If kickbacks are not given, a significant number of adoptions may be lost. Indeed, sales representatives openly confess that they do not particularly like the idea of providing professors with kickbacks, but they must often make the offers just to remain competitive. All of the sunk costs of publication can be lost without kickbacks. In short, there are both offensive and defensive reasons for engaging in bribery of professors, all inspired by the competitive process and the university that pays little attention to prices students have to pay for course materials.

Of course, publishers can be expected to bribe selectively. There are dangers involved in campus kickbacks. On some campuses, publishers run a risk of being caught and having their sales representatives barred from campuses; such fears may explain the kickback ruses. The adoption must be worth the kickback plus the risk cost associated with the kickback. This means that kickbacks are typically tendered at large state universities and private colleges where there are prospects of significant-size adoptions (at least one hundred copies, sometimes thousands of copies annually).[10] Kickbacks will also usually be tendered to professors in charge of large sections or members of departmental adoption committees.

The larger the class size per faculty member, the larger the potential kickback, everything else equal. However, a greater risk of being caught and a greater penalty imply a smaller kickback by the publisher with a larger kickback expected by the professor. Nevertheless, fewer faculty members involved in an adoption decision lower the risk of being caught. Consequently, the single professor in charge of a very large section (500 or 1,000 students) is a prime candidate for a substantial kickback and is in a very favorable bargaining position with publishers.

The fact that faculty members are bribed should not be a surprise because adoption decisions are largely private decisions of faculty members. Rarely are such decisions, if ever, questioned by students or scrutinized by university officers who seem to be more concerned with their professors' publication and research records than with their work in the classrooms. Administrators rarely become involved in decisions about textbooks because they have confidence in the professional integrity of their faculty members and because textbook adoption may be considered within the purview of academic freedom.

Of more importance is the fact that many administrators have few private incentives to detect textbook kickbacks. Adoption decisions, even bad ones

---

[10]Many sales representatives never show up on the campuses of small colleges, much less make an effort to bribe the faculty. Furthermore, to the extent that faculty members on small campuses know more of what their colleagues are doing, bribes may be a riskier form of doing business on these campuses.

based on kickbacks, will not, to any significant degree, adversely affect their student enrollments and university revenues. University education is heavily subsidized: the price students pay for tuition, fees, room, and board is typically far less than the students would be willing to pay, even at the margin. Heavy subsidization of education is often revealed in excess demand and selective admission policies. A shortage of university slots for students means that an extra price not captured by university tuition and fees can be extracted from students. As noted in an earlier chapter, this extra price can be extracted in the form of greater work demands imposed on students and little professorial attention given to teaching. It can also be extracted through higher textbook prices, even textbook prices that are inflated by kickbacks. So long as the added price remains relatively low (total textbook expenditures represent a relatively minor part of total student expenses[11]), university enrollment can remain virtually unaffected by any increase in textbook prices. The shortage of university slots may be reduced, but so slightly reduced that no one in higher administration or the funding agency (for example, the state legislature) may be able to detect the cause of the decrease.

THE SOURCES OF GROWING KICKBACKS

The emerging problem of kickbacks in the textbook-selection process may be attributed in part to the general decay in integrity across all professions. It is, perhaps, only wishful thinking to believe that faculty members and publishers possess any greater professional integrity than people in plumbing, journalism, politics, or law.

However, the source of growing kickbacks in academia may be more easily identified. It may be fundamentally and significantly related to the rise of expansive modern university (or megaversity) systems over the decades of the 1960s and 1970s. Growth of universities has increased real faculty salaries in many disciplines and, accordingly, may have drawn into faculties a larger number of people who are only marginally concerned with teaching and the maintenance of professorial integrity and who are relatively more concerned with maximizing their income. Many may be unconcerned with the sources of their incomes, whether money comes, for example, from selling their rights to consulting time or their rights to textbook adoptions.

The expansion of universities has also meant a growing depersonalization of universities, reducing the probability that misconduct will be detected or that meaningful penalties will be exacted.[12] Perhaps more important, uni-

---

[11]Textbook expenditures for an academic year will often total no more than $500, which amounts to less than 10 percent of total university expenses at most public institutions and to as little as 2 percent of total university expenses at exclusive private institutions.

[12]The connection between group or institutional size in terms of membership and the viability of ethical rules of reasonable conduct has been explored with an appropriate review of the literature in Richard B. McKenzie, *The Fairness of Markets: The Search for Justice in a Free*

versity expansion has also led to larger class sizes, increasing the attractiveness of kickbacks as publishers' promotional tools and enhancing the bargaining power of professors who teach large sections.

THE LOCUS OF BLAME

Sales representatives generally understand that their tendered kickbacks are, to a limited extent, wrong. At the very least, most seek to camouflage and legitimize kickbacks in a variety of ways, preferring to make the kickback with food, drink, and educational hardware rather than in cash. However, their perception of *wrong* probably extends to their recognition that the professors involved are violating their fiduciary relationship with their university. After all, the sales representatives are agents of their publishers who want their books adopted by the most efficient means possible, and, as noted, kickbacks to faculty members can be less costly than other available promotional methods. To sales representatives, a kickback may be no more inherently wrong or professionally repugnant than an expenditure on a glossy brochure.

To professors, however, kickbacks may be construed as a breach of trust, if not a violation of an explicit contract. Professors are agents of their universities who are employed to make professional judgments about their courses that are independent of their direct private interests—to the extent reasonably practical. In other words, within the framework of their contracts and commonly recognized professional norms, professors are paid to make decisions on, for example, textbook adoptions, with the interest of their students in mind. Their salary incorporates a premium that should compensate them for the income they refuse to accept from kickbacks tendered by publishers (or by students or educational hardware suppliers).

From this perspective, accepting a kickback from a publisher for an adoption may be morally equivalent to accepting a kickback from a student for a higher grade. Both represent a violation of contract, as well as of trust and professional integrity. A textbook kickback can result in double payment, which is the reason many faculty may find these kickbacks so attractive and irresistible. At least for the short run, a faculty member is paid once in terms of the premium incorporated in his or her salary and then again through the kickback. If such conclusions are not valid, we must wonder why the kickbacks are not widely and openly publicized by professors and publishers.[13]

Society (Lexington, Mass.: Lexington Books, 1987), chap. 2. See also James M. Buchanan, "Ethical Rules, Expected Values, and Large Numbers," *Ethics*, October 1965, pp. 1–13; Roland N. McKean, "Economics of Ethical and Behavioral Codes" (Charlottesville, Va.: Department of Economics, University of Virginia, 1974); and Mancur Olson, *The Logic of Collective Action: Public Goods and the Theory of Groups* (Cambridge, Mass.: Harvard University Press, 1971), especially chap. 4.

[13]This line of analysis, of course, assumes that the adoption bribes are unannounced and held secret from administrators and those responsible for paying university bills, namely students, legislators, and donors.

Faculty members, especially economics professors, may respond that the kickbacks represent efficient trades between professors and publishers and between departments and publishers. "The ability of disc jockeys to obtain payola," writes economist Ronald Coase in discussing the economics of compensation in the broadcasting industry,

> would lower the salary for which they would be prepared to work for radio stations and would therefore increase radio station profits. But disc jockeys would receive a reward for the extra work in which they engaged to obtain payola and so their earnings would also rise. Payola would benefit both operators of radio stations and the disc jockeys.[14]

Kickbacks could conceivably lower the prices of textbooks, since these payments would be less expensive than other forms of sales promotions. Textbooks are very much alike, and it does not seem to matter very much which textbooks are adopted. Prices of textbooks are set competitively, meaning that they will not be raised because of the existence of kickbacks. In other words, kickbacks are Pareto efficient.

This line of argument can at least be considered in light of differences between the radio and education markets, all of which raise questions about the efficiency as well as the fairness of kickbacks. First, the efficiency-based argument for kickbacks ignores the fact that agreed-upon rules may have been violated.[15]

Second, the kickbacks are almost always unannounced, indicating that kickbacks may often be (but not necessarily always are) a form of fraud. Kickbacks violate the grounds on which students and their parents, legislators, and donors make their payments to universities.

Third, any argument that kickbacks are efficient overlooks the fact that there are third parties, including students, alumni, and other supporters of the universities. Kickbacks paid to faculty members and departments marginally reduce the ability of universities to extract payments in other forms (tuition and higher work standards) and, to that extent, reallocate university resources in ways that may not be efficient. Through deception, faculty members and departments within a university can exploit the publicness of the

---

[14]Coase, "Payola in Radio and Television Broadcasting," p. 308. When the payola argument is applied to universities, there are two critical assumptions. First, university labor markets are competitive in the sense that wages are determined by the forces of supply and demand within reasonable limits. Second, the kickbacks are known to administrators and professors in general; indeed, they encourage them. The value of the kickbacks are then reflected in a greater supply of professors and in reduced wages for affected faculty. Efficiency in the allocation of resources is achieved by administrators and professors knowingly deciding how and from what source compensation will be paid.

[15]An argument that adoption bribery is efficient because it improves the welfare of both parties, the publisher and the professor, could be driven to what is likely to be considered (by most professors) an absurd conclusion: the selling of higher grades is also efficient because it benefits both parties, the student and the professor. The line of argument ignores the long-run consequences on reputation and quality of graduates.

reputation of their university, a reputation asserting that adoption decisions are made on academic grounds, rather than on private interest. If kickbacks became sufficiently widespread, over time university reputations can be damaged through an accumulation of independent decisions by individual faculty members and departments that at times result in adoptions of marginally inferior books; the damage to reputations can lower the demand for university education. Reduced demand can, in turn, lower the quality of students in classes and can lower the academic standards of universities.

Over the long run kickbacks can lead publishers to substitute on the margin kickbacks for the currency, cogency, and accuracy of their textbooks, which can marginally destroy the value of a university education. Because of the attractiveness of kickbacks, publishers may reason that such matters as the usefulness of their textbooks to professors and their students will not be as influential in determining adoption decisions. Accordingly, publishers may be inclined to sacrifice the quality of their texts for kickbacks in their sales promotions.

POLICY OPTIONS

The central theme of this essay is that kickbacks for textbook adoptions can be inefficient, as well as a wrong, and wrongheaded, policy. Kickbacks on textbook adoptions can amount to a form of fraud for universities that portray faculty decisions on textbooks as being reflections of professional integrity and independent of the financial interests of faculty members.

A governmental ban on academic kickbacks would not likely lead to improved market efficiency. Universities operate under market conditions different from that of the general economy. Obviously, faculty members can be paid (as they are paid) in many ways. There is no reason to believe that market efficiency would be improved by governmentally ensuring that *all* universities provide the same types of compensation. At the same time, it does not follow that academic fraud should be permitted solely in the name of academic freedom. The only viable policy option that will accommodate the varied circumstances of textbook adoption decisions is the strict application of laws against fraud. Universities will need to clarify their kickback policies, if they intend to allow kickbacks to continue. "Let the student (or parent) beware" may be the warning many universities and colleges should post at the campus gates.

CONCLUDING COMMENTS

Nothing that has been written is intended to imply that kickbacks are widespread. However, neither are they an uncommon practice. No one really knows the extent of the practice; more information on the subject is sorely needed. All that is really known is that in universities kickbacks are a growing phenomenon. Where kickbacks are not announced, they represent a potential form of academic fraud.

Nonetheless, a subsidiary point of this discussion is that the emergence of adoption kickbacks in covert forms should be expected to accompany growth in universities and increases in the size of university classes. In many important ways, it is not unreasonable to say that largeness in nonmarket settings breeds corruption.[16] Students who are not paying the full price of their education have only a partial incentive to be mindful of corruption. Administrators, physically detached from their funding sources and from their faculties whom they manage only casually, also have limited incentive to uncover corruption within professorial ranks.

However, it is not unreasonable to expect adoption kickbacks to proliferate. Universities are continuing to expand, and class sizes seem to be limited only by the potential wattage of public-address systems. More and more, faculty members are becoming aware of the income potential of their adoption decisions. More and more, publishers are learning that they must also enter the competitive kickback arena and they are finding faculty members willing to participate in creative disguises.

Where universities give the impression that decisions on textbooks and faculty income are independent, it is not unreasonable to expect that, at some point, students and parents will learn of kickbacks accepted by their professors and sue their universities. Unfortunately for professors who are not tempted by kickbacks, such legal actions are likely to lead to more administrative meddling in departmental affairs and greater administrative control of adoption decisions.

Just as unfortunately, for those universities that wish to restrict their faculty from accepting kickbacks, available solutions are few. These universities could control the sizes of their classes, but there is little hope that such a solution will be viewed as cost effective. The only other solution is for universities to announce strong opposition to adoption kickbacks and to take strong and immediate action—firing professors who accept kickbacks or filing criminal charges against professors who violate antikickback policies. Given bureaucratic inertia, however, most universities will probably wait until the kickback problem has become a legal crisis before investigating the problem. Universities are not likely to adopt policies to solve the problem unless they are induced or forced to take such action.

QUESTIONS TO PONDER

1. Would you object if you were told that your professor received a kickback for the adoption of this book? Explain your answer.

---

[16]This point is developed in general terms in Buchanan, "Ethical Rules, Expected Values, and Large Numbers."

2. Would it be more or less efficient for a university to allow kickbacks but announce the kickbacks to their students?

3. Do you agree that payola in the radio business would improve economic efficiency? Would laws against payola improve economic efficiency? What would be the consequences of eliminating current laws against payola?

CHAPTER 24

Does the NCAA Exploit College Athletes?[1]

The National Collegiate Athletic Association (NCAA) is under increasing attack for its rules governing the recruitment and retention of athletes. Few inside or outside colleges and universities seem to be satisfied with the NCAA's rules, criticizing the NCAA for being both too strict and too lenient in the rules it makes and enforces. And cheating on NCAA rules appears to be widespread, if not rampant, as evidenced by the number and prestige of colleges and universities that have been penalized for rule infractions in recent years.

Most academic administrators and much of the general public appear to be worried that the NCAA has failed to establish reasonable academic standards college athletes must meet to attend college and to restrict the payments, overt and covert, that member colleges and their supporters can make to athletes.[2] As columnist Frederick Klein has noted:

> Young athletes (we're talking about teenagers here), some with meager academic credentials, are enticed to campuses with the promise of an education, and then tied to team-practice schedules that don't give them time to pursue one. Many are placed in Mickey Mouse courses, awarded grades they don't earn, or both. When their eligibility for sports expires, they are cast adrift.[3]

---

[1]This chapter is a revised version of an article published jointly by Thomas Sullivan and one of the authors, Richard McKenzie [*The Antitrust Bulletin* (Summer, 1987), pp. 373–399]. The authors of this book are indebted to Thomas Sullivan for his contribution and for his permission to republish the article here in revised form.

[2]Three of 110 proposed rule changes created an unusual amount of controversy within the ranks of NCAA colleges in 1985 and 1986. The three most controversial rule changes are: (1) Freshmen entering Division I colleges would be required to have a grade-point average of 2.0 in their high school core curriculum and a minimum combined score on their Scholastic Aptitude Test of 700 or 15 on the American College Testing program. (2) A drug-screening program (with tests and penalties) would be instituted for national championships and football bowl games. (3) Boosters would be barred from all contact with prospective athletes. Charles S. Farrell, "NCAA Members to Vote on 110 Proposals to Change Governing Rules Covering College Sports," *Education* (November 20, 1985), pp. 29–32.

[3]Frederick C. Klein, "Designated Villains," *The Wall Street Journal*, October 16, 1985, p. 28.

On the other hand, many members of the media and economics profession appear convinced that existing NCAA rules represent an egregious, as well as inefficient, attempt by colleges to monopolize their athletic labor markets and to suppress the wages and fringe benefits paid student-athletes.[4]

After noting that in 1984 the U.S. Supreme Court found that the NCAA violated the nation's antitrust laws with its rules governing the televising of football games, University of Chicago economist Gary Becker stressed that "the NCAA's real monopoly power is over athletes":

> This is why the association's rules on payments to athletes are a more serious restraint of trade than were its restrictions on televising football games. The NCAA limits not only the number and size of scholarships but also such matters as compensation to athletes for summer employment, when colleges can approach high school players, and when transfer students from other colleges are eligible to play. These rules are designed mainly to reduce the competition among colleges for players in football and basketball—the two top revenue-producing college sports.[5]

Almost all critics detect significant hypocrisy in the NCAA's enforcement activity; several have called for reform including outright payments to student athletes on the grounds that "[m]aintenance of the present system can only continue to produce victims, not beneficiaries. A young athlete who couldn't get in the door of a college otherwise is underpaid while he is there and too often denied compensation that any school can afford, an education with which he can discern hypocrisy and avoid its consequences."[6] After listing several colleges recently found guilty of violating NCAA rules, the *New York Times* editorialized for open payments to athletes:

> The full roster of known wrongdoers is much longer [than the seven colleges listed], and for every college actually caught, dozens go undetected. The rules

---

[4]See Armen Alchian and William R. Allen, *Exchange and Production: Competition, Coordination, and Control,* 2d ed. (1977), pp. 210–12. The authors of this book made the mistake of adapting the cartel argument in their own textbook, Richard B. McKenzie and Gordon Tullock, *Modern Political Economy* (1978), p. 271. Clemson University economist Robert McCormick has written:

> [T]he real reason for the NCAA's existence is to cartelize college athletics. Like all good cartels, the NCAA has rules limiting competition between institutions that prevent the monetary value generated by fine athletes from going to the athletes. . . . The NCAA cartel makers are determined to make sure that competition does not break out that would allow very talented young athletes to be compensated for the valuable services they provide. [Robert E. McCormick, "Colleges Get Their Athletes for a Song," *The Wall Street Journal,* August 20, 1985, p. 27.]

[5]Gary S. Becker, "College Athletes Should Get Paid What They Are Worth," *Business Week,* September 30, 1985, p. 18.

[6]Larry E. Howell, "College Athletes Are Underpaid," *The Wall Street Journal,* October 29, 1985, p. 31, a letter to the editor in response to Frederick Klein's column "Designated Villains."

require pretending that the players are really students, a patent lie at many institutions. So why not just let universities hire players to wear their colors and earn a decent living while they prepare for the pros? Selfishness is one reason. . . . But if the country won't go cold honest, let it at least recognize that many players are not serious students, need to be recruited with money and paid at least something while in school.[7]

The hypocrisy in the NCAA system is, according to some, patently evident in the differential treatment of a music student and a student-athlete. Both may have narrow academic goals, but only one—the student-athlete—is not permitted to sell his or her talents at market value.[8] As columnist Edwin Yoder has noted,

If you're a college student working on the student newspaper with a view to a career in journalism, taking a bit of pay for it will not affect, let alone impair, your "eligibility" or your eventual marketability as a professional. But if you're a basketball player, participating in what is theoretically a parallel "student activity," all hell breaks loose if you openly take a dime for doing it.[9]

Mr. Yoder added that while outright payments might "dash the phoney romance of 'Amateurism,' . . . a bit of honest corruption would be a drastic improvement over what we have now."[10]

The criticisms of the NCAA are plentiful; our purpose in this chapter is not to add to them. On the contrary, our central purpose is to reassess the conventional claims of economists that wages of student-athletes are suppressed by the NCAA as evidenced by the existence of NCAA rules and the persistence of flagrant cheating.

Our reassessment leads to strikingly unconventional conclusions: Most important, athletes' wages are not materially suppressed by the NCAA. Indeed, NCAA rules likely enhance the demand for student-athletes and increase their wages and employment opportunities in college athletics. We conclude that market economists have overlooked important checks on the powers of the NCAA to exploit athletes exist and that current moves to force the NCAA to permit its member colleges to pay athletes competitive wages are misguided. Athletes' wages can be expected to be adjusted over time in response to market forces.[11]

---

[7]"Colleges Majoring in Scandal," *New York Times,* April 17, 1985, p. 22, editorial.
[8]McCormick, "Colleges Get Their Athletes."
[9]Edwin M. Yoder, "College Athletic System Corrupt," *Greenville (S.C.) News* (June 28, 1985), p. 4A.
[10]Ibid.
[11]There is nothing in our argument that suggests that the NCAA member-colleges should not make payments over and above tuition and room and board. Our thesis is simply that market forces can be expected to determine the extent of payment. A requirement that the

We begin by reviewing the conventional economic argument on how an employer cartel, which the NCAA is alleged to be, can suppress worker wages. This cartel theory relies on the uncritical acceptance of an unfounded presumption that 850 or more colleges can form through the NCAA an effective, workable cartel and that this employer cartel can be maintained even without legal restrictions barring entry into the athletic labor markets by other sports associations that permit competitive wage payments to athletes. We find no legal barriers to the emergence and entry of alternative sports associations into athletic labor markets.

In the absence of legal barriers to entry, the NCAA rules are prudent measures by colleges to increase the demand for intercollegiate athletics and college education. The NCAA rules are an efficient contract among participants in a joint venture; they are similar in character and purpose to the rules franchisors impose on their franchisees.

In fact, the observed cheating on NCAA rules is to be expected, as it is in franchise markets, because of the common benefits the colleges' joint sports venture entails. Cheating by colleges is evidence of the public-goods character of the objectives of the NCAA rather than prima facie evidence of a cartelized labor market.[12] Penalties on violators of NCAA rules are no less necessary, and no less expected, than penalties franchisors impose on franchisees.

THE CONVENTIONAL CARTEL ARGUMENT

Economists have leveled three major charges against the NCAA. First, the NCAA operates as an employer cartel that suppresses athletes' wages. Second, it creates market inefficiency and transfers income from athletes to coaches and colleges. Third, the NCAA breeds hypocrisy and cheating on rules. Implicit in these criticisms is the charge that temporary problems of over- or underpayments to athletes are not subject to self-correction through market pressures. Hence, the presumed monopsony power of the NCAA must be corrected from outside the collegiate athletic market through, for example, antitrust prosecution or new laws that would correct the NCAA's market power and force colleges to pay higher wages to athletes.

The NCAA as a Cartel

The argument that the NCAA is a working cartel that suppresses athletes' wages (including fringe benefits) is grounded in the conventional microeconomic argument that labor-market competition among independent

---

NCAA be forced to allow payments of any particular amount, or bidding for athletes through the abolition of rules, is misguided.

[12]Public goods are goods the benefits of which are shared by all within the relevant community.

employers dissipates quasi rents that would otherwise go to employers.[13] The wages paid athletes by all colleges is raised by their bidding against one another in an effort to employ additional athletes when the wage is below the athletes' marginal value. Competition may help employ more athletes than otherwise would be employed, and the efficient employment level may be achieved.[14]

In the competitive process, however, revenue from sporting events is transferred from colleges (or, more precisely, their athletic departments) to athletes. In technical terms, the labor market competition results in reciprocal *pecuniary externalities* imposed by colleges on each other.[15]

For colleges contemplating the formation of a labor market cartel, the competitive results are an unnecessary increase in the wage bill and an unnecessary reduction in the profits from college athletics. If they were not dissipated, the sports profits could be used to increase the salaries of coaches and athletic directors or could be transferred to nonathletic programs.

To keep the potential sports profits out of the hands of athletes, according to the NCAA's critics, colleges have an understandable desire to suppress their intercollegiate athletic competition. The NCAA's rules on the employment and payment of athletes are seen by some as workable devices for suppressing colleges' demand for college athletes and, thereby, labor-market competition and wages.[16]

Ideally, the NCAA should form a cartel and act as a monopsony to *maximize* profits. Through the development of appropriate employment rules (such as market restrictions on the payments that can be made to athletes and the number of scholarships that can be granted), it should depress the intercol-

---

[13]Quasi rent is the amount by which the wage rate exceeds the resources' opportunity cost, or next best alternative employment.

[14]The efficient employment level occurs when the marginal value of the last worker employed equals his or her marginal opportunity cost. The efficient employment level is achieved when no further trades between employers and employees can be made, which graphically occurs at the intersection of the supply and demand for labor curves. In competitive markets, the wage rate, which is subject to competitive pressures, drives the market to the intersection of their supply and demand curves. At that intersection, the marginal value and cost of the last worker are equal.

[15]*Pecuniary externalities* are financial costs competitors suffer from bidding for scarce resources and goods and services. They result in improved market efficiency.

[16]One set of authors write in technical economic terms,

The essence of these rules is that players cannot be paid according to their marginal revenue product [MRP]. Rather, they are paid a uniform wage in-kind, consisting of a scholarship, room and board, and expense allowance, and so on. The problem is that, in an era of modern college athletics, many (if not most) players have MRP's in excess of the value of their stipulated payments. Seen in this light, the NCAA is a mechanism by which schools capture rents from student-athletes.

Arthur A. Fleisher III, Brian L. Goff, William F. Shughart II, and Robert D. Tollison, "Crime and Punishment: Enforcement of the NCAA Football Cartel" (Fairfax, Va.: Center for the Study of Public Choice, George Mason University, working paper, December 1985).

legiate demand for student-athletes below competitive levels until the marginal cost of the last athlete hired equals his or her marginal value.[17]

Market Inefficiency and Income Transfers

The expected market consequences of the NCAA rules include reduced wages and employment opportunities for student-athletes, greater profits for colleges, market inefficiency, and a transfer of income from many low-income athletes to higher-income coaches and other members of the athletic staffs.[18] Because of the suppressed labor-market demand, wages and employment opportunities for athletes will fall, and fewer athletes will be hired because fewer will be available for employment at the lower wages.[19]

Because student-athletes are paid less than their market marginal value, monopsony rents will be collected by colleges. The intercollegiate athletic labor market exhibits inefficiency because the number of athletes actually hired is less than the competitive level and the marginal value of additional athletes will exceed their opportunity costs. The gap between the marginal value and opportunity cost of athletes necessarily means that some athletes are forced to employ their talents where they are less valuable than in college athletics.[20]

In addition, critics say the NCAA as an employer-cartel suppresses the incomes of some of the more disadvantaged college students because many athletes are black and come from low-income backgrounds. These income transfers are occasionally denounced by economists who typically maintain analytical neutrality. For example, Professor Becker writes:

> The NCAA's efforts to justify its restrictions on competition for athletes should be viewed with suspicion because they increase the financial benefits colleges receive from football, basketball, and other sports. I would have expected greater hostility from Congress and the courts to a policy that lowers the earnings of young blacks and other athletes with limited opportunities.[21]

---

[17]When viewed from the perspective of all colleges in the athletic labor market, the marginal cost of the last student-athlete hired exceeds the wage (and his or her marginal value) by the amount of the reciprocal pecuniary externalities. By suppressing the labor demand and hiring fewer athletes through the development of NCAA rules, colleges can reduce their collective marginal cost of labor until it no longer exceeds the athletes' marginal value. When the colleges' cost is reduced by more than their revenue, their collective profits must rise.

[18]Nonathletic members of the colleges' administrations and faculties are thought to support the NCAA wages rules because of the presumed transfer of rents from the athletic programs to the nonathletic programs.

[19]Graphically, the demand for labor and wages fall below competitive levels because of the NCAA's rules. The suppressed wages will cause athletes to move down their labor supply curves.

[20]The extent of the market inefficiency equals the difference between the collective value of all athletes that are not hired under the cartel but would have been hired under a competitive labor market minus their combined opportunity costs.

[21]Becker, "College Athletes Should Get Paid."

And Professor Robert McCormick notes:

> Some student athletes, especially blacks, come from very poor families. The NCAA only allows school scholarships to pay for tuition, room and board, and books, and prohibits students from working during the school year. One would think that administrators would be ashamed to prevent these students from being given small sums that would allow them to dress and socialize like the more well-heeled students. Perhaps it salves the consciences of some university presidents to deplore the plight of black workers in South Africa because of the exploitation they promote on their campuses.[22]

Cheating on NCAA Rules

If the NCAA is perceived as a cartel, cheating on NCAA rules is to be anticipated. Each school can reason that because athletes' wages are below their market value, additional profits can be made by skirting the NCAA rules and paying more than the NCAA allows—attracting better athletes, larger attendances, more lucrative television contracts and greater national publicity. Understanding its own incentives to cheat on the cartel rules allows each college to further reason that other colleges will be induced to cheat and that it must cheat to remain competitive.

Indeed, the coaches who may benefit through higher-than-competitive market salaries from the cartel rules will have a real personal incentive to cheat or to allow cheating to persist by those around them. Coaches who do not cheat or allow, and even encourage, cheating may lose their salaries laden with economic rents to others who are willing to cheat and, therefore, are better able to attract larger attendances, television coverage, and national prominence.

THE COUNTERARGUMENTS

Although it is clear that a monopsony can suppress worker wages, it is not at all clear that the NCAA is a monopsony or even an employer cartel capable of acting like a monopsony. As argued below, proponents of the cartel theory of NCAA rules draw several highly dubious, if not seriously defective, conclusions founded on the unsubstantiated presumption that the NCAA is a monopsony.

The Mistaken Presumption of Underpaid Athletes

Proponents of the cartel theory implicitly, if not explicitly, conclude that resources are misallocated because athletes are underpaid for their services. The presumed prima facie evidence is the NCAA rule that restricts colleges from offering more than the equivalent of room, board, and tuition. However,

[22]McCormick, "Colleges Get Their Athletes."

the critical pay variable determining the allocation of resources is the *expected*, not *actual*, pay of athletes. The expected pay of college athletes is typically greater than their actual pay by an amount equal to their scholarships plus the present discounted value of future income from professional employment.

Granted, few college athletes make professional teams. Many football and basketball players, however, could turn professional before their college eligibility is finished.[23] The fact that many athletes—including most of the better athletes—voluntarily use up their college eligibility before turning pro suggests that their extra year or years spent in college sports provide valuable on-the-job training and media exposure, and a resulting increase in their expected lifetime income that more than compensates for the loss of income during their college years.

Herschel Walker, for example, played his junior year at the University of Georgia when he could have turned professional and earned several hundred thousand dollars, if not more than a million dollars. Because he stayed at Georgia his junior year, he must have expected the nonmonetary benefits of an extra year in college (including the prospects of receiving the Heisman Trophy, which he did receive) and the added lifetime income from the greater experience exceeded the professional salary he would have received had he turned professional.[24]

For athletes with less talent than Herschel Walker, the years of college experience may be more valuable because they offer more opportunities for improvement of skills, media exposure, education. The increase in the present discounted value of the less-talented athletes' future income may be greater than for many of the more talented athletes.[24]

The Mistaken Interpretation of Cheating

Proponents of the cartel theory of college sports mistakenly conclude that the existence of cheating is prima facie evidence of an employer cartel that exploits athletes by materially depressing labor-market demand and athletes' wages. The existence of rules and the persistence of cheating, however,

---

[23]Indeed, the value of college experience to athletes is clearly indicated by the number of high school athletes that could follow the lead of basketball player Moses Malone and try out for the professional ranks directly out of high school. Admittedly, there are few high school athletes that could successfully make the transition as did Malone, but that is, again, only a way of asserting the value of college athletics.

[24]Admittedly, there are restrictions on the ability of players to enter the National Football League (NFL) draft. (College football players cannot be drafted until they have used their college eligibility or until they are declared "hardship cases.") However, such draft restrictions also could be construed as devices to ensure the long-run viability of college athletics. In addition, the NFL draft restrictions do not prevent colleges from seceding from the NCAA and paying players what are thought to be competitive wages. If anything, the NFL restrictions represent barriers of entry to the NFL for players, not barriers to entry for collegiate sports associations or barriers to exit from the NCAA.

could be the product of voluntary collective efforts of member colleges to engage in a demand-enhancing joint venture. The joint venture may be characterized as the enhancement of the colleges' competitive athletics and internal and external support for nonathletic, as well as athletic, programs, which can be most effectively accomplished by ensuring that college athletics remains amateur. The members may believe quite correctly that the public's demand for college education may be significantly reduced by the creation of professional or semiprofessional college sports.

The joint-venture problem and the rules that emerge may be comparable to the quality-control problem faced by most sellers of brand names and franchises. For example, McDonald's restaurants collectively produce a joint product, that is, a reputation for fast service for foods of a certain type and quality in reasonably clean facilities. Like the NCAA, the McDonald's Corporation also has detailed rules and restrictions for their franchises to follow. These restrictions cover such details of operation as cleanliness of the kitchens and dining areas, the recipes for the products served, the parking facilities, and the amount of time customers should have to stand in line. The restrictions establish uniformity in product and service with the intent of enhancing the reputation of McDonald's restaurants, increasing the demand for McDonald's products at all outlets and increasing the corporation's profits.[25]

The individual franchises are willing to consent to the prospects of paying the penalties for violations because they understand that McDonald's overall reputation across all franchises is important to their own individual franchise profits. The franchisees willingly accept the restrictions on their own behavior to ensure that there are limits on the behavior of others.

At the same time, each franchisee has an incentive to cheat on the restrictions. By cheating—that is, for example, by not cleaning regularly or by adding soy bean meal to their hamburgers—an individual franchisee can lower their own production costs and can raise their own profits. Each also can rightfully reason that the franchisor's reputation in general may be only marginally, if not inconsequentially, damaged by its own violations. Each franchisee understands, however, that all other franchisees have a similar incentive to cheat. If the benefits of improved market demand did not more than compensate for the added costs franchise owners incur to avoid penalties, the restrictions would presumably never be accepted. (And franchises would not command such high prices.)

Like the McDonald's restrictions, NCAA rules and regulations can be viewed as means to enhance the reputation of all associated with college athletes—including athletes and nonathletes—by keeping college sports non-

---

[25]Admittedly, McDonald's does not restrict wage payments made by franchises to their employees. However, it does restrict the prices they can charge.

professional.[26] NCAA members willingly accept restrictions on payments to athletes to enhance the demand for college athletics, college enrollment, and contributions to athletic and nonathletic programs. Each NCAA member understands, however, that every other member has an incentive to cheat on the rules of the joint venture. From this perspective, penalties are required because, as in the case of McDonald's restaurants, cheating can be expected when the benefits from the joint venture are common to all participating members.[27]

To the extent that the demand for college athletics is enhanced by the NCAA's system of rules and penalties, the demand for athletes will increase their sports opportunities. More college teams will survive and prosper.[28]

The Mistaken Presumption of Monopsony Power

Proponents of the cartel theory mistakenly assume that because the NCAA includes 850 members—virtually all major collegiate sports teams—it has significant monopsony power that enables member colleges to suppress athletes' wages. The proponents acknowledge that colleges have substantial private incentives to cartelize their markets. They overlook, however, the

---

[26]Exactly why the member-colleges believe the NCAA will further the interests of the colleges through a joint venture is of no consequence to the argument. There may actually be various types of benefits received by different schools, just as there may be various types of benefits received by the different McDonald's franchises. The critical requirement is that benefits from a joint venture are perceived.

[27]As would be true of all ventures in which joint action results in benefits to all that have some durability (through, for example, the creation of a "reputation" for amateur sports), individual participants—for example, players—have an additional short-term incentive to free ride by cheating. Each athlete can reason that if he or she accepts side payments, his or her payments may never be uncovered and, even if they are uncovered, may have no detectable effect on his or her own expected income over the expected relatively short time involved in a college education. The reputation benefits for amateur sports in college may evaporate with rampant cheating; each athlete can reason, however, that he or she will have long completed his or her college career when the joint-venture benefits do evaporate. That is to say, there are inevitable tensions between the short-term interests of athletes (and coaches and, for that matter, all others whose stay at colleges is perceived to be short-term) and the long-term interests of colleges as institutions.

[28]In addition, more athletic talent at lower wages will be available for the professional ranks, which may explain professional teams' support of the NCAA system of rules and regulations. Proponents of the cartel theory of college sports have a difficult time explaining professional teams' support of the NCAA rules. If the NCAA were a cartel that suppressed wages and employment opportunities for athletes, the supply of athletes available for the professional ranks would be reduced, increasing the wages professional teams must pay. Also, when wages are suppressed by a cartel, we do not anticipate a surplus of labor that would spur nonprice competition in the form of talent improvement. If anything, a cartel that seriously suppressed wages would induce a reduction in athletic talent available to the college and professional ranks.

critically important, and patently obvious, fact that the NCAA members are not a *single unified* firm, but are a collection of many independent firms with different cost structures and different market demands. They have the same incentive to improve their profits by cheating on the cartel—even forming alternative collegiate or semiprofessional sports associations that permit explicit wage payments to athletes—as they do to form the cartel in the first place.[29]

In other words, the proponents of the cartel theory fail to explain how any effective, exploitive sports cartel can be maintained in the long run in the absence of forced membership or barriers to exit from the NCAA by member colleges, and barriers to entry into the sports market by alternative sports associations.[30]

If the NCAA seriously depresses athletes' wages, the temptation of member colleges to drop their membership and form another association that permits competitive wage payments would appear to be overwhelming. Proponents of the cartel theory cannot escape with the argument that several teams must agree to form an alternative association. Their argument that the NCAA actually is an effective cartel suggests that such an endeavor is a viable possibility. In addition, conferences and the College Football Association (CFA) that are a part of the NCAA are already well organized to secede from the NCAA as a unit and to establish alternative sports associations that would allow payments to athletes if the NCAA is not responsive to market forces and member schools. The existing associations—the National Association of Intercollegiate Athletics (NAIA) and the National Little College Athletic Association (NLCAA)—could take advantage of the alleged NCAA's exploitation of athletes and allow payment.

If athletes were seriously exploited under the NCAA, the seceding teams or conferences may reasonably expect that their exit would induce other

---

[29]Even Professor Becker acknowledges the legitimacy of the incentive to cheat on cartels:

> Since collusion, even if by merger, is the only way to internalize and thus incorporate these effects, one might expect every industry to evolve into an effectively monopolized one. But just as all firms together have a strong incentive to depart from the competitive solution, each separately has an equally strong incentive to depart from monopoly solution. . . . Since all firms want to expand output, collusion has a tendency to break down because of "chiseling" by the members. Each firm, in effect, hopes that all others act monopolistically while it acts competitively.

Gary S. Becker, *Economic Theory* (1971), pp. 99–100. Professor Becker recognizes that the effectiveness of a cartel depends on the costs imposed on violators for departing from the cartel agreement. In the sports market, this means that the NCAA would have to have a means of imposing sufficient costs on colleges for seceding from the NCAA and setting up their own sports association that would allow for payment of athletes to more than cover the benefits of seccession.

[30]Many economists who argue that the NCAA is an effective employer cartel would be the first to contend that it would be extremely difficult, if not impossible, for a collection of 850 firms in any other industry to maintain an effective cartel in any other product or resource market.

teams and conferences to follow suit.[31] Those that do secede will be the ones attracting the more sought-after athletes and presumably would benefit from larger attendance and television contracts to the detriment of remaining NCAA colleges. In fact, entrepreneurs outside of college athletic departments searching for sports profits should be willing to organize the necessary critical number of schools.[32] The openness of the association market is important because the emergence (or the threat of emergence) of alternative sports employment opportunities would cause wages of athletes to rise to approximately competitive levels.

The logical extension of the proponents' own cartel premise leads to the inescapable conclusion that if there were not something intrinsically important to colleges in their efforts to maintain the pretense, if not the substance, of amateur athletics in colleges, the NCAA rules would not last long in the absence of significant barriers to exit from the NCAA or to entry into the sports association industry.[33] And these barriers would have to be legal.

COLLEGE ATHLETICS AS AN OPEN MARKET: A LEGAL REVIEW

A review of antitrust law supports our central thesis that the NCAA acts not as a cartel but as a demand-enhancing joint venture. Court rulings on collegiate athletic restrictions are not only compatible with our view of the function and purposes of the restrictions, but they also indicate that no legal barriers exist in antitrust law to prevent entry of rival leagues, conferences, or associations of leagues and conferences. That colleges voluntarily enter conferences and join the NCAA as member colleges for the purpose of producing an entertainment product of a given kind and quality through joint control and regulation is evidenced by experience and legal approval.

The fact that colleges join the NCAA or combine in conferences to implement rules and regulations governing the production and marketing of college sports does not make the colleges per se "competitors in any economic

---

[31]The NAIA and the NLCAA could expand their sports programs considerably by allowing for payments.

[32]It would appear that officials of the NCAA or athletic associations in other countries would take advantage of their experience with running sports associations and their understanding of the exploitive rules of the NCAA and seek to organize alternative sports associations by enlisting the support of colleges, if not of their conferences.

[33]Proponents of the cartel thesis might react, as they have reacted in private conversation with the authors, that if member colleges are capable of cohering over the long run within the NCAA to produce a joint product, they are every bit as capable of cohering within the NCAA to cartelize the market for the purpose of suppressing athletes' wages. The argument is a non sequitur, mainly because of the brand-name benefits of being associated with the NCAA. Membership in the NCAA would collapse if there were no brand-name benefits—no demand-enhancing benefits—associated with membership: Few schools would long endure the penalties (which run into the millions of dollars), that the NCAA imposes for infraction of rules.

sense," even though they "compete on the playing field."[34] Without cooperation and regulation, college sports may not exist at all, or if existing, would
not be as healthy an enterprise as they are. Joint action is a precondition to
the existence and success of the product, if for no other reason than that
athletic games require rules to define the boundaries within which competition will be allowed to prevail and to make the game interesting and mutually
beneficial to the participants and fans.[35] That restrictions on players are
needed may only prove the existence of ancillary or incidental restraints
necessary for the success of the joint venture.[36] Antitrust law has long sanctioned restraints that are ancillary or incidental to otherwise lawful combinations. (The legal analysis is extended in the appendix to this chapter.)

By their nature, games require rules that amount to restrictions on competitive impulses. Rules against the restriction of payments to athletes may
be seen from this perspective as materially the same as rules against changing
the goal line or payments to referees intended to affect their calls during the
game. Restrictions on payments of many kinds may be useful devices for
increasing the extent to which competitive energies are directed toward improving players' skills and the quality of competitive play.

CONCLUDING COMMENTS

Our analysis leads inextricably to the conclusion that the conventional
economic wisdom regarding the intent and consequences of NCAA restrictions on the recruitment and retention of athletes is wrong and misleading.
The conventional wisdom is wrong in suggesting that, as a general proposition, college athletes are materially underpaid and are exploited, that cheating on NCAA rules is prima facie evidence of a cartel intended to suppress
athletes' wages, that NCAA rules violate conventional antitrust doctrine, and
that barriers to entry ensure the continuance of the NCAA's monopsony
powers over athletes. No such barriers exist. In addition, our reading of the
Supreme Court's decision in *NCAA* indicates that the NCAA would be unable
to prevent through the courts the emergence of competing athletic associations (see the appendix). The actual existence of other athletic associations
indicates entry is not only possible but also practical if athletes wages were
materially suppressed.

Conventional economic analysis of NCAA rules also is misleading in
suggesting that collegiate sports would be improved if the NCAA were denied the authority to regulate the payment of athletes. Given the absence of
legal barriers to entry into the athletic association market, it appears that if
athletes' wages were suppressed, alternative sports associations would form
or expand, and the NCAA would be unable to maintain its presumed monopsony market position.

---

[34]*Smith v. Pro Football, Inc.*, 593 F.2d 1173, 1179 (D.C. Cir. 1978).
[35]Ibid., p. 1179.

From our interpretation of NCAA rules, it does not follow necessarily that athletes should receive any more compensation than they do currently. Clearly, market conditions change, and NCAA rules often must be adjusted to accommodate those changes.[36] Absent entry barriers, we can expect the NCAA to adjust, as it has adjusted, in a competitive manner its rules of play, recruitment, and retention of athletes.[37] Our central point is that contrary to the proponents of the monopsony thesis, the collegiate athletic market is subject to the self-correcting mechanism of market pressures. There is reason to believe that proposed extension of the antitrust prosecution to the NCAA rules and/or proposed changes in sports law explicitly or implicitly recommended by the proponents of the cartel thesis would not only be unnecessary, but also would be counterproductive.

QUESTIONS TO PONDER

1. Is there an economic difference between ruling out side payments to referees and ruling out side payment to players?
2. Can athletes be better off by having restrictions on their wages?
3. If athletes are exploited by the NCAA, why don't private firms develop sports teams?

---

[36]Indeed, to the extent that the NCAA is successful in increasing the demand for college athletics, we would expect athletes' wages to rise. Given the increase in the price of attending college relative to the prices of other goods, the wages of athletes have effectively risen over time.

[37]Farrell, "NCAA Members to Vote," pp. 29–32.

APPENDIX
The Legal History

In this chapter we maintained that antitrust law has for a long time sanctioned restraints on trade that are ancillary or incidental to otherwise lawful combinations. Our purpose in this appendix is to support that claim with a review of court findings. Contrary to the claims of the cartel proponents, the nontelevision restraints of the NCAA are not in violation of U.S. antitrust, at least as interpreted by the courts to the date of this writing.

The ancillary restraint doctrine was established as early as 1898 as an accepted American rule of interpretation of the Sherman Act.[38] In *United States* v. *Addyston Pipe and Steel Co.*,[39] Judge Taft held that a contract or combination that produces an ancillary restraint is nevertheless reasonable and lawful as long as the main purpose of the contract, transaction, or combination was lawful and the restraint is limited in time, place, and manner of enforcement. The underlying rationale of the ancillary-restraint doctrine is based on the premise that the incidental restraint enhances the efficiency of the main agreement.[40] Throughout the history of the Sherman Act, the doctrine has enjoyed wide application and acceptance, including the sports market.

In *Smith* v. *Pro Football, Inc.*,[41] the District of Columbia Circuit applied the doctrine to its initial analysis of the National Football League (NFL) regulation of the player draft. The court recognized that the NFL was a legal combination in the traditional antitrust sense. Joint cooperation was essential for the production of professional football. Normal market forces did not operate in the sports market because teams and leagues are not "interested in driving [other teams] out of business, whether in the counting-house or on the football field, for if the league fails, no one team can survive."[42] The joint venture produced a new product; it also produced restrictions on the actions of members of the league and players. A rule of reason was used to judge the legality of the regulations necessitated by joint venture.[43] Critical to the court's anal-

---

[38]*United States* v. *Addyston Pipe* and *Steel Co.*, 85 F. 271 (6th Cir. 1898), *aff'd* 175 U.S. 211 (1899).

[39]Ibid.

[40]See generally Robert Bork, *The Antitrust Paradox* (1978), pp. 26–30.

[41]593 F.2d 173 (D.C. Cir. 1978).

[42]Ibid., p. 1179.

[43]The court ultimately held that the player draft was an unreasonable restraint of trade because of its anticompetitive impact on the market for players' services. Ibid., p. 1189. See

ysis was the characterization that sports leagues operate as joint ventures with the purpose of producing new products and increasing demand, not as a cartel that restricts output or supply. The joint-venture analysis of *Smith* was recently followed when the Supreme Court considered the restrictions of the NCAA on college sports.

In *NCAA* v. *Board of Regents*,[44] the Supreme Court, in a broad and sweeping decision, recognized the important role the NCAA plays in regulating collegiate sports.[45] The Court, specifically noting the NCAA's regulation of "standards of amateurism, standards of academic eligibility, regulations concerning recruitment of athletes, and rules governing the size of the athletic squads and coaching staffs,"[46] ruled that the NCAA was an association of colleges that compete against each other for athletes, fans, and television revenues.[47] But the Court was candid in recognizing that college sports is an "industry in which horizontal restraints on competition are essential if the product is to be available at all."[48] Quoting Robert Bork, the Court said "[S]ome activities can only be carried out jointly."[49] The product marketed was "competition itself—contests between competing institutions."[50] Finding that incidental restraints were essential for the production and success of the product, the Court reasoned:

> Of course, this would be completely ineffective if there were no rules on which the competitors agreed to create and define the competition to be marketed. A myriad of rules affecting such matters as the size of the field, the number of players on a team, and the extent to which physical violence is to be encouraged or proscribed, all must be agreed upon, and all restrain the manner in which institutions compete.[51]

On college football, the Court was specific in approving the nontelevision regulations of the sport: The regulations enhance consumer demand and choice, including the choices available to athletes.[52] Because college football

---

also *Mackey* v. *National Football League*, 543 F. 2d 606 (8th Cir. 1976); J. Weistart and C. Lowell, *The Law of Sports*, secs. 5 and 7 at pp. 114–8, sec. 510 at p. 128 (Supp. 1985) (criticizing the narrowness of *Smith*'s rule-of-reason analysis); Robinson, "Recent Antitrust Developments—1979," *Columbia Law Review* 80 (1980).

[44]104 S. Ct. 2948 (1984).
[45]Ibid., p. 2954.
[46]Ibid.
[47]Ibid., p. 2959.
[48]Ibid., pp. 2961, 2959. See also *Broadcast Music, Inc.* v. *CBS*, 441 U.S. 1 (1979); *Continental T.V., Inc.* v. *GTE Sylvania, Inc.*, 433 U.S. 36 (1977).
[49]104 S. Ct. at 2969, citing Bork, *The Antitrust Paradox*, p. 278.
[50]Ibid., p. 2961.
[51]Ibid.
[52]Ibid. The Court struck down the NCAA's television contracts, finding that they restricted output and demand without producing offsetting procompetitive benefits. For an analysis of output as the key factor in balancing the competitive effects, see Sullivan, "On Nonprice

is a part of the academic tradition, the Court found that ancillary restraints produced by the NCAA joint venture were essential "in order to preserve the character and quality of the product."[53] Absent mutual agreement by colleges on the regulation, the "integrity" of the product would be compromised and "might otherwise be unavailable."[54]

The Court concluded that the integration produced by the NCAA joint venture, while placing some limited restraints on colleges and athletes, actually promoted increased competition and output by producing a product distinguished from other sports entertainment, this is, from professional sports entertainment. The result enhanced consumers' and athletes' choices. On balance, the joint venture's nontelevision regulation increased competitiveness. The restraints, maintaining the "competitive balance among amateur athletic teams,"[55] are a "justifiable means of fostering competition among amateur athletic teams and are therefore procompetitive because they enhance public interest in intercollegiate athletics."[56]

At bottom, the Supreme Court sanctioned many nontelevision regulations issued by the NCAA. Because the Court found that the "preservation of the student-athlete in higher education adds richness and diversity to intercollegiate athletics,"[57] it is willing to give the NCAA "ample latitude to play that role," a role "entirely consistent with the goals of the Sherman Act."[58] This conclusion was premised on the Court's implicit finding that amateurism and education are components of a market product, the promotion of which is procompetitive.[59] As long as the NCAA regulations are designed for, and have the effect of, enhancing the market product and preserving sports amateurism and education, they will receive favorable re-

---

Competition: An Economic and Marketing Analysis," *University of Pittsburgh Law Review* 45 (1984), p. 771.

[53]104 S. Ct., p. 2961.

[54]Ibid.

[55]Ibid., p. 2969.

[56]Ibid. The Court rejected Justices White and Rehnquist's argument that the NCAA regulations were noneconomic in nature (nonmarket goods) that produced a social benefit in promoting amateur athletics. Instead, the majority said antitrust laws only permit an examination into the competitive impact of the restraint, not whether they promote public interest or other values. See *National Society of Professional Engineers* v. *United States*, 435 U.S. 679 (1978); Sullivan, "The Economic Jurisprudence of the Burger Court's Antitrust Policy: The First Thirteen Years," *Notre Dame Law Review* 58 (1982), pp. 1, 16–18.

[57]104 S. Ct., p. 2971.

[58]Ibid. See also *Gunter Hartz Sports, Inc.* v. *United States Tennis Association, Inc.*, 665 F.2d, pp. 222, 223 (8th Cir. 1981); *Neeld* v. *National Hockey League*, 594 F.2d, pp. 1297, 1298–1300 (9th Cir. 1979); J. Weistart and C. Lowell, *The Law of Sports*, sec. 5.11, p. 757 (1979).

[59]See, e.g., *Hennessey* v. *NCAA*, 564 F. 2d, pp. 1136, 1151–53 (5th Cir. 1977); see Note, "Antitrust and Nonmarket Goods, The Supreme Court Fumbles Again," *Washington Law Review* 60 (1985), pp. 721, 729; Note, "Antitrust and Nonprofit Entities," *Harvard Law Review* 94 (1981), p. 802. R. Haveman and K. Knopf, *The Market System* (1966), p. 209.

view from the Supreme Court.[60] Since *NCAA*, the antitrust outcome centers on the restraint's effect on output *and* consumer demand and preference.[61]

This legal review is not intended to suggest that the NCAA does not have some modicum of market power or that market power is a precondition to liability under Section One of the Sherman Act. The Court in *NCAA* answered each of these concerns. First, the Court found that the NCAA did have market power in the regulation of television contracts.[62] Second, the Court explicitly said market power is not a prerequisite for liability under a Section One charge,[63] as is required under a Section Two claim. Although the Court did not decide whether the NCAA has market power over nontelevision aspects of the sports regulation, for our purposes the issue need not be debated. Even if the NCAA has monopoly power, which is debatable in markets for athletes, monopoly power alone is not illegal. The question is whether that power is exercised and, if so, whether the result is a predatory or exclusionary practice—one that deters entry of a potential competitor by raising the costs of entry or one that discourages existing rivals from increasing output.[64] The focus is on whether the monopoly conduct is designed to destroy or smother competition. The exercise of monopoly power does not refer to monopolistic pricing in the absence of entry barriers, but to the creation or preservation of market power by means that are anticompetitive.[65] On this point, the Supreme Court decision in *NCAA* is clear.

---

[60]This might include more severe collective restraints if the NCAA was faced with "intraband competition from other products, produced by another association or league as may be developing with the College Football Association (CFA) whose purpose is to promote the interest of major college football schools." Ibid., p. 2968 n. 55. See generally, Weistart and Lowell, *The Law of Sports*, 760–762, 768–69.

[61]104 S. Ct., pp. 2963–64; Sullivan, "Economic Jurisprudence of Burger Court's Antitrust Policy."

[62]104 S. Ct., p. 2966.

[63]Ibid., p. 2965.

[64]See, e.g., *United States* v. *Griffith*, 334 U.S. 100 (1948); *Berkey Photo, Inc.*, v. *Eastman Kodak Co.*, 603 F.2d 263 (2d Cir. 1979), *cert. denied*, 444 U.S. 1093 (1980); *United States* v. *Machinery Corp.*, 110 F. Supp. 295 (D. Mass. 1953), *aff'd*, 347 U.S. 521 (1954); E. T. Sullivan and H. Hovenkamp, *Antitrust Law, Policy and Procedure* (1984), pp. 431, 455; H. Hovenkamp, *Economics and Federal Antitrust Law* (1985), pp. 135–38.

[65]Sullivan and Hovenkamp, *Antitrust Law, Policy, and Procedure*, p. 455. See also 2 P. Areeda & D. Turner (1978) sec. 403 at p. 271; 3 P. Areeda and D. Turner (1970) sec. 710, at pp. 148–50 (reduced output by the monopolist will be offset by expanded output by other competitors); *Berkey Photo, Inc.* v. *Eastman Kodak Co.*, 603 F.2d 263 (2d Cir. 1979), *cert. denied*, 444 U.S. 1093 (1980). The analysis should not differ for monopsony as compared with monopoly. A monopoly buyer, a monopsonist, is one who has the ability to reduce demand by forcing the seller to sell at a lower price. The contention is that the NCAA is a monopsonist that forces the athlete to sell his or her service at a lower wage than that prevailing in a competitive market, resulting in a deadweight loss similar to that achieved by a monopoly seller. Ibid., p. 17–18. For reasons discussed herein, the monopsony theory is contrary to actual practice found by the Supreme Court in *NCAA*. Questions also exist whether the Sherman Act covers buyer cartels or monopsony power. During the debates, Senator Sherman said, "There is nothing in

Again, the Court in *NCAA* recognized that certain market products cannot be produced without cooperation between competitors.[66] Specifically, the NCAA's non-television regulations over college sports were held lawful because they enhanced output by increasing consumer and athlete demand.[67] Contrary to a finding of monopolization (e.g., market power plus exclusionary practices), the Court concluded that the NCAA's nontelevision regulations were ancillary but essential restraints that actually promoted and more evenly distributed the market product of sports competition.

Implicit in this analysis is the finding that the NCAA did not act to reduce output or earn monopoly profits, as is the case with a traditional cartel or single-firm monopolist. Indeed, the creation and success of the rival CFA, which has the purpose of promoting the interest of major football colleges,[68] belies the notion that the NCAA's conduct increased the cost or deferred the entry of a rival competitor. The nontelevision means used to achieve the integration of the NCAA's joint venture produced efficiencies, not anticompetitive consequences, through reduction of transaction costs. The result was an increased demand for amateur sports. Like other joint-venture agreements, member colleges in the NCAA or CFA are able to obtain certain economies through lower costs that benefit not only the participating colleges but also consumers and athletes.[69] The result is the creation of a new product market.[70]

This same economic approach used in *NCAA* is evident as well in more recent Supreme Court antitrust jurisprudence. The one theme recurring throughout the recent cases is that economic efficiency is a valid business justification for conduct engaged in by a monopolist or by joint venturers.[71]

---

the bill to prevent a refusal by anyone to buy something. All that it says is that people producing or selling a particular article shall not make combinations to advance the price of the necessaries of life." 20 Cong. Rec. 1458 (1889) *quoted in* Hovenkamp, *Antitrust Law, Policy and Procedure*, p. 18. More recent authority is to the contrary. See e.g., *In re Beef Industry Antitrust Litigations*, 600 F.2d 1148 (5th Cir. 1979), *cert. denied*, 449 U.S. 905 (1980).

[66]See generally Sullivan, "On Nonprice Competition"; Easterbrook, "The Limits of Antitrust," *Texas Law Review* 63 (1984), p. 1.

[67]104 S. Ct., p. 2969.

[68]Ibid., p. 2954. The CFA was formed during the same period of time that the NCAA's power to regulate was on the increase. To be sure, the CFA, made up of five major conferences that emphasize football, was created to increase the influence of the major football colleges within the NCAA structure.

[69]Hovenkamp, *Economics and Federal Antitrust Law*, pp. 111–13. The economies might include: (1) operation at an efficient scale, (2) avoiding high market costs, (3) reducing market costs or improving market opportunities, and (4) avoiding the free rider problems such as in the advertising of the product.

[70]See e.g., *Broadcast Music v. CBS*, 441 U.S. 1 (1979); *Appalachian Coals, Inc. v. United States*, 268 U.S. 344 (1933); *Chicago Board of Trade v. United States*, 246 U.S. 231 (1918); *Buffalo Broadcasting Co., Inc. v. American Society of Composers*, 744 F.2d 917 (2d Cir. 1984).

[71]See generally Sullivan, "Economic Jurisprudence of Burger Court's Antitrust Policy." See also *Northwest Wholesale Stationers, Inc. v. Pacific Stationery and Printing Co.*, 105 S. Ct. 2613 (1985);

During the same Court term as when *NCAA* was decided, the Court recognized in *Cooperweld Corp* v. *Independence Tube Corp.*[72] that integration and collective cooperation between related firms can produce efficiencies. Addressing the issue whether a parent corporation and its wholly owned subsidiary would conspire within the meaning of the Sherman Act, Chief Justice Burger reasoned that:

> Coordination within a firm is as likely to result from an effort to compete as from an effort to stifle competition. In the marketplace, such coordination may be necessary if a business enterprise is to compete effectively. . . . [To deny this reality] would serve no useful antitrust purpose but could well deprive consumers of the efficiencies.[73]

In *Northwest Wholesale Stationers*,[74] the Court unanimously ruled that per se illegality does not result from a horizontal concerted refusal to deal unless the defendant "possesses market power or exclusive access to an element essential to effective competition."[75] This relaxed standard of analysis was accepted in spite of a longstanding per se rule of illegality for horizontal concerted refusals to deal or groups boycott.[76] The justification for the changed legal standard again was an efficiency rationale—that the challenged practice might "enhance overall efficiency and make markets more competitive."[77] Speaking for the Court, Justice Brennan observed that:

> [N]ot every cooperative activity involving a restraint or exclusion will share . . . the likelihood of predominantly anticompetitive consequences. . . . [C]ooperative arrangements [may] seem to be "designed to increase economic efficiency and render markets more, rather than less, competitive." The [purchasing cooperative] arrangement permits the participating retailers to achieve economies of scale in both the purchase and warehousing of wholesale supplies, and also ensures ready access to a stock of goods that might otherwise be unavailable on short notice. The cost savings and order-filling guarantees enable smaller retailers to reduce prices and maintain their retail stock so as to compete more effectively with larger retailers.[78]

Aspen Skiing Co. v. *Aspen Highlands Skiing Corp.*, 105 S. Ct. 2847 (1985); *Cooperweld Corp.* v. *Independence Tube Corp.*, 104 S. Ct. 2731 (1984).

[72]104 S. Ct. 2731, 2740–43 (1984).

[73]Ibid. The Court held that a parent corporation is incapable of conspiring with its wholly owned subsidiary under Section One of the Sherman Act.

[74]105 S. Ct. 2613 (1985).

[75]Ibid., p. 2621.

[76]See, e.g., *Klor's, Inc.* v. *Broadway-Way Stores, Inc.*, 359 U.S. 207 (1959); *Fashion Originators Guild of America, Inc.* v. *FTC*, 312 U.S. 457 (1941).

[77]105 S. Ct. at 2620–22.

[78]Ibid., p. 2620.

Finally, in *Aspen Skiing*,[79] the first monopolization case decided by the Court in nearly 20 years, the Court said a monopolist has "no general duty" to deal with a competitor. The right is not unqualified, however. As long as the conduct is not predatory or exclusionary, the monopolist can compete vigorously on the merits.[80] But the monopolist cannot deliberately refuse to deal with a competitor that it has dealt with before, when that refusal would change the "character of the market" and hurt the competitor, in the absence of an efficiency justification.[81]

In *Aspen Skiing*, the Court ruled against the monopolist because it failed to offer any business justification for the refusal to deal. From the lack of an efficiency defense, the Court concluded that the defendant decided to forego short-run profit for the long-run effect of weakening competition.[82] In characterizing the conduct, the Court decided that: "If a firm has been 'attempting to exclude rivals on some basis other than efficiency,' it is fair to characterize its behavior as predatory."[83] Thus, it is clear from *Aspen Skiing* that had the monopolist engaged in the restraint for the purpose of promoting efficiency (reducing long-run costs thereby increasing demand for the product), the Court may well have deemed the refusal to deal lawful.

Read together, *Cooperweld*, *Northwest Wholesale Stationers*, and *Aspen Skiing* are authority for recognizing cooperation and integration as means of achieving cost-reducing efficiency objectives. Unlike raw cartels or single-firm monopolists, partially integrated associations, such as the NCAA joint venture, can increase output and consumer demand. The Court in *NCAA* found no less. Economic efficiency is sanctioned under the current antitrust laws, even when advanced by a horizontal agreement or a monopolist. Consequently, the NCAA's nontelevision regulations are inapposite to the traditional cartel goal of reducing output and increasing price. Allocative efficiency is promoted and, as the Supreme Court has held, the predisposing characteristics of cartelization are not present in the NCAA nontelevision regulations.

In short, legal barriers do not prevent the continuation of the present NCAA regulations or the formation of alternative, competing leagues or as-

---

[79]105 S. Ct. 2847 (1985). See also *Lorain Journal* v. *United States,* 342 U.S. 143 (1951) (the right to refuse to deal not unqualified).

[80]See generally *Transamerica Computer Co.* v. *IBM,* 698 F.2d 1377 (9th Cir.), *cert. denied,* 104 S. Ct. 370 (1983); *Berkey Photo Inc.* v. *Eastman Kodak Co.,* 603 F.2d 263 (2d Cir. 1979), *cert. denied,* 444 U.S. 1093 (1980); *Telex Corp.* v. *IBM,* 510 F.2d 894 (10th Cir.), *cert. denied,* 423 U.S. 802 (1975).

[81]105 S. Ct. at 2857–60.

[82]Ibid., p. 2860. See also Sullivan and Hovenkamp, *Antitrust Law, Policy and Procedure* (Supp. 1985), p. 52.

[83]Ibid., p. 2859. The Court accepted the Areeda and Turner analysis that " 'exclusionary' conduct comprehends at the most behavior not only (1) tends to impair the opportunities of rivals, but also (2) either does not further competition on the merits or does so in an unnecessarily restrictive way." as quoted in ibid., p. 2859 n.32.

sociations from continuing or entering the market to compete against the NCAA for production and marketing of college sports. The emergence and presence of the CFA (or, for that matter, the National Association of Independent Colleges or the NLCAA) is substantial evidence of a lack of barriers to entry.[84] The current state of antitrust law encourages robust competition on the merits through efficiency-enhancing conduct. The NCAA's and CFA's regulations are paradigms of this type of competition.

---

[84]Defenders of the cartel thesis seem to imagine that the NCAA has been able to maintain its monopsony stranglehold over member colleges through academic accreditation controls that require NCAA approval of the member colleges' athletic programs. For example, Professors Alchian and Allen write, "The answer [to the question of how the NCAA maintains control] is that any college violating the athletic 'code' could find its academic credentials threatened." Alchian and Allen, *Exchange and Production.* It is difficult for us to handle such concerns in any other way than to say the imagined controls simply do not exist.

Index